Fresh Wounds

Fresh Wounds

Early Narratives of Holocaust Survival

Edited by Donald L. Niewyk

The University of North Carolina Press   Chapel Hill and London

© 1998

The University of North Carolina Press

All rights reserved

Manufactured in the United States of America

The paper in this book meets the guidelines for
permanence and durability of the Committee on
Production Guidelines for Book Longevity of the
Council on Library Resources.

Library of Congress Cataloging-in-Publication Data

Fresh wounds: early narratives of Holocaust survival /
edited by Donald L. Niewyk.

  p. cm.

Includes bibliographical references and index.

ISBN 0-8078-2393-7 (cloth: alk. paper)

1. Holocaust, Jewish (1939–1945)—Personal narratives.

2. Jews—Biography. I. Niewyk, Donald L., 1940–   .

D804.195.H64   1998

940.53'18—dc21   97-17725

                        CIP

02 01 00 99 98   5 4 3 2 1

To the memory of DAVID P. BODER

Contents

Acknowledgments

My heartfelt thanks go to the individuals and institutions that helped make this book possible. Special recognition belongs to Sybil Milton, former senior historian at the Research Institute of the United States Holocaust Museum, who brought the Boder interviews to my attention when I was working on an earlier research project. She was the first to recognize their significance and urge their publication. Both she and Charles W. Sydnor read earlier versions of the manuscript and offered many valuable suggestions for improvement. The staff of the Simon Wiesenthal Center in Los Angeles generously allowed me to use Boder's own transcripts of the interviews. Anne Caiger and her colleagues in the Department of Special Collections, University Library, University of California at Los Angeles, provided access to David Boder's papers. Edwin M. Matthias and the staff of the Motion Picture, Broadcasting, and Recorded Sound Division, Library of Congress, made it possible for me to hear the original recorded interviews. Particular praise is due the division's technical projects' engineer, John E. Howell, who spent countless hours over a period of twenty years reconditioning a wire recorder and transferring the interviews for playback on modern equipment. Judy Mason assisted mightily with the word processing. A sabbatical from Southern Methodist University and a grant from its University Research Council enabled me to complete research and writing. Students in my Holocaust course during the 1997 summer semester imaginatively suggested the title of the book. Finally, I am grateful to the University of North Carolina Press, and particularly its executive editor, Lewis Bateman, for agreeing to publish the manuscript and carefully preparing it for print.

A Note on Editorial Methods

Boder's questions, which have been reproduced only when necessary to clarify the narrative, appear in italics. The editor's interpolations are placed in brackets. Unless otherwise noted, the footnotes are the editor's. The interviews required such extensive editing that employing ellipses in every case would clutter the text. Their use has been minimized. Such matters as punctuation, capitalization, and spellings of proper names have been regularized. Note, too, that retranslation into more idiomatic English is so extensive in this version that no effort has been made to identify the passages that deviate from Boder's early transcripts. The interviews, grouped by country, are then ordered chronologically and topically.

Fresh Wounds

Introduction

Every student of the Holocaust knows the crucial importance of survivors' testimonies in reconstructing the crime. They bring us as close as we are likely to get to the multifaceted essence of the experience, whether that involved being abandoned or helped by one's neighbors; concentrated in ghettos or sent directly to labor camps; witnessing actual mass murder or the piecemeal brutality of "extermination through work"; escaping the Nazis or enduring the worst that they could do. It may be, as some have said, that close attention to survivors' accounts buys texture and historicity at the expense of coherence. If so, it is a risk we need to take if we are to grasp the complexity of the process and approach an understanding of what happened to the victims. Far better that we let the survivors shape our image of the Holocaust than leave that task to novelists and film makers.

Accounts by Holocaust survivors are most readily available as published memoirs and recorded interviews. Each has its virtues. Written memoirs impose style and structure on the chaos of memory. Oral recollections, such as those set down in this volume, put a premium on spontaneity and raw directness.[1] Both have this in common, however: most of the accounts available to us were set down long after the events they describe. They continue to appear today, more than fifty years later. Only a handful came into being in the immediate postwar years.

The delay was understandable. Some survivors did not then want to talk about what they had gone through, but those who did had trouble finding a sympathetic audience. After the initial shock and outrage over the revelations of Nazi atrocities wore off in 1945, the world consciously tried to put the war behind and concentrate on reconstruction. Survivors who emigrated to the United States were urged not to dwell on the past but to start anew. Those who moved to Jewish communities in Palestine (and, later, Israel) met with disapprobation for their tardy Zionism and for allegedly having gone "as lambs to the slaughter." Everywhere it was easier to keep silent or repress traumatic memories rather than risk being misunderstood or disbelieved.[2] Widespread interest in what survivors had to say developed only in the 1960s when a new generation, jolted by revelations at the trial of Adolf Eichmann in Jerusalem in 1961, began asking questions about

1. On the usefulness and variety of oral sources on the Holocaust, see Langer, *Holocaust Testimonies*.

2. Bergmann and Jacovy, *Generations of the Holocaust*, pp. 4–12.

the Holocaust. By then memory might return imperfectly, sometimes in bits and pieces. It could take years for survivors to fit them back together and understand them well enough to relate.

The late appearance of survivors' accounts has raised questions about their reliability. Although no memory is ever likely to be perfect, even in the short term, it must be conceded that accuracy diminishes with time. A vast literature on the psychology of remembering has documented the fallibility of long-term memory and its vulnerability to a broad range of interfering stimuli. The vividness of remote memories depends heavily on rehearsal, i.e., thinking and talking about them; and yet studies have shown that the more frequently they are reproduced, the less accurate they become. Unpleasant facts may be forgotten or repressed. New information can interfere with memory, modifying and distorting it. Once incorporated into the original memory, it cannot be distinguished from what is actually reconstructed, especially after much time has elapsed.[3] One of the most eloquent and insightful Holocaust survivors, Primo Levi, came to accept this as a sad truth. Although he once celebrated the reliability of his own recollection of events,[4] in his last book he conceded the frailty of memory and noted that he and other survivors had "ever more blurred and stylized memories, often, unbeknownst to them, influenced by information gained from later readings or the stories of others."[5] It should be emphasized that there is no suggestion here of deliberate fabrication. Blurred remembrance is rather "the predictable result of many years of conscious and unconscious refashioning of the past little by little, including assimilating the roles of other actors who have since died."[6] Nor should this be interpreted as an attack on memoirs and interviews recently set down. Their importance is incontestable, and they will naturally be held up to the historian's usual critical scrutiny. The point here is to underline the special value of the few survivors' accounts rendered shortly after the Holocaust ended.[7]

The interviews with Holocaust survivors that make up this volume were

3. Spence, *Narrative Truth and Historical Truth*, esp. pp. 86–94; Ross, *Remembering the Personal Past*, pp. 97–181 passim; Loftus, *Memory*; Parkin, *Memory and Amnesia*.

4. Levi, *Moments of Reprieve*, pp. 10–11.

5. Ibid., *The Drowned and the Saved*, p. 19.

6. Henige, *Oral Historiography*, p. 111.

7. Two survivors whose 1946 interviews appear in this volume subsequently published memoirs of their Holocaust experiences: Kuchler-Silberman, *One Hundred Children* and Matzner, *The Muselmann*. Comparisons are instructive. Kuchler-Silberman's published account differs from her interview chiefly in terms of the former's richness of detail. Matzner's book, on the other hand, leaves out important information that he gave in the interview.

gathered in 1946 by the American psychologist David P. Boder. It was the first oral history of its kind and the only one done before Yad Vashem began its work in Israel a decade later. Moving from camp to camp set up for displaced persons in France, Italy, Switzerland, and Germany, Boder interviewed 109 victims of Nazi persecution, the majority of them Jews. Although he drew together a unique and valuable collection of sources on the Holocaust, he succeeded in publishing only a handful of the interviews during his lifetime. The audience simply was not there. Since Boder's death in 1961, his work has been largely forgotten. This volume presents thirty-six of the most important of his interviews of Holocaust survivors.

In some respects David P. Boder was an unlikely originator of such a project. Sixty years old in 1946, he was nearing the end of an academic career that had not previously touched on social psychology or matters of trauma and recovery. He had been born to Jewish parents in Latvia when it was part of the Russian Empire, but his last close surviving relative there, his mother, had died at an advanced age just before the outbreak of the Second World War, and there is no evidence that he lost family members during the Holocaust. And yet, a fuller view of his life story provides clues about why this man, of all people, should have gone to Europe after the war to interview survivors.

Boder was born in Liepaja, Russia, in 1886. Educated at Vilna, Leipzig, and the Psycho-Neurological Institute at St. Petersburg University, his studies were interrupted by World War I, during which he served in the army of the Tsar. In 1919 he fled the Russian Civil War with his daughter, Elena, and his second wife. Reaching Mexico by way of Siberia and Japan, Boder taught psychology at the National University of Mexico until he secured a permit to enter the United States in 1926. After completing a master's degree at the University of Chicago and a doctorate at Northwestern, he began teaching psychology at the Lewis Institute in Chicago, later renamed the Illinois Institute of Technology (ITT). There his role was confined largely to teaching in a service department, and it cannot be said that he was a major figure in psychological research in the 1930s and 1940s. Perhaps his chief claim to fame at that time was as founder and director of the Psychological Museum at the Lewis Institute/IIT, which popularized research techniques in his field.

Hence Boder, an Eastern European Jew who doubtless had experienced anti-Semitism, victimization by war, and the life of a refugee trying to build a new life far from home, could readily identify with the human wreckage of Hitler's genocidal war. Additionally, the somewhat marginal position Boder occupied in his field freed him to branch out into areas of inquiry shunned by mainstream researchers. Contemplating his career, one gets the impression of a man open to taking risks and willing to reinvent himself, even at an age when most people contemplate retirement. Finally, the subject of Boder's master's thesis, the psychology of language, betrays a longstanding interest in linguistic analysis.[8] Indeed, Boder went to Europe specifically to discover what words survivors would choose in telling their stories. Fluent himself in German and Yiddish, he must have thought himself well qualified for the task.

Nothing, however, could have prepared him for all the impediments to actually doing it. In 1945 it was not simply a matter of jumping on a plane or boat for Europe. One had to get State Department permission to enter the liberated and occupied zones, and bureaucratic obstacles delayed Boder's departure for more than a year, until July 1946. By that time his leave of absence from IIT was nearly up, and its president was insisting that he be back before the end of September to meet classes bulging with recently returned veterans.[9] Boder's efforts to supplement a modest research grant from the Psychological Museum fell flat. The American Joint Distribution Committee rejected his application because the project was not limited to interviewing Jews.[10] When Boder finally arrived in Paris, lugging an early version of the model 50 wire recorder, he found that working conditions in the overcrowded refugee centers were anything but ideal. People came and went in the storage areas and administrative offices where he conducted the interviews (background noise frequently intrudes on the recordings); bored refugees often tried to eavesdrop (Boder can be heard chasing them away); and determined individuals occasionally barged into the sessions demanding to be included.[11] The recorder proved even more balky than usual now that it was dependent on a still shaky European power grid filtered through converters and transformers. Under the circumstances it was no small accomplishment for Boder to conduct more than one hundred interviews and travel hundreds of miles in just two months.

Boder later explained that he tried to stay away from persons whose stories were represented to him as exceptional. "I wanted the rank and file experience—not the unusual story. I would limit my stay to about two days in one place, partly because the narratives would begin to show signs of preparation and lose their spontaneity, and partly because of the desire to record the experiences of individuals in many and dissimilar groups." Employing a nondirective style of interviewing, and unbound by any interview questionnaire, Boder asked his subjects where they were when the war began and let them take over as much as they were willing to do. "I would sit behind the person, so that he would not be influenced by

8. A version of Boder's thesis was published under the title "The Adjective-Verb Quotient."

9. Letter of introduction from Henry T. Heald, July 12, 1946, David P. Boder Collection, UCLA Library, box 1. (Hereinafter referred to as "DBC.")

10. Boder to Joseph C. Hyman, July 17, 1945, DBC, box 1.

11. "Spool Book," p. 126, DBC, box 15.

the facial expressions of the interviewer. No other persons were permitted in the room where the interview was taking place, and never was the person interviewed permitted to resort to the use of prepared notes." [12] The technique often worked well. Many of the interviews lasted several hours and required little prompting from Boder. But in a significant minority of cases he had to drag information out of his subjects, and even then the results were sometimes disappointing.

Back in Chicago, Boder set about seeking funds to get the interviews translated and published. A series of grants from the United States National Health Service from 1947 to 1957 enabled him to translate seventy of the most important interviews and deposit mimeographed and microcard copies in a handful of large research libraries. [13] Publication was another matter. Editor after editor told Boder that the public was surfeited with information about Nazi atrocities and that books such as those he was proposing did not sell. When in 1949 the University of Illinois Press decided to publish eight of the interviews, six of them of Holocaust survivors, Boder had to agree to forego his lengthy content analysis and limit himself to a very short introduction. [14] The book, *I Did Not Interview the Dead*, won a prize for its artistic design from the American Institute of Graphic Arts but received few reviews. In 1952 his editor informed Boder that the book was selling poorly and that there was no chance of its being reprinted. [15] All Boder's subsequent efforts at getting additional interviews published came to nothing. In 1957 his application for yet another renewal of his federal grant was turned down, and the translation project was left uncompleted. By that time Boder had retired from IIT and moved to Los Angeles, where he occupied an unpaid position as a research associate in the psychology department at UCLA. In the last years of his life he unsuccessfully applied for grants to translate key works in the history of Russian neurophysiology. [16] Boder died in Los Angeles in 1961, the year of the Eichmann trial. By the time the world began to take notice of the genocide of the Jews, Boder's efforts had been all but forgotten.

The reader should know that this version of the interviews differs from Boder's in several respects. Most obviously, it is selective, consisting exclusively of accounts by Jews who survived Hitler's attempted genocide and who had some-

12. Boder, *I Did Not Interview the Dead*, pp. xii–xiii.

13. Boder, *Topical Autobiographies of Displaced People Recorded Verbatim in Displaced Persons Camps*, 16 vols. (1950–1957).

14. Boder to Hananiah Harari, October 4, 1950, DBC, box 18. Boder later began to publish his content analysis in "The Impact of Catastrophe." This was to have been the first in a series of four essays, but none followed.

15. Miodrag Muntyan to Boder, May 12, 1952, DBC, box 24.

16. Boder to Department of Health, Education, and Welfare, March 20, 1959, DBC, box 21.

thing important to say. Those who "froze up" or were unable to tell coherent stories during the sessions have been excluded, as have been the accounts of anti-Communist Soviet citizens, members of various religious sects, and other Gentile refugees. Just as significantly, this version edits and revises Boder's translation. Boder insisted on a starkly literal, verbatim rendering of the original language, searching it for evidence of what he called "deculturation" and various types of trauma. Here the objective is to let the survivors tell their stories as clearly and as intelligibly as possible, always in their own words, but with much redundant material excised and, in a few cases, the narratives reordered for chronological coherence. Those for whom every hesitation, repetition, and convolution may be heavy with meaning ought to consult the original recordings or transcriptions. Moreover, Boder's command of English, while usually competent, was never entirely idiomatic; after all, he had been forty years old when he entered the United States. Here every effort has been made to honor Boder's fidelity to the distinct character of the original text while rendering it in more precise and idiomatic English.

The reader will also note that these oral accounts do not include all categories of Holocaust survivors. Whoever could return home in 1945 usually did so, and Jews from Greece, Italy, France, Holland, and other Western European countries rarely turned up in "Displaced Persons" (DP) camps. Much the same was true of survivors from the prewar Soviet Union. These are interviews of Jews who, for the most part, could not or would not go home again, those from Germany and Eastern Europe or who had been refugees from those places in Western Europe before the war.

That in itself is a broad category, presenting problems of organization. Most Holocaust victims went through such varied experiences that neat classifications are impossible. The best approach is to group the victims according to where they were when the Nazis tried to gather them up. No other single factor was as important in determining the fate of the Jews, for the length and severity of Nazi rule varied greatly from country to country. So, too, did Gentile attitudes toward Jews, the availability of hiding places, and the proximity of safe foreign havens.

We begin with Poland, where German rule was unparalleled in its duration and brutality, even though we should distinguish between its western and eastern halves. Jews in the former experienced nearly two years of comparatively benign pregenocidal German policies between 1939 and 1941, which lulled some of them into a false sense that things would get no worse. Their coreligionists east of the Bug River first tasted Nazi racism at about the time of its radicalization as Hitler turned his armies against the USSR. Ultimately virtually all of Poland's Jews came to experience the full force of ghettoization, forced labor, and extermination. Only the few who fled eastward with the Soviets were spared. Ninety percent of Poland's 3.3 million Jews were murdered during the Holocaust, and survivors in Poland experienced the most intense wave of postwar anti-Semitism in Europe. Hence it is not surprising that Polish Jews contributed more than half of the interviews contained in this volume. These are followed by a single representative of Lithuanian Jewry, which was treated in essentially the same way after the German attack in June 1941.

Jews who lived in Germany on the eve of the Holocaust are represented in the five accounts that follow. They divide into two groups, those who once had been German citizens (or, before 1938, Austrian citizens) and those who had been aliens, usually members of the sizable Polish Jewish minority in Germany. The former, especially elderly Jews married or well connected to non-Jews, sometimes enjoyed privileged treatment, including incarceration in the "model ghetto," Theresienstadt in occupied Czechoslovakia. Most non-German Jews were expelled in the late 1930s and theoretically should have shared the fate of Eastern European Jewry, but in practice many of them had come to know the Nazis and the outside world too well to let matters take their course in Poland.

All three of the interviews with Jews from France were of women who had found refuge there before World War II from harsh conditions in Eastern Europe. As noncitizens they were the first Jews to be rounded up and handed over to the Germans by officials of the collaborationist Vichy regime. On the other hand, they and their cohort usually had a better chance of survival than if they had stayed behind in parts of Eastern Europe where German rule was direct and far more brutal.

These interviews are followed by two with Slovakian Jews, victims of a state created by the Nazis and run by local fascists who gladly handed their Jews over to the Germans in two separate waves, one in 1942 and another two years later. Those who survived the first wave naturally stood a better chance of hiding or holding out. Something similar must be said of accounts by Hungarian Jews that close the anthology. Sheltered from deportation until 1944 by a Hungarian government that was anti-Jewish and allied with Hitler, but disinclined to participate in genocide, Hungarian Jews who were not then immediately exterminated at Auschwitz stood at least a fighting chance of enduring the death throes of the Third Reich.

Seeing the Holocaust through the eyes of the victims is fraught with difficulties inherent in all forms of "history from below." How typical is one person's experiences, or those of several dozens, when, after all, *millions* of people were swept up in Nazi genocide? No two of their stories would be the same, and some of the worst would never be told. (As Boder put it in his title, "I did not interview the dead.") These difficulties can never be completely overcome, but minimizing them requires some effort to summarize what has been learned so far about Nazi policies and the responses of victims and bystanders.

The remainder of this introduction is devoted to a broad overview of the Holocaust, fitting the interviews into the big picture. Books about the Holocaust that provide only the briefest historical background before plunging into

Nazi genocide slight the importance of long-term Jewish-Gentile relations in determining the fate of Jews under Nazi rule. It is commonly understood that
well before Hitler the Jews were an unpopular minority almost everywhere in
Europe, widely despised for their religious differences, liberal politics, and business prowess. That was certainly true in Eastern Europe, and nowhere more
so than in Poland, where the large Jewish minority was significantly overrepre-
sented among bankers, industrialists, the intelligentsia, and the professions. There
and in Hungary and Romania, governments routinely conceded to popular anti-
Semitism in the 1920s and 1930s with laws narrowing Jewish rights. Later, under
German rule, significant portions of the Eastern European populations would
help the occupier torment the Jews or else refuse to help them. Not surprisingly, several interviews in this collection confirm the widely held impression that
Ukrainian guards were among the most feared in ghettos and camps. Unfortunately, Boder's practice of beginning most of the interviews with the outbreak of
war left these complex interrelationships largely unclarified. A somewhat fuller
perspective on Jewish-Gentile relations will emerge from our exploration of East
European bystander reactions during the Holocaust itself, and, as we shall see,
they were by no means one-sided.

German Jews, of course, felt Nazi anti-Semitism long before the armies began
to march. Policies designed to isolate the Jews and make them despair of any
future in Germany had as their goal the victims' "voluntary" emigration. However, for a number of reasons having to do mainly with not wanting to alienate
traditional conservatives at home or popular opinion abroad, the Nazis were slow
to unleash these measures. Not until the pace of "Aryanizing" Jewish property ac-
celerated in 1937 and actual violence broke out during "Crystal Night" in 1938 did
it become unambiguously clear that the Jews would have to get out, and by then
the hour was late. Nor were many foreign doors open to them. Elderly Jews such
as Hildegard F. and Friedrich S. were understandably slow to face the daunting
task of starting new lives (nos. 24 and 25). Many German Jews in small towns and
villages moved to the shelter of big-city Jewish communities in hopes of holding out, as did Jürgen B.'s family (no. 23). Alien Jews in Germany like David M.
and Jacob M., however, faced expulsion or concentration camps as Hitler moved
toward war (nos. 26 and 27).

During the first two years of armed conflict, the German dictator still planned
to solve the "Jewish problem" through emigration. Madagascar and Siberia were
his favored dumping grounds for Jews who could not arrange more salubrious
sanctuary. Jews throughout German-dominated Europe were registered in preparation for the exodus that was to follow the expected swift military victory.
In Poland, where German rule was far more direct and brutal than in Western
Europe, ghettos—those characteristic features of the coming Holocaust—were
established to concentrate and isolate the large Jewish communities and ready

them for speedy extrusion. This doubtless painful process at least had the advantage of shielding the Jews from harassment by German officers, Polish anti-Semites, and especially ethnic Germans who lived in Poland. Although German policies were not yet genocidal, Rachel G.'s description of forced labor and reprisals in Warsaw documents their murderous results (no. 11). Julian W. describes conditions so execrable in Lodz that Jews willingly entered the ghetto in February 1940 (no. 15). Ghetto administrations took over crucial tasks of rationing scarce food supplies and providing basic social services. A glimpse of the latter is caught in the eyes of Israel U., then a homeless orphan in Lodz (no. 14).

At some point in 1941—historians disagree about exactly when and why—Nazi Jewish policy changed from emigration to extermination. Unless Hitler had been planning genocide all along, as now seems doubtful, the change was organically linked to his war against the Soviet Union. It may have been euphoria over initial victories in the East that precipitated the Final Solution, or perhaps it was induced a few months later by rage over stiffening Russian resistance and intimations of ultimate German defeat. General plans for the mass murder of Jews, completed at the Wannsee Conference in January 1942, provided for swift death in extermination centers or else slow death in slave labor camps. But the whole enterprise was to be kept secret as much as possible. The Nazis had learned long before that ordinary people, Germans included, rarely could stomach violence against Jews, and of course the victims themselves were to be kept in the dark in order to heighten their vulnerability.

Naturally word leaked out and made the rounds via the rumor mill and, starting in June 1942, Allied radio broadcasts. Did Jews then know about plans to kill them? The question bears heavily on issues of compliance and resistance during the Holocaust and charges that, far too often, Jews meekly accepted their fate. Evidence in these interviews suggests that some Jews knew, or suspected, the worst of the Germans. Certainly that was true of those who lived near the death camps, as did Udel S. not far from Auschwitz in Eastern Upper Silesia (no. 2). Armed with this knowledge, Rabbi Solomon H.'s small community in Eastern Poland resisted deportation, with disastrous results (no. 20). Word about Treblinka was also partly responsible for the Warsaw ghetto uprising in 1943, as several interviews attest.

But especially for Jews who lived far from the killing fields, knowledge of genocide was either absent or repressed. In 1943 Jürgen B. arrived at Auschwitz from Germany in a state of ignorance (no. 23). The same was true of Edith S. arriving from France (no. 28). Pinkus R. explains that as late as 1944 the Germans were still successfully disguising deportations from the Lodz ghetto as destined for work camps in Germany (no. 17). At about the same time Hungarian Jews arrived in Auschwitz believing it a relocation center or work camp. George K. had heard about crematoria over the BBC but dismissed the reports as atrocity propaganda (no. 33). Few outside Eastern Poland and the occupied areas of the USSR knew about the murders there of hundreds of thousands of Jews and others by SS Einsatzgruppen (Special Action Squads). No one at the time could see the big picture. Ignorance combined with incredulity and denial ("It may be happening to other groups of Jews, but it won't happen to us") to keep hundreds of thousands, and perhaps millions, of potential victims in the dark about genocide.

Nazi officials, intent on sustaining the Jews' ignorance and exploiting their uncompensated labor, sealed those they did not kill outright in ghettos and work camps to produce for the Reich. The situation in Kovno described by Ephraim G. was typical of most ghettos; possession of a work card was essential to keeping one's family together and avoiding deportation to some uncertain fate (no. 22). Even very young Jews like Israel U. in Lodz hastened to master skills that would earn them the coveted cards (no. 14). Rachel G.'s job as an occupational retrainer assured her a privileged position in the Warsaw ghetto (no. 11). Most ghetto jobs involved industrial drudgery. And yet, Roma T. must have wished she had one of them. Her assignment was to clean out Warsaw apartments vacated by deported Jews; those who had been unable to make the trip had been shot by the Germans (no. 19). Evidently, though, work was not always the order of the day. Nechama E. describes idly waiting for months in a small town in Eastern Poland where, it seems, the ghetto served principally as a holding pen (no. 7).

Ghetto affairs were conducted by Jewish Councils created by and responsible to the Germans. Control over work permits, food allocations, ghetto police, and deportation lists gave the councils power literally over life and death. The very fact that they managed the ghettos and made them productive for the Germans has led to charges of complicity in genocide, and it cannot be denied that Jewish leaders who stood up to the Nazis did not last long. The trend in modern scholarship is to view the Jewish Councils in less negative light than once was the case, acknowledging their efforts to save at least a remnant of the Jewish people and their well-founded fears of immediate mass slaughter should the Jews not comply.

In 1946 that was not yet the view. Very few of the survivors Boder spoke with had anything good to say about the Jewish Councils. Fairly typical is Udel S.'s condemnation of the regional Jewish Council in Eastern Upper Silesia for lulling Jews into a false sense of security. Typical, too, is his personification of the council in its chairman, Monek Moren (no. 2). That role in the Lodz ghetto was played by Chaim Rumkowski, whose energetic and intrusive personality made him a lightning rod for everyone's frustrations. Israel U. tempers his criticism of "King Chaim" when he points out that his administration established an efficient food rationing system and kept the Germans happy with ghetto production until August 1944 (no. 14). Pinkus R., however, hints at the corruption that inevitably crept into the system in Lodz, as it did in other ghettos (no. 17). The overwhelming impression left by the ghetto stories is of endless and mounting tensions caused by brutal mistreatment and fears for the future compounded by overwork and undernourishment. If the reader has time to read only one ghetto experience, make it Ephraim G.'s moving description of the Kovno ghetto (no. 22). Above all, what he has to say about the monstrous German response to defiance by Kovno Jewish leaders ought to make us thoughtful about the chances for successful overt resistance in the ghettos.

At the time no one could know that only one of the ghettos would survive to the end of the Holocaust. The exception, Theresienstadt in Czechoslovakia, had been unique almost from the beginning. The Nazis made it into their "model ghetto" to house elderly Jews who had fought for Germany in the Great War or who, like Hildegard F., had German spouses (no. 24). Friedrich S., a retired engineer from Vienna, attests to the active, and often extremely able, cooperation of ghetto inhabitants in making the town as livable as possible (no. 25). That helped the Nazis use Theresienstadt as a propaganda tool and to fool Red Cross inspectors. At the same time such cooperation enabled thousands of its Jews to survive until the Germans handed the ghetto over to the Swiss Red Cross during the last days of the War.

Ordinary German Jews, as well as their coreligionists in Western Europe, were granted no such privileges. In 1941 German Jews began to be sent to Eastern European ghettos, where their fate was often no different from that of their hosts. Indeed, one of the best descriptions of the black market in Lodz comes from Jacob M., deported from Hamburg in 1941 (no. 27). Other Jews in Germany were kept at home in concentration camps only to be sent eastward in 1942. A few exceptions were made for skilled workers in German armaments plants, such as Jürgen B., but that ended in 1943 (no. 23). In occupied countries such as France, however, a great deal depended on the cooperation of local officials in identifying and apprehending Jews. The collaborationist Vichy regime willingly responded to German requests for assistance, starting with roundups of the large population of alien Jews. All of the accounts from the Jews in France attest to the hostile attitudes of most French police and bureaucrats, although none is more vocal on the subject than Fania F. (no. 30). Conditions in French detention camps that held Jews for deportation to the East seem mild only in comparison with what awaited them in Poland.

Jews deported from Polish ghettos, French detention centers, German concentration camps, and cities and towns all over Hitler's expanding empire were put through a selection process, usually in Poland, to determine who was to work and who to die. This might happen at a major installation such as Auschwitz or at a comparatively minor transit or work camp. Those victims lucky enough to make the initial cut would go through the experience again and again as the weak were weeded out to make room for fresh slaves. Not surprisingly, the four camps devoted solely to extermination—Chelmno, Belzec, Treblinka, and Sobibor—are scarcely mentioned in the interviews; virtually no one had survived them. On the other hand, the two camps that combined "crematoria" (as the survivors almost inevitably called the gassing and burning installations) and forced labor facilities, Auschwitz and Majdanek, are well represented.

The survivors forcefully remind us that Auschwitz was not one camp but a complex of administrative, industrial, exterminatory, and support centers. The original camp, Auschwitz I, contained the central offices where a few fortunate Jews, Nelly B. among them, might secure comparatively comfortable work assignments (no. 29). Birkenau (Auschwitz II), about two miles away, with its barracks and "crematoria," was constructed by prisoner labor starting in 1942 and never finished, as we learn from one of its first Jewish prisoners, Helena T. (no. 32). A bit farther away was the "Buna" (synthetic rubber) factory at Monowitz (Auschwitz III) where, as George K. informs us, contact with Germans and Polish civilian workers sometimes ameliorated harsh labor conditions (no. 33). Israel U. and Adolph H. were assigned to different satellite camps, run by Auschwitz but some distance away, that supplied the main camps with food and coal (nos. 14 and 34). Work at Auschwitz was of every imaginable kind. The most important thing in terms of survival was that it be indoor work. One gets a sense from Hadassah M.'s description of women prisoners at Auschwitz being driven to clean out fish ponds just how short the lives of those doing outside work were likely to be (no. 9).

The smaller camp at Majdanek, near Lublin in Eastern Poland, also used poison gas but at first was oriented more toward extermination through work. Jews who survived it, like Jurek K. and Roma T., were there for only short periods (nos. 8 and 19). Nechama E., who was sent back to Majdanek as part of a clean-up squad, confirms that all its surviving Jews were massacred by the SS in its "Harvest Festival" action in November 1943, not with gas but by shooting (no. 7).

Auschwitz and Majdanek were unique in that they were the only Nazi camps that combined large scale gassing and forced labor facilities. No one there for any length of time was unaware of the "crematoria." Among the most ghastly scenes described in these pages are those set at Auschwitz as hundreds of thousands of newly arrived Hungarian Jews were gassed and burned in 1944. The ovens were quickly overtaxed, and prisoners whose job it was to dispose of the bodies were forced to employ open pits, turning the landscape literally into an inferno. Hadassah M. and Edith S. were certain that gassings done at that time were so hurried that many of the victims were dragged from the gas chambers in a stupor and burned alive (nos. 9 and 28). Although it is not possible now to confirm that this really happened, it would appear that in 1946 many Auschwitz survivors were convinced that the Hungarian Jews still breathed when they were thrown into the flames.

Auschwitz and, to a lesser extent, the other extermination centers have become synonymous with the Holocaust. And yet, hundreds of thousands of victims never were anywhere near a gas chamber. They either spent most of the period working in ghetto factories or else were sent to one or more of the hundreds of Nazi slave labor camps located throughout occupied Eastern Europe and inside Germany itself. Relatively neglected in historical research, these camps were so numerous and diverse that no one has yet cataloged them all. The interviews give some insights into that diversity. Some, such as the early "Organization Schmelt" camps (named for SS General Albrecht Schmelt, Himmler's "Special Representative for the Employment of Foreign Labor in Upper Silesia"), were exclusively Jewish and characterized by treatment that was often less hellish than what came later. The same was true of Jewish work camps that were at first loosely tied to Gross-Rosen, the easternmost of the prewar German concentration camps.

In 1943–44 these Jewish camps were redesignated outposts of the mother camp and hence placed under concentration camp discipline, meaning that guards drawn from the German army were replaced by SS men. Something similar happened to the approximately 160 Organization Schmelt camps, many of which were then liquidated and the remainder divided between Gross-Rosen and Auschwitz. This reorganization invariably worsened camp conditions, although the deterioration of Germany's military situation also played a part. Abraham K. gives details of this transition at Markstadt and nearby Fünfteichen, satellites of Gross-Rosen, as the German armaments firm Krupp expanded its Bertha Works in eastern Germany late in 1943 (no. 1). Udel S.'s telling of his relocation from Auschwitz to Fünfteichen suggests, however, that these outposts rarely became as brutal as the main branch (no. 2).

The interviews usefully remind us of the prominent involvement of German private enterprise in exploiting Jewish labor. Firms such as Krupp, I. G. Farben, and HASAG ran giant factories in Poland and Eastern Germany under SS management. The slave labor camps attached to them were not always single sex nor exclusively Jewish, but Jews were heavily represented and treated worse than Poles and others. Fairly typical were the ammunition plants run by HASAG at Skarzysko-Kamienna in central Poland, described by Roma T. (no. 19). Jurek K., who watched his father sicken and die there from overwork and malnutrition, knew what "extermination through work" meant (no. 8). About 8,000 Jews worked there at any one time; at least three times that number died there between 1942 and 1944. Circumstances were no better at state-owned concerns, as Kalman E.'s experiences at the Hermann Göring Works at Starachowice attest (no. 6). An interesting comparison is possible with the Slovakian Jewish labor camps, experienced by Baruch F., where conditions were still tolerable (no. 31).

Harsher working conditions and increasingly intrusive SS supervision also characterized the forced labor camps in Germany itself, as Fela N.'s experiences at a series of textile mills show (no. 3). Some of the worst circumstances prevailed at work camps in Germany during the last months of the war. Sigmund R. and Jürgen B. thought they had known the worst in Poland until they were evacuated to Germany in 1945 (nos. 5 and 23). This impression was not uniform, however. Jacob M. found work in a German ammunition factory "paradise" compared with Auschwitz (no. 27). Nechama E. may have survived because the Germans removed her from Bergen-Belsen to work in an aircraft factory as the war wound down (no. 7). Contacts with sympathetic civilian employees in these workplaces sometimes made a crucial difference to the chronically underfed slaves.

The Germans and their accomplices who supervised ghettos, work camps, and extermination centers are glimpsed occasionally, although sometimes only from afar. The handful of Jews lucky enough to get jobs in camp offices sometimes found their German bosses correct and agreeable, as was true of Helena T. at Auschwitz (no. 32).[17] Elsewhere the brutality of the SS and the German police batallions could be appalling. Nechama E. describes a drunken holiday raid by Germans on a small Polish ghetto that can only be described as a perverted form of sport (no. 7). And yet, German guards, some of them SS officers, could treat their charges decently and even humanely; see in particular the interviews of Abraham K. and Pinkus R. (nos. 1 and 17). Several of Boder's informants, Udel S. among them, give examples of both beastly and compassionate behavior by the perpetrators (no. 2). The evidence, here and elsewhere, does not lend itself to easy generalities about all Germans.[18] Certainly members of other nationalities joined in tormenting the victims, as the interviews with Slovakian and Hungarian survivors attest. George K., for example, alludes to Hungarian police and army officers abusing and looting Jews during the roundups of 1944 (no. 33).

Jews in ghettos and forced labor camps were far more likely to come into close daily contact with officials who were, like them, captives of the Nazis. These officials carried out German orders in return for privileges—more and better food, exemptions from deportations or harsh work details—that could be withdrawn at any time. This had the great virtue, as the Germans saw it, of minimizing demands on their own manpower. Hence in ghettos Nazi policies were enforced by ghetto officials and Jewish police forces under the overall supervision of the Jewish Councils. Following the collapse of the councils' strategy of cooperating with the Germans, these officials were often targeted for reprisals, especially the Jewish police who had rounded up their neighbors for deportation while sparing

17. Lore Shelley's study of twenty-seven prisoners who worked in the political section of the Auschwitz administration shows that just over half of them were (like Helena T.) Slovakian Jews sent to the camp early in 1942. Presumably their early arrival and knowledge of German influenced their assignment to the offices. See *Secretaries of Death*.

18. See the debate aroused by Daniel J. Goldhagen's indictment of virtually the entire German nation during the Holocaust, *Hitler's Willing Executioners*.

members of their own families. Jacob M. describes Jewish prisoners at Auschwitz seeing to it that newly arrived members of the Lodz ghetto police did not survive the camp (no. 27).

In the forced labor camps a complex hierarchy of prisoner administration made them inmate-run to a surprising degree. Capos supervised work crews and block seniors oversaw the prisoner barracks. These and other prisoner trustees reported to the camp senior, also an inmate, who in turn was responsible to the SS. Capos and block seniors in particular have the reputation of having been corrupt and brutal, and the interviews often confirm it, but with unexpected twists. For these posts the Germans often preferred German professional criminals—thieves, murderers, toughs of all kinds—who were usually the most feared prisoner officials. And yet, Jürgen B. credits one of them with saving his life at Auschwitz (no. 23). Jews occupied such positions more frequently than is commonly suspected, and with them, too, the record is mixed. Abraham K. documents astoundingly savage treatment at the hands of fellow Jews, although he senses that the capos and block seniors, too, were victims of the Nazis (no. 1). K.'s ruminations on the nature of evil in this context are particularly worthy of attention, although not everyone will be as forgiving as he is.

Jews may have been best off under non-Jewish capos and block seniors who were political prisoners, principled opponents of the Nazis who did not need to prove themselves worthy of their position by targeting Jews. Anna K. credits her Auschwitz block senior, a Polish political prisoner, with saving her life when she was gravely ill with gallstones (no. 18). Control by political prisoners of Buchenwald concentration camp in Germany also made a significant difference for Jews held there. Bernard W., one of only a handful of Jews who spent the entire Holocaust at Buchenwald, knew that best of all (no. 4). The survivors make it clear that without the cooperation of political prisoners, Jews and non-Jews, in the running of the camps, it would have been much harder to maintain hygiene and protect individuals from arbitrary acts by professional criminals among the prisoners and the SS guards themselves.

Survivors are more broadly generous with their praise for camp medical personnel, themselves prisoners, who managed to save lives even when basic medicines and dressings were scarce or totally absent, as was usually the case. Doctors, nurses, and medical orderlies were often the only persons in a position to shield patients from SS officers eager to murder incurables with fatal injections. Fela N. owed her life to such protection (no. 3). Other lives were saved by members of the "Canada" detail, present at the Birkenau ramp to take the newcomers' belongings to be sorted. Israel U. recalls these prisoners whispering to him and others to lie about their age if necessary to maximize the chances of being selected for work (no. 14). Jacob M. witnessed a newly arrived woman being forced by one of the old hands to give her child to an older woman and proceed along the ramp alone (no. 27). She could not have known that older women and all women with children, regardless of age, would be sent to the gas chamber. The prisoner had given her a chance to live.

Having close friends or family members with you could be a crucial advantage in German work camps. Friends who supplied extra food and encouraging words kept Edith S. from joining the ranks of "Moslems"—camp slang for prisoners who had given up and were certain to die (no. 28). As often as not the friendships were made right in the camps; Benjamin P., for example, benefited tangibly from ties with the orchestra conductor at Monowitz (no. 10). Strong Jewish family ties often led siblings and parents and children to stay together as long as possible. Israel U. recalls the Germans trying to separate relatives and friends during the initial processing at Birkenau (no. 14), but that was almost impossible to do when large transports were arriving, and even when prisoners were separated it was sometimes possible for them to reunite once in the camp. Hadassah M. and her sister helped each other make it through three of the worst camps, Majdanek, Auschwitz, and Ravensbrück (no. 9). Pinkus R. was separated from his family at Auschwitz but managed to reunite with his two teenage sons and keep them all together straight through to the DP camp (no. 17). It should be added, though, that family solidarity could also put a Jew at risk. Jurek K. returned to the Warsaw ghetto to be with his parents even though he had found a hiding place with sympathetic Poles and knew that Warsaw Jews were being deported to Treblinka (no. 8). Baruch F. survived precisely because he defied his parents and left home to live in the forests of Slovakia (no. 31).

By now it should be clear that the Nazis had greatly narrowed the choices open to victims but not eliminated them altogether. The interviews abound in examples of opportunities seized and risks taken. Jacob M. lied about his skills to get a good job (no. 27). Prisoners like Nechama E. and George K. jumped at chances to do extra work for their block seniors in return for additional bread and soup (nos. 7 and 33). That is also how Adolph H. survived the notorious Jawiszowice coal mines that fed the Buna works at Auschwitz III (no. 34). Developing and exploiting barter economies and black markets in ghettos and camps kept Abraham K., Rachel G., Julian W., and many others alive (nos. 1, 11, and 15). Knowing German as well as other languages was useful in managing the polyglot forced labor camps, and promoting their language skills won coveted office jobs for Nelly B. and David M. (nos. 29 and 26). The survivors often attributed their survival to luck, and that certainly played a part, but the evidence suggests that pluck could be every bit as important.

Survival strategies were put to stringent tests during the last days of the Holocaust as the Germans moved their prisoners into the contracting Reich, hoping to prolong their employment as slave workers or else use them as bargaining chips in negotiations. These transfers often had to be done partly or wholly on foot since what was left of Germany's rolling stock was reserved mainly for the military. Hence survivors of Auschwitz and all the labor camps associated with it and Gross-Rosen were marched to rail heads in Germany and Czechoslovakia and then moved west in (mostly open) railroad cars in the dead of winter. The death toll in this relatively little studied phase of the Holocaust was appalling. Nervous SS guards, understaffed and with the Russians on their tail, shot anyone who faltered. Adolf H. recalls that half of the group of prisoners with whom he marched out of Auschwitz, forced by their guards to bed down in the open, did not get up in the morning (no. 34). The lucky ones arrived in German camps that still could provide a modicum of food, medical care, and orderly administration. Buchenwald remained one of them to the end, and Nechama E. and Udel. S. indicate that the same was true of Theresienstadt (nos. 7 and 2). The Red Cross managed to get a number of inmates released to Sweden from the women's concentration camp, Ravensbrück, Edith S. among them (no. 28). But Jews dumped in the hopelessly overcrowded convalescent camp at Bergen-Belsen found a far worse situation, as Fela N. makes clear (no. 3).

And then, at the very end, for some there was still more marching to be done. The SS remained under orders to keep their charges from being liberated, and whenever possible they took them away again. At Buchenwald the prisoners themselves foiled a portion of these final death marches, enabling Jurek K. and Mendel H. to tell the tale (nos. 8 and 16). They had feared that their guards would shoot them rather than let them fall into enemy hands, and that is just what did happen to thousands of victims who could not avoid the last-minute evacuations. But not always. Pinkus R. recalls that the SS man who evacuated his work squad from a German labor camp found carts on which to carry the sick and ultimately let all his charges go (no. 17).

Evidence that Jews acted to save themselves and their friends from death while in German hands has never satisfied critics who fault them for not taking more aggressive action against the Nazis. Why did they not fight back, engage in sabotage, form underground resistance networks, or at the very least escape when the opportunity was there? Failure to do so has been traced variously to the Jews' alleged pacifistic culture, their lack of arms, the hostility of Gentile neighbors, and draconian German policies. The interviews shed some light on all these issues, including the Nazi enforcement of "collective responsibility," punishing large numbers of Jews for the acts of one or a few. Rachel G. gives examples of this in the Warsaw ghetto (no. 11). But the interviews also show that fighting back was not quite as rare as some assume. Isaac W. speaks for hundreds of Polish Jews who were able to retreat with Soviet forces in 1941 and then don Red Army uniforms to avenge their fellow Jews (no. 21). Baruch F. and his brother joined large numbers of young Jews who broke out of work camps to take up arms during the abortive Slovak National Uprising in 1944 (no. 31). Nathan S. must have been just twelve or thirteen when he began acting as a scout for Soviet partisan units in Eastern Poland (no. 13). Nor should the battle of the doomed in the Warsaw ghetto be forgotten. Benjamin P. shows that lack of weapons and ammunition ultimately forced the fighters to take cover and wait to be burned out (no. 10).

This lack of weapons meant that most Jewish resistance would have to be unarmed resistance. This took several forms. One was trying to avoid deportations from ghettos by hiding in "bunkers"—cleverly disguised rooms in attics, basements, or behind false walls—during the later phases of the Holocaust. Their inadequacy for long-term concealment, especially for families with small children, comes out in Udel S.'s memories of Bedzin (no. 2). Ephraim G. recalls that the ghetto police in Kovno became adept at discovering these hiding places (no. 22). Under very different conditions in France, Edith S. worked in the Jewish underground to hide Jewish children in the homes of cooperative Frenchmen (no. 28). No one familiar with these and other survivors' accounts is likely to reach the conclusion that Jews responded passively to Nazi persecution.

A few Jews, such as Lena K. and Rachel G., concealed their identities and posed as Poles, although this required excellent command of the Polish language and help from Polish friends (nos. 12 and 11). Even with such friends it was possible to fall victim to Poles who preyed on Jews trying to pass outside the ghettos, as happened to Roma T. (no. 19). And yet, complete strangers came to the aid of Anna K. (no. 18). Sweeping judgments of Poles and other Eastern Europeans during the Holocaust are difficult to sustain in the light of these experiences.

Escape from ghettos, trains, and work camps was difficult and in some situations impossible. Obstacles to breakouts that were attempted emerge from the interview with Kalman E. (no. 6). But if one could escape, what then? How could one survive without food, water, and shelter? Gentiles might help, but most did not; they were impoverished, too, and if caught suffered the same fate as the Jews. Nechama E. managed to jump from a train she believed was taking her to Treblinka only to see no alternative to walking to the nearest ghetto and waiting for the Germans to make their next move (no. 7). Rabbi Solomon H. attempted to save part of his flock by leading them out of their Eastern Galician ghetto and establishing a family camp in the woods, but very few of them survived the winter (no. 20).

It was still risky but far easier to escape and hope to survive in the confusion surrounding deportations in the last days of Nazi Germany. Some, like Helena T., were able to melt into lines of German refugees moving in the same direction as the prisoners (no. 32). Others took advantage of bombing raids to disguise themselves as Germans, and, especially in the case of women, German officials no longer found it easy to tell them apart. Nelly B., unable to walk very far, actually got help from Nazi welfare agencies (no. 29). Stranger still was the flight of

Benjamin P. Disguising himself as a wounded SS veteran, he took a job as overseer on a German farm only to have a few anxious moments after liberation convincing the Russians he was who he said he was (no. 10). The prize story, however, is told by Sigmund R., who escaped from a death march out of Dachau with a few friends and brazened his way across southern Germany to Switzerland as the Reich teetered on the verge of collapse (no. 5).

Naturally most survivors had no chance to liberate themselves, and for those who were not too sick to know what was happening at the time, the moment of liberation was unforgettable. The Russians come off no worse than the Americans in the memories of the liberated. At Buchenwald liberation gave rise to one of the few occasions for concentration camp humor. The story appears in several versions in these interviews and involves Buchenwald commander Hermann Pister calling the camp from Weimar to order the prisoners executed and being assured they had been (or would be), or else roundly insulted by newly freed prisoners who answered the phone. It did not happen that way, but for the survivors the story was a priceless source of mirth for years to come. On a more serious note, two of the survivors, Israel U. and Benjamin P., acknowledged taking revenge on German civilians following liberation (nos. 14 and 10). P. also returned to Auschwitz to torment his former tormentors. These reprisals, understandable under the circumstances, are rarely mentioned in subsequent memoirs.[19] It was, perhaps, easier to talk about them with a sympathetic American in the immediate aftermath of the war.

Women's experiences of the Holocaust are well represented in the interviews. Fourteen of the thirty-six survivors who speak in this volume were women, which roughly reflects the nearly two-to-one ratio of men to women in the DP camps. Certainly women were less likely to survive, targeted from the beginning of genocide as bearers of future generations of Jews. Especially for them, much depended on staying out of German hands, and it cannot be denied that survivors like Rachel G. and Lena K. showed imagination and flair in seizing life-saving opportunities to "pass" as Gentiles (nos. 11 and 12). Women with children and without the help of Gentile friends had it much tougher. Raisel M.'s mother courageously (and presciently) defied her husband, who wanted to lead his family back to the ghetto from which they had escaped, and in doing so probably saved Raisel's life, but could not save her own (no. 13).

Jewish women who were unable or unwilling to escape were more likely to be selected to die because they lacked work skills required by the Germans, and obviously pregnant women and women with children were routinely sent straight

---

19. But see the journalistic account, based on some solid research, of Jewish survivors who persecuted Germans in Poland after liberation. Sack, *An Eye for an Eye.*

to the gas chambers. And yet, those who were selected for work may have been somewhat better prepared for survival than were men.[20] The traditional "women's work" for which they had been trained—repairing clothing, promoting cleanliness, fostering warm social relations—came in handy in forced labor camps, as Fela N. makes plain (no. 3). At the same time, we should avoid any temptation to romanticize the subject. Women were sexually vulnerable, and Roma T. recalls that Jewesses raped by SS men were sometimes killed to cover the crime (not of rape but of "race pollution") (no. 19). Women who concealed pregnancies in the camps often gave birth under unspeakable conditions; Edith S. gives but one example (no. 28).

If anything, children were even less likely to live. In ghettos they were usually allowed to remain with their families, although the Germans sometimes organized special deportations of young children. In the camps those under ten were regarded by the Germans as "unproductive eaters," and except for those in the short-lived Auschwitz Gypsy and Family camps, the latter described by Hadassah M., they would not be spared (no. 9). As Nechama E. learned to her sorrow, it did not pay to form emotional attachments to children who somehow managed to survive for short periods in the camps (no. 7). Older children might be spared if they lied about their age and especially if they convinced the Germans they could work; it also seems likely that very young Jews like Edith Z. were regarded by their masters as more pliable subjects (no. 13). Several of Boder's informants, barely in their teens at the time of the events they described, mastered lifesaving work skills with breathtaking speed, giving special meaning to the cliché about "growing up fast."

Liberated survivors who returned home to Eastern Europe to look for family members and perhaps start life over encountered a world in ruins and more than a little antagonism. Homes and apartments that still stood had long before been taken over by others who were loath to give them up. Soviet occupation and the imposition of Communism outraged Polish, Hungarian, and other nationalisms, while the stereotype of Jewish sympathy for the Reds heightened anti-Semitism. Bernard W. encountered an implacably hostile postwar atmosphere in his Polish home town, while Rabbi Solomon H. made no headway in restoring religious life in Warsaw given the intensity of ill feeling among the Poles (nos. 4 and 20). Udel S. was only one of thousands of Polish Jews for whom the Kielce pogrom of July 1946 was the last straw (no. 2). At about the same time Lena K. was giving up on her school for Jewish orphans in southern Poland. Harassed and attacked both individually and collectively, they left for France and, eventually, Palestine

20. On this subject see the excellent essays by Sybil Milton and Joan Ringelblum in Rittner and Roth, *Different Voices: Women and the Holocaust*, pp. 214–249, 374–418.

(nos. 12 and 13). Sincere Communists like Rachel G. might hope for a better future based on radically transformed economic and social institutions, but most Polish Jews joined Hadassah M. in resisting appeals to stay from the government-sponsored "Central Committee of the Jews in Poland" and, when necessary, left without official permission (nos. 11 and 9).

At the time survivors made the decision to chance lives as refugees in Western Europe, they could not have known how long it would take to find permanent homes. They believed themselves to have been victimized by the Nazis more than any other single group, and they could no more understand why they were expected to go on being denizens of "camps" than they could fathom continued limits on immigration into Palestine and the United States. For the victorious Allies, however, Holocaust survivors were only one component of a far larger refugee problem. In 1945 Jews constituted less than one percent of the fourteen million refugees from Hitler's War, although by 1947 they made up a far larger proportion—perhaps as much as one third—of the approximately 700,000 unrepatriated displaced persons in Europe. The British, who interpreted the westward migration of Holocaust survivors after 1945 as part of a well-orchestrated Zionist plot to undermine British rule in Palestine, were not particularly welcoming of Jews in their zones of occupation. Benjamin P. and Isaac W. provide glimpses of life in British DP camps in Austria as well as insights into problems of accepting the prolongation of regimented camp life after liberation (nos. 10 and 21).

Jewish refugees clearly preferred the American camps set up exclusively for Jews and often made great efforts to reach one. Helena T. describes the camp at Feldafing set up for Jews in a former Hitler Youth camp south of Munich (no. 32). There they did not have to rub shoulders with DPs from Ukraine and the Baltic states, some of whom might have helped the Nazis kill Jews. Others, like Jürgen B. and David M., were allowed to live independently in German homes (nos. 23 and 26). Perhaps the happiest interviewees were those living in small, autonomous shelters and camps in France, Italy, and Switzerland, supported by American Jewish charities and the United Nations Relief and Rehabilitation Administration. There conditions might be as pinched as in the bigger camps, but at least life was brightened by a greater sense of community and self-determination.

No single vision of the future sustained these survivors during the years of postliberation waiting. For a few it was an apocalyptic image of new lives for Jews in the coming state of Israel. Some were Zionists of long standing. Pinkus R. owned property in Palestine and had made plans to move there even before the war (no. 17). The post-Holocaust collapse of Orthodox Judaism's rejection of Zionism comes through in Rabbi Solomon H.'s report on the religious idealism combined with Jewish nationalism that prevailed in a kibbutz camp (no. 20).

Other survivors spoke with genuine optimism about starting over in the United States, South Africa, or Latin America, their destination often determined by the location of relatives. Still others said nothing about the future (Boder did not always draw them out on the subject) or appeared reluctant to make plans.

It may be significant that several of the survivors actually drew some inspiration from their experience of the Holocaust. Veterans of the women's camp at Birkenau, Edith S. among them, stood in awe of the memory of Mala Zimetbaum, who, recaptured after escaping the camp, publicly defied her executioners (no. 28). Roma T. remembered something similar happening at Majdanek, leading to momentary defiance among the prisoners (no. 19). Benjamin P. had reason to dwell on some of the worst behavior of Jews during the Warsaw ghetto uprising, including Jewish turncoats helping the Germans flush out the survivors, but he also relived the heroism of the nameless woman who died holding off the Germans in the early hours of the revolt and so inspired her comrades to fight with equal valor (no. 10). Auschwitz survivors who were in Birkenau in October 1944 remembered the Sonderkommando revolt, sometimes, like Anna K., in larger-than-life terms (no. 18). These and other courageous acts, perhaps raised from mere history to legend, helped establish the psychological basis for confidence that a time would come when Jews would exert some control over their own future.

Reading these survivors' stories both validates some recent trends in Holocaust scholarship and suggests directions for further research. Conspicuous among the former are tendencies toward exonerating Jewish leaders and prisoner trustees from charges that they cooperated in their own destruction. Certainly some Jewish Council members, capos, and block seniors were venal, and some of them made errors, but most did the best that could be done under the circumstances and are better viewed as victims rather than collaborators. Something similar must be said of the retreat from condemning Jews for not resisting. The chances for successful resistance were severely limited, but what could be done commonly was done, whether hiding in "bunkers" or forests, smuggling food or bribing officials, adopting false identities or doing extra work for extra rations. As many of these survivors could attest, just staying alive was resisting.

Much still remains to be learned. A deeper understanding of pre-1939 Jewish-Gentile relations in Eastern Europe would shed more light on why help was offered or withheld during the Holocaust. Further inquiries into what Jews knew about genocide and when they knew it might reveal that large numbers of them were genuinely unaware of what the Germans had in store for them. The ignorance of new arrivals in Birkenau in the *last months* of the camp speaks volumes. Additionally, we need to know more about the Holocaust outside the big camps and ghettos. Lodz and Warsaw, Auschwitz and Majdanek are fairly well understood, but what do we know about Dabrowa-Gornica and Miedzyrzec, Skarzysko-Kamienna and Markstadt? Finally, the psychology of the killers ought to capture more of our attention. Recent and extremely valuable studies of Holocaust perpetrators have portrayed them as reluctant killers, ordinary men motivated chiefly by deference to authority and conformity to the group. Some of those encountered by survivors included here resemble that characterization, but not all of them by any means.

Poland

I   Abraham K.

Although large numbers of Jews lived in the Polish district of Eastern
Upper Silesia, the Holocaust there (except of course for Auschwitz
itself) is comparatively unknown. It had been part of Germany before 1918, and the Nazis reincorporated it into the Reich in 1939. Its
100,000 Jews, spread over more than forty Jewish communities, were
then placed under the administration of a single Central Jewish Council.
The Germans appointed Moshe (or Monek) Merin to head it. An active
Zionist before the war, Merin organized Jewish police units to enforce
the occupiers' demands, hoping to save at least a portion of his Jews by
making them indispensable to the German war effort. Hence he maintained strict order and organized work in the ghettos, rounded up the
unemployed for shipment to various camps, and violently suppressed all
overt forms of Jewish resistance. Against this background, Abraham K.
sketches an unforgettable story of desperate Jewish measures to stay
alive and avoid deportation to labor and extermination camps in 1942
and early 1943.[1] He also takes us inside the smaller slave labor camps in
Eastern Upper Silesia and documents the transition from army to SS
control.

K.'s hometown was Dabrowa-Gornica, a factory center near Katowice just east of the 1939 Polish-German border and about thirty-five
miles north of Auschwitz. It was home to about 5,000 Jews. His Hasidic
family sent him to a private heder, but his education was cut short by
the German invasion. Too young at eleven to be included in the early
deportations of Jews to slave labor in Germany, he soon learned the
metal trade to help maintain his family and keep it from being sent away
from their home together with other "unproductive" Jews. Ultimately
he could not avoid being transported to Markstadt labor camp and then
to Fünfteichen, both satellites of concentration camp Gross-Rosen,
where Krupp was expanding its huge Bertha Works. During the last
months of the war he was taken to the main camp for a short time and
then to Buchenwald, where he was liberated in April 1945.

K. is haunted by treatment of Jews by their fellow Jews during the
Holocaust. Whether as Jewish Council members, Jewish police in the

---

1. Parts of this interview appear in Boder's *I Did Not Interview the Dead*, under the
pseudonym "Abe Mohnblum."

ghetto, or as block seniors at Markstadt, Jews strike him as more vicious and corrupt than some Germans. He occasionally loses sight of the directing Nazi hand behind every action. But Abraham is also thoughtful about the temptations placed before these individuals, wondering what he himself would have done in their position and whether their actions, too, were only human. What is more, he subsequently witnessed the still worse conditions that prevailed in concentration camps where the SS ruled more directly and the prisoner administration was largely non-Jewish.

At the time of his interview in Geneva in August 1946 the eighteen-year-old Abraham K. was enrolled in a training program for mechanics sponsored by the ORT. We pick up the interview with his description of German roundups of Jewish workers in Dabrowa in the early months of German rule.

Workers were needed for Germany, young people between eighteen and fifty. They didn't send an order to the Community Council because they were afraid they couldn't trust the council with such a thing. And so they went through with it themselves. Early in the morning, it was about 4:30, they sent a certain number of policemen, and they simply got us from the beds. I still remember when they came into our house. Fortunately my father wasn't home at the moment. And they came in, and they pulled off my blanket and asked "How old are you?" And I said, "Born in 1928." "Oh," they said, "go back to sleep," because that time such boys were not yet taken. Pretty soon there was another raid, [and] it became an everyday thing.

Finally the German police created a Jewish militia [police force] to keep order on the streets. And its first duty was to serve the Jewish Community Council. Raids were now done by the Jewish militia. They would get an order that so and so many Jews had to be delivered to go to a work camp or to Auschwitz—there already was an Auschwitz, and we had heard about Auschwitz. So they would give an order to the council and instruct them to make out a list so they themselves should settle everything. Now when a raid had to take place, they would get the police from the council in Sosnowiec[2] and would expedite everything. It was arranged so that when they would arrest a man, a Jewish militiaman would lead him under the arm, and an extra police cordon would surround the locality so there would be no disturbances.

2. This was Moshe Merin's Central Jewish Council of eastern Upper Silesia.

What kind of people were chosen for the militia?

That was a decision of the Jewish Council. The council named a certain Monek Merin director of the whole district as far as Lodz. He was the manager of the whole Jewish community. He was a Jew. I don't know how he worked himself up so high. He had influence with the Gestapo and everywhere had his say. He had his own automobile, he had a chauffeur, and he led the life which he certainly could not have afforded before the war. He took in people whom he knew before the war, his friends and his relatives. He was not a highly educated person. His character was not so good. That later became evident from his deeds. He gave good jobs to his best friends. They had pull, and they fared well. Because from all the supplies that were allotted to the Jews they still could live [well]. They really did not have to take too much away from everyone in order to live a very good life.

It was the same thing with the Jewish militia. Jewish functionaries, already in the Jewish Council, got in their friends, and these looked around in turn and named them [their friends] as candidates. They were inspected, whether strong enough, in good health. Above all whether he would not feel embarrassed to drag a Jew through the streets to take him to prison, because there was a Jewish prison, and when he has to club a Jew, he would also not be embarrassed to do it. These were the Jews they would look for in the first place. They didn't have to search very hard because there are enough people of this kind.

With the organization of the Jewish militia it became much worse than before. It became especially bad for those who had no acquaintances among the militia, and that was nearly the whole population, because a militiaman did not mistreat his own family. But the general Jewish population suffered much more because a German policeman [who was] given the address of a Jew wouldn't know the man. He didn't know where he could hide and so on. He goes there, if he doesn't find anybody, he comes back, files his report, and the issue is closed. A Jewish militiaman would watch the Jew, he knew him yet from before the war, he knew where he was or where he could hide, and so they were much worse.

I want to tell you just a little episode at which I myself happened to be present. The Jewish militia did not feel that they were merely functionaries to execute what was demanded from them. They also felt that they were better, more important people. In Dabrowa-Gornicza there was a shop where shoes were manufactured. This industry was founded by a German who was the manager, and only Jews worked there. Large numbers of workers would arrive from Bedzin[3] [in] special Jewish street cars. Every two hours a street car would go especially for the Jews. No Germans, no Poles could board. There were Jewish conductors, and the Jew-

3. A larger industrial town a few miles west of Dabrowa-Gornicza.

ish militia always controlled the street cars so that nobody would smuggle bread or anything else. Because it always used to happen that there was a difference in price between one city and the other. In most cases bread was cheaper in Dabrowa than in Bedzin. And so they always controlled the trams to watch that nobody should smuggle anything. There happened to be on the car a Jewish militiaman, tall of stature, and of strong build, and it was early in the morning when the working men were traveling to work. The cars were badly overcrowded. The Jewish militiaman felt himself to be better than we, the people, and he wanted us to make room for him. But the train was so packed that people were standing on the steps. So what does he do? He tells a man to make room for him. The man said, "Have a bit of sense, it's impossible, we are all pressed together like herring." But the militiaman didn't say much, he just struck him. A person doesn't immediately consider the consequences, and he struck back. But the [militiaman] was much stronger, and he beat him, and when they arrived in Dabrowa, he took that Jew to the Jewish police station, and they beat him up to such an extent that the man was unrecognizable.

[Later the beaten Jew managed to get to his workplace, only to have the Jewish police try to arrest him there. But the gateman called the manager.]

The German manager gave orders that nobody was to come in. That was a fortunate thing because otherwise I do not think we should have seen [the worker] alive.

If one were to ask me, "If they had asked you to become a militiaman, what would you have done?" today one can never be sure that one would simply have replied, "I don't want to do it." Because a human being is only a human being. If one stands over him with a gun and he is being threatened, one cannot be responsible for the deeds that one may perpetrate. And in such light one also has to see the Jewish militia. They did horrible things, too, in which I think all people are alike. There are only a few heroes.

The raids kept on and on, and they took on increasingly threatening aspects. They took more and more Jews, and when it came to it, they took old people, sick people, people who had no occupation. The order was that on a Saturday afternoon they should appear in the synagogue. The synagogue wasn't a synagogue anymore, just an empty house. Later it was even converted into a horse stable. The thing made a terrible impression, and people thought, now the worst is coming, because it was known that they were being led directly to their death. Those who had the slightest chance went into hiding. Many were afraid even to hide. So gripped were the people by terror that, even though they knew that they were going to a certain death, they were afraid to hide.

Ah, but then why were they afraid to hide?

Many were hurt, and many were brought back to the square, and they were transported to Auschwitz. That was one reason, and second, the people were mis-led. [The Germans] ordered the Jewish functionaries to calm the people. They were told that they were being sent to a place where they would have light work, according to their ability to perform, and in this way they would be interned for the duration of the war. This also led to the fact that many people just didn't go into hiding. They thought, "If they catch me here, my life is lost right now; there possibly I will survive the war."

I was lucky. I was accepted to work in a metal shop, on trial to see whether I was at all fit for this kind of work. I wanted to work, but there was nowhere to get the training. There was no chance to learn. One had to *produce*. It was a mu-nitions factory belonging to a German, and they gave me a certificate that I was admitted for a tryout, a blue card for people who were working for the Germans.

I endeavored to produce the most; that, I believed, would help me to remain at home. Things quieted down a bit, but then came my father's turn. He was doing nothing; he was sick, but since my mother, my sister, and I were working, that is, the majority in the family, he was permitted to stay at home.

What was your mother doing?

My mother was also admitted to a war plant. She worked on uniforms for the Wehrmacht. Since a cousin of mine was an overseer over the [uniform manufac-turing] shop, we had "pull." He put my sister to work among the first girls, and that is how she remained home. Otherwise, several hundred girls were sent to Grünberg.[4]

[The Jewish police continued roundups and deportations of older Jews, from which K.'s mother escaped only by leaping out of a second story window and running away.]

Well, we remained home, and only young people were around, because all the old ones had been sent away. The mood was terrible. And we somehow felt that things wouldn't last long. One day we heard that [another raid] would happen. Again I went to the night shift and slept in the daytime. It so happened that my mother also worked on the night shift. My sister was on the day shift, and the two of us worked during the night.

4. A forced labor camp exclusively for women, one of ninety-three "Organization Schmelt" camps run by the SS in eastern Upper Silesia.

Where did you sleep?

At home. Because in the daytime it was not so dangerous to sleep at home. Twelve o'clock noon somebody knocked. I slept very soundly. I did not hear a thing. Customers were always coming because my mother had to work at home too because one couldn't even buy bread from her earnings at the shop. She was a corset maker.

Who, in those times, wore corsets?

There was already a ghetto. That is, the Jews had to live in a concentrated fashion, in a certain section, but they were not permitted to go out on the streets where non-Jews lived. On the other hand, the Poles could come in. She worked for Christians. That was not permitted. But, as the Poles could move through those streets, it was possible to work for them. As long as I talk about it I will tell you how that work would proceed. When my mother worked in the daytime, she would return home by five o'clock and work then until 1:00 or 2:00 [in the morning]. When she was through with her work, her sewing machine was hidden, because it was not permitted to us to have sewing machines. The machines had to be surrendered. But her life depended on the machine. We had to take this risk, whether we wanted to or not. So after work we would hide the machine in the attic or in the cellar. And so at that time, too, my mother thought that it was possibly a customer calling for some work, or wanting to order something, so she quickly opened the door.

[A German policeman arrested K. and took him to nearby Bedzin and then, with other Jews, to a transit camp at Sosnowiec. From there they were sent to Markstadt, a workcamp near Breslau.]

They were building a plant for Krupp. There were already 2,000 Jews when I arrived. A lot more workers were needed. The work had started, and they needed a lot of workers; and the Poles were already all taken, so they had to take the Jews. One hundred twenty-nine of us were sent over there, among them twenty-nine women. These women were mostly the ones who had somebody among the men, engaged, or good friends. There were several hundred women, but these had arrived at other times.

That time we still traveled in passenger cars. It was already winter, it was cold. When we arrived there we saw nothing. We came to the square, and there comes the chief of the guard. [He] didn't look in any way terrible. We were accustomed to uniforms, but here comes a man with a leather jacket. And he spoke in a firm voice, a voice of command. He spoke German. And here I noticed a Jewish star. I understood that he was a Jew. He didn't make any special speech, but he immediately called around the pushers, the Jewish capos who were appointed, and told them to which barracks they should go.

What did you call them—"pushers"?

Yes, *Schieber*.[5] And they told us to step forward four abreast. Until then, from the railroad station to the square we had marched five abreast [so] we stepped forward in fives. We didn't know the customary orders of this camp. There were three brothers among us, and they wanted to stand together so they could sleep together. But since they stepped forward in fives, every fifth person had to step aside. One of these brothers was separated from the other two. And the capo hit him real hard. That was a Jewish capo. That torments a person. It makes one a revolutionary. Here he is a Jew, and he beats me. He is the same as I am, but because he has more to eat and because he was in the camp longer he has to behave that way. And I couldn't do a thing. I couldn't open my mouth. It does something to a person, to a bystander more than to the one who is actually beaten.

And then a German policeman, one of those who had brought us to Markstadt, stepped forward and told the pusher, "I brought these people up here, and I didn't have any trouble with them. They have only been here a few minutes, and already you have beaten them." It was sad to see a German put himself in our place and have more understanding for us than a so-called brother.

The camp was surrounded by barracks, behind wire fences. In those times we were still guarded by the German Wehrmacht, and round and round were also barracks of civilian laborers such as Poles, Czechs, Frenchmen, and also Germans. In the morning when they would wake us at about 5:00, roll call would take place. But I didn't yet know what a roll call was. We were told that as soon as we heard three whistles we should present ourselves for roll call. What? How? I didn't know. I only knew that we had to appear. And so we stepped forward for roll call. We were counted. They checked whether anybody was missing. And we went back; we were told that at 9:00 everybody had to be in the barracks because they would call for us.

At 9:00 the pushers came. They belonged to the camp management who always stayed home; some were from the night shift, because there were pushers for the people who worked nights and slept in the daytime. But when the pushers heard that a new transport had arrived, they wanted to know what kind of people we were. There were also people who had lived near us at home, and they might have known some of the new prisoners.

---

5. The word suggests sinister figures such as racketeers and profiteers.

Were they Jewish?

Yes. The camp of which I am talking was exclusively Jewish. At 9:00 they came for us. We were told we were going to the barbers, and they would shear us and clean us up. Well, we had to line up. When we marched across the camp, here and there one would get beaten, according to custom. In general, whenever a new transport arrived, I found out later, it was customary to beat them, and they were told all kinds of things so that they would be seized by terror. When we arrived in the washroom, two barbers were ready with their machines. And a man came in with a whip in his hand, beautiful boots, a good jacket, dressed warm and beautiful.

Was this a German?

No, a Jew. And so one of the pushers from the night shift—he happened to be a very nice chap. He knew, so he said, "This is a *kat*." *Kat* in Polish is an executioner. I couldn't understand what he meant. In reality a lot of people were being executed, being killed, but I just couldn't imagine it. . . . I stepped back immediately so he shouldn't look at me. I didn't want to look at him. We were led—fifty people at a time—into a small bathing room. At the most, under normal conditions, maybe fifteen people could have entered. We had to leave our things outside, and we, without even a towel, were not permitted to dry ourselves. We had to get out and dress quickly and go to—well excuse me I have forgotten. Before that, we had to pass through the barber. The barber shaved off all our hair, and after that we went into the bath. We were led into the blocks again.

We were told there would be another roll call, a special one for us to fetch our food cards. In this camp there was a rule that every one of the inmates was given a monthly food card with which he could get his dinner. It had the dates on it. Every day the date was punched out. And if one would lose such a card, he would eat no dinner. We got there, if I remember exactly, the 25th of February [1943]. We stood in line waiting for our food cards, but the question was not about cards. They were taking down what one was, where one was from, what kind of trade one had, and so on. It lasted for hours. They called out the names, and finally we got our cards, went to the counter, and fetched our dinner.

When I stood in line for my dinner I saw an orderly. There were two kinds of orderlies, one kind who were stationed in the camp, and others at the construction plant. This one was a camp orderly who always stayed home and treated the sick in the sick ward. I saw him carrying a large dish, about a liter and a half in size and packed full. Well here is what I saw. Red turnips, potatoes with their peelings—and rotten—and something else red. And I thought he was carrying it for the dogs! I couldn't imagine that it was food for humans. But when I came up to the service window, I was immediately convinced that that was cooked for me. At that time I couldn't imagine that I would ever get accustomed to such fare.

But afterward I learned that it is so. We saw dozens of prisoners, inmates of the camp, trudging toward our hall. We didn't know why. Soon we had a chance to find out for ourselves. They had been in the camp for a year. They knew that we wouldn't want our rations. And so they waited for it. Such people had the good fortune to eat our dinner.

And that again did something to me. I asked myself, what in reality is a human being? [In the camp] he doesn't notice that the potatoes are rotten, whether the food is hard or soft. He takes it. He waits in line for it. They simply fight each other for the food. When two were waiting or watching one person—new to the camp—till he shoved his plate away, both of them would throw themselves at it. Sometimes the plate would break, and nobody had anything.

So that's how it was the first day, and I just prayed to get to work again. I thought maybe on the job things would be better. In the evening there was a roll call for assignment to the various firms. Tomorrow we would know when to step forward, where to go. The twenty-nine women were exempt as they had been assigned to the kitchen and the laundry. As personnel of the camp, they did not go outside to the plants. And there had to be 100 of us, but one man was missing. I saw the camp senior get excited, so he immediately called the pushers [with] two whistles. Imagine a large square where there were about 3,000 people. It didn't take five minutes, and everybody was assembled and stood like one man.

Were these pushers the same thing as capos?

Yes, [although actual] capos were only in concentration camps. In our place there were no capos, only pushers. Then there were also group leaders. There were various categories. A pusher, for instance, was the superior of a group that worked in one firm; then there were group leaders [who] were subordinated to the pushers. One has to say that the pusher was responsible for all the Jews in his division. On the other hand, the group leader could shift his responsibility to the pusher.

Well then, a man is missing?

Yes, and they all gathered together. Immediately a command was given that it should not take more than five minutes for that man to appear. It didn't take a second, and the pushers all disappeared! And it didn't take five minutes, and the man was caught! What has happened to that man? Among those twenty-nine women was his wife and his sister-in-law. He had gone over to his wife for a moment and didn't hear that roll call was taking place. When the pushers came with this man [the camp senior] asked him in the vilest language, in Yiddish . . .

He spoke Yiddish?

Yes, all of them spoke Yiddish. The inner management of the camp was all Jewish.

There wasn't much of a debate. A stool was brought. They made him take off his pants. Two men held him, and then another *kat*—this one's name was Moshe Nachtinger, another false name—had the honor to flog this man. The first time in my life I had seen such a beating. A whip with twisted steel wire about half a meter long so that when one would beat with it on the back it would wind itself down around the stomach, where it made large cuts. Can you imagine steel wire and covered with a piece of leather? It was the first time in my life that I heard an older person, a grown up, wail and cry and plead in such a manner. I had only one wish. I only wished then to get the authority to avenge him for five minutes. I was taken by such a rebellious mood. Something was going on in my heart. What can one do? One has to keep his mouth shut and see to it that one is not getting a beating himself.

Afterward they began to assign people to various firms. We already knew what to do: to listen when [the names were] being called, run out from the line and get into another formation, and watch that there be only four in a row so that one should not happen to be the fifth; otherwise one would get such a beating that he couldn't stand in formation at all.

Then each pusher was told that he should check up whether we knew the name of our firm. And he asked everybody. To many it didn't occur to remember. Nobody was much interested in it. So when one forgot, he would get what was coming to him. [Then] we went to fetch our ration for tomorrow because in Markstadt the ration was always fetched in the evening for the next morning. The ration consisted of 330 grams of bread [11.6 ounces], a piece of margarine, and, once or twice a week, 25 grams [less than an ounce] of sausage.

Did they give you the same thing every day [for dinner]?

Yes. With such a ration one could not live longer than about three months if one worked for twelve hours [a day]. First of all, one would get thin and weak. The second consequence was that one would begin to swell, first the feet, then the face, then the eyes, forming large bags under the eyes. And the third consequence was that one would go to the sick ward and die. Or he would be killed before that at the plant because such a man, of course, could not work anymore. And at the plant they were not interested whether a fellow was sick or weak. He had to produce, and that was all.

And so the first workday came. It was a construction company that was building streets, transport facilities; in other words, it was all just common labor. I was given a shovel. In general it was terrible there. Imagine a big field, an even plain without any hill in sight. The wind was blowing, and we were very badly dressed. It would so to speak throw us off our feet. We were working all day up to dinnertime. I still remember the first day when I got those 330 grams of bread. I still could split it up. I convinced myself to distribute the bread so that I would eat some of it in the morning, some of it at nine o'clock, and something again before dinnertime. Not like the others, who devour everything all at once, and then they get swollen.

Where could you keep the rest?
I still had pockets then. I still had my civilian clothes. I only had to cut a piece from the back and front and sew a white rag underneath in the form of a Star of David. Every piece of clothing that could be separately worn, for example a pair of pants or coat, had to have the cutouts in the form of a Star of David, and a white rag would be put underneath so that it be well recognized from afar that the person was from our camp.

Now after the noontime the *Polier* would come. That is the main master of the project. [On the first day] he told us that several carloads of slag had arrived, and they had to be unloaded, and we should come immediately. And did I get black that time! The stuff was still hot. It just came out of the foundry. It was loaded immediately on trucks and driven to the highway. The wind was blowing, and everything got into my eyes. I almost couldn't see anymore; the hours appeared so long that the day seemed like a year to me.

We were lucky. We were working for a firm that only worked from 7:00 to 5:00, and we went home again. We fetched our dinner, and we got gradually accustomed to the work and to the food as well. And then one would eat a plateful, or two, or three, and—if we only had it—many more.

Now I want to talk about the general conditions in [Markstadt]. At 5:00 we had to get up and dress very quickly and wash—that means whoever wanted to wash; at the beginning everybody would wash himself because they were still accustomed to that from home. At 5:30 there was roll call on the square. There was a custom in this camp that people had to appear in three different groups. First the groups that marched away from the camp. I belonged to one of these; we marched at six o'clock. There was an early shift group, and they left at 5:00. The late group went at 6:30; those who worked near the camp and did not need more than half an hour for their walk. We would step forward according to the firms in which we worked. The camp senior would appear fifteen minutes to six; he quickly would give two whistles so that the pushers should assemble, calling them according to the firm. For instance he would call a firm [name], and then the pusher would report, saying "twenty-two" or however many, [and] distribute the work slips to the foreman. The foreman had to sign that everybody was at work, and the pushers would approach their divisions, and exactly at 6:00 the camp commandant with his thick belly would come in very elegantly. The camp senior had to make a report [with] everybody still standing at attention with caps off.

And was he a Jew?

Yes. He had been in the Polish army, and he did it very efficiently: "Herr commandant, there are so and so many Jews ready for work; so many for the hospital; and so many for the early shift; so many for the day shift; and a total of so many." When that was done, the guards would assemble, and the chief of the guard would appear before his division; he had his assignment to lead us to work.

Were the guards SS?

No. At that time it was the Wehrmacht, people either on leave or those who were somewhat sick or could not fight anymore on the front. When we came to our plant, each one who worked in the firm went to his foreman and had to stand at attention. The foreman would come out and look at us and then assign each one to his place. There were various plants. There were plants where they looked just for skilled workers—of course, their situation was much better. [Other] divisions had mostly road labor. If the division was large, more guard masters would come with us. I worked for quite a long time for this firm in transport and road construction.

We worked until twelve o'clock without any interruption, constantly being coaxed by the foreman and by the guard, listening to their yells; every mistake was immediately taken notice of, and we simply were trembling at our shovel. At noon we had half an hour; those who had such a strong will that they had saved some bread would eat something while the others had to look on, and each one had the desire to tear the bread out of his mouth. At 12:30 we returned to work. During the day there would come various officers to check on the guard, and at the same time they would also check up on us; and when they disliked somebody or in general to instill fear, they would write down their names and a note would go to the camp and punishment would be meted out by the Jewish executioners in the presence of the camp commandant.

And for what reason would they do it?

Well, for example we could not live from the ration allotted to us. There were a number of civilian workers in the camp who tried to turn some tricks. If one still had a good shirt from home, one would sell it and run around without a shirt. If one managed to snatch a cigarette, he would sell it for bread, which was considered a great crime. One would get beaten for such a thing. The number of strokes depended on the camp senior.

Did something of the kind happen to you?

Yes. I worked with a firm that constructed railroad tracks and communications. I had to repair the tracks, and I had a few cigarettes on me. So a Czech, a civilian, not a prisoner, passed by and asked me whether I had some cigarettes. They knew that we had cigarettes. Sometimes we would get an allotment of cigarettes. Since I didn't smoke, I collected them. I looked around whether the guard wasn't there and went with him to the toilet to give him the cigarettes. But the guard had observed me. He slowly followed us and quietly opened the door. The [Czech] wanted to give me bread. The guard came in: "What are you doing here?" and I said, "I was just stepping out." He said, "Yes, you are swindling, you are trading," and I couldn't say a word anymore, I knew what was in store for me. He immediately wrote down my name, then he undressed me, asked me if I had any money on me or such things, but he found nothing, and then a report went to the camp. He found the cigarettes, took them away, and when I returned to the camp, I was immediately called to the "cold food room" where the cold meals were handed out.

The camp senior came in. A few other boys were waiting. Five boys had returned to the camp but without a guard. The rule was that they should call for a guard or join another group or report. They didn't do it. And there was one who had stolen some turnips that had rolled away from a car at the railroad station. When they were beaten, I became so terrified that I let down my pants and laid down [before my turn]. I struggled so much that I threw the two [men] who held me to the floor. The stool under my stomach slipped out, and we all three fell. When I got my allotment, I couldn't get up anymore. [But then] I had to get up, because they continued beating, and finally you would get up. I put on my pants and went to my barracks; the people with whom I lived put on cold compresses; the next morning they could see what I had on my body. They called it a map, black and blue lines that formed a map.

Returning again to work conditions. After lunch we worked until five o'clock, and about six o'clock we were home again. They fetched our dinner. One could go and bathe. In the winter there was some hot water. There was a special bath master who had to see to it. The rooms were not heated. There was no coal. Every day there were two other people who would go and get the "cold food," clean up the rooms and by 10:00 it was "lights out," and everyone had to be in his bed. After all, all night there had to be a night watch. There were twenty-six men in one room, so we arranged [it so that] at every hour another one was holding watch. About every third day one had to take over the watch for one hour. It was only one hour, but imagine that in the middle of one's sleep—and we really didn't have too much time for sleep—one had to get up whether it was cold or not, with nothing to wear to watch for an hour.

Most harmful were those three *kats*. Every night they would go through all the rooms and would look for some dust and would look under the bed if there wasn't some straw; and we had to arrange things in such a manner that we would not move because otherwise there was immediately a piece of straw under the bed. In each room a trusty was responsible for the room; if things were not just so, he would be the first one to be punished. And a little piece of straw; if that was found, the room trusty was so badly beaten he would remain lying on the floor. Then they would take each one of us twenty-five and they would get their portion for the straw.

We had no good brooms, we had to find brooms ourselves; gather weeds in fields and make brooms of them. When one would go to bed, he would look below to see whether by lying down he didn't in any way dirty up or that a piece of straw hadn't fallen down. They [the *kats*] came in the first night; we were still new. They didn't find anything [so] they took up something else—some dirty feet. They immediately beat up the room trusty [so badly] that he had to be taken to the sick ward, and every one of us got twenty-five [blows].

What do you mean, "everyone?" It wasn't their fault that one had dirty feet.

Was anybody asked if he was guilty? Did one have the right to defend himself? We wouldn't dare to say a word. In the beginning we tried—we didn't know yet, so we tried to defend ourselves [with the result that] we would get still more. But of course they would not beat that many people in every room.

At the beginning I would never fall asleep without hearing screams. It does something to a person, and he becomes like paralyzed. The night was terrible.

Our clothes were reasonably good at first. When one constantly wears the same clothes they get torn, become rags. There was a tailor shop; the women worked there. But when one has only one pair of pants and they are torn, in what can one go to work? One could give it up for repair only when one wouldn't go to work. There was a plant that did not work on Sunday; then Saturday night 3,000 would turn over their clothes. How much could they mend? Rarely could we get something from the tailor shop. The tailor shop mostly worked for the camp personnel. They would make nice clothes, and in the shoemaker shop . . .

What personnel, the SS?

No, the Jewish block seniors, the division pushers would order nice boots, all kinds of other things for themselves.

Did the Germans permit that?

Yes, that was precisely the principle and the plan; if they feed and dress one Jew well, this person would always be afraid to lose his job; and his life, too, depended on that. If he lost his position, he would go down just like the others, and he was ready, rather, to kill a hundred others. The Germans didn't have to bother with the whole camp population at all; just appoint one Jew, and then he would arrange everything in the best order to their satisfaction and very often, much beyond their demands.

Although I had seen the Jewish militia at home, I never could imagine that one Jew could do such things to another Jew. If I should imagine what I would have done in their place, I am by no means sure today [that I can say] "No, I would not have accepted such a position." One was only under Jews, and still one Jew was ready to kill the other for a little bread, just out of irritation; the other fellow was not considered a human being . . .

[K. was close to tears, and there was a long pause during which he pulled himself together. He then explained that late in 1943 he learned of the liquidation of the Dabrowa ghetto, which had occurred in June of that year.]

Meanwhile, when they were making that district Jew-free, a transport of fifty [Jewish] militiamen arrived in Markstadt. Many people took their revenge. Although many of them [the prisoners] lived under bad conditions and themselves were oppressed, they still did what they wanted, that is, they would beat up the [former] militia people because they knew well what they had done to their families at home.

If one prisoner beat another prisoner, was he punished for it?
It all depended on the mood of the block senior. They were glad if people were fighting, and then they would come and kill both of them.

In March 1943 rumors came that all civilian camps under the Wehrmacht—ours was still called a civilian camp because we would not wear prisoner uniforms, wearing only the Star of David—had to be subordinated to the SS. And while we were at [Markstadt] we had built a new camp, not knowing for whom [or] what kind of camp it would be. It was the concentration camp Fünfteichen, five kilometers away from Markstadt. One day several SS officers came and started a selection. A doctor came, and if one wasn't very well, he was sent immediately to Auschwitz, and the rest, 1,800 people, they sent over to Fünfteichen. Well, a new life started there.

Did you continue working in the same factory?
Yes, because they needed us; we produced a great deal.

You told me before that the whole organization of Markstadt was such that nobody could live there longer than three months. How long were you there?
I was there a year.

How do you explain that?

I worked with civilians, I sold my shirt, sometimes I would beg so I would get a little piece of bread, a bit of soup; I simply begged. Some people had pity—then I would get cigarettes from the camp. I would trade them, and so it went.

So how would you sell them to the civilians? Is it possible that the civilians couldn't even get cigarettes?

No, in Germany it was very difficult to get cigarettes; even the Germans bought cigarettes [from us]. Then there were many who applied themselves very hard, and the foreman would bring them some food; he would not question whether it was a Jew. There were many such cases. And those who had no "luck" and had to live only from their rations, they just didn't survive, because it was just impossible.

And how many of your twenty-six did survive?

I don't know anymore. Those times I didn't think anymore of the twenty-six—one thinks only of himself.

And so we got to [Fünfteichen]. We marched in; everybody had to take a stool from the old camp. They didn't have any stools—it was a new camp. When we marched in, [an SS man] stood there and said, "Jews here, right? You are still marching today, but I can guarantee you that in two weeks you won't be marching anymore."

Fünfteichen belonged to the command of Gross-Rosen. When we arrived there were already a few Russian prisoners. There we were regular prisoners in prisoners clothes, those striped clothes. Six hundred Jews arrived a few months later from Auschwitz. They came to work in the buildings which we had built before. They immediately installed machinery and were manufacturing cannons. Since such prisoners were considered dangerous, they were put in closed shops where they could not escape. Otherwise the capos and the whole management of the camp were Poles and Germans. Also prisoners. But these were professional criminals who had spent ten or twelve years in prisons already before the war, and now they had advanced themselves and become block seniors. So what can one expect from such people? When we arrived and they heard that we were Jews, they had the best opportunity to show their morals and to deal with us just as they pleased, because they were given complete authority. And I was assigned to block 17. Here we had a Pole from the Ukraine, a real bandit, a real criminal. And with dirty language, the only one he knew with his intelligence. Right away he started to beat us, and it was just terrible.

We were all exhausted, and there was so much blood on the floor, so he ordered [us] to wipe off the blood and line up in rows inside the room, and so we had to stand all night. He chose a deputy block senior, and they slept in shifts, one two hours, the other two hours, and they stood guard over us so that nobody should sit down. And when somebody sat down, he did not see another sunrise. Then they ordered us to the blocks.

We got breakfast. Well the breakfast was better than in the Jewish camp because we got hot soup in the morning. After the soup we had to clean up the block, make the beds. The block was divided into three parts, the eating room and on both sides sleeping rooms. At the start each one of us had a bed to himself [with] a blanket; the beds had to be in the best order, flat as a table. And when something was not just so, the person was given some *experience!* When it was reported that the beds were ready, he [the capo] would come in, and when he couldn't find anything [wrong], he would chase us all out of the sleeping room, do something to a bed, call us back: "Look what kind of beds you make."

Nobody could defend himself. We had brought various eating utensils with us from the Jewish camp, so he threw it all out on the garbage heap and said, "When you go to work you have to organize dishes, you must organize everything." But I didn't yet know what that meant. Well, it simply meant that we had to steal it. The block senior demanded that we steal at the construction works, and when we were caught at the construction works, then they would come to the block senior, and he would beat us for it. Whatever you did you were beaten for it.

I want to tell an episode which made a great and good impression on me. A father and son were on our block. The father was already fifty years old, and I don't know how he got to Fünfteichen. He was already a bit swollen. And he had a son who was very strong. While in the Jewish camp he worked in a good plant, and he knew how to take care of himself. Otherwise he worked around the Czech barracks, and at the beginning, the Czechs had a lot to eat, so they would throw away some moldy bread on the garbage heap and from that a person could nourish himself well. One was lucky when one could find such things. So he was sufficiently strong. And the father, because he was old and couldn't move so fast, would always fall the first victim. He was beaten so badly that he really couldn't take it anymore. And on a day that the father got the first beating the son couldn't stand it anymore. Somehow he got up courage, and he stepped forward: "Herr block senior, why do you beat my father?" And as soon as he heard it he raised his club, but he didn't strike him yet. "What, you dare to ask me such a question? You know that I have the say over the life of your father, and your life, and over the lives of these 150 cursed Jews; and that I can do what I please. You dare to tell me something?" So [the son] said, "Herr block senior, you may beat me as much as you like, I won't say a thing, and I won't cry, but let my father alone." And I don't know how it made an impression on [the capo], but he did not touch the father anymore. On the contrary, he gave him more soup, and he gave the son an assignment inside the block, and he could always scrub the floors, and he would get more to eat. Of course, one can't say that if everyone had done that he would have gotten away with it, because many certainly acted in a similar manner and were killed for it. Such things were not tolerated in the camp. But this one got away with it.

Of the 170 men where I was, there were fewer and fewer every day. The beating wasn't all. They wouldn't let us sleep. Every evening when we would return he [the block senior] would detain us in the eating hall. One couldn't go out to the toilet; we could go only in groups and only when one would take the responsibility for it, and every evening we were up until one, two o'clock, and at 5:00 we had to get up.

No matter how much you force him, a human being still always has a limit. When they beat us so much, and with little food, one just didn't have the strength to work. We simply would fall asleep on the job. The foremen understood. Finally they saw that beating didn't accomplish anything. The construction authorities interceded with the camp commandant, and an order was issued by the commandant that at nine o'clock everybody must be in bed and no more beating. Oh, when we returned and heard the news we were all gladdened. We said Messiah had come. But [the block senior] said, "Yes, I can't beat anymore, but I will inspect for lice. Whoever has lice will not go to sleep until he has no more lice." Well, we had them by the thousands. You can't imagine. And for one to get them all off would have taken an eternity.

How would you get them off?

Well, we just had to squeeze them with our fingers. And that he made us do. And there wasn't anybody who had no lice. And so we were up until two o'clock again, and then he took pity and let us go to sleep. And we reported it, so an order came that he shouldn't do that either, and we should be able to go to sleep at nine o'clock. This lasted for a week. We had more peace in the block, and the block seniors just couldn't stand for it. They had to beat us. That was their urge like a person has to eat, so they reported to the chancellery [the clerical bureau] that we were not conforming to the requirements of the camp; that we no longer kept order, that we let dirt lie around, and so on. So they arranged it that beating was again permitted, but no killing. Only *dry* blows that [would show] no marks afterward. So right away he [the block senior] prepared two clubs at the door, so when the first two [prisoners] arrived, he immediately stretched [them] over a chair and beat them. And so in three months we saw nothing but beatings, killings, more killings, nothing to eat, and hard work. During the first three months they took 800 men to the crematorium.

We got accustomed to it again. We got to know the foremen and started trading again. In this camp it was better in that we were getting more cigarettes. Good workers would get more, each according to his work. And it also depended upon the foreman from whom we would get some premium coupons, worth a mark or two, and use them to buy cigarettes [in the] canteen. It went so far that some did real business with the foreman, and they would get premium coupons worth several hundred marks. For them they could get a lot of cigarettes, and they would give the cigarettes to the foreman, and the foreman would give them chocolate in exchange, or alcohol, and that they would bring to the camp and give it to the block seniors, and so they would make friends with them.

The foreman was not a prisoner?

No, he was just a civilian. And so they [the foremen] would get together with the block seniors and "associate" with the Jews. The Jews were useful to them, and so a time came that nearly half of the block trusties were Jews, and in the kitchen the majority were Jews, and nearly the whole office personnel were Jews. The Jews almost took over the camp, and it became much easier for the whole camp. We weren't threatened so badly anymore. Oh yes, they beat people, because the Jewish block trusties would also beat people. But one was beaten not specially *as a Jew*. I also started some trading, I also got bonus coupons because I worked well, and the foremen started to like me a bit. Sometimes they would give me a bit of bread, and they started to give me premium coupons.

At what were you working at that time?

At Hellgolder's, a Viennese company. We would lay out cold and warm sheets together and make roofing material. This was very dangerous work. These were like asbestos sheets. The sheets were a mixture of wood shavings and some poison. We could not step on them when they were freshly laid. If one stepped on them, one would fall down. We built the roofs for the Krupp plants. That was the only firm. And we had many cases of falls. Many who fell from the roof were dead on the spot.

Well, I got accustomed to the work. I can say I had luck. I got accustomed to running over the roofs. We were not permitted to run on the sheets, but we had to run on the planks that were laid. For two years I worked for the same firm. I was very much liked there, and at the end I got a lot of premium coupons; I would buy cigarettes for them in the canteen, and sometimes I would buy bread with them and sell the bread again in the camp for more, and so I would earn something. And so I managed to get ahold of some marks because in this camp money had value, because many civilians worked in the plant, and they could make use of the money. That's how we could say that business became big. We already knew that here you could get food, here you could get bread, and people were trading. And finally I earned one hundred marks. These I gave to an acquaintance who worked in the kitchen, that he should intervene with the chief of the kitchen so that he should take me in as kitchen help. That meant that evenings when I came home from work I would go there to work.

The enemy was very near us, and we had to evacuate in January 1945. For the journey we were given 500 grams of bread, a piece of sausage, two blankets, and we marched. Whether one had shoes or not, nobody bothered about it. In the deepest snow we ran forward. We left on a Sunday afternoon at 3:00 under SS guard, and we ran until 2:00 at night without sleep, but then the SS got tired, so they drove us into a barn where hardly 500 men could crowd in. We were 5,000 altogether, so they put two such barns at our disposal. If one had enough strength, he killed another one so that he could sleep on top of him, so that he had more room. When we got up in the morning, the dead were stacked like railroad ties. Stacked up and abandoned. And so we marched five miles, and we didn't get anything more to eat. Many fell on the way, and those who couldn't keep up anymore would step aside waiting for death.

How would he wait for death?
He stands by himself under a tree, his eyes shining like reflectors. And he waits for the moment when the whole formation will have passed by till the hindmost guards arrive who will shoot him. A man with his full mental abilities, who knows what is going on, and he waits for death. And so every three, ten meters one saw somebody standing under a tree, or sitting down, and such a man would be shot and thrown into the ditch. We arrived at Gross-Rosen no more than 4,800. Eight hundred died on the road or were shot.

2　Udel S.

The Upper Silesian city of Bedzin where Udel S. was born in 1915 is just a few miles from Abraham K.'s hometown. In the 1930s it had nearly 60,000 inhabitants, about half of them Jews. S. mentions initial German atrocities there in September 1939 but provides details only for the period after 1941, when Nazi policies caused the Jewish population of Bedzin to double. Not only did the Germans ship Jews from small communities in the surrounding area to the city; they also put off construction of a ghetto there until January 1943, which made it for some time a refuge for Jews fleeing harsher persecution elsewhere in Poland. S. points out that in 1942 the Jews in Bedzin heard about Auschwitz from an escapee and apparently believed what they were told. And yet, apart from constructing hiding places to avoid deportations to the nearby killing center, S. recalls more resignation and denial than resistance among his fellow Jews. He holds Moshe Merin responsible for lulling the Jews into a false sense of hope that deportation meant being sent to work someplace else.

Udel S. remained in Bedzin until the Germans began to liquidate the local ghetto on August 1, 1943. Perhaps the most affecting passages of his interview describe attempts by his family and others to evade the deportations by hiding in cleverly concealed rooms in their ghetto apartments. Especially for those like S. who had children, the results were usually tragic. After a few days, hiding became impossible; S. and his family, together with many of their neighbors, simply gave themselves up. Sent to Auschwitz with five members of his family, only he survived. One of his most vivid memories of Auschwitz was the cruelty of the Jewish capos there. He was then sent to work at the Krupp arms plant at Fünfteichen, the same camp that held Abraham K. (although there is no indication that they knew each other there). When it was evacuated in the early part of 1945, S. was sent via Gross-Rosen to Flossenbürg concentration camp in Germany, and he ended up being marched from there to Theresienstadt in Czechoslovakia, where he remembers conditions being still comparatively good. Among his memories of the last days of this "model" ghetto was the arming of Jews by Czech guards, who until then had worked for the Germans.

As S. saw it, postwar Europe could only be viewed as a land of exile, one that "burned," in the colorful Yiddish term that traditionally referred to anti-Jewish violence. Two of his brothers gained entry into Palestine by impersonating members of the "Jewish Brigade" of Palestinian Jews who had volunteered to fight Hitler in Europe. Udel S., however, returned to Bedzin to discover the fate of his remaining family. There he experienced the persistence of Polish anti-Semitism at first hand. At the time of his interview in September 1946 at Henoville, France, S. had just arrived to take charge of an ultraorthodox kibbutz financed by American Jewish charities. There 120 Jews like himself learned carpentry, tailoring, and agricultural skills in preparation for new lives in Palestine.

I was in Bedzin from 1939 to 1943. In various ghettos. Sometimes in a large ghetto up to April 1943, when ghettos surrounded with wire fences were established. When the Germans arrived in Bedzin, I was at home. We were a family of twelve, ten children and my father and mother. At first we lived unmolested. The first few weeks various misfortunes happened to other Jews. They [the Germans] burned the synagogues and the prayer house, and a number of Jews were shot right away; they burned down various streets where the Jews lived, but nothing happened to our family then. Right away, the first day when they marched in, they took 170 Jews and shot them.

Did you see it?
I did not see it, but afterward when we came outside, we saw Jews sitting in poses like it would be Saturday night; they were sitting in their silk coats, with their heads leaning against the wall, and they [had been] shot, not once, but several times. Entire pieces of flesh were torn away.

Who buried them?
The official Jewish undertakers. In the cemetery. In four [mass] graves, women and men separately. [The Germans] did not permit digging so many graves if each one would have been buried separately because it took too much time.

At that time it wasn't yet known for what purpose the Jews were sent away. It was said that the Jews were being resettled to other districts where they could continue to live. But [in 1942] information leaked through that such a thing as Auschwitz had been created. A woman from Bedzin managed to escape—in what way is not exactly known—but she escaped from that hell, and she reported exactly how things occurred there.

From the beginning of 1942 misfortune also started to fall upon our family. We were ten children. All of us—the youngest one was thirteen years old and the oldest one was thirty-five—they started sending away one by one. One brother was sent away to labor service. This means he was sent away deep into Germany;

he was getting hardly any food except for 200 to 300 grams of bread a day, barely anything else, and so he had to work eight, ten, or even twelve hours a day. This was not yet considered too terrible because after all the people were still alive. We still were able to maintain contact with our children, we were able to write letters to them. In 1942 my father died a natural death at home. [On] the 12th of August 1942 they ordered all the Jews of Bedzin to assemble on three squares. At that time they were 57,000 Jews.

The squares were surrounded and guarded by the Gestapo with machine guns. And they started a selection. People who were working were assigned to [group] one; they had papers from the authorities, and that meant that they may live. But older people, children, or those [the German officer] generally didn't like the looks of were assigned to [group] three; these were set apart, and from them transports were formed—two, three thousand Jews—and sent to Auschwitz. Group two meant the doubtful cases. When the German was unable to decide from a person's papers whether his work was sufficiently important, then these people were ordered aside for the time being, and at night the proprietor of the plant would arrive, and if he would report that he needed the people, then such people would be released, and they would continue going to work. Because they had set up certain workshops in Bedzin like in America [employing large numbers of workers] which worked for the German Wehrmacht. Such people still had the right to remain at home.

[S. mentioned the role of Monek Merin in the roundups of Jews in Bedzin. Boder interrupted to get more details.]

Monek Merin was the leader of the Central Office of the Jewish Community Councils. He maintained contact with Berlin, with the Gestapo, with everybody. He had full rights to travel wherever he wanted to. He was a congenial Jew; he meant well at first, but later he was the executor of all the orders of the Gestapo. He knew that the Jews were going to Auschwitz, and he would assemble these Jews. He would send the old people to Auschwitz because he judged that an old person was already useless, he wouldn't bring anybody into this world, while young people could reproduce. But in time it became clear that he was simply a traitor to the Jewish people. If he hadn't confused our minds, if he hadn't talked us into thinking that there was a chance for salvation, we possibly would have organized for resistance. But he lulled us to sleep so much that we did not organize any resistance, and we went like sheep to the slaughter. Without any resistance whatsoever. And so things went on until April 1943. [Then] for reasons which we could not ascertain, the Gestapo took this same Monek Merin with all the other [Jewish] authorities and sent them, too, to Auschwitz. And we Jews remained without leadership, without anything.

The first trouble took place the 22nd of June. They surrounded the whole ghetto [which was located] outside of the town. Seventeen thousand Jews still lived there. And they took 4,000 of the most splendid young people, the Jewish youth, and they were immediately sent to Auschwitz. We already knew of the danger, we were prepared for it; and when I saw that the horror was imminent and there was no salvation of any kind, we made bunkers, hideouts for ourselves. For instance we excavated, constructed various kinds of cellars. We constructed [double] walls, so with the first threats of danger one could hide. Because as soon as Russia entered the war, we had information that America and England had allied themselves with the European powers, so we thought that help was near and we would be able to hold out two, three, or even four months in the hideouts. But time has shown that that was a mistake, and we were unable to hide.

The 1st of August 1943 we were informed that Bedzin was to become Jew-free. No Jew should be found in Bedzin. At that time I still had a sister, a brother, and a wife with a child of fourteen months, and an in-law with me. I had constructed a hideout, and we were lying there for seven days.

Tell me a bit, I can't well imagine these hideouts; how did people live in them?

We arranged [one] right in the apartment. Suppose for example a room was four or five meters long. We would separate one meter, and we constructed a new wall. Along the wall we would place a cupboard [or] a wardrobe, and inside, in the back, we would make a kind of opening through [which] one could get in; and there we simply would lie on the floor all day. People would go out at night, and the lucky ones came back. The unlucky one was shot. Because during the evening the ghetto was surrounded. As soon as they would hear a shot they would turn their searchlights on that point and begin to shoot. Many people were killed, but every day they would send away a transport, 2,000 Jews, to Auschwitz. I was hiding for seven days. My child died in the bunker on account of lack of proper nourishment. It was August, the weather was very hot . . .

Did you have a window?

No, no window. We made little holes between the bricks through which air could come in. For a grown-up person it could be sufficient, but for a child, he would become suffocated . . .

Wasn't there a danger that a child might cry?

Precisely. For example in the case of my brother, the mother herself simply choked the child to death. They were hiding in a very small bunker. And they heard the Gestapo come into the apartment. The child was about two years old [and] tried to cry, so the mother, thinking that it was just for moment, plugged up her little mouth. But because the Gestapo remained upstairs longer [than expected], and there were nineteen grown-up people below in the cellar, she held her hand so long that the child suffocated. She simply choked her own child to death with her own hands. In the case of my child it was different on account of lack of air and sucking poison and gall from the mother.[1]

How old was the child?

Fourteen months old. And so when the child died, we became convinced of the futility of remaining longer in the bunker, because the child was our only hope; there was no purpose for us to live. That's how my wife felt, and we decided to come out and surrender to the Gestapo. They received us very politely; they did not beat us. And so we six went, we even asked him [the German] whether we should take our bundles, so he said, "Yes, because you are young people, and you are being transported to work."

[S. and his relatives were then sent to Auschwitz by train. The trip lasted longer than usual] because we made stops at various stations, and the train had no clearance to proceed ahead. Soon children began to suffocate in these cars. We arrived at Auschwitz and stopped at the ramp. We disembarked and they told us to wait. On one side stood trucks, on the other side stood SS men with their guns, and in the center stood a Gestapo man with a little stick. And he was pointing. The one to whom he pointed toward the right had to go to the trucks, and it was known that he was going directly to the crematoria. They were throwing people alive and dead, children, all together in these trucks as if they were not people; they were thrown just as if they were all dead. From [my] car they took out thirty-four suffocated people.

I and my brother and my wife, we were fortunate that we were assigned to the left side, and it was said that we are still going to the camp; there was hope for us to live. And we never saw the people who were loaded on the trucks again, but within an hour we saw the same trucks returning with the dirty clothing of these people. It was said that these people had already gone through the gas chambers. We were all lined up four abreast and transported away on foot toward the inside of the camp.

[Boder wanted to know who from S.'s family was sent to the gas chambers at that time.]

My mother-in-law, my sister, and my sister-in-law—although she was eighteen years old, she did not look so well; she was what they called a "Moslem," a person who looked very emaciated and had no right to live.

We arrived at Auschwitz at two o'clock. We were led into special blocks, so-

---

1. Folk wisdom at the time had it that emotional stress poisoned a mother's milk.

called barracks, erected of wood. As soon as we entered, the ruler of Auschwitz came: "Quick! Hurry! Move it!" in German. "Strip completely!" And in a minute one had to be completely undressed, and soon their clubs were striking our back, and we were driven into what they called the washroom to bathe. At the bath they sheared off our hair *everywhere*. This was done by Jews, well-seasoned, old prisoners. French Jews, Belgian Jews, those who had managed to achieve a certain post, a certain rank. One of them was a barber, the other a clerk, and the like, and they proceeded with this work. They called one squad the Canada squad. That was the squad that emptied all the railroad cars of all the transports. They gathered all the gold, diamonds, dollars. These people used to take away the food from the whole transport, because everybody would take food for himself, so they had food without limit. And they too were Jews, Polish Jews. Then there also was a gas squad made up of Jews who serviced the crematoria.

We arrived at the west barracks, and as I have remarked before, we were taken and completely shorn, every hair. Just from the shearing one could see that "Auschwitz" had begun. The shearing took place with terrible tortures. They did not shear like humans, but simply were tearing, and people were screaming from suffering. But after all, we understood that we were in Auschwitz. We bathed, everyone got a ragged shirt, a pair of pants, and a coat to wear. No shoes, no hat.

What were these things, specially made?
No. These were the things of the people who were gassed, specially prepared with "KL" written on the back [so] that no one should be able to escape.[2] And they led us to the quarantine to prepare us for work. As soon as we arrived there, they put us six people to a "container," a unit of three beds, one over the other. Boards just knocked together. The bed was about a meter and half wide and two meters long. One blanket was spread underneath, and one blanket was to cover. And afterward they started to call out the people and give them numbers, numbers on their arms made with a special thing that looked like a pen. And it had a point, and it would get under the skin. One didn't feel pain anymore because a man was not a man anymore.

What does that mean . . . ?
One did not feel pain anymore, neither this nor a good blow, a good slap, a good knock on the head. One had resigned himself to anything. One was not concerned whether he goes to the gas chambers or someplace else.

Every Saturday selections took place. People had to strip completely, a German doctor passed through the lines, and [if] boils of various kinds, skin erup-

2. KL = Konzentrationslager, German for concentration camp.

tions, and things like that were found, these people were immediately sent to the gas chamber. Even if he was working. My brother went after a selection along with my wife.

Were you and your brother together?

We slept in one bed. I saw him the Saturday when he was selected; Sunday morning he would be sent to the gas chamber, but unfortunately I could not find a way [to help him], I could do no more than weep and wail. I had to look on, not only when my brother but all my friends, all my comrades, relatives were sent away. I want to point out one thing here. When people were selected, and it being known that they would be taken Saturday night, there was curfew on the block. It was prohibited to step out from the barracks, and one heard the screams like one solid wail. Because the people were taken right there and then, naked, on the trucks and transported to the crematoria. And the screams were like one solid wail, but again it was the same thing. We had to sit around saying nothing because what did we have to defend ourselves with? And what could we accomplish? One was fortunate to get his 200 grams of bread. This was the only hope of survival.

I spent three months in Birkenau, and the things I saw no man can imagine. Once one of my comrades was standing and working, and an SS man approached him with a gun and asked him whether he was thirsty. Of course he replied, "Yes." So he called over a second comrade, a certain Udel Tshernetsky from Bedzin, and he shot him, and then he said, "Here, now you may drink your brother's blood." This I saw with my own eyes.

What were you working on these three months?

Not the same thing every day. We carried rocks from the railroad station in the camp. We were digging ditches, to beautify the camp. Because the Germans were ready to "bury" the people, but the camps had to look nice. So we made lawns, concrete [walks], all under the supervision of capos.

And who were the capos?

Jews, Frenchmen, Germans. They were Jews . . .

French Jews?

Yes. They were worse, these French Jews, than the Germans, unfortunately. It was this way. They simply had such a drive to live. Because he [the capo] was getting an additional ration of bread and an additional dinner, so he was ready to beat the life out of a person, and he indeed was beating people that way. And after three months I felt that my strength was waning; I observed that we were becoming fewer and fewer. [He corrects himself:] We really did not become fewer in numbers because every day new people arrived. The camp had to have a stable population. So the weak ones were immediately sent to the crematoria and fresh [contingents] brought in.

And there came a day when they picked 650 Jews, the healthiest ones—it was alleged that they were the healthiest ones—and we were sent to a Krupp plant near Breslau, in Germany. There a period began that I might call a better life for us. In spite of the fact that it was terrible enough, we were given work like human beings. We were already working men, we got more to eat. They beat us an awful lot.

Why?

Just for no reason, because we were Jews. Frenchmen and Czechs, Christians worked there. Members of the labor service. They were not beaten, they ate better, they had freedom of movement. But we Jews, we had to wear special prisoners' clothing, garments with special blue and white stripes, special round little caps, special wooden shoes, so that one could not have contact with anybody. We were led to work under SS guard; every day we had to make fifteen kilometers, seven and a half [each way]. We departed at 6:00 in the morning, and we returned at 8:00 at night. Each roll call lasted an hour and a half. When we returned at 8:00 at night, we had to stand until 9:30 "to check whether the number was correct." Then we were given dinner, and we lay down. At 4:00 in the morning we were made to rise for roll call, and in ten minutes everybody had to stand in formation ready to march to work again. And so it lasted for quite some time.

In our camp we manufactured cannons whether we wanted to or not. But in time Russia started a counteroffensive. The camp might fall. An order was issued that we should evacuate Fünfteichen to an unknown destination. We were all put in formation—7,000 people were in the camp then—everyone was given a blanket, one kilo of bread, and we started a march on foot. We left Fünfteichen on the 21st of January, and we marched seven days without being given any more food. Every day we marched thirty kilometers in wooden shoes. It snowed constantly, but we marched on. Whoever had no strength to go on was shot on the spot. If he fell, he was given a bullet and thrown off the road. And we marched on. The 28th of January we arrived in the famous German camp Gross-Rosen. This was a camp laid out as big as Auschwitz, but they had no gas chambers there; there were just crematoria. When we arrived, the camp already contained 34,000 people. We experienced three horrible weeks. We became polluted with vermin. It was simply impossible to get rid of them. Lice, fleas, bedbugs, worms, everything you ever can think of, because we no longer slept in beds there. We lay stretched out on the floor with a little bit of straw under us. During this time the transport of 7,000 people to which we belonged was reduced to 4,000. The 3,000 people were either shot during the march or died out in the camp.

And in February we had to abandon Gross-Rosen, too. They loaded us into trains, open gondolas, and the snow and rain poured down from heaven as if without mercy, and we were not getting any more food at all. And every morning when we opened our eyes with daybreak, we had to throw two, three people out of the car because they had died overnight. And so we traveled for eleven days, in one station, out the other station, until on the fifteenth day, it was the beginning of March, we arrived at Flossenbürg, the famous camp on the Austrian-Czech border.[3] The camp was located on a mountain 1,500 meters high. It was something terrible. By the time we entered that camp there remained of us no more than 1,700 people.

From how many?

One doesn't know exactly; one estimates the number of people. From the 7,000 that left the camp [Fünfteichen], 3,000 fell during the march to Gross-Rosen. When we arrived at Gross-Rosen, they took us to a special sector, and they knew exactly [how many]. After Gross-Rosen, 2,300 people fell.

[At Flossenbürg] they took us into a barracks; they told us to undress completely—that was in March, and they ordered us to run. We were running, 1,700 people, entirely naked, in snow, water, mud, through the streets of the camp. After we had run 400, 500, possibly 600 meters uphill, we were led into a kind of washroom, they called it, a kind of cellar. Ukrainians stood there, also internees, and they poured cold water all over us with hoses. The windows were open, and soon, momentarily, people started to die.

Why?

Of exhaustion, from not having eaten for fifteen days; in fifteen days we had but 600 grams of bread.

But how can one go for fifteen days with only 600 grams of bread?

Every night we spent in a different place. People would find a little piece of turnip, a little kohlrabi. One also ate raw potatoes that one could snatch on the road. A leaf here and there, just like animals. A human being really can't imagine it, but I went through all this, and I know exactly how it was. Those alive were sheer skeletons, simply skin and bone. One didn't want to lay down on the bare cold floor—the floor was of stone—so people took the dead men and put them together, and we, the living ones, lay down on the dead ones.

So we remained there in the washroom until ten o'clock the next morning. No more than 1,140 of the 1,700 came out of the washroom alive; the rest died, all of them. And when we came out of the washroom, we went through the same pro-

3. Should be "the German-Czech border."

cedure as in Auschwitz. Again we were moved into various blocks. In these blocks it was worse than in Auschwitz, because in Auschwitz the blows, the beatings, were not as cruel. They had a special kind of German murderer in Flossenbürg. And in addition it was the time when the Germans started to see that they were losing the war, so they started avenging themselves without end. They were killing us, they were beating us. Every day we were removing ten, fifteen dead people from the block. So they announced that whoever would carry the dead to the crematorium to be burned—it was a provisional crematorium, a make-shift . . .

How did it look?

A pit was excavated in the forest, provided with an iron grate, iron bars. On these five [bodies] were laid out, and they burned underneath. Above them was another grate, and again people were laid out, and from the fire that burned underneath, the people on top were burned. This was without a chimney, without anything. As soon as a person died, a dentist would come over, pull out the gold teeth, and [the body] would be carted—yes, they would write down the number of the one who died—and he was burned. And since I suffered from hunger, this terrible thing came to pass. [I] enlisted [with] a group of forty people, and they brought us to the dead to [be taken to] the crematorium, and we received an additional dinner. That was called the stretcher platoon. There were some special stretchers, one man laid out one way, the other the other way; we carried two bodies at a time. More we were unable to carry.

After a stay of three weeks, an order came that we should march on. We got good, entirely new clothing but all of it marked with stripes.[4] And we were sent over to Dresden on foot. There we got better food. It happened that we had a good commander en route; we marched, a little party of only 400 men, so whenever we came to a place, he procured food for us. We went through heavy bombardments. Once in Aussig, in the Sudeten country, the Americans bombarded in broad daylight. One didn't know whether to cry or laugh. On the one hand, we suffered casualties, and about forty of our people were killed; on the other hand, we were gratified when we saw what the war made of Germany.

In Dresden we came to a provisional camp, and it was already April. We were there two weeks, and then an order came that we had to march again. And by now we remained only two hundred ninety-some people, because within this two week period again some had died. And we wandered on along the Elbe, the famous German river, in the Sudetenland. There many people jumped into the water [drowned themselves] because it was impossible to bear any longer. At that time I weighed 37 kilos [about 82 pounds]. Today I weigh 72 kilos [158 pounds].

4. Boder noted that these stripes had been painted on ordinary clothing with supposedly indelible ink by special prisoner painting squads.

3   Fela N.

Fela N. was one of thousands of Polish Jews who were sent to work in Germany during the early part of World War II and actually spent the entire Holocaust period there.[1] She had been born fourteen years before the German invasion in Wojstawice, a small community in the Bielsko district of southern Poland, southwest of Krakow. At some point during her childhood the family moved to the nearby city of Andrychow where they lived a solid, middle class existence. The Germans divided the family almost immediately, and as it turned out, irrevocably. In 1941 Fela was sent to slave labor in the first of several textile mills inside Germany, the last of which was part of Gräben, a satellite of Gross-Rosen concentration camp. She shows how conditions for her and her coworkers went from bad to worse as SS control became more nearly complete. She views herself as one who steadfastly retained her dignity through every ordeal, confounding some of her tormentors.

Evacuated westward to Bergen-Belsen at the beginning of 1945, Fela N. experienced the rapid disintegration of conditions in this hideously overcrowded camp, packed with growing numbers of forced workers from all over Hitler's collapsing empire. Anyone who reads her description of sanitary conditions there will understand why she found three months in Belsen far worse than the entire previous five years. There Fela experienced firsthand the sadism of the beautiful but mad Irma Grese, who had already established a reputation for brutality as an SS guard at Auschwitz.

Fela N. was living near Paris and studying to become a dental technician at a school run by Jewish charities when she gave her interview in August 1946. Her parents and two brothers and two sisters died in the Holocaust; only she and a younger brother survived. Boder commented: "This once lovely and sheltered girl hides her insecurity and bewilderment behind a determined regal bearing and a rigid emotional control. To contemplate how different her life might have been is to realize afresh the dimensions of the catastrophe that has befallen her." We begin with her deportation to Germany in 1941.

---

1. This interview appears in Boder's *I Did Not Interview the Dead*, under the pseudonym Fela Lichtheim.

I was sent to camp Birkenheim. That was the district of Auerbach in lower Silesia. There was a big factory, a big textile plant. Germans worked there. And there were already a hundred girls in the barracks. And other hundreds arrived from our city and from the different towns around. And so I felt for the first time that everything behind me was lost. The gate closed, and I entered into a dark hall. There stood beds and beds and more beds and nothing else. And so my second life began. I worked there for half a year. At two looms.

Were these electric looms?

Yes, electric looms. I had to service the machines myself, had to fix everything, had to get the material. I knew the machines well. The German foreman taught me. The food wasn't very bad nor was the cleanliness, but only very little freedom. We saw no people at all. The gates were covered with sackcloth and shutters so that we shouldn't see the street. We only saw the little garden where we sat and the barracks.

Did they allow any books or papers?

No, nothing. Once in two weeks we were allowed to write a letter. A postcard and that was all. And Sunday when we were free, we were permitted to lie on the bed, or in that little garden. We barely had room for ourselves and nothing else.

Were you permitted to sing?

Yes, that we were permitted. That was during the first year in the camp. Things were not yet so bad. It wasn't yet a concentration camp. It was a so-called [work camp] where one worked very hard. In the winter we could not dress well. We could put something on, on the way to the factory, but in the factory we could not wear a pullover or a jacket. One would become stiff. You see, they were afraid that one works badly when one is warmly dressed. One has less movement, and it was believed that one works less and makes lots less meters of goods when one moves slower. When you are lightly dressed, you can move faster.

Was the factory heated?

No! No! No! It was not heated at all. There were frightfully large rooms with long, long rows of machines, just machine after machine. We were not permitted to talk all day, not even to each other. Even when the girls were not watched, the motors, the [noise of] many motors would not permit us to talk.

And before our eyes was a very large clock so that we should know the time, that we should know that we have to work from 7:00 to 12:00 and from 1:00 to 6:00 in the evening. And it was done for the purpose that the time should appear to us longer. If one has a clock before his eyes, time goes much slower.

What happened when anybody got sick? Was there a doctor? Was there a hospital?

No, absolutely no. There was only a nurse and a very small sickroom of two or three beds. When one was sick, one had to be *really* sick, so that one could remain a day or two. When you *really* had gallstones or heart trouble, you would be put there for a few days until you were well again and could work again.

We worked there six months, and then came an order that fifty girls were needed in another camp, in Weidenburg in lower Silesia. So we were sorted out, and I was in the group that had to go. And so I left this camp and went to another camp. This was not a weaving plant but a spinning plant. There was nobody [there]. It was a new camp. The barracks were just put up. There was nothing, no beds, not a thing. We had to beg for everything. They didn't want to give us any water, not a dish. They believed that because we were Jews we didn't need anything, that we kept dirty and could live like animals. And so we had to fight for each saucer, for every little dish, for every blanket to cover ourselves.

In a few months the situation somewhat improved. It happened that a woman camp commander arrived. When she saw how neat we kept and that we were just like other people with whom one could talk, when she understood that we were not what people were saying about us there in the factory, she took the matter up with the director and we were given various things.

Who was this camp commander?

She was a German woman, not an SS woman. She was a plain German woman.

Did it ever happen that some girls refused to work?

No, everybody wanted to work because every girl was in good health. Not very eagerly. But when one was forced, one was put before a machine and stayed there and worked. And in time we would get accustomed to the work. The people with us were not too bad. We worked together with the Germans, outside workers, free people, free Germans, and from time to time we could slip a word to them. And we were there eighteen months.

Were they [the German workers] friendly to the prisoners?

Not all of them. Some were dangerous. Some spied to see whether we were talking to the other Germans. We had to be very careful.

Did they pay you for the work?

No. Absolutely nothing. We had our own kitchen, and the girls cooked in the kitchen. We never got any soap. We still had some things from the other camp. When we came to that first camp, we still had all our things from home. And we had soap and some other things that we needed. And they did not take away from us, so that we had everything.

The time came when all the little camps were concentrated into larger camps. And our camp consisted of only fifty people, and we had to go to a different camp, Gräben. That was a flax camp, twelve kilometers from a very big and famous camp, Gross-Rosen.

Only women?

Yes, only women. And there we were again for more than a year and a half. But then the bad times started. That was a concentration camp with very strict rules, and we definitely felt that we were not human beings. Not Jews, just animals, just at the mercy of the Germans.

The work was very hard; I suffered very much. The halls were large. We worked there the whole winter. It was terribly cold. I had nothing to wear. They took away everything. The SS came one day to the manager of women. We were told to get out of bed and get out in the yard. They counted us up, and they talked to us. The SS people told us that they saw that we are in good health and fine looking and that they wouldn't do us any harm. They would give us our things back, that we should work well and no harm will be done to us.

That was in December 1944. And they told us that we should remain outside. And while we were there all the SS men and all the SS women went into the barracks. They took away everything. They opened all the lockers, they turned over the beds. They made an inspection, and they just threw together our best things, cut them with scissors. They just ruined everything.

And then what?

We didn't understand it at all. Just a moment before they had told us everything would be all right, that we would have our things, and that we would be able to dress the way we wanted to and so on. And that was just a trick on their part so that we should just forget ourselves for a moment, and then they did such a thing to us. And then they told us to go inside. So we were left with nothing to wear, except the things we had on. And there were many girls who had been getting ready to go bathing, and they had put on some kind of morning dress, and they had left the other things inside, in the barracks. And they remained that way. All completely naked, except for a morning dress.

Most of the things they took away, and they made a warehouse. They told us that each week we would get a shirt, a pair of stockings, a dress, an overcoat in case it should be cold; and, of course, we had to submit. We were not permitted to have anything. But afterward the rooms were again put in order, and they told us that none of us would dare have more than a pair of stockings, a pair of underthings, or more that one shirt. We should not dare to have more than what was being given to us. And that was a big blow for us, because we were not accustomed to such conditions. Anything that we had from home was so dear to us, because these were the only tokens of remembrance. And it was difficult during the war to make something. Still they had ruined everything. And they liked to see it so. And they told us to get on with our work. We were then on the night shift. Without food, without sleep, without washing ourselves, still they told us to go on to the factory, go on with our work as usual.

And a very hard winter came, and we had to stand at the machinery that was thousands of times bigger then ourselves, in frost, and in hunger; and we had to stay there and work. Twelve hours, from 6:00 in the morning until 6:00 in the evening. The next week it was 6:00 in the evening until 6:00 in the morning— with only a quarter of an hour for rest.

Were they working on Sunday?
They worked most Sundays. They told us that we were free, but wagon-loads of flax would arrive from the fields, and we had to go to work and unload everything, and unload all of that in the biggest and worst frost.

What were you doing with that flax?
That was processed by machines and a better flax would come out. Then it was processed by other machines, and then it would come to the spinnery and from the spinnery to the weaving plant. So it went on.

And how long were you at the flax plant?
About a year and a half. There I was terribly sick. I once fell off my bed, because we had two-level or three-level bunks. I was on the night shift, and I wanted to get up early. I was still half asleep, and so I fell down and I caused a very small wound on the bone. I paid no attention, I thought it would heal in a couple of days. I had been working in dust, terrible dust. That was the worst thing, because this dust got into our noses and our lungs. We could not talk or breathe there. We couldn't even see each other, there was so much dust around. So the dust got into the little wound; it became larger from day to day. Pus developed, and I had a temperature of 40° [104°F] and had to stay in bed. I thought and hoped that in a week or two it would get well. It lasted two and a half months. I could not walk. I was very weak, and so I remained in bed for two and a half months in the barracks.

You were not in a hospital? Did the doctor come to see you?
No, absolutely, no. I didn't want him. If I had asked for a doctor, a German doctor would have come, and he would have said that I had to go to Auschwitz, as being unfit for work. And that's what happened after a certain length of time.

How was it that they allowed you to stay in bed?

Well, in the morning roll call your name was called. So the medical trusty, a Russian woman, would say, "N. is sick, she is unable to work." And they believed her, and every day the SS camp senior would come to the barracks to see whether somebody hadn't remained there. She would go into the room for the sick to see especially that somebody wasn't pretending to be sick. She herself would examine the people. The reports from our camp were going to Gross-Rosen because we belonged to the concentration camp Gross-Rosen, and everything that happened in our camp had to be made known to the commandant of Gross-Rosen. For example, every day a list of the sick and also of the ones who were well and able to work went over [to Gross-Rosen]. And so my name went there often, almost every day during the two and a half months. I was sick, constantly sick, and they didn't like it very much. An order came that I should be sent to the Auschwitz crematory because I was unfit for work and it was impossible to keep me longer. They didn't tell me that. They knew how sensitive I was. They were afraid that I would do something; they didn't tell me anything. Only after liberation I was told that I was to have been sent to Auschwitz[2] within a few days. All were very grieved, and still they couldn't do anything. It surely would have happened that way.

Within a few days an order came that the whole camp had to go to transport. It was again one of those times when all the camps were being abandoned, and again people were driven away because the Russians were near. And so we, the sick, had to get up, and those who were well also had to get up, and we had to pack all our things, everything we had. We were given a little piece of bread, a bit of margarine, a bit of marmalade, and so we started to transport on foot. We didn't know where we were going. And we were marching thirty-five kilometers a day without a stop, without a halt for rest, without anything—with SS men, with soldiers, with all the SS women who were with us. We were driven day and night, day and night.

Were the SS men also marching on foot?

Yes, also on foot. Often it would happen that automobiles would pass. They would take all the SS men. Only two or three soldiers remained with us to watch us, and the rest were driving a few kilometers ahead and then waiting for us again in some town.

Were all the people from the camp able to march?

That's it, we were not. I myself couldn't walk.

2. Auschwitz, of course, was no longer functioning as a mass extermination camp at that time. The phrase "sent to Auschwitz" was the generic one for being killed.

Was it winter or summer?

It was winter. It was in January. And before we started out—we knew that someday we would have to march—many girls had made themselves socks and caps out of blankets.

Did they permit that?

It wasn't permitted. We were hiding them. They would have killed us if they had known that we had made these things. And then, on the day of the transport when she [the camp chief] saw that we had these things on us, she did not care anymore. She was already leaving the camp. And that was in part our salvation because it was terribly cold.

One night we came to a village where they permitted us to sleep in a barn. But we were 500 girls and barely 150 could get in. The rest remained outside. So we lay down on the cobblestones and in the snow. It was just a miracle that many did not fall asleep forever.

And so we marched and marched until we came to Janow. I don't know where it is. I just know the name of the city. There they put us in railroad cars, but such cold cars, open gondolas, dirty. Where barely 80 people could get on, they put 150 of us in each car. We were lying one on the other. We were yelling. We began to cease being human because we knew it was just impossible otherwise. We would shout at each other, "Move on! Make room!" We had to talk rudely to each other. It just didn't go otherwise. They did it all on purpose so that we should become mean to each other. Well, we did not beat each other, but it wasn't far from it. And the conditions were terrible. In general no food, and traveling day and night. It was snowing, and we were wet through and through.

The soldiers and SS men had a separate car. Not a passenger car, but a closed one, and there they had a stove. There they cooked and prepared various things to eat. They drank coffee, and we had to look on. And so we traveled for several days.

When we stopped at a station we asked permission of the woman camp commander to wash ourselves, because we hadn't washed ourselves for two, three weeks. When the trip was first on foot, she permitted us to wash, and it was January. We undressed and we went into the pond. So we washed ourselves in icy, ice-cold water. She marveled at us. Everybody marveled at us. They didn't want to believe that we were Jews. All that they had heard was that the Jews are dirty. They are unfit to keep clean. The young and beautiful girls had to use such water! With a knife we had to break through the ice so that we could wash a little bit. We cleaned our things and returned to the dirty railroad car.

So we traveled several weeks more without food, without anything. They gave us some cold preserves without bread, without anything. It was salty. No water. It really was a miracle [to survive]. One girl asked a soldier to give us some water from a pump or a well! At every station there was so much water, but they wouldn't permit us to fetch it. Sometimes when the train was standing, we went over to the locomotive, and we scooped up that dirty water, oily warm water. It was so greasy from the oil, but we grabbed it so nobody would see us, and we drank that water, that dirty water.

One night at 3:00 we arrived in Belsen [Bergen-Belsen]. We stood there in the open. We were told we had first to bathe because they were afraid we might have lice. So we 500 girls divided into five groups, and each group went separately. They let the girls out from different doors so that they could not talk to us and could not tell us anything of what they had been doing, so that we could be prepared. And that precisely was bad. And then my turn came. We were undressed, completely naked. We were permitted to take only our shoes.

Who did that? Men made you undress?

Those were men. They were special prisoners, still lower than we were, so they should have the satisfaction of doing it to us. But we responded with ironic laughter. Women were also present, Jewish women who had to work there. The women were taking away the things. They put them on a stick, and the things went into a special oven where they were disinfected so no lice should remain on them, although we had no lice at that time. They undressed us and told us that we will get our things back. So we went in bathing. We wanted to take a shirt or something else for a towel, but they did not permit us to do it.

We went in just so. We could take only our shoes. But at that time we had no good shoes. Mine were big, very big wooden shoes. Three pair of feet like mine could go into such shoes in which I had worked for months in the camp, and these we could take with us. I still had some pictures from home, my mama, my papa, and my brothers and sisters and many, many other pictures. But I specially wanted to take those of my family with me. They didn't permit me to do so. They immediately burned them all, except for a few small pictures that I hid deep in the shoe so that they could not find them. I saved these few pictures which are so precious to me and are full of deep memories.

And so I went bathing under the shower, and there were men present. They laughed! They mocked us! They went amidst the wet bodies and they—[Boder noted that she slapped herself on the buttocks]. And no towels were given, no soap, we just washed ourselves that way in the [hot] water. And after the bathing they took us into a hall where the water was frozen on the walls. We stood in that hall for hours and waited until the things came from that oven, from disinfection. That is how we dried ourselves. The water on our hair froze to the head, and the drops of water froze on us. We huddled together so that we could warm ourselves a bit. We really could not believe that people could do such things to us, move us after such very hot water to such a cold hall, where there was only water and frost. We had to get dry by ourselves. I was all blue from the cold.

We waited two hours until our things came, and they were really not our things that came. I did not get my dress but a dress that belonged to another girl, and some other girl got my things in turn. Everything was mixed up. We got a shirt, a pair of pantaloons, and a dress. They did not permit anything more. Everything else we had to abandon. We were chased and beaten, so we should go faster.

Who beat you?

The soldiers. They were just soldiers, not SS men. Plain soldiers. We didn't know the way to the barracks. It was very far from the bathhouse. We arrived in the barracks, and it was pitch dark. We couldn't see the door or anything. They pushed us in like pigs, locked us up, and went away. And so in the dark we looked for some bed, for a table. One couldn't find anything. But the next morning when daylight appeared, we saw that the room was empty, that we had nothing. We had only the floor and the walls. Broken glass in the windows, and the wind blew from all sides. We sat down on the dirty floor, and our life started anew.

From January to April I was in Belsen. But these months cost me much more than the three and a half years spent in other camps. In the other camps I could wash myself. We did not suffer from hunger. We could go around clean, I could keep my things in order. Here we were 500 girls in one barracks. Soon 500 more arrived, 200 more, 100 more, every day—Hungarian people, Russian people, all kinds, old people, healthy people, and sick people, all together, one next to the other! One girl had lice, the other did not have any, so now she had lice, too. And so it was. Horrible! Horrible! And so we sat there for months on the dirty soiled floor.

Didn't you work in Belsen?

Absolutely no. Only the Ukrainians.

Women?

Yes, they were very strong, twenty-five to thirty years of age. They worked in the fields, in the gardens. It was a very, very big camp and extended for kilometers. Before, it had been a military installation. Later they made it a concentration camp. There the people were concentrated to be led to their death, to be driven to their death. There was a crematory where they burned only the dead people. They didn't have to burn the people alive because thousands and thousands were lying before the blocks every day, dead from typhus.

Before your block?

My block and various other blocks. After I was in the block a few days, they ordered some of the girls to go to another block, so I went there. We didn't know where and what for until we noticed that it was a block on which was written, "Here reigns death." It was a typhus block. In it were only old Gypsies, Hungarians. They all had typhus, and we were still all well. We still looked human. This block led us to all evil. I was there with Gypsies. They were reasonably friendly with me. These were German Gypsies. It was dirty, terribly dirty.

Were there many Gypsies?

There were a lot of people. There really weren't so many Gypsies, but they were all mixed up. There was a terrible mess of people. I still was well that time. I still had a little piece of blanket that I was beating out every day. I cleaned it. I still had in my possession a little comb, a toothbrush, some toothpaste, and my hair brush.

Toothpaste? Where did you get toothpaste?

We got it sometimes in the other camps, not very good paste, but you could still clean your teeth with it. I had that and nothing else. My overcoat and a piece of blanket. Not *my* overcoat, *some* overcoat and a little piece of blanket and I brushed them every day. I brushed them with my hair brush.

Did they let you out of the barracks during the day?

Only in front of the block. It was fenced off with barbed wire, because that was a typhus block. It was contagious, and so other people shouldn't get near there.

Did any of the girls with you get sick?

Five hundred of us came to Belsen and 122 remained. There was a special list made of us. The rest died from typhus or from sheer dirt. I, too, came pretty close to it. I remember the day when I saw the first lice on myself, on my blouse. I couldn't believe it, I cried like a little child. I had never had lice on me, and I couldn't believe it. Other people had lice, but I shouldn't have had any. And so the others, sitting near me, laughed at me! "Today you have one, tomorrow you will have two, and in a week you will have thousands!" And so it was. But then I didn't have any more strength to remove the lice from me. They crawled over me like ants—and although I looked over my things twice a day so that I should have some rest at least for five minutes, at night I couldn't sleep. We were not sleeping with our legs stretched out, because there was no room. We slept sitting up. People were sitting in rows, back to back—the legs, just very little space for them.

So we sat for months, for weeks without real food. At the end we didn't get any bread. For six weeks we had no bread, only a little bit of soup if you could call *that* soup—water with turnips and without salt. Once a day a very small cup, and we had to fight for it. And there were terrifying scenes. So frightful! There were my girl friends with whom I had been in the other camp—such beautiful girls, young girls. In the other camp we had sometimes enjoyed a little humor. We danced, even gave some plays. There were very gifted girls among us. I too, was one of them.

For instance, I arranged various theatricals. If a girl had a birthday, for example, we always would arrange something. And we sang or put a little verse together so we could bring about a little joy. And that all passed through my mind while I was in Belsen. And I saw the same girls who had danced with me, who were so gay before, so full of will to live in spite of the hard life. Then we still had believed in freedom. Now one after the other died.

At the block where I was, the face of every girl near death was so changed. I could recognize that such a girl would die soon, only from hunger and from filth. How often I was called to come over! People, they called, "Come over to me!" I couldn't do it because I felt my heart would break. You couldn't see the person, just the eyes, eyes and lice. You didn't see anything else, just lice all over her. And we were all in tatters, no clothes. You would look over your things. Everything would be cleaned up, all beaten out to the last piece of blanket. And you would sit down. In a moment the same thing all over again. People had terrible skin eruptions. After I was freed, I was full of skin sores. My body was covered with wounds. It was terrible. Many girls, many of my girl friends went insane.

People were yelling at night, "Where am I?" They were calling, "Mama!" They were calling, "Brother!" You had to hold your ears, not to listen to such screams. You didn't want to believe it, and every day the Germans would come in, the German women—for roll call. Every day they called us for roll call. I can remember Irma Grese. I knew her personally. I didn't know that she was called Irma Grese. After liberation I saw her picture in the paper. These things have been written about, how she dressed and what kind of a face she had, and so I know that it was she. I remember her very well. She did such terrible things, specially with our block. Her face, you know, was so beautiful. Large blue eyes and beautiful golden hair. Beautifully dressed in such a trim SS costume and a stick in her hand and a large dog. She would come to us every day, and before she would arrive we had to wait three, four hours for her. From 8:00 in the morning to 11:00 in the morning we were called to the camp square without washing, without food, without anything. We had to stand there in the rain and snow and frost, that was all the same. Stand lined up, four or five abreast. The block senior was inside the block and waiting until *she* came. We had to stand, we couldn't sit down. We wanted to sit down even on that wet, muddy ground. But we had to stand at attention till Irma Grese came. Then she would come. She had once prohibited us to have anything on our head.

What do you mean by "anything on our head"?

A kerchief or some covering. We really didn't have kerchiefs. Everything was taken away from us, but we had little rags that were cut out from the blankets, gray blankets. It was fortunate that we could have such a little piece. And standing outside for hours in the snow or in the rain we would throw such a thing over our heads. We needed it. She had prohibited this. Those girls who were doing it, would hide behind. They would not stand in the first rows, but in the fifth row behind. She could not count at a distance with her eyes. But she had to put her whip on every head. That is how she counted. One after the other.

Did she beat you with the whip?

So, one, two, three (demonstrating the strokes), and nobody could move. And when she would notice that some girl would have that little piece of blanket on her head, she would approach her immediately with a smile and would tear down that piece of blanket with the person together. She would call her dog. The dog would jump at the girl and gnash his teeth as if he was going to bite. Irma Grese did not permit him to bite. She did not want that. She just wanted to horrify us. She wanted to cause anguish and terror, and that was much worse. So she would throw down this blanket together with the person and kick her and beat her with her whip. She should know not to do it again once it was prohibited. And then, afterward, when Irma Grese would talk to the block senior, she would ask how many people there were, how many had died and so on, and so on, and show such a beautiful countenance, such a kind face. Indeed, nobody could tell that just a moment ago she had made such scenes and was so bad, that she could be so merciless to other people. As if we were somebody worse than the block seniors!

I can just tell you that the block seniors were no better! Before the war maybe they were selling onions and garlic on the streets. Now they were big personages in our camp. We who had been going to universities and museums were not treated like human beings. They thought we were Jews, born of course, in cellars somewhere, that we didn't have mothers. We didn't know what a white bed was! We didn't know what good soup was! That is what they all believed. And I am telling you that the block seniors who ordered us around were not different, they were worse than any of these girls, these children. What hurt us so badly was that they put us at such a low level. When we wanted to *go out* we had to report. To ask permission to *go out* we had to stand at attention and say, "Frau Camp Senior," or "Leader," something of the kind, depending on who the SS woman was. It was up to her to say yes.

What do you mean, "to go out"?

Well—to relieve oneself. If she was in a mood to say yes, all right. If she would say no, we would have to go back. Nothing would help. They could make us do whatever they wanted. That means we continued in the block, lying on the filthy floor, no food, just waiting from morning till night, night till morning, just listening to the shooting.

Where are your parents now?
My papa—when he was taken, we still had letters from him. I sent him packages. Afterward his camp was Dachau, and at that time all mail was blocked. We couldn't write. We lost track of him. We don't know anything about him. My mother surely is not alive anymore. She was about fifty years old. My mother would have been fifty-four now. But she was in Auschwitz and surely is not alive anymore.

A whole transport of the women had gone to Auschwitz. My older sister was with her husband in Baranowicze. During the war I still received some little mail, and all at once that stopped, and those horrible things were going on. Germans murdered people there, too, and I don't know anything about them up to this day. It is seven years since my sister's last letter and eight years since I have seen her or my brother-in-law. Also my brother, a married one, he had a little boy two years old. He also was deported in 1942 from where he used to live and was sent away to the Ukraine. He is not alive anymore.

Tell me, how were you freed?
I was liberated in Belsen on the 15th of April. I can tell you! I haven't told you half of what I went through in Belsen. Believe me, I could not tell you as much about the three and a half years of captivity as about the few months I spent in Belsen. And about the people I have seen, as well as about myself. It is horrible. One cannot describe it in words, because words hurt too much. I looked like a seventy-year-old woman. I was unable to move. I was all run down, emaciated, unwashed for weeks, without undressing. In that one dress and coat I was lying on the floor. I wanted some water for a drink, but I couldn't get it. I had diarrhea for two months, and then I had [intestinal] typhus.

Where were you lying? In the hospital?
No, absolutely no. We were not being treated. They wanted it that way. Sure, every day a few soldiers would come in to see that the bodies were thrown out in front of the block. They were not immediately transported to the crematories.

What do you mean in "front of the block"? Weren't the dead people removed?
Yes, here were four special women, Hungarian women whose job it was to do it. When a woman would die, that was immediately reported. The four women received a bit of soup for it, because they were still reasonably strong. They would take a gray blanket, put the dead person on the blanket and throw her out in

front of the block. And so these bodies would lie sometimes two weeks, sometimes three weeks—until fifty or a hundred or two hundred dead had accumulated. Then Jews came, men under guard, and transported them to the crematory. And often I would pass the crematories—because at night we had to fetch those kettles with soup. Every day there was another shift. We saw mounds and mounds of dead. It was unbelievable—dead with whom the crematory could not keep up. There were mountains of dead, and from the air came all the sickness. These typhus diseases swept through the camp where people lived, where thousands and thousands were still moving around. People went out to search for some potato peelings. They went around begging for something. There was cooking going on in the kitchen, and one would go and beg for a bit of soup. So one would see all those terrible things.

Who freed you?
The English. In April, when we didn't expect it at all. We didn't expect any liberty. We absolutely did not know that liberation was so near. And it came to us. We didn't have any contact with anybody. All at once we saw the SS men and the SS women carrying white bands on their arms.

4   Bernard W.

Jewish men sent to Germany shortly after the conquest of Poland often did their slave labor in actual concentration camps. One of the most articulate accounts of survival at Buchenwald is provided by Bernard W., a Polish Jew who spent five and one-half years in the German camp. The young artist, who had studied at the Warsaw Academy of Art, was drafted into the Polish army in 1939 at the age of twenty-three, only to have his unit surrounded by German forces in the early days of World War II. W. managed to escape and return to his home town of Tomaszow-Mazowiecki, but not for long. There were many like him, and the Germans swept the newly occupied territories for young Poles to be sent to camps in Germany.

Buchenwald was probably the most efficiently organized and least brutal of the German concentration camps—the best of the worst, one might say—by the time Bernard W. arrived in October 1939. A major scandal the previous year involving corruption among the SS and the professional criminals that had constituted the camp elite had led to housecleaning and opportunities for the political prisoners to take control. Otherwise W. might not have lived to tell this story. (W. seems to have perceived these changes most acutely in 1943, by which time an influx of foreign prisoners had changed the ethnic composition of the camp underground, but the crucial developments had occurred before his arrival at Buchenwald.) However, he is far from uncritical of the men with the red triangle who helped run Buchenwald, finding some as brutal and venal as the "greens." Equally surprising is his account of library resources and informal classes that made it possible for Buchenwald inmates to pursue intellectual interests, psychology in W.'s case. More conventional is his description of work conditions in the camp that drove some prisoners to take their own lives—"murdered by suicide" in W.'s trenchant phrase. He attributes his own drive to go on to his faith in the future of Zionism.

Bernard W. and thousands of other prisoners from Poland were initially accommodated in a temporary "small camp" improvised with tents and barbed wire fences on the edge of Buchenwald's roll call square. Food and hygiene were far worse than in the main camp, and work in the stone quarry was even more brutal than usual. Prisoners who did not deliberately run through the sentry line to be "shot while trying to escape" almost inevitably fell sick with dysentery, but frostbite got Bernard sent to the infirmary for a second time. We may speculate that one reason he emerged alive, and with a successful throat operation thrown in for good measure, was SS admiration of sketches he made there. At the same time we should not lose sight of the proficiency of prisoner doctors who worked under anything but ideal conditions. W. may also have been one of the camp's skilled workers, for in most cases only they were exempted from the transfer of all Jews from German concentration camps to Poland in October 1942.

Bernard tried in vain to evade evacuation from Buchenwald during the last days of the war. He escaped from a death march, hid from the SS, and was liberated by American forces just when he thought he had reached the limits of his endurance. Following an abortive effort to pick up the pieces of his life in Poland, he led a group of fellow survivors through the British occupation zone of Germany, hoping to reach Palestine by way of Holland. Arrested at the border, they were subjected to what W. considered a renewal of the concentration camp experience. After three months he was released, moved to Italy, and joined a kibbutz housed in a castle at Tradate, halfway between Milan and Como, where he was interviewed. There he prepared for a new life in Palestine. We join W.'s story with his description of a brief career in the Polish army.

When war broke out between Poland and Germany, I was drafted into the army. I lived in Tomaszow-Mazowiecki a hundred kilometers [southwest of] Warsaw. Our battalion was taken prisoner by the Germans near Warsaw. I succeeded in escaping from captivity by donning civilian clothes and going home. The road was very difficult. In the towns through which I passed I saw thousands of Jews shot, thousands of Jews wounded, and also thousands of Jews who were being led to execution. Luckily, I succeeded in getting home. That was two days before Rosh Hashana. My brothers and sisters and my parents were very happy that I had remained alive and returned home from this war.

And, alas, I was home only one day. The Germans found themselves a method. They would search out all young people from seventeen to fifty-five, and under the pretense that they were taking them for labor, they loaded them into a large truck and drove [them] away. And this happened to us, too. We went by truck to Czestochowa [where] they beat [us] very much, and afterward they sent us to a prison in Posen. We were there three weeks under very frightful conditions. We were beaten. While getting off the train we were beaten so that . . . never in my life did I dream that a man could survive such beatings. Never in my life did I see an animal beaten as we were beaten.

After three weeks we left again and arrived in Germany. We didn't know what we came for. We were told that we were going to work. And we arrived in a concentration camp. Buchenwald. The first [thing] I saw there made a terrible impression on me. I saw bloody people being chased and beaten. I saw people tied in chains by a window and [forced to] stand that way a whole day, the pants let down. In terrible positions and terrible conditions. We arrived first in a town, Weimar, eight kilometers from the camp. We got off the train and went on foot. We had to hold our hands up and run on the double. And the guards who were escorting us beat us. And the people who were not able to keep up were shot right on the way.

Did you see it yourself?

Oh, that I saw myself. On the second day there we were registered. Everyone had to declare from what town he was, his ancestry, and how old he was. We arrived in a large roll call square on [which] stood four tent barracks, very large. One barrack could hold a thousand people. And these barracks were enclosed by a wire [fence] supplied with an electric current. The first days we still received something to eat. Afterward hungry times began. In the morning we got up at three o'clock, and we had to stand outside till eleven o'clock, not dressed, in the cold when it was raining. These were constantly cloudy, autumn days.

The third day that we were there we had to go out to work. We had to run down a large stone quarry, very deep, and fetch very large stones used for road building. Whoever couldn't take a large stone was so [badly] flogged and beaten by the SS men and also by the German capos that he immediately became bloody and fell to the ground unconscious. I saw very many cases that people were seeking death. They couldn't endure those beatings anymore. Without our having done anything to deserve it, the capos or the SS men called out prisoners and flogged them to death.

Who were the capos?

Germans, very many political Germans [who] wore a red triangle. There were also capos who wore green triangles. These were criminal prisoners. They had committed great crimes.

The political ones also?

The political ones also. A certain political capo—his name was Herzog[1]—has hundreds of Jews on his conscience. He killed them just with a club or his fist. Strong people! They, alas, couldn't defend themselves. But when that capo got

1. The capo Herzog, a former member of the French Foreign Legion and regarded in the camp as a homosexual sadist, was universally feared in Buchenwald.

out—he had been released—another capo came, also a political [prisoner], a certain Vogel. He conducted himself more sadistically yet.

What do you mean by sadistic conduct?

When a man is taken and told to lie down, pull down his trousers, and given twenty-five blows on the naked . . . so that the man can't get up anymore, and then hit in the face with the fist so that he is entirely covered with blood. And if that man is not dead, he has to carry a very large stone approximately two hundred meters upward from the stone quarry. And if he can't walk, then he is hit in the head with clubs and on the hands where he holds the stone. And if the stone falls from his hands, he is again beaten. And if he is still so strong that he does not fall, then they take the cap off his head and throw it [beyond] where the SS sentries stand and order that man to run and fetch his cap. When the man runs to fetch his cap, he is shot like a dog by the sentries. And under these conditions we worked for two weeks. Very many of my comrades found death during that time. Many have also sought death. They couldn't look at that and endure all the ways in which we were tortured.

[Later] conditions were so bad in the tent camps that dysentery broke out. The Germans were afraid that it could spread all over, [so] they isolated us. In the beginning I was not sick, but later at the end [of 1939] I did become sick. We received very little to eat. People were dropping like flies, it was so bad. From our town 107 Jews had been arrested with my transport. Seven Jews remained alive.

What did they die of?

From hunger and cold and from beatings that we frequently received. When our circumstances became very well known—at that time there were still relations between America [and Nazi Germany]—we were let out from the small tents. We came to the big camp. Luckily, I got into the sick ward because my feet had frozen, and one of my toes was cut off. There, thanks to my being an artist by profession, I succeeded in remaining for three months. I made many drawings there.

When I came out, I was assigned to a detail of Jewish stone carriers. And I endured very hard times there. All day we had to [run] up and down with stones. When we got up there with the large stones and had put [them] down, we had to run down on the double into the quarry. And we received beatings from the German capos and from the SS men. And that was day in, day out, day in, day out. The people—our comrades, Jews—ran at the head of the formation. We had no more hope of holding out and sought death. It was this way. The sentries who stood around would shoot at everybody who came near them or who wanted to run through. And very many of our people were murdered by suicide or were forced by the capos to seek [death] because it was too hard.

After a year and a half Buchenwald started to be built up. Barracks began to be erected. I got into a detail working at masonry as handy man, as helper. We carried lime up three stories. We carried bricks. We also carried stones, and we were beaten. And when, after that very hard day, we returned to the block, every day we were so beaten up we couldn't move. And yet we had to stand for roll call on the square. And when all that was finished and all the Aryans [the non-Jewish prisoners] returned to the blocks, we had to go out yet for night work. And that was still worse. The German capos beat us so much that very few people returned home from that night work.

At that time Buchenwald was developing inside, too. Canteens were being built. Various cellars were being built for the kitchen. And the Jews had to do the hard jobs. The very hardest labors, [such as carrying] stones. The Jews had to act as horses to pull carts. The Jews were so beaten, and the carts were so loaded that we couldn't pull them. All day long at the dray columns all you heard was "One, two, three, four. Left, two, three, four." Then in the year '42 a training school opened for masonry apprentices. And Jews were entered in this school. Two hundred Jews reported that they wanted to become masons. The Jews had to begin building factories where later on arms were also manufactured. And also, toward the end of the year '44, they wanted to manufacture V-1s. Luckily, they were blown sky high by the air attacks of the American forces. For a long time I worked at masonry. And they did a lot of chicanery. We starved a lot. Aryans received supplements. From Jews the supplements were taken away.

What do you mean by "supplements"?
Three times a week each prisoner who worked received a quarter of a loaf of bread and a little piece of sausage as supplement to that which he received in the block.

And we were tortured very much at work. For every trifle we received twenty-five blows on the naked [buttocks]. That was a normal punishment. And besides that the SS men would allow themselves to beat so that one would fall dead in an instant. In the year '39 they took twenty Jews down the quarry and shot them for nothing. They claimed that they wanted to learn how to shoot. Later, when the Russian prisoners of war arrived, they searched out the Jews [from among them]. And the Jews were immediately shot.

When a Jew received a certificate to go to the sick ward, well, he already knew that it meant his death. He would not come back anymore. Once they wrote up fifteen people—young people, the oldest was twenty-five years old—and gave them a note to go to the sick ward. There they received injections. In a few minutes they weren't alive anymore.

[After a pause to change the spool, Boder asked W. about a neck scar similar to that left by a goiter operation.]

That I got in Buchenwald. Already in the year '39. I was operated on in the sick ward at the same time when they amputated the toe from my foot. I was completely swollen and that swelling was cut through, and I only know I was completely festered. It was from the cold. It was this way. We were not permitted, even when we were sick, to go to the sick ward, because if one had been there a few times it was a sign that we no longer had the right to live. If a prisoner was [there] twice or three times in a month, then he received a document, and he had to report to the sick ward in the morning. He never returned to the block. We knew that he had been sentenced to death by injection.

By the time the German retreat had begun, the treatment had changed somewhat. It was in 1943. It had eased a little. And also in Buchenwald the offices had been taken over by the political prisoners. This was also a certain alleviation because up until then the "greens," the professional criminals, had held all the power over the prisoners. But among the prisoners the Jew was still considered inferior.

Among the political prisoners?
Among the political prisoners! Only in rare cases was a Jew looked upon as an equal with a German. It was a rare case that a German Communist should not consider himself first a German and only then a Communist. The Germans were always first of all Germans and only then "politicals." And behind that mask of "political" various dirty tricks went on among the political prisoners. They, too, wanted to make a good name for themselves with the SS. They treated [us] worse than dogs. Only when the situation had changed in the last years, they began to think a little differently. But when the German army was still victorious, then it was very bad for us. Not that we [believed] that we would ever get out of the camp, but that we were absolutely unable to defend ourselves.

In the meantime the camp had enlarged. In 1939 the camp numbered 7,000 prisoners. In 1944–45 the camp already numbered 167,000 prisoners. A part of these prisoners were also in outside details, Dora,[2] and various other camps. Any prisoner who did not conduct himself accordingly there [in the main camp] went on transport to another camp [one of the Buchenwald satellites]. And that threatened a much earlier and a very bad death.

In 1945, when the Americans were already near, one day it was said that no more details were to leave for work. And we were also hoping maybe we, the Jews, would manage to stay alive. And we heard over the loudspeaker—that was when we were in the blocks—"All Jews fall in on the roll call square." And we

2. Dora-Mittelbau, a satellite of Buchenwald near Nordhausen in the Harz Mountains. Its subterranean factories, built and manned by Buchenwald prisoners, made V-2 rockets. This and other satellite camps accounted for more than half of Buchenwald prisoners by 1945; in spring of that year the main camp reached its peak of 80,000 inmates.

could already hear the shooting of the American troops nearby. And the commandant had promised all the prisoners that he would hand over the camp as it was, that nobody would be in danger. All at once . . .

Whom did he promise that?
To the political prisoners.

Could they talk to the commandant?
Yes. They held various offices. When we heard [the announcement], we felt that our only chance to save our life was gone. We did not go out to the square. We left the blocks, and we scattered over the whole camp. Some of us ran to the small camp;[3] some hid wherever they could, in the cellars, in various holes. And that night when we were hiding that way, there was also a terror bombing raid. And we thought, "Maybe they will succeed in blowing up the whole camp, the SS as well." We no longer wanted to sell our life that cheaply. The second day, in the morning, the whole camp was told to fall in for roll call. The Jews, too, had to fall in. When the whole camp was at roll call, we heard, "All Jews remain standing. All others step out." When we heard that, we ran down on the double. And a part hid in the political blocks. A part hid in the small camp and part in the sick ward.

In the small camp we tore off our Jewish insignia—a "Jew Star," a red triangle [over] a yellow one—and sewed on other temporary numbers, because there was a large number of prisoners who were without insignia and half dead. And there was great confusion in the camp because very many outside details had come in from other camps; the American troops were in the vicinity, [and the Germans] had to evacuate numerous camps. But the American troops did not come [to Buchenwald]. So they began to evacuate the small camp. I, myself, no longer had any chance of remaining in the camp, and I did not want to be recognized by the SS as a Jew, so I, too, went out with a transport.

It was the 10th of April 1945. We arrived in Weimar, and we boarded the trains. We got nothing to eat. We left hungry. The road from Buchenwald to Weimar was covered with many prisoners who had been shot by the SS. On the second day American [planes] shot up the locomotive, and we continued on foot. Hundreds of kilometers.

And the SS went along?
Yes. They were changed many times. Any prisoner who could not continue walking or had stopped for a moment was immediately shot. The road was covered with hundreds of prisoners. One fine day, it was the 13th of April, I contemplated my chances. I looked upon death, and I saw that I had no way out. So

3. The Buchenwald quarantine.

I decided, tonight I must run away. If they shoot me, then I am out of luck. If not, then perhaps I will succeed in remaining alive. And that evening I ran away. It was not far from a village, Eisenberg.[4] The SS were firing at me, but they did not hit me. And I fell down in the field. It was already very dark, and I lay there near a small tree.

Later I heard many people running. I heard many shots, and then it became quiet. Later I saw [lights] on the highway and all over. That was the SS with dogs looking for the prisoners who had escaped. For them it was a great danger to let a prisoner get away alive. And I also heard very many shots. Every prisoner who was found was immediately shot. I lay that way all night long, weak, famished. And at dawn, when it became light, I saw them keep on looking. Approximately forty meters away from me they shot one prisoner after another, whoever was caught. I lay that way for two days and two nights. I thought, "I cannot endure it anymore. It does not pay to live anymore, and I might as well go to the SS. They would shoot me." I did not want to torture myself anymore and die of starvation. I wanted a quick death. And I got up. I took a few steps and fell unconscious. I was much too weak from hunger.

And while lying that way I saw very many military coming out from the woods and from all over. They went out without weapons. I was wondering, "What is this?" And suddenly I saw a few people walking, and I recognized that they were prisoners, too. And they came over to me. I got back some strength. They said, "Look in the woods. The Germans are running away." So we went into the woods. I saw very many weapons thrown away [and] everybody running away. And I found a few pieces of sugar that a German had left with his entire rucksack. And suddenly we saw many German soldiers of the Wehrmacht [and] the SS, standing and listening to the bells pealing. We understood that something must have happened. We went over [to them]. The Germans extended their hands and said, "So, now we are comrades. The Americans are already here. You have suffered. We have, too. We are comrades." We said nothing and passed by, and American troops were already there. I was there [in Eisenberg] three days, [living with] a land owner. Later we were taken [by the Americans] to Erfurt. A camp was already there. We were cared for by UNRRA and the Red Cross.

There are a few things which you told me before this interview. First you said you had studied psychology in Buchenwald. How did that come about?

I had very good friends. Jews. People from various corners of the world. And in their spare time they would impart much of their knowledge to us. And Buchenwald had a library of thirty-five thousand works in various languages.

4. Twenty miles east of Weimar.

Each prisoner had the right to get books from that library. And thanks to these books I had the opportunity to further my knowledge.

When and where did you read?
Every evening I read in my free time. I always had an hour, or half an hour, to read about three times a week. One did not have time every day. Because roll call seldom passed normally. Two, three, four, even five hours we had to stand on the square, in rain or in cold because the count did not always check, and if a prisoner was missing, or the Germans were in a bad mood, we would have to stand all through the night.

Tell me, you had family in Poland. Didn't you go back to see what had happened there?
Yes, I was in Poland [for] two and a half weeks. I was also on that street on which I had lived. I was also at the flat in which I was raised. I was in the yard. I was not allowed to pick the fruit which was our own property.

Why not?
Because I am a Jew. Any Jew who still owns anything in Poland had better leave because if he remains, then death threatens him. And it was too painful for me when I saw strange people having my property, living in my flat. But the most terrible was that I found no one anymore. From a family which had numbered seven persons, I alone remained. That shook me so that I did not want to remain anymore. And the attitude of the Poles toward the Jews was none too friendly either. Any Jew who was on the street—when they met him, they said: "Patrz sie, znowu kot."[5]

I returned to Germany [and settled in] Segensdorf, a Jewish camp where we had established a kibbutz, a very active one. I wanted to go to Palestine, and I left with a group of forty-six persons. Alas, we were stopped at the Dutch border by English patrols, and we went to an internment camp. In reality it is a concentration camp where the biggest war criminals, SS, Nazi criminals were. I was there with Krupp, von Buelow, various Gauleiters, generals. The English wanted to get very many things out of us. Who is our leader? Who is sending us to Palestine? They gave us one loaf of bread for eight [people] for a whole day. We lost [between] 15 and 20 kilos [33 and 44 pounds] each. The Germans could receive packages. We could not. The Germans sent letters. We were not permitted to receive any letters or send letters to anyone.

We were tortured that way for three months. They interrogated us for twenty-

5. Roughly, "Look, the cat again."

five hours at a time. They undressed us completely during the search. There were instances when they beat us, too. We had it still worse than in the concentration camp. However, the feeling that we Jews were imprisoned under the same roof with the biggest war criminals, that was the worst. They said, "Unfortunately we have no other camps." And that was a big lie! There were many camps where they could isolate us. Fortunately a Jewish captain, an Englishman, found out that Jews were imprisoned there. And that was lucky for us. He made the effort to free us. They released us; cars from the Joint came and took us. From there I came right here.

5   Sigmund R.

Once in Nazi hands there were few opportunities to escape. Should one come, it had to be seized in a moment's time. Sigmund R. did just that, although only at the end of a long ordeal.

Sigmund R. was born in 1926 in Austria and spent his childhood in Belgium, but he was taken to Poland in 1934. His choice of Yiddish for the interview suggests that his parents were natives of Poland. The family lived in Krakow when the Germans made that city the capital of their "General Government" in 1939. R.'s father fled to the Soviet-occupied zone of Poland, while the rest of the family stayed behind. They were among the thousands of Krakow Jews who succumbed to German pressure to relocate "voluntarily" in 1940, moving in with an aunt who lived in a nearby town. A year or two later (R. is vague about dates) he reported for forced labor in the vain hope that the Germans would then leave his mother and aunt in peace. Sent to Mielec, one of dozens of forced labor camps in southeastern Poland that were later taken over by Auschwitz and officially redesignated "concentration camps," R. evidently became proficient in the manufacture of aircraft parts for the Germans, which greatly enhanced his chances of living.

R.'s memories of endless drudgery as a slave worker in Poland are almost completely overshadowed by the truly wretched conditions he encountered at a work camp in Germany during the last months of the war. At the end, when he was among those evacuated from Dachau, his chance came. Left momentarily unattended by a guard, Sigmund R. and a small group of compatriots simply walked away and made for the Swiss border. With courage born of desperation, they claimed that they had become separated from a Red Cross transport bound for Switzerland and brazenly demanded help from German officials to complete the journey. There actually were such Red Cross transports at the time, and police and railroad officials may have known about them, but in any case everyone wanted these inconvenient wayfarers out of their hair. R. is unclear about how he and his comrades cleared the border, but it seems likely that Swiss officials used their influence with German colleagues who, after all, could not have been too eager to go down as war criminals during the last days of the Third Reich.

Once in Switzerland the Swiss Red Cross gave R. every assistance. After passing through several camps, he began to study mechanics as well as other subjects designed to prepare him for life in Palestine at an ORT school in Geneva, where he gave his interview. We begin with his deportation to Kamenz, a camp near Dresden, during the last year of the war.

In Kamenz I had it the worst. We were there quite a few months. There the food was very bad. The treatment also was very bad. Also even the prisoners themselves, the *goyim* [Gentiles] were very mean. They could not stand to look at a Jew. And besides that, the guards were all Hungarians. The Hungarian SS guards were very mean. They beat us with rifles. They had volunteered [for the SS]. Every Sunday we performed gymnastics in the morning. And if one did not do it well, he was beaten for it. And so at the beginning there we received a loaf of bread for four people. The loaf weighed something like a kilo [2.2 pounds]. And toward the end, when it became very bad, we were given such a loaf of bread for eight men. Later even for ten men.

How was it divided?
We were given a whole loaf and told to divide it.

What kind of tattoo do you have here?
This was made in Poland. In Mielec. Mielec was a "civilian camp," but later it was changed into a KZ. Then everybody was given a tattoo on his hand.[1]

There was a mechanical section [at Kamenz]; we worked with lathes. Later, when we heard that the Russians were approaching, the work stopped. It was already winter then. We were sent to dismantle barracks, the wooden houses that were there. [They were] piled up. We had to carry it for maybe half a kilometer to the unloading place. And a truck came there, and we had to load it on. The food there was very, very, very bad. It was plain water. It was generally bad in all the camps, but there it was worse than anywhere else. We received an eighth of a loaf of bread; on this we lived the whole day. We lay on straw [that] was altogether neglected. There was a lot of dirt in it. Nobody cared anymore. Toward the end, when they ordered the camp evacuated, a lot of people were annihilated. Also, a lot became sick, so that out of about 1,500 men only 650 people were left. People who were completely sick, people who simply couldn't walk anymore were given hypodermics, put to sleep. A few hours after the injections the man was dead.

Were they taken to the sick ward? Or . . .
They were taken up on the second floor into the sick ward.

1. A number of the Yiddish speaking survivors spoke of being tattooed "on the hand." In fact the tattoos were placed on the prisoners' forearms.

Did [they] know what was going on?

Those people [the first victims] didn't know. However, later on we saw that they did not come down anymore, and once we noticed one being carried down we knew that those who were called had it done to them.

And what was done with the dead?

There was a boiler for central heating, fired underneath, and the people were thrown in there. They were burned. Once it had been a textile plant. I don't know for sure what kind. And the factory was liquidated [refitted], and we were there some four or five months. Afterward the Russians approached. We were evacuated to Dachau. We traveled for fourteen days. We weren't given even a drop of water. In Dachau I was altogether weak. We didn't work anymore. We were already like Moslems; everybody was. Only a few were still well. And only these were taken and sent away with a transport. Because lately the Americans bombed the place terribly—Munich, the whole region. We knew every time that the Americans came at 12:00 midnight and bombed the region. When they flew over our camp, they always threw flairs that illuminated. And so they saw what was going on on the ground. They knew where the camp was. The camp was never bombed.

And so it became worse and worse. The Americans came nearer. We were 2,000 Jews there, but 1,000 could not walk. They had swollen legs, or else they were swollen all over. They were so weakened they really couldn't take a step. We were called to roll call. All the Jews in Dachau were called together. They were called out by name. The first roll call was on the 24th [of April 1945]. On the 25th we were again called together. And on the 27th, in the morning, we were awakened very early, five o'clock. We were made to stand in rows and later taken to the railroad cars. To every car was a hundred people. They did not have any more freight cars, so they provided [fourth class] passenger cars for the trip. However, they piled in so many, we were hardly able to stand.

And so we traveled as far as a certain station in Austria. There the tracks were blown up, and we had to get off. They told us that we still had to walk twenty kilometers to the next station, so that we could continue to travel. We were ordered to march. We marched six kilometers. It started to snow. It was already dark. They started to billet us with the peasants, there where they keep straw and all such things. Our railroad car was exactly the last to be billeted. Every soldier was told to take a few men, go to the village and look for quarters. A soldier went with us, too. We were something like nine men. While he went upstairs to look for quarters, we walked away. Simply walked away.

And you were able to walk through Germany?

We had prepared an excuse that the Red Cross wanted us. Before we left we were given packages from the Belgian Red Cross. There were canned foods, cigarettes, some biscuits, and that was the whole package. We wandered the whole night till we came to a German village, and someone came up to us on the road, from something like the Security Police. . . . I don't remember exactly who he was. And he took us to the mayor. There we were, so we said we were lost from a transport, and our transport was supposed to go to Switzerland.

Weren't there any SS in the town?

All of them were at the front. We told the mayor that the Red Cross *demanded* that we go to Switzerland. He became confused so that he believed our story. He even gave us a little soup there, and he led us to the road that goes to Switzerland. He told the soldier to let us go on this road because the Red Cross wanted us to go to Switzerland. Well, we went along the road, and we came to another village. We wanted to stay overnight there, but the mayor didn't want [us] to. He was very mean, that mayor. He said he had many soldiers, and he didn't have room for us.

And so we walked on. We had no choice, and we came upon a peasant who was working. We went over and begged him to let us stay in the barn overnight. He said he had a small barn, where he keeps fodder that he needs for the cows and the horses. And it is very small, and all of us would not have enough room. We said, "No, there surely will be enough room." And so he let us in. He later even brought us a little milk, and in the morning we found out that he was a railroad employee. So we asked him whether he could arrange it so that we could travel to the Swiss border. He said, "Yes, I will be able to arrange everything." He said we should come to the station, and we would be able to board the train. So in the morning we got up, washed up, and ate something.

What kind of clothes did you wear?

I had civilian [clothes], but the others had those striped suits. We came to the station. There we sat and waited for the train. We got on . . .

Without tickets?

Well, without tickets. He ordered it, so that we could ride without tickets. This was a small station, and he was the railroad employee [in charge]. We rode as far as Bregenz [?]. There we got off and went straight to the German police, and we told them to give us some certificate so that we could travel on to the Swiss border. He [the officer] said he couldn't give us any certificate, [but] he could give us a ticket to travel on.

Did you tell him you were prisoners?

Yes, we told him. Later he told us to go somewhere, some office, where we were supposed to get the money. There we received the money, and we went to buy the tickets. The train wasn't leaving till nine o'clock. At 9:00 we came to the train station, and we . . .

[Boder was obviously amused]: And you were not afraid?

[Laughing] What was there to fear? We took a chance to the finish. If we succeed, we succeed! If we don't, we don't! And so at 9:00 we went into the sleeping cars, and later, about ten o'clock, we were in Feldkirch, near the Swiss border. There we knew we had to wait till the morning. In the morning we went over to the border.

Were there no SS men?

No. The Wehrmacht stood at the border. And so we saw that we couldn't go over. We saw some sort of higher official there. We asked him to arrange for us to pass because we are completely exhausted, and we only want to get to a Red Cross hospital [and that] we were invited by the Red Cross. And he said that he would take care of everything. We had a few potatoes with us, so we even cooked them there. And this was our breakfast and our dinner. Later, we started to move to the border. In general not many people were permitted to pass. Every day a few. They were mostly foreigners. And when we saw them moving, we also started to push ourselves near the fence. We started to cry for help. And so a German sentry came over. We told him we only wanted to get to a hospital because we were completely exhausted. Well, he said he couldn't do anything. He called over the Swiss sentry. The Swiss sentry called over the officer. We told him we only wanted to get to a hospital, so he immediately ordered to let us pass.

And there we were! Soon we were given biscuits to eat, coffee to drink, light things that we could eat. Right away a certain doctor came, a Jew, and he talked with us. There were even journalists from America. I think there was even a Jewish woman journalist. And later we were taken into a truck and driven to a hospital in Buchs. We were there something like two weeks. We were treated very well there. We didn't eat any bread because it was forbidden by the doctor, but we ate biscuits and light things. Later we recovered and received some civilian clothes and bread. And after the two weeks we went to a quarantine camp, Gaticon [?]. We had to stay there three weeks. But it was very bad in this camp. First, the food was no good. There was very little; they only cooked potatoes. Nothing else. We did not get meat at all, so we ate potatoes and the fifth of a loaf of bread that we received.

How many people were there?

About a hundred people. All were from concentration camps. After the three weeks we went to Waedenswil. A woman doctor came there and took us out, because we wanted to go to a religious camp where one eats kosher. And so we were sent to Atterberg. It was very good there. And we studied a little and worked a little there. Something like every six weeks we went on three, four days leave.

Where did you go on leave?

At Waedenswil we were sent to Zurich on the first Saturday; I was assigned to a family there, and I went there often. And later a home for boys from concentration camps was established near Lausanne. A very nice region. It is very hot there, [but] we did not work very much there. I worked at house service. I only cleaned the house. And half days we studied a little there—the *Pentateuch*, *Rashe*, the *Talmud*. We were there something like three, four months, and later we arrived at the ORT school in Geneva. It is not a home. It is private. We are something like twenty persons. However long it will take, it will take. Then I hope I'll be able to go to *Eretz*.[2]

2. *Eretz Israel* = the Land of Israel.

6   Kalman E.

Kalman E. experienced most of the Holocaust years in his hometown of Starachowice, an industrial center about ninety miles south of Warsaw. There the Jews were placed in an open ghetto between February 1941 and October 1942. Then those not needed for work were sent away, to Treblinka as it turned out, and the remaining 5,000 were pushed into barracks adjacent to the prewar ammunition factories, now renamed the Hermann Göring Works, to serve the needs of the German military.

Fourteen-year-old Kalman E. was one of the "lucky" ones, the only remaining member of his family not sent away with the others. He says little about what it was like in the Starachowice camp, but he has fairly vivid recollections of the prisoner revolt that occurred as the Germans prepared to liquidate the camp and move their slaves westward in July 1944. Fearful that they were about to be killed, the prisoners set fires and rushed the fences, only to be recaptured or shot down by the hundreds by the Ukrainian guards. Not one is known to have escaped and lived to tell about it. Kalman survived to be evacuated to Auschwitz/Birkenau with the others, and from there to Germany where he was liberated by the Americans somewhere in Bavaria.

This interview was recorded at Chateau de Boucicaut, just outside Paris, where about sixty young survivors, mostly from Buchenwald, lived under the direction of the ORT. It must have been one of Boder's most difficult. It was not enough that his recorder acted up more than usual. Kalman E. told his story loosely (necessitating more than the usual amount of editing for this version) and turgidly; he tried to begin the interview by imitating the tone of a radio announcer, stating that "Comrade E." was at the microphone, and he clearly sought to dramatize his story to the hilt. Parts may strain credulity. Commenting years later on the "somewhat artificial pathos" of E.'s interview, Boder wrote: "He is definitely a pleader, but of a cause which even *then* was not too popular."

We begin with the flight of E.'s family from Starachowice in September 1939 in an unsuccessful attempt to stay ahead of the Germans. At the time he would have been no more than eleven years old. His father had died some time before. He and a brother and sister were supported by his oldest brother, a cobbler, and his mother, who "traded a little in dry goods."

As soon as the Germans entered our town we immediately left for a small town in which very few people lived. Since our town was a manufacturing city with large factories, people were very scared. Two weeks later when the Germans were already there, we could not make a go of it in the small town so that we had to return. Soon during the journey we were stopped by Germans and searched. The few belongings that we had were taken away from us on the road and distributed among the Poles, the Gentiles. And afterward, when we came back to the town, we did not find anything in the house any more. Everything had been robbed by neighbors. And there were very few people [left] in the town.

The next day—it was on Yom Kippur—we saw the old synagogue that had been standing for years and years lit up in flames. In the middle of the night on the second day the synagogue was still burning. And whoever came out to [try and] save the synagogue was beaten, and also a few people were shot. As propaganda, people had to sign [a statement] that the synagogue had been set on fire by our-selves. And later on the Jews were separated from the Poles. The Jews had to live in special houses on special streets where no Pole was allowed to enter. And soon very hard living conditions began. Later an order was issued from the German au-thorities that all Jews had to wear [arm]bands. And whoever did not have a band on his arm got ten years punishment or else was shot on the spot. It often hap-pened that a Jew in that crowded ghetto could not sustain himself and his family [and] was forced to go out on the forbidden streets. Unlucky Jews were shot.

[Early in 1940 E. was put to work in a factory managed by a German.]

We would work very diligently. He would stand and watch. All at once he comes over, gives us a *Nagan* [a rubber truncheon], and says, "Beat your comrade!" I take it and beat him. He says, "That is not how one beats," takes the *Nagan* out of my hand, and gives me such a hard blow that I could not lift my hand any-more. He says to me, "That is how one beats. Now do you get it? Now beat your comrade." And afterward he said for two people to fill up a railroad car with coal and for two people to lay down on the floor and be entirely covered. When they were covered with coal, he laughed at us and ordered us not to dig them up. They should come up by themselves. And if they cannot, they can just stay there.

All of a sudden Jews from all over began to arrive in our town on trucks, on trains. People were being resettled. One bright morning at five o'clock the whole town was surrounded, and an order was given that in ten minutes not one Jew was to be found in his home. And many Jews were prepared for it. We "slept with our clothes on"—trousers, jacket, shirt, everything ready, and a small bundle at the head [of the bed]. We took that bundle and ran out at once. The whole family. There the Germans were already waiting with guns, with grenades in their hands. It looked for a minute [like they would] kill us. But we were following orders, and it did not take ten minutes [for us] to come out. I looked back once at my home, and I said, "I will not see this house again."

We went out to the market place. This is a large square in the center of town. All the Jews were assembled there. We already saw Jewish blood flowing in the streets and bullets flying. When we were already assembled on the square, we saw an old couple walking. They no longer had the strength to drag their feet. So a German took them into a house and with one bullet shot both of them. Put one next to the other, and shot both. Looking around the town again, we saw children lost from their mothers and mothers lost from their children. They were calling, the mothers to the children and the children to the mothers. But those children whom the Germans noticed died [were killed] immediately on the spot. The panic lasted four, five hours. It was terrible. Also while [we were] standing in rows, the Germans came over and immediately took off the better things. I myself was dressed in my best clothes. They soon took off my jacket and my boots, and they asked if I did not have any money or anything else.

How old were you then?

I was fifteen years old when all that happened. That was in the year 1942, in the tenth month. Luckily, I had a pair of old shoes that I had taken along in my bundle. I put them on and watched how the blood flowed and the little children [were] taken by the feet and thrown against the wall.

Later on when the afternoon came, everybody was tired standing on that square. Suddenly an auto with five SS men arrived, and they said for all young men from eighteen to twenty-five to fall in to be taken to work. I was a boy of fourteen years [*sic*]. I was not supposed to step forward. But suddenly an SS man was passing, and he took a liking to me. He gave me a sign with his revolver, and I had to step out from the ranks, and with a heavy heart I looked at my mother and was incorporated into the ranks of the workers. Once more I wanted to turn and take a look at my mother. I soon got it over the head with a riding crop; to this day I still have a souvenir of that instant.

When we arrived in the new camp, we were spread out in two places, we [men] and the very few women separately. An order came to hand over whatever we still had. We went over to the other side. The things we left on the place on which we had been standing. And later on a few SS men arrived and gave an order, "In the name of our Führer ten people will be shot." And immediately ten people were selected. And they said that the same thing would happen to every Jew who did not hand over his possessions that he had hidden on him.

How were the people selected?

He [the SS man] passed through. Whoever he pleased he made a sign with the revolver in his hand. And [that person] had to step out in spite of knowing that he was going to a certain death.

Did he pick older people, younger people . . .

Whoever caught his eye. There was no difference whether young or old. It could have been anyone.

Did those people say anything before they were shot?

All that we heard was "Shema Yisroel," nothing else. Afterward we were arranged in two rows and led past five SS men [who] had the job of searching all our belongings. Tore our shirts, tore our shoes. Our hair was searched. Wherever there might be a chance [to conceal something]. They even looked under [the soles of] our feet if one had not pasted on any valuables with adhesive tape. We were led into barracks, a hundred people to a barrack. The barrack looked low. One little electric bulb. Three-tiered beds, without straw, without anything, just wood. Two people received one little bed 1.2 meters long and 60 centimeters wide.

Everybody was thinking about what had happened to his parents and to the other people who had remained there on that square. The night fell slowly, and everybody [lay] on the plank beds, bewildered, confused, brooding. There was no question of sleeping. There is no hope. I myself must summon courage to live through that moment and be able to relate to the Jews in every corner of the world what has happened to us. In the middle of the night everyone sits exhausted, in thought. Suddenly we hear a shot. A guard, a Ukrainian, got a fancy and shot a machine gun burst into our barrack. But, thank God, it only cost three [dead] and two wounded. We had no water. To go out [to the toilet] was a threat of death.

Dawn was slowly nearing. We all arose, and we wanted to go to work. We thought that if we remained lying, they would take it for sabotage, that we did not want to go to work. So we all got up and went to work. As we walked out the door, the Ukrainians heard it. They immediately surrounded our barrack and fell upon us like murderers, beating with rubber truncheons. "What do you think, Jews? Do you think you can get out of this camp? You're going to stay here. You're going to croak here!" And with terrible blows [they] chased us back. At six o'clock a Jew came who had been living in Starachowice for a long time. An elderly Jew around forty. He was made temporary overseer of the camp.

Who made him? The Germans or the Jews?

The Germans. [Corrects himself:] The Ukrainians. He told us to get dressed and go to work. In five minutes everybody was ready, because nobody had slept, nobody had undressed. As we went out through the gate we received bread and a little bitter, cold, unsweetened coffee. When we arrived at work, the Ukrainians received us with bad beatings. We immediately got the worst kind of work. We were assigned to ovens of two thousand degrees of heat. They made ammunition, shells for cannon. And whoever did not complete the norm, the number that he was supposed to make—that was two thousand to three thousand shells—had to stand sixteen hours. And if [he] did not finish in sixteen hours, he had to remain for twenty-four hours. That is how it was going on every day. In a short time very, very many people had fallen who did not have the strength to endure all those things.

At work, the Gentiles told us the terrible agony that was experienced by the people who had remained there on the square. Because until then we had had no information, and later on we had some information from people who had returned—who had been taken as far as Treblinka and after that returned. And part of those people were also working there in the factory, driving the engines from one factory to another. An acquaintance, a Jew, was acquainted with such a machinist, and he told him about the terrible tortures that the Jews had suffered. First of all, 150 people were packed into a small railroad car. Entirely closed, nailed shut, doused with chloride. That Christian reported the impossible thing that 50 percent would arrive at that place half dead.

There were two girls who worked in a factory, one from Borzecin [?] and one from Lodz. And one girl had an elderly mother of forty years. The two girls were very beautiful. And a manager, a young German, in the factory had his eye on the girls and wanted . . . wanted to make use of these girls. But he did not succeed. Therefore he sent a telegram to the camp [administration] that the two girls committed sabotage. And the two girls were taken out of the camp—the camp was on a hill—and thrown down from a tower, and they were shot in midair. The old mother heard about the misfortune. She climbed a tower which was not occupied by the sentries and leaped down. It was a terrible moment in the camp. Besides that, there was a camp commandant by the name of Althoff. He was a murderer. He drove down every day, and he could not eat breakfast if he did not see the blood of ten Jews. And it was the same story every day.

One woman, after being in the camp four months, gave birth to a child. And an order came that the child was not permitted to live. If the child lived [at the end of] two days, the mother, too, would be shot. Then there were instances when from lack of cleanliness and from hunger many people became sick with typhus. Finding this out, [Althoff] came into the block where the sick lay and shot these people in their beds.

[As the Russians approached Starachowice, the Germans consolidated several work camps and prepared to move their slaves west.]

There were two more small camps [manufacturing] shoes and clothing for the Germans, and a smaller shop for wood working. Altogether 300 people worked there. These were also taken over to us, to the big camp that numbered up to two, three thousand people. When they brought the 300 people to us, a girl looked around . . .

How many women were there?

Women made up 20 percent in the small camps. In our camp there were 40 percent women.

A young girl, born in Lodz, looked around at the conditions in which she found herself [and] said: "Jews, time now counts in minutes. Perhaps we will be able to escape. And whoever dies will die a hero's death. But I believe that many will remain alive." This girl impulsively threw herself on the German commandant of the Ukrainians and tore the revolver out of his hand. And she started shooting, not at the people, but in the air. In the same moment the guards ran up and completely surrounded us and began firing on the people. But thank God, there were no dead. The girl was only slightly wounded. And with great difficulty we succeeded in saving the girl from death.

Tell me, how did you succeed?

A great deal of work was done on the Germans. It cost us a lot of money. The Jews gave up their last possessions.

Where did they get these possessions?

The Jews had left [them] with the Gentiles. And many still brought [them] to the Jews, because they were working in the same factories. They would return [them] to the Jews. And every Jew handed over the money they had left in order to save the young girl. The chief was a big glutton for money. He loved money and gold very much. And the Jews were not sorry to hand over the last possessions they had. This girl is still alive today in Germany.

When the Russians had come closer, the Germans considered it dangerous for us to stay. At night an order came that not one Jew was to go to work but had to stay in the camp. A terrible scare gripped the whole camp. Everybody walked around brooding and said, "These are our last moments. The Russians are approaching, and the Germans know that they have lost the war. They will finish us all off on the spot." In the afternoon a decision was made by the Jews to get away from this camp. There were definite rumors that we would be shot if we remained till the next morning. At night everyone was awake. The police [Jewish trustees] came into each barrack and said, "Jews, the last moments of our lives are approaching, and so we have one way out, to break out of the camp. There is a forest not far from the camp. It is quite certain that many Jews will die, but this cannot be helped. If we do nothing, the entire camp will perish. There is no place where we could be taken, and the Germans will not let us live."

At night, [with] everything ready—a little bundle, hammers, pliers, axes—[we] went over to the fence. There was no strong guard. And so on all four sides Jews watched for the moment to be able to go over, tear out the fence, and escape into the forest. It went on like that for four, five, ten minutes. After that people came running from all four sides, breaking the boards and cutting the wires. And a few people succeeded in escaping. At the same moment gunfire began falling from all four roofs, from the towers where the guards stood, and many, many were shot and a very small part escaped into the woods. But the majority of Jews were afraid to risk [it] because death would be certain and swift.

Where were you?

I myself was lying under the barrack, not far from the wires, watching for the moment I could escape. But I noticed that terrible shooting. And a lot of people were shattered and torn to pieces from the grenades that were thrown. Feet, hands, it even tore off someone's head. In a few seconds the whole camp was surrounded by Ukrainians and Germans. Escape was out of the question. Everybody [was] chased into the barrack. Everybody was silent, more dead than alive, and waited for the moment to arrive. Because there was no thought, no hope that we would remain alive. Finally we saw the dawn. We were allowed to go out to wash, and back again into the barrack. An hour later we were all lined up and all our clothes, everything that one had on, was taken away so that the people would not be able to escape. We were left in just a shirt and a pair of shorts.

On the same day, in the afternoon, [we] were able to find a moment when there was a light guard, and a few people approached the gate [and] the fences. And like snakes they slithered over the fence in order to escape into the forest. Thirty people succeeded in getting across; ten people were caught on the fence and shot. Afterward the camp was surrounded with a stronger guard, and the forest was surrounded, and they were shooting with machine guns and [throwing] hand grenades. We in the camp were again chased into the blocks. The ten corpses were soon taken off the fence and laid out in the middle of the square, where they lay twenty-four hours.

[To their relief, E. and his coworkers were not killed but evacuated to a string of labor and concentration camps in Germany.]

7   Nechama E.

With this interview we turn to survivors from the major Polish cities of Lodz and Warsaw. In both, the Jews were placed in large, closed ghettos in 1940. Nechama E. of Warsaw was perhaps the most cheerful and open of the survivors. Evidently the twenty-three-year-old woman had come to terms with the loss of all the other members of her large family. Recently married and visibly pregnant, she eagerly awaited her turn to emigrate to Palestine.

Her story, one of the most varied, comprises several types of ghettos, slave labor camps, and extermination centers. She begins as Warsaw fell to the Germans in 1939, recalling how Poles pointed her out as a Jew to Germans and threw her out of food lines. But Polish anti-Semitism was not unremitting. Following her jump from a train that she believed was carrying her and hundreds of other Jews to Treblinka, a Polish police-man working for the Germans directed her to a nearby ghetto rather than turn her over to the German patrols, which would have meant being shot on the spot.

Nechama E.'s escape from the death train was the first of many bold and risky acts to stay alive. Sick in the Auschwitz infirmary, she avoided being selected for the gas chamber by hiding among the Christian patients. Later, at Bergen-Belsen, she courted death by stealing turnips to keep from starving along with the other inmates. She also took chances for others, notably in the case of a stranger's child who attached herself to E. Others helped E., particularly the Jewish prisoners of war at Majdanek who stole medicine to help her recover from malaria. On the other hand, her story contains little indication of more active resistance to the Germans. The bodies sprawled in the streets as E. entered the Miedzyrzec ghetto suggest that some of the Jews there may have tried to run away when the Germans came to deport them. By then fragmentary information about extermination centers had reached some of the ghettos. But if so, that was the end of defiance. During the period when flight might have been possible, E. tells us that she simply "sat" in the ghetto, hiding from deportations but otherwise passively waiting for something to happen. Nor is there any indication of organized resistance to the ghetto's Jewish Council or its Jewish police force during the eight months E. was there.

E. also has something to say about the perpetrators. The murderous

Christmas eve raid by the SS on the Miedzyrzec ghetto more nearly resembles a perverted game than the dutiful act of reluctant murderers. Moreover, if E. was spared from the crematorium at Auschwitz as part of an effort to provide witnesses to "humanitarian" behavior by the Germans, it suggests that already in 1943 at least some SS doctors were preparing to save themselves from the full force of postwar justice.

After returning to Poland in 1945, E. joined a kibbutz, married another survivor, and together with her new husband took the underground road through Czechoslovakia and Germany to a cooperative camp near Como, Italy, run by the Hachsharah with the aid of the American Jewish Joint Distribution Committee and UNRRA. That is where she spoke with Boder. We begin with her deportation by train from Warsaw in September 1942.

Two hundred persons were packed into one railroad car. Everyone riding in these wagons saw death before his eyes at any instant. We lay one on top of the other. One pinched pieces from another. We were tearing pieces. Because everyone wanted to save oneself. Everybody wanted to catch air. One lay suffocating on top of another. We were in that railroad car a whole night. We grew very thirsty. It became terribly hot. Everybody undressed. There were small children who began to cry terribly, "Water!" So we started banging on the doors, screaming. So they began to shoot inside, from all four sides, while traveling. They were sitting on the roofs, on the steps. Very many people died. I was sitting and looking at one taking a bullet, another taking a bullet. I, too, expected to get hit in a moment. And I saved myself by hiding under the dead. The blood of the killed was flowing over me.

A little girl of four years lay there. "Give me a little bit of water. Save me." And I could do nothing. Mothers were giving the children urine to drink.

Is it really true?

I saw it! I did it myself, but I could not drink it. I could not stand it anymore. My lips were burned from thirst. I thought, this is it, I am going to die. So I saw the mother doing it, and the child said, "Mama, but it is bitter. I cannot drink it." So she said, "Drink, drink." And I myself imitated it, but I was not able to drink it. But what then? There were girders inside the railroad cars, iron girders. From the heat, condensation was pouring from the girders. One lifted the other up. It was high up, and we licked off the girders.

It was very stifling. There was that little window, a tiny one, so we wanted to open it. Every time we opened it, they would shoot in. There were small children, and they were all suffocating. We could not stand it anymore. Early in the morning, just before dawn, my mama began crying very much. I was with my "little" brother, eighteen years old. She begged us to save ourselves. Many had files, knives, hammers along with them. The boys took a saw and cut out a hole. And we took the bars off the windows. And we started to jump. No. What does "jump" mean? One pushed another out.

[The Germans] immediately started shooting. Many were shot. Out of a hundred people there could remain ten. My little brother jumped out five minutes before me, and he was shot. When I jumped out, I fell into a ditch. And I remained lying completely unconscious. And the train passed. I came to. It was at night, around three in the morning, so I. . . .

And your mother herself did not jump?

No. My mother could not. She could not jump with the small child. And a woman of sixty, she could not jump.

I came to. I got back my wits, so I went to look for my brother. In the meantime some sort of Polish militia man arrived and told me that I should quickly run away because the Gestapo was all around. I would be shot there. He told me that I had jumped near Radzin and Lukow.[1] So he told me to go to Miedzyrzec ghetto.

I began to walk toward Miedzyrzec. When I jumped out, I met a little girl. She also jumped. While jumping she had caught on a piece of iron, and she tore her entire leg open. And the two of us started to walk. Yes, after getting up I went to look for my brother. He lay shot. He had a bullet here, in the heart. I could not move away from him, but that Christian said that I should go away quickly. The struggle for life is stronger than anything. I left my brother on the road. I do not know what happened to his bones. And I went on. I had walked with the little girl for about three hours. It was dark. Through woods, through fields we crawled, crawled, crawled.

That little girl was a stranger?

I don't know that little girl at all. She was about fourteen years old. She did not feel the pain for terror. After having walked for perhaps ten kilometers, the two of us sat down where the road leads into a forest. The child said that she could not walk anymore. The leg hurt her. We didn't know what was going to happen. In the meantime I had heard Gentiles saying that Germans prowled on this road looking for Jews. And I saw it was bad. So I took the child. I carried her perhaps, who knows, a kilometer or two. I myself did not have any strength. I was barefoot. My shoes had remained in the railroad car, because I had undressed. I did not have the time to put anything on. I was completely naked and barefoot. And

1. Although E. and her companions assumed that their destination was Treblinka, the location of her jump suggests that the train may have been headed for Majdanek or some other slave labor camp in Eastern Poland.

that child remained in the field. And I went away. I could not help at all anymore. The child had fallen, and I could not do anything to help anymore. I went away.

I do not know myself how many kilometers I had covered. I came to the Miedzyrzec ghetto.[2] It was the day after a large deportation. When I entered the ghetto, I became faint. It was at night. I did not have anywhere to go. I regretted very much that I had jumped off the train because at every step, wherever I went, shot people were lying. Broken windows, all the stores looted. Terrible things had happened there.

I lived in that ghetto eight months, in deathly fear. I registered with the Jewish Council, and I sat! Every four weeks there were new deportations. Jews were brought in from the small towns all around. And there was a sort of assembly depot for Jews. And from there all the Jews were being sent to Treblinka. There I lived through three terrible deportations. During the first deportation I hid in an open attic and lay there for four weeks. I lived on just raw beets. I did not have anything to drink. The first snow fell then, so I made a hole in the roof and pulled in a little snow by hand. And this I licked.

Were you there alone?

No. There were about twenty people there. There was a father with a mother with child. There were some others in the attic. We had nothing to eat. We found raw peas. I had pared the beets, and afterward I gathered the rinds of the beets because I had nothing more to eat. And I nourished myself that way for four weeks, till there was a deportation. It lasted four weeks. After the deportation we came down from the attic. At that time a lot of Jews had also been shot. It was a terrible thing to see. We were taken to work removing the dead.

Who were the SS? Germans and who else?

Only Germans. Just Germans. There were a few Ukrainians, too, but not many. All the streets were splashed with blood. In every ditch Jewish blood had been poured. We started looking for something to eat so we . . .

Was there no Community Council?

At that time the chairman had been taken away [and] shot. There were Jewish police, too. So [the Jews of the ghetto] were shot little by little. During each deportation ten, twenty were taken and also transported into the railroad cars. And they were shot [or] sent away. Those who escaped were shot. So there was no-

2. Miedzyrzec Podlaski, a town of about 12,000 mostly Jewish inhabitants, served the Nazis as a regional center for concentrating Jews prior to deportation. The first deportations from the town occurred during the last week of August 1942, and the ghetto was liquidated on May 2, 1943.

body to turn to. Everybody was hidden in the cellar. Everybody was afraid to go out. Many were lying in hiding there still a few weeks after the deportation. They did not know that they were already in the clear. When we came down, it was sort of peaceful for about two months. For two months time we lived on what the Jewish Council gave to those who were strangers [Jews who were rounded up from neighboring towns and assembled in Miedzyrzec for deportation]. Every day they gave them a kilo [2.2 pounds] of potatoes and a piece of bread. Every day we lived in great fear. People walking in the streets were shot at.

I had to support myself. I carried water for the Jews who lived there. And for that I received a few pennies. I lived in a large hall [that had once housed] a circus; all the deportees lived there.

In short, it dragged on till winter, till Christmas eve.[3] Then there was a frightful night to live through. Drunken Gestapo came down from Radzin. There were perhaps, who knows, thirty people altogether in that house. I was sleeping there with about fifteen persons in our room. In the middle of the night we heard shooting. We lay in great deathly fear. And they were knocking on our door. And I did not know why they could not enter through the door. In the morning I got up. I opened the door. A shot person fell into my room. When we came [into the other rooms] everyone lay shot. Two children with a father who were sleeping in bed, everything was shot! A man lay with his stomach completely torn open, his guts outside on the ground. And later Jewish police came in. The Germans had left, and we had to clean up the blood and all that.

There were also two men who had [escaped from a forced labor camp and come to Miedzyrzec]. One had received four bullets in the neck, and one six bullets. And the one who received six bullets was in agony for about four hours. He tried to choke his other friend. He had gone completely out of his mind. And he died. The second one who had remained alive, who had received the four bullets, was in agony for two weeks. He had puss, and there was no doctor. He lay so long till white snakes [worms] appeared on his neck. Worms which smelled bad. And he was pleading for death, to be shot. We covered our mouth and nose so as not to smell. We took off the bandage and took off the snakes. Then it became a little easier for him. The same day, in the afternoon, he died.

I lived through another deportation. I was not able to hide anymore. I was led away to a synagogue. There was a large synagogue. There all the Jews were assembled. It was terrible in the synagogue. [The Germans] simply came in—if they heard a cry, they shot in. They threw grenades. They beat. They struck. They did not give us anything to drink. We had to relieve ourselves on the same place where we slept! I was there a whole night. I saw it was bad. I did not want to go to death. I went on fighting against it. I went over to a window. It was on the

3. Later E. says these events happened on New Year's eve.

first floor. We took two towels, I and another girl. We lowered the towels from the windows, and we crawled down and escaped down into a cellar, and there we again lived through the second deportation. It only lasted three days, and then we went out again.

Again we lived there a few months. During the last deportation I was not able to hide anymore. I was led away into a transport [and] taken off at the Majdanek camp. We were all lined up. The young women were taken to the Majdanek camp. The men were taken to another camp. The children and the mothers they kept another two weeks. And then one bright and clear day they came with trucks and took away all the mothers and all the children. Many mothers still tried to save themselves, but they could not. All were taken. We know for certain that they were led to the crematorium. The [women's] camp was in the fifth sector, and the crematorium was there [next to it].

I was in Majdanek two months. We were so starved! At first we did not yet know what it meant to be in a camp. At six in the morning, a German SS woman came and started to chase [us] with a large strap, beating everybody. We were lying on the beds, grieving, wondering where our mothers, fathers, and children were. We were crying. Then a German woman came in and beat [us] over the head to go out to roll call. It could happen that we would stand four, five hours. People were being kept so long because not everybody knew yet what this was about. Many children of about sixteen years hid in an attic. They were afraid to come out. They thought they were going to be shot. And for that we stood five hours as punishment! Later nobody hid anymore. They said whoever hides will be shot.

Did you work there?

Yes. We were sent to do garden work. We were sent to carry the shit which . . . there were no toilets there, so we carried it in buckets. We were given nothing to eat. They were hitting over the legs. They were beating over the heads. The food consisted of 200 grams [7 ounces] of bread a day, and a little soup of water with nettles. The hunger was so great that when a cauldron of food was brought, we could not wait for it to be distributed, but we threw ourselves on the food, and that food would spill on the ground, and we ate it with the mud.

After two months they began to select the healthy who were able to work. They tested the heart. Whoever had the smallest blemish on the body did not come out from there. Only 600 women were picked out, and I was among them. This was in July.

I was taken away to Auschwitz. The conditions were then already a little better. Fewer were being packed into a railroad car. They were putting sixty into a wagon. [After] arriving at Auschwitz, we were led into a large hall before taking us to be bathed. All the women had their hair cut off. For the first time in Auschwitz. In Majdanek I was not shorn, just in Auschwitz. And they tattooed numbers on us. And a little triangle. We had very great anguish because we had our hair cut off. How can women live without hair? And we were dressed in trousers and in blouses. We were terribly hungry. We went to work in a detail called the "Death Detail." Why? We went to work, the 600 women from Majdanek. It took a month, and there remained no more than 450. We died out of hunger. We worked carrying large stones on barrows, building a highway. They gave us nothing to eat. We were beaten terribly. There were German women who were also prisoners [i.e., prisoner trustees]. They were imprisoned for prostitution. They said that every day they must kill three, four Jews.

I worked that way for three months, until I became sick. I had gotten malaria. I went around for two weeks with a 41° fever [about 105°F]. I was afraid to go to the sick ward because it was said that if one goes there one does not come back anymore, one is taken away to the crematorium.

I saw that I could not stand it anymore. My legs were buckling under me. Each day I got more and more beaten because I did not work. I could not eat anymore. I gave [my bread] away to other girls. I decided to go away to the sick ward. There were no medicines. I lay around for about four weeks without medicine. There was a doctor, also a prisoner, a Jewess. She was not able to help at all. She had no medicines. None was given to her. I pleaded for a drink of water. They did not want to give it to me because the water there was rusty from pipes. If you drank that water you became still sicker. I passed the crisis, and during that time there were three selections. They came to take the sick to the crematorium. During each time I lived through much deathly fear. I hid myself. Christian women were lying there, so I climbed over to the Christians, into their beds, and there I always had the good fortune to hide.

Did the Christian women let you?

Yes. There was a Christian woman, a very fine one. She was there for political reasons. She was also very sick. She was already near death. And . . . she was not taken. Christians were not taken to the crematorium, just Jews. [Christians] had it much better. They received aid from the Red Cross. They received packages from home, and we nothing. We had to look on how they ate. If there was a kind one, she would occasionally give us, the sick, something. And that is how I was saving myself in the sick ward.

My sickness was very terrible to describe. Complications set in afterward. I had many boils on my body. I had scabies. And I had nothing with which to cure myself. At one time I lay already completely dead; the Christian women made an outcry that I was already going to die. So a woman doctor came up to me, and she brought some sort of an injection, and she gave it to me.

A Jewish doctor ?

Yes. After that injection I became a little stronger, and I got out of bed. I nursed the other sick. I did not have much strength, but I was already able to walk around a little. Three weeks had passed. An order came to deliver the names of all the sick. They came to that sick ward where there were only typhus patients, and all were taken out. Not one remained. It was on the night of Yom Kippur. All were taken, undressed, wrapped in blankets, thrown on the trucks like sheep, and driven away in the direction of the crematorium. We all went and looked, so we saw how the women were singing *Kol Nidrei*. They were singing the *Hatikvah*. When they said good-bye, they said, "We are going to death, and you take revenge for us." They were still pleading to be left. There was a girl eighteen years old, and she was crying terribly. She said that she was still so young, she wanted to live, they should leave her, they should give her some medicine to heal her scabies. And nothing helped.

How many sick were taken?

Four hundred persons. An entire block.

Could the crematorium be seen burning?

Of course! When we went out at night we saw the entire sky red, the glow of the fire. Blood was pouring on the sky. We saw everything. We knew. When we went to the shower hall, we recognized the clothing of the people who had left and returned no more. In the warehouses where we were issued clothing we recognized the clothing of the people who had been taken away. Sometimes, when we would go out at night to relieve ourselves, we saw how transports were brought with mothers and children. The children were calling to the mothers.

The next morning a German doctor appeared. I became very scared. All who were in the block became scared—we were all sick from malaria—because it was said that the others were taken yesterday, and today they would take us. He came in with a list and called out my name and another twelve Jewish names, and to that another fifty Christian women. And he said that we who were sick with malaria, who show a positive sickness—because there were positive and nonpositive [forms of malaria, and] a blood test showed that I had a positive malaria—were going to Majdanek, back to Majdanek.

I did not believe it. In the evening all of us were taken, seventy-odd people. We were put on a truck and driven to the train. While riding on the truck all of us believed that we were going to the crematorium. We had thought that it would be an open truck, and we would be able to see where we were being taken, but ultimately it turned out to be quite different. We were taken in a closed one. Driving past the guard we heard, "Seventy-odd prisoners for Lublin."[4] So we already knew that we were being taken to Majdanek.

We were led into a freight car, which is used for transporting cattle. Among us were many ethnic German women[5] who had also been imprisoned there in the camp. They were [there] for prostitution.

What color triangle did they wear?

Black.[6] Very mean! Very mean! They beat this way. They hit this way. Inside the railroad car two sentries with rifles were posted to guard us. So [the ethnic German women] had some sort of intimate relations with them. They received food from them. They made a little ghetto. They put us into a small part of the railroad car and took the bigger part for themselves. And in our part we were squeezed one on top of another. We nearly crushed ourselves to death. En route two girls died. They were very weak. We had no food. And they were full of those scabies. They were taken down in the middle of the night at Majdanek, and they were dead.

We arrived there, eleven Jews. We were taken to the first sector, taken to a Polish sick ward, undressed, bathed, and put into beds.

Who did that? Men or women? Prisoners?

Women. Prisoners. Christians. There were no Jews anymore. Because when I was there the first time, there were still 30,000 Jews. Returning I found out that there were only 300 women and 55 men.

[E. then described what those surviving Jews told her of the SS massacre of all other Jews at Majdanek and several nearby slave labor camps.]

And next morning these women had to clean up all those who remained, the shot. They were doused with gasoline and were burned in the pits. And afterward [the 300 women] had to take the clothes which everybody recognized from her mother, her sister, her children. They cried with bloody tears. They had to take those clothes and sort them. And everybody was thinking, "Why did I not go together with them? Why did we remain alive?"

[Boder wanted to know more about the 300 women.]

4. The Germans always referred to Majdanek as "Concentration Camp Lublin."

5. "Ethnic Germans" were residents of Eastern European countries who identified themselves, and were accepted by Nazi authorities, as racially German.

6. The Germans used black triangles to mark "asocials," among whom they included prostitutes, "shiftless elements," chronic alcoholics, and the like.

[The Germans] came to the square where they were standing and picked out the most beautiful, the youngest, and healthiest women. And 55 men, prisoners of war who had [fought] for the Poles. All Jews. And these 55 Jews helped us very much, the women who had returned from Auschwitz. We were completely non-human! We looked like skeletons. And they put us on our feet. In the things that they sorted from the dead was very much gold, very many diamonds, whole bars of gold. This they [bartered with] Christians [who] received food packages from home, from the Red Cross. And with that [the men] nourished us.

Tell me, you were all searched. You had to undress. How was it possible to find gold on the dead?

A Jew had it sewn in underwear. In the sole of the shoes. In the hair. They searched and they searched, and they did not find. Sometimes it was sewn in the sleeves. After death, when they went to look through the clothes, then all that was found. When we became healthier, we were transferred to the fifth sector, and we lived together in one block with these 300 women. I became cured because [the] men took salves which the Christians received from the Red Cross, stole it from them and brought to us.

Why did they take those who had positive malaria to Majdanek?

They said it was a whim on their part.[7] Thirty thousand they burned and thirteen they led to life. And I was fortunate enough to be among these thirteen. And we were also thinking, "Any day we will be burned." Every day we saw them bringing others to the crematorium, from the entire Lublin region. [They were] gassed first and then burned. If there was no gas, they would shoot and then burn. We thought there were no more Jews, only we few have remained. We thought that they had already exterminated all the Jews from Europe.

After we had been in Majdanek for eight months, an order came: the 300 women survivors of the action must go to Auschwitz. And we, the thirteen tattooed women [i.e., the ones who had come from Auschwitz], of whom eleven remained, were to go someplace else. And we began to cry very much. "Why aren't we being taken with them? We are Jews, too." She [the SS woman] answered, "You have seen too much and know too much to be able to go with those women." So [we] saw our death coming.

Two days later we were taken away to Plaszow. They added another 300 women from Radom. There were little children, too. In Plaszow they took away the small children [and] the pregnant women. There was a famous hill. They were

7. As Boder stated in his notes on the interview, survivors were sometimes called upon to testify to the "humanitarian" actions of certain Nazi doctors in postwar war-crimes trials. Fears of defeat and retribution may explain why this group of prisoners was kept alive.

taken to the top and undressed. There were no crematoria. They were shot, and afterward we carried boards and made a fire, and they were all burned.

[When Boder expressed amazement, E. fairly shouted at him.]

Yes I carried the boards. We carried the boards, and we saw how they shot them. If anyone had gold teeth, they pulled the teeth out. Plaszow [was located on the site of] the Jewish cemetery. They made streets out of the tombstones. They shot people every day at first. I was all alone. I had it very hard, but I remedied it a little. I went to scrub floors in the blocks. People gave me a little piece of bread to eat. All at once twenty men arrived from Auschwitz. I asked about the 300 women from Majdanek. [One of them] told me at once, "Alas, they are no more." In the middle of the night they all [had been] called together and led into the crematorium.

While I was in Plaszow, a transport was brought with small children from Krasnik. I took a great liking to a little girl. Her name was Chaykele Wasserman.

How come children were brought without mothers?

The Russians were approaching Krasnik, so [the Germans] liquidated the camp. And that child's mother had escaped, and she was shot. And many children were all without mothers because the mothers were immediately taken away. And the children were brought to Plaszow. I took that little girl. I was with that little girl for four months. That child was very dear to me. I loved it very much. That child could not go anyplace without me. I was thinking, "I shall live through this war. I will be very happy with such a pretty and smart little girl." She was eight years old.

What did the child do then all day?

Nothing. The child went around on the street. It was not even called to roll-call. After a time [the guards] came and took all the children away from us. And that child was very clever. She lowered herself down an open privy and hid there. When the inspection was over, women went to the latrine. So the child began yelling they should call me, and I went and pulled out the child. The child stunk very badly. I washed her up, dressed her in other clothes, and brought her to the block. She was overjoyed. "Now I shall remain alive!" But, alas, it was not so.

The Russians were approaching Plaszow, and I was taken to Auschwitz the second time. We arrived in the middle of the night.

And the child with you?

I took the child along. What will be will be. All night long the child did not sleep. She did not want to eat anything. She just kept asking me, "Does gas hurt?" If not, she is not afraid. But I cried very much. I said, "Go on, silly one! There is a children's home. You will be there." She says, "Yes, a children's home! You see, there is the crematorium. It burns. They will burn me there." It was very painful for me. I could not sleep. But suddenly the child fell asleep in my arms. I left the child lying on the ground and went over to some man who worked there in the shower-bath, and I pleaded with him. I lied to him. I said it was my sister's child, and he should help me save the child. So he said, "Tomorrow morning you will all be undressed, and you will all be led before the doctor. He will make a selection. And you will tell the child to hide in the rags when you undress." And that child was very clever. She did not even take off her shoes. She hid in the rags. And I waited that way till the evening, till I saw the child all dressed up. The child got out from under the rags and came to me. The German doctor had left.

How did she wash herself and everything?

There were Jewish women in the shower-bath. She was washed. Clothes there were very plentiful, from the many children burned. . . . She was dressed very nicely. "See," she says, "again I have stayed alive. I shall again stay alive." And together with the child I left for the block. There was nothing to eat. The cold was so cutting, one could get sick. They chased us out bare to the inspection. And the child, too, had to go. The child was counted as a grown-up person, but that child had much grief. She was not numbered. After three days a doctor by the name of Hessler[8] came, and selected women to be sent to Germany. I was taken away. And that child cried very much. When she saw that I was being taken, she screamed, "You are leaving me. Who will be my mother now?" But, alas, I could not help any. I could do nothing with the German. I asked, and he said, "If you want to go to the crematorium, you can go with the child. And if not, then go away." I felt very bad. I cried very much. And the child was crying. And I parted from the child and left. The child remained with the older women. It was said that deliverance was coming, the Russians were approaching, and [prisoners] would not burn in the crematoria anymore. I do not know. I believe it is a lie. I don't know what happened to the child. I know only one thing: I left.

The child said good-bye to me, and I was led away to Bergen-Belsen. In the year '44, in winter. I was in Bergen-Belsen three months. The hunger was a terror. We went to the garbage heap and picked the peels from the turnips that were cooked in the kitchen. And if you chanced to grab a turnip . . . I was very daring. I fought strongly to stay alive. Outside the gate was the kitchen with wires so

8. E. may have been thinking of SS physician Kurt Heissmeyer.

you would not be able to get near. I risked it. I got out through the gate where they were shooting and grabbed a turnip. And a minute later they shot a girl who grabbed a turnip. I knew that the moment I grabbed it the bullet might hit me, but hunger was stronger than death. I returned to the block. People, corpses assaulted me that I should give them some too. I shared it with them. We rejoiced.

After three months a German came again and selected Jews. I did not know what to do. But I only wanted to go on, on. They collected 200 Hungarian women, 300 Polish women, and we were led away to Aschersleben, near Magdeburg. There was an airplane factory. Everything had been bombed. There was a camp commander, a very mean one. There were foreigners. Prisoners of war. Dutch, French, Yugoslavian. And they worked there. They were free. And they helped us a lot. They would give a little piece of bread, whatever they could. If one was caught, nothing was done to him, but the woman was taken, had her hair cut off, and received a good beating. And they [the foreign workers] said, "Do not worry. The Americans are already approaching. It will not be long, and you will be liberated." Well, we did not believe anything. We were without hope and indifferent. But they would bring us newspapers. We saw that it is really so, that the Germans were in a bad way, that the Americans were approaching. We began to believe a little.

There was a foreman, a German civilian. And when he saw that we took so much interest in politics and that we knew what was going on in the world, he said "Yes, yes, don't think so much. There will come a time when you will all go with bared breasts to be shot." We cried terribly. But it was not so. For HIM it was death!

Heavy air raids had begun. Every night we were led into a forest to a bunker. We were working the night shift. Snow was falling. Three, four times a night they sounded the alarm, and we had to get out and run to the forest. In the middle of the night they suddenly woke all of us up and called "Everybody out!" Everything was burning around that little town. From the airplanes which were bombing. A prisoner told us quietly, "Children, three kilometers from here are the Americans." But for us there was still no joy. They dragged us on [all the way to Theresienstadt]. We were completely in tatters. We made socks, we dressed ourselves from the blankets we had. We were very dirty. We were beaten. They screamed at us, "Accursed swine! You are filthy! What sort of people are you?" We were thinking how would they look if they were on our level.

In Theresienstadt there were only Jews, many Jews from Germany. There were very many old women who were [in mixed marriages of] Germans and Jews. They had Jewish sons, SS men, serving Hitler. She was Jewish; the husband was a German. And that is the reason they remained alive. All old, gray women. We were there eight weeks. There was very little food. And the Germans prepared a large crematorium, but they did not have enough time to do it. One fine day they called all the Jews together. A German came and said that if he would be escorted to Switzerland, [extermination] would not be carried out. The Swiss Red Cross would take us over, and all of us would be saved.[9]

Two hours before the entry of the Russians the Germans drove through, the SS men with tanks, with weapons, and began to fire on the whole camp. All of us were hiding. We thought, "This is the end." But two hours passed. We heard the Russian tanks were there. And we didn't believe it. We went out, whoever was able. There were a lot of sick who couldn't go. We went out with great joy, with much crying. We had lived to see the moment of liberation.

But then a real death began! The Russians had opened all the German storehouses, and they said, "Take whatever you want." And the people began to eat, too much, greedily. And that was harmful for them. There was a great epidemic. Hundreds of people fell a day. In about a month half of the camp had fallen. There were stables full of dead people. People crawled over the dead. It stank terribly. There was a severe typhus raging. And I, too, got sick. I lay in the hospital four weeks. I had spotted typhus. All night I lay and cried, "What will I do now? What did I survive for?" But my fate had not been completely lost. I still had hope.

I left Theresienstadt with a transport for Poland. In Warsaw I immediately joined a kibbutz. There in the kibbutz I married my husband. My struggle is for one thing only, and this one thing has remained for me: To come, together with my husband, to Eretz Israel and to build a Jewish home together with all brothers and sisters.

9. Theresienstadt's commander, SS Major Karl Rahm, hoped to save his neck by striking a deal that would have turned the ghetto over to Swiss officials. Already 1,200 of Theresienstadt's Jews had been transferred to Switzerland in February 1945. Rahm was hanged as a war criminal in 1947.

8 Jurek K.

The power of family ties during the Holocaust, especially for very
young Jews, can scarcely be exaggerated. Jurek K. escaped from a German deportation train, recovered from a gunshot wound with the help
of a compassionate Polish peasant, but made his way back to his parents
in the Warsaw ghetto in 1943, well after it had become known that the
Germans were exterminating Jews at Treblinka. Jurek's age was difficult to determine; he said he was twelve when the Germans attacked
Poland, thirteen in 1943 when he was sent to Majdanek, and seventeen
at the time of his 1946 interview. His confusion was understandable
after a long period during which he lied about his age to assure being
assigned to work. He was the only child of a Warsaw Jewish industrialist
and his wife. Their factory had been bombed by the Luftwaffe in 1939,
but their savings sufficed to see them through ghettoization, build and
maintain a hiding place in the ghetto, and spirit a five-year-old relative
into hiding with Gentiles. Jurek told of his escape from the train and his
return to the Warsaw ghetto as an afterthought to his memories of the
ghetto uprising, which he spent in hiding with his family. In fact, the
earlier events may be the most telling part of his story.

Following the suppression of the Warsaw ghetto uprising in May
1943, Jurek K. was sent to Majdanek together with his parents. There
his mother was separated from her husband and son and probably perished. During the short time the two males remained at Majdanek, they
worked on the *Scheisskommando* that carried human excrement from the
cesspools to the camp gardens. Although it is sometimes argued that
the SS left members of this work detail alone in order to avoid contact with the filth and smell, Jurek's interview shows that the guards
found ways of tormenting them as they struggled with the unwieldy
vats. Then Jurek and his father were sent to work at the giant HASAG
ammunition factories at Skarzysko-Kamienna. There Jurek watched his
father sicken and die from overwork and undernourishment, the fate of
thousands more like him.

As the Russians approached Skarzysko late in July 1944, the Germans
evacuated his work group to Buchenwald. Jurek evaded the evacuation
of Jews from Buchenwald in April 1945 with the help of a Czech block
senior. Resettled in France with the help of Jewish charities, he was

studying to be a dental technician in Paris and living in the ORT home at Chateau de Boucicaut at the time he gave his interview. We begin with his initial deportation from Warsaw early in 1943.

I was taking lessons from a teacher, privately at [his] home, because Jews were not allowed to go to school. And while walking to [the teacher's home] the Ukrainians surrounded the streets, seizing all the people whom they wanted to send East, and they caught me. And so, unfortunately, I fell into such a transport. I was caught and taken to the transfer terminal. But at that time it was not yet so bad. They loaded us into the train, and we were told that we were going to Treblinka.

There were children only?
There were grown-ups, too. At the time we were about two or three thousand people. And so we were sent away. It was said that we were going to our death at Treblinka. I knew that if one has to die, better let it be another death — not to be gassed. Soon some Jews who had concealed files inside their shoes [began] to file through the bars of the train [windows]. They cut the bars, and two people jumped. What happened to them I don't know, because I only heard shots. The Germans were firing at them. The main thing is that after ten minutes I had thought it over. I had considered it. I knew that I had left my mother and father at home. And so I decided to jump. This is it! What will be will be. I got out on the roof, and the Ukrainians were standing on the steps of the train. They didn't see it, because the windows led to the roof of the train.

What was it, a passenger car?
No, no, it was a freight train.

Then how could you climb on the roof?
Because the people helped. One put his hands under [he demonstrated a hand hold] and you climbed up that way. Everybody wanted to see somebody save himself. And so I got out on the roof. I was lying down, afraid that the Ukrainians might see me. I lay that way until I saw that the train was going up a hill. Here it was better to jump, because if one jumps on a level stretch, one can fall under the train. But if one jumps on a hill, one falls [and] rolls right down the hill. And so, I thought it over well and jumped. I don't remember anymore, but I felt a sharp pain in my legs. And I heard a shot. After perhaps two or three hours I came to, and I saw two children playing nearby with a large hoop, playing, running, jumping. I started yelling, and the children ran away and brought an old Gentile with them — it must have been their father. The father took me into the house. By

chance I was lucky, because he was a very decent Gentile. And he made me a . . . how does one say it? A bandage on the leg, because it appeared that I had a bullet in my leg as far as the bone. Here. I can show it to you.

He is now showing me a bullet wound on the leg.
And the woman bandaged me. The peasants there had various medicines. They brought it and put it on, and I was with them four days. They gave me good things to eat and to drink. They had everything. I still had a few zlotys on me. I wanted to pay. They wouldn't take it. After four days—this was about eighteen kilometers from Warsaw—I said that I wanted to go back home. And so the Gentile took a cart with two horses. He drove me about ten kilometers, [and then] I walked to Warsaw. I still had money.

Did you pay him anything?
No, nothing. He didn't want to take anything. But I remembered his address, so I wrote him a letter two or three weeks ago. I have not received an answer from him yet.

And so I got to Warsaw. I bribed a Polish policeman. I had eight hundred zlotys, so I gave him two hundred. He let me into the ghetto. He led me through. I looked terrible, my face all lacerated because I had fallen on my face while falling on the grass. Everything torn. I ran into the house. You can well imagine the joy on seeing me walk into the house. Everybody was already certain that I was not alive anymore. After two weeks everything had already healed. The leg still hurt.

[A few days later the Warsaw ghetto uprising began. K. and his family concealed themselves in a basement hiding place until they were burned out and taken to the transfer terminal to await deportation by rail.]

I, who had already been [there] once, didn't imagine that it would be so terrible, because when I was there before it was not so bad. Now the Ukrainians were standing on every step. One had to take off his hat before them, stoop, bow before them. If one did not, he immediately got it over the head with the rifle. So we were taken upstairs. They made a search. The men were undressed; the women [too]. They looked for money. They were always looking for money, money and diamonds.

And the women and men were kept together?
No, no, the women were taken into a room separately. They were searched for money. Luckily, they didn't find anything, because my mother didn't have anything on her anymore, and she was returned again to us to our room. Two days we stayed there in the transfer terminal. We were not given anything to eat, but

everybody had what he took along from the bunker with him, a few rusks and other things. We lived on that. After that, we heard the train was arriving, and everybody had to go outside. We were arranged in pairs and threes, and we were packed into the train, 120 people in one closed railroad car. We could not breathe at all. And so after a journey of two hours, three people in our wagon were already asphyxiated. The Ukrainians were playing with us. As soon as the wagons were closed they shut the windows completely—there were iron windows that could be shut. And they said that whoever wanted the window opened had to give [them] money. Some people were found who still had some money. They gave away the pennies so the window would be opened, to let in a little air. And people were fighting and beating each other because everyone wanted to get close to the window. Everyone wanted to catch a little air.

After riding for four hours, people could not bear it anymore. A few people had already fainted. The train stopped at some station. The locomotive had to take on water. We didn't have a drop of water. We begged, we cried through the windows to the Gentiles, "Bring us a bottle of water. We will give you money." A little boy wanted to give water. The Ukrainians shot him right on the spot. He remained lying right there with the little bottle in his hand.

And after a time we arrived in Majdanek. I can't say exactly how long we rode because we had no watches. People did not think at all about time. People thought just about getting out [of the train], be it Treblinka, be it Majdanek. The train was immediately surrounded by the gendarmery, and we were all chased out. Into every car ran a few Ukrainians, and they took and chased everybody from the cars with rifles. They did not look who it was, whether a woman or a man. They just struck, beat over the heads with rifles. They chased everybody out—"Run, run fast!"—[and formed us into] a single line on a platform.

We were supposed to go to a house to bathe. You can imagine . . . , how is it possible after riding such a long time where we didn't have a drop of water, were so weakened. Suddenly here we are told to run. And so we did run. Many people did fall to the sides while running. They ordered [us] to run still faster, still faster. The bathhouse was a long distance away. We were sure that we were about to be sent into a gas house where we would all be gassed. So, people started saying good-bye to one another again. And we were separated. The women, the men, the small children up to ten years were taken separately.

Who did that?
The SS. With large whips they took and separated the little children. And we were sent into the bath to wash. A search was made again, completely nude. They looked into the nose, ear, mouth. Looked whether we had money. On many people they still found money in the mouth. They found diamonds. They found some tiny diamonds stuck inside the ear.

What did they do when they found something?

They just took you and beat you. They didn't do anything [worse]. And after the bath, we were given a good beating. And if they saw a young boy, he was asked, "How old are you?" They asked me, and I said, "Sixteen," even though I was only thirteen years old. He looked at me. So he said, "Well, let it be. Let him stay." So I remained there with my father, and we were sent into the same block. I was lucky that I was sent inside along with my father.

Yes. And your mother?

My mother was sent away separately, to another sector, with the women. Already the second day we were sent to work. That means we carried shit in special buckets in a special holder, two people to a holder. One had to run and jump with it, make various gymnastics. There and back, there and back.

And from where were the feces taken?

From the toilets. There were no toilets like here. There was a ditch with a large board. And everyone did it together there. When we scooped it out, we had to run with it [for] half a day, until dinner. And after dinner people had to take everything out and throw it away outside. After a day of such work, people could not stand on their feet anymore. Whoever did not run well or jump well, if it was not to the Germans' liking, he immediately got clubbed, beaten. It was not work that is of some use. This was work so they could exterminate people. To weaken people.

Every day was the same. At 4:00 people arose. A roll call was made [to see that] nobody was missing. If one was missing the whole camp was immediately left standing until the missing one was found. It happened once that one did escape through the wires. I don't know how. So we stood outdoors for fourteen hours waiting till they caught that person. From 6:00 in the evening till 8:00 in the morning. The Ukrainians left with the dogs, and they caught that man about fifteen kilometers away from the camp. The dogs almost tore that man apart.

Fortunately, either the Russians were approaching or something; it was said that the camp was being entirely evacuated.[1] This was in 1943, I believe. The same night eight dark trucks covered entirely with black tarpaulins had left the women's camp. And terrible screams were heard from the women. After them another three trucks followed with all the small children that had been selected at that time. And the trucks drove in the direction of the gas chamber. Because during the time that I worked in Majdanek, when [we] had to go out of the camp on the way to work, we had to go by a house. On it was quite openly written

1. This rumor was erroneous. Majdanek was not evacuated until July 1944, approximately a year after K.'s departure from the camp.

"Gas Chamber." Everyone could see. And those trucks went in the direction of the gas chamber with all those women and children. From that time until now we have had no news from those people. That means that they were surely gassed or burned. I don't know what the Germans did there.

And it was not possible to write letters between the women and men?
Absolutely not! The men were in four sectors. Every sector consisted of twenty-two barracks. Every sector was separated from the other with a wire fence. And the women were in the fifth sector, also separated with a wire fence so that we could see them from afar, but to talk was forbidden. For the least word there was punishment, either by hanging or by shooting.

Did you see how people were being shot?
No. I didn't see that. We saw one who went over to the wires to talk with his wife. He was instantly shot. Every fifty meters around the wires there was a tower. Inside that tower sat two Ukrainians with machine guns. They watched that no one escaped, or people shouldn't talk, and so on.

[K. and his father, together with other prisoners, were sent to Skarzysko.]

For thirteen months I worked on a locomotive. The driver was a Pole, and I was a stoker there in an ammunition factory. And we shuttled the wagons with the ammunition. My father got a very hard job. He had to carry shells. And I saw that my father would not last much longer.

How old was your father?
My father was born in 1896. And so my father became constantly thinner and thinner. I, as a young boy, could perhaps last longer than my father, because [he] was very tall. He needed a lot to eat. And, unfortunately, there was not enough to eat. We got 120 grams [about 4 ounces] of bread per day and 2 liters [just over 2 quarts] of soup. That soup wasn't soup but clear water. One fine day I saw that my father's face was completely swollen. It was said that it was from too much work and this and that. We went to a doctor there. There was a sick ward. The doctor said it was from hunger. Unfortunately, he did not know if there was any hope of saving my father.

Who was the doctor? Was it a Jewish doctor?
A Jewish doctor, a murderer. He, too, was a murderer. They were all murderers. The leaders of the camp, though they were Jews, were all murderers. The worst sort of Jews. Bandits who before the war did not have any way of making a living. Thieves put into the camp and made to be our leaders.

Still a doctor is . . .

But he had such a disgusting character, a murderous character, that Jewish doctor. And so he told me frankly that there was not a bit of hope. I had to bid good-bye to my father.

When I worked there outside on the locomotive, it always happened that the Pole brought me a little piece of bread or something. They weren't in a camp. They came from the outside to work. It was also forced labor. I always hid [the bread] and carried it to my father. But I didn't have that much, to be able to give father a great deal of help. After a month's time I saw my father become more and more swollen. And after two weeks he went to the hospital. The hospital consisted of two halls, one for men and [one] for women. There was a little hay on the floor, and the people lay there on the hay. They lay, and they died there. And that same Jewish doctor immediately looked into [his patient's] mouth. If he had some gold teeth, he right away pulled the teeth.

And so my father went to the hospital. Every day after work I went there, and I saw that, alas, there was no more chance to save him, because with every minute he would become . . . [Here the spool ended abruptly.]

After [he] had been lying there for two weeks, I went into the hospital to visit my father. My father wasn't there anymore. I immediately understood that my father had already died. And you can imagine my heart. How I looked then. I knew that I was alone then. Out of the entire family I was now all alone. And so I saw there was no other counsel. Crying wouldn't help any. Again I went to work.

After thirteen months the Russians were steadily approaching the camp. Already shooting was heard. Day and night we saw fire in the distance. And so everybody thought that we were already liberated. After two or three days the Germans gave an order that the entire camp was being evacuated. It was impossible to hide oneself there because this was the kind of camp where everybody watched. If one should be missing, nobody would be evacuated. He would be searched for until he was found. And so we had no other choice. We had to present ourselves, and we had to leave. We were again packed into [railway] wagons, this time not a hundred and twenty as before, but a hundred people to a wagon. And we were taken to Buchenwald.

We were the first transport of Polish Jews which arrived in Buchenwald. But there were already many Jews in Buchenwald who had possibly a lot to say there, because a few Jews were already block seniors and so on. The prisoners received us rather nicely, because Buchenwald was a *political* camp. It was not a camp for extermination like Majdanek or Skarzysko. This was a camp for *political* prisoners. The prisoners did whatever they could for us. And they did most for the younger ones up to seventeen, eighteen years. [They] immediately ordered food, because we were so starved. We were soon given something to eat. I was [there] eight or nine months. I don't remember too well.

Buchenwald consists of two camps, a big camp and a small camp. The small camp was much worse than in the big camp. Only people who worked not so hard, but sat [around], had little to eat, and so forth were in the little camp.[2] We, the younger ones, were transferred to the big camp. I was in block twenty-three, a special block, a "Jew-block" the Germans called it. I was there two months. I rested up before I went to work, thanks to the Jewish prisoners who had arranged everything so well that we shouldn't have to go to work immediately, but rest up for a couple of months. Then we went to work. The work was not so hard. The work consisted only of carrying a few bricks, because the Germans were building various bunkers and so forth there. They were building kitchens.

And so it went until one day Anglo-American aircraft arrived and bombed. They were probably so well informed that they did not bomb the camp but everything all around the camp. That means the SS armories and all the points important [to the] Germans. The Germans were shooting at them. I saw one airplane shot down, but the SS armories, all those munition factories were destroyed. But, unfortunately, an incendiary bomb fell on the kitchen in the camp. And the kitchen began to burn. And we prisoners knew that were the kitchen to burn down, we would have it very hard. We would be evacuated from the camp. We wouldn't have a place to eat.

And so after exactly eight months we found out that the Americans were moving at a fast clip toward Weimar, nine kilometers from Buchenwald. On the other side the Russians were approaching Berlin. There was great joy in the camp when we heard that. The people who worked outside the camp told various news that they had heard. There was, for instance, one SS man. He happened to be a good SS man who every day told those prisoners what was happening in the world, that the Americans were moving forward, that the Germans were on the run, and so on.

When the Germans saw that the Americans were moving forward, they ordered that the entire camp be evacuated. Everybody, without exception. Now we knew that we must not allow ourselves to be evacuated, because the Americans were already very close. We ran from one block to the other. We were hiding and did not let ourselves be evacuated. But the Germans came into the camp, surrounded entire blocks, sent everybody up to the gate, and [told us] that we were going to Theresienstadt. The two Jewish blocks went first. It was announced over the loudspeaker, "All Jews assemble on the roll call square!" The few younger boys all escaped from the Jewish block and ran down to the small camp. There there was also a Jewish block under a Czech block senior, a very good man. There was no other like him. He received us in his block, and [when] the Germans arrived

2. K. may not have appreciated the extent to which the men in the small camp were sick, starved, and used up. The small camp was Buchenwald's quarantine.

and asked if this was a Jewish block, he said, "No, I don't have even a single Jew here. Only Christians—Yugoslavs, Poles—Gentiles only." And he had to sign that he had [no Jews]. The Germans no longer knew exactly which of the blocks were [made up of] Jews, because all the papers had been burned during the bombing. And [in fact] we were all Jews there. He had not a single Gentile!

Night arrived. We went to sleep. And at night we heard terrible shooting. For the first time we saw a Russian airplane flying over the camp. We signaled. We threw our hats in the air. And the Germans who were in the towers around the camp hid their heads into their collars. They were afraid. The next day we heard shooting coming steadily closer. And from our block we saw, far away, tanks passing by. We did not know whose tanks they were, German or American. And we saw the Germans who were standing in the towers—they were not Germans [but] Ukrainians—running down from the towers and running into the woods. When we saw this, the prisoners risked their lives and took scissors and cut through all those electric fences. And they ran straight down to where we saw the tanks coming. I was with my two comrades. We ran over to one tank. From afar [the tank driver] probably saw such people for the first time; [he] stuck his head out and marveled. He didn't know what sort of people we were. Were we animals or people? We were dressed in prisoner uniforms. We ran over and started to talk to him. We found out that he was a Jew. Right away he gave us something to eat. Canned food and chocolates and other things. As one says, he lifted up our hearts.

We returned to the camp, and we didn't find one German anymore. All had escaped into the woods. We took axes and stones and beams and ran into the forest to look for the SS. In the first two hours we found seventeen SS men hidden in the woods, one [up in] a tree. He didn't want to come down. They took all the weapons from another SS man [and] shot him down from the tree. Three higher ranking officers had been caught. All the SS were herded into one block, and a few people were detailed to guard them. Now the Germans had to remove their hats for us, because we forced them [to]. And they were abused until the Americans came into the camp.

The Americans came after two days. Before that the prisoners themselves held the camp. Ach! It is impossible to imagine the joy. We carried them in. Picked them up and carried them in. We tossed them up in the air. And really, the joy was so great that one can't imagine.

Jurek, how did you get to Paris?

After the liberation of Buchenwald, all the youngsters were taken and transferred to the SS armory which was still standing. We had it very good. Every day we would run to the Germans, into the town. They were abused. They were harassed, the Germans there in the towns all around. One day a car came with representatives of UNRRA. At that time an American rabbi, Rabbi Marcus, took us over. Before that there was Rabbi Schechter [who had] arrived in Buchenwald first. It was Passover, or something. He distributed matzoth at that time. Services were conducted that day. Rabbi Marcus accompanied the entire transport as far as Paris. He took us through in a train. After the German-French border, we got a luxury train, first class. And we traveled as far as Ecrennes [?], ninety-two kilometers from Paris. There we were under the care of the OSE. We rested up a little after all the agony that we had endured. We were there two months. And now we are here in Paris, in Chateau Boucicout.

9   Hadassah M.

Polish Jews who had money could hope to bribe their way out of painful situations during the early years of German rule, as several interviews already have made plain. But wealth by no means assured escape
from the Nazi net. Hadassah M.'s family was prominent in Warsaw's
gem and precious metals trades, which gave them skills and access to
valuables that helped them avoid deportation until near the end of the
Warsaw ghetto in 1943. But whatever remained of their wealth probably disappeared in the ransoming of M.'s husband from the SS torture
squads. In hiding during the last days of the ghetto, she and her family
were betrayed by other Jews, and she and a younger sister were sent
to Majdanek, where they were assigned to the work crew building the
crematorium. She was twenty-nine at the time.

After three months at Majdanek the sisters were moved to Auschwitz, arriving at a very "lucky moment" indeed; by summer 1943 the
camp had temporarily run short of laborers, and the mass extermina-
tions had been suspended. They managed to stay together and were
assigned to the justly feared task of clearing aquatic vegetation from
fish ponds near the camp. One of Hadassah M.'s deepest impressions of
Auschwitz was the gassing in 1944 of large numbers of children held at
the family camp at Birkenau. Postwar research has confirmed her impression that they had been kept alive solely to deceive the Red Cross,
which had been pressing for an opportunity to inspect Auschwitz. Once
the Red Cross dropped its demands — perhaps satisfied with what the
Germans showed its representatives at the model Theresienstadt ghetto,
or else caving in to German resistance — the children and the adults who
lived with them in the family camp were liquidated.

The sisters managed to stay together during the last months of the
war as they were sent to Ravensbrück, the German concentration camp
for women, and then to one of its satellite work camps northwest of
Berlin. There they were liberated, twice, in a sense, first by the Americans and then by the Soviets. They returned to Poland and settled in
Lodz where Hadassah organized a Zionist kibbutz for the orthodox
Agudat Israel, which was then shedding its earlier opposition to Jewish
nationalism. There she ran into revived Polish anti-Semitism and encountered opposition from the official Central Committee of the Jews
in Poland, sponsored by the new Communist government and dedi-

cated to persuading Jews to stay and (as they confidently hoped at the time) help build a new Poland free from racial strife.

Hadassah M. was interviewed at a home for displaced Jews at Henonville, about thirty miles from Paris. Still a passionate Zionist, she managed the camp kitchen for her own large kibbutz and a Lithuanian yeshiva located there. We join the interview with her description of the last deportations of Jews from Warsaw as the Germans prepared to liquidate the ghetto early in 1943.

In 1943, January 18th, there was a great conflagration. They took [the people from] all the workshops away. Nobody could save himself. Except for one workshop. Schultz's. That workshop was left unharmed at that time. And the entire ghetto was emptied out.[1] I was not at home then, and in my absence they took all my children away. The oldest child was ten and a half, the next seven, and twins of four years. One had died a short time before.

[At Schultz's workshop] people worked at furriery, shoemaking, [and] various trades. One of the largest shops. At that time I still had an uncle, a brother, and a sister. We were [living] together. In 1943 after the ghetto purge we perceived that the time was coming for Schultz's as well. During the second Seder night we went down into the bunker, entirely under the ground, very deep underground. Without windows, air, or anything. Thirty-odd people were living in that bunker. We had been preparing for months in advance. We knew that a moment would arrive when they would make Warsaw completely Jew-free.

On the 13th of April, after having been in the bunker a few weeks, we were discovered.[2] Another bunker had been discovered, and there someone was found who reported us. We no longer had any alternative, and we had to start going out.

How did people sleep and eat there?
We had made makeshift beds. As for eating, we lived on whatever we could. Because food did not enter one's mind. They took us out on a Friday at one o'clock. [Earlier] the same day people who were discovered in bunkers were taken to the headquarters of the Jewish Council and shot. Fate wanted us to remain alive, and we were taken out and searched. We couldn't take anything along with us, and besides that, we didn't want to because we knew that we were going to Treblinka. Or rather we thought that we were going to be burned like the people

1. About 7,000 were deported from the ghetto at that time, leaving more than 50,000 Jews in Warsaw.

2. If M. is correct about arriving at Majdanek on May 1, 1943, she may be mistaken about the date of her arrest. It is possible that it occurred during the first days of the ghetto uprising, about a week later.

before us. But they led us to the transfer terminal, the assembly place for all the people whom they had gathered together, and on the same day we were put into railroad cars. In my wagon there were over a hundred people. The car couldn't take in anymore than fifty-odd.

Men and women?

Men, women, and children. Thirty-nine people suffocated from the heat. Because there [was only] a very small window far up. Many people jumped out, not because they wanted to save themselves; they wanted to perish in the open air. When dawn came, we saw that we were being taken, not to Treblinka, but in the direction of Lublin, that means to Majdanek. We arrived in Lublin, and from there, guarded each fifth row by two soldiers with large dogs, with rifles ready, we were led to Majdanek, which is a few kilometers from Lublin. When we arrived, we were the first transport of Jewish women. Men were already there, Slovakian Jews. At that time this was a completely new camp. We were among the first Jews in Majdanek.[3]

We arrived on the 1st of May 1943. We lived under very hazardous conditions. They took away our shoes, and we had to stand all night on a field barefoot. Majdanek has a climate which has strong winds, high [extreme] temperatures. Throughout the night ten centimeters of frost lay on the ground. They examined our feet [to make sure] we didn't put a piece of paper underneath. In the morning we had to run, not walk, to work, chased after by a young SS woman with a giant dog. Her name was Brigida. It is possible that in all that time we did not find a woman quite like her. Her meanness exceeded all human understanding. The work crew numbered around 1,500 people. Whether it rained or snowed, we had to stand and work. Whenever she noticed anything, she released a dog. We were bitten, our clothes torn off. And when one returned to the camp bitten, the next day she was taken to the crematorium, because people who weren't completely well, or had the smallest rash, didn't have the right to live. We were given absolutely no medical help. Whoever gave us the least bit of help was punished.

And what did you work at?

We worked in the field. Later on we worked with bricks. We were helping, alas, to build a new crematorium near the bath. At that time they were gassing the people in the bath where we bathed. And they were burned in a pit, an open ditch. We ourselves were present when we took out still unburned pieces, parts of people, and took them on the trucks and threw them in the water. The ashes

3. By that time Majdanek had been in operation for more than a year, and already more than 40,000 Polish, Slovakian, Czech, and German Jews had been sent there. Naturally, not all of them were still alive when M. arrived in May 1943.

[were] either thrown in the water or they were strewn in the gardens. And so this [pit] was not enough for them, and we ourselves had to help carry bricks at night to build the crematorium. I was in Majdanek three months, [and then] I was sent to Auschwitz. We were told that we were being sent to factories to work.

How many people were traveling with you to Auschwitz?
Over a thousand people traveled with my transport. Women and men. We had already been selected the night before. At 12:00 at night—we were already asleep —they ordered us to dress quickly. We didn't know where we were being taken. The men of that sector knew [thought] that we were being taken to the crematorium. One man had a wife among us. He was a doctor, a Jew, and he knew exactly where we were being led. So he poisoned himself. But as we were being led on the road to the crematorium, an SS man arrived riding a white horse, and he gave some kind of an order, and we were led back again. When we returned, we didn't find that doctor anymore. The next morning they took us to Auschwitz.

When we arrived, we were assured that we had come at a lucky moment, that Jews were not being burned anymore. I worked for three months in Auschwitz.

When were you tattooed?
Immediately on arrival.

Was your hair cut off?
Wherever a hair was found.

Who did the cutting?
Women. But men were standing by, SS men, capos, people who were working there in the bath.

In the morning we went into the water and stood up to our neck [and] gathered the grass by hand and carried it to the shore. It was taken out on the field [and] dried. I don't know what they used it for.

How many people were working in the water?
In my time this work crew numbered 250 people. Two hundred were in the water at a time, and 50 people were working outside [on land]. When not in the water, we were carrying barrows, heaped up to capacity; from 7:00 till 12:00 we weren't permitted to rest. We had to go around, and ten Christians stood with shovels, and everyone threw in a shovel, so that, God forbid, we shouldn't be able to rest, not at the loading and not at the unloading.

Tell me about the water. How did you work in there?

We went into the water with our clothes on. Only the shoes were taken off. If it happened that someone said that she wasn't feeling well [and] could not go into the water, she was thrown in just as she was—she couldn't even take off her shoes.

In Auschwitz my block was right across from the crematorium. Perhaps thirty meters separated the crematorium from me. I had occasion to witness everything. It was entirely open. They didn't even try to cover it up. Quite late they covered [it] with small trees so that we shouldn't be able to see and hear everything. The transports arrived there, huge transports. In ten minutes by the clock we already saw the fire coming from the chimneys. We knew if the transports were of fat or lean people. Because if black smoke came from the chimney, it was a lean transport; if fat, there was a huge fire going that could be seen from distances of tens of kilometers. There were seasons when the ovens weren't able to burn as many transports as there were, [so] they dug ditches, pits . . . almost as if they were burning people who were still quite alive.

Without having the people gassed?

At the end they were giving very little gas. The people were only like they had lost consciousness. They even begrudged [them] a little gas. We had occasion to hear all the cries of *Shema Yisroeil* and sometimes the singing of the *Hatikvah*. I myself saw how the oven [gas chamber] was being opened and the people were being pushed in. I also had occasion to see the gassed people lying outside, a whole heap. In the beginning we thought that maybe it was just the people's clothing; only when we came closer we saw [they were] all gassed people.

You happened to pass by, yourself?

No. Our work crew passed along the road that time. So we observed quite well. There were also cases that out of giant transports nobody, nobody was let into the camp alive. Children were altogether out of the question. If they want to claim that they only burned weak people, the living witnesses can tell that they took away the most beautiful, the youngest, the healthiest people, still sufficiently capable and strong [enough] for work. There was a time when they installed a children's block. The children were given the finest and best, but it was only when they had to present proof for an inspection or such. During one nice, bright morning the children were taken away and all burned.

In 1945, when the Russians were already breathing down our necks, we were aroused from sleep in the middle of the night and had to march on foot. That night we covered thirty kilometers, without any rest, running, not walking. We weren't given anything for the road. We were told to take along our blankets, but we had to throw them away in the middle of the road because our strength had given out. If one wanted to rest a moment on the road, if she only nodded her head, she was taken out and immediately shot. Very many men fell at that time, more than women. After covering thirty kilometers that night, we were given fifteen minutes to rest in the morning. After that we walked a whole day, again a whole night, and we were loaded into railroad cars. Whoever couldn't make it in the cars fast enough was also taken away and shot. We traveled five days in entirely open railroad cars. During the entire five days we lived on a little snow. So many of us were packed in that there was no place to sit down. We had to stand.

Were there SS in each railroad car?
Yes, each car was guarded by SS men. They had a bench for themselves in the same wagon where they could lie down quietly.

We stood still more often than traveled. Whether it was raining or snowing we traveled uncovered. When one needed . . . there wasn't any [toilet] either. If one had a can to do what one had to . . . After five days of dragging us around that way we arrived in Ravensbrück. In Ravensbrück we lived under threatening conditions—dirty, nothing to eat, again beaten. In Auschwitz we were beaten with clubs for no reason whatever. In Ravensbrück the same thing happened to us, but this was still worse, because we didn't even have anywhere to sleep. After four weeks we were sent on to Neustadt, seventy kilometers beyond Berlin. There was an entirely new camp where we didn't have any conveniences, the most necessary that a person has to have. And we again met up with blows and with beatings.

Did you work there?
Not at the beginning. There was a commandant whose greatest pleasure—he was a great sadist—was to beat up someone so badly that she couldn't get up. Later on work began. People were assigned to ammunition factories and to dig trenches. I worked at the trenches in such difficult conditions. We got 80 grams [2 ounces] of bread a day. We walked seven or eight kilometers to work. And on the 2nd of May we were liberated.

Tell me about the last few days. Did you notice that you were going to be liberated?
Rumors reached us. But we were already so resigned about everything; we didn't imagine that someday the happy moment would come. Every one of us remained entirely alone. But the moment of liberation did come. A few minutes before the Americans arrived, all the SS men disappeared, and we were left alone. They didn't tell us anything. Still, it was lucky for us that they didn't take us out of the camp so that we should have to walk farther. Because if they had moved us at that time, not even 10 percent of us would have survived. Because the people were so exhausted. People were sitting and eating grass from hunger. We didn't even have the strength to get up.

So in the morning the Americans came in?
First the Americans drove through in trucks and calmed us. Later on the Russians arrived, and the Russians stayed. All the German women were released half an hour before [liberation]. Only the German prisoners. The entire day we knew that [the liberators] were already quite near. They [the SS] broke open the magazines then. They still had time to shoot one Gentile girl.

Why?
Because she had come close to the magazine.

How long did you stay in the camp?
Two days, but [then] we lived for another few weeks right outside the camp in the house where the SS men had lived because we simply had to come to ourselves so that we might have the strength to go on. From the camp we traveled on foot, everyone with a little hand cart that we had taken away from the German civilians. We walked for about ten kilometers, and later we met a cart on which people were riding, and they took us on.

Who was with you?
My sister was there, and a few more young girls whom I had to keep under my protection. Everyone was traveling separately to one's home.

What did the Germans say when you took their little carts?
Many were still so shameless that they didn't permit it. But they were simply afraid of us. They had to let us do whatever we wanted. Later they created a militia for themselves so that nothing should be taken away from them anymore.

Then we traveled toward Stargard and from there by train to Lodz. I had no reason to go to Warsaw. I was given reports that Warsaw was, as it is in fact, an empty, desolate field. And unfortunately I knew that I wouldn't find anyone of the family anymore. So my sister and I and the few girls that I had with me settled in Lodz. Right away they found some relatives and some friends from their town, and they got settled. [But we did not] find anyone even in Lodz, [so] we joined *Agudah Israel.*

Were you always with them?
Yes. From before the war. And we began to do our work, because we saw that we had to create a home for those people who were returning from the camps, who were deeply shaken, everyone alone. We created the first *Agudah Israel* kibbutz in Lodz. When I opened the kibbutz I was with four people. More people arrived, and by joint work we were able to create a home for all those who were completely alone after returning from the camps. We saw to it that as far as pos-

sible we should be able to send people out of Poland, to *Eretz Israel*, where our air is. Because in spite of everything we didn't have a peaceful life in Poland. A Jew couldn't go peacefully out in the street. Carnages and slaughters had begun again.

How do you explain it? The Poles wanted to be free of the Germans. They knew that the Germans were attacking the Jews. How does it come that a Pole should do the same thing?

The Germans left a legacy which it seems will remain in Poland, in spite of the government being strongly against it. But it [the government] isn't strong enough to stand up against the dark masses which still reign and maintain themselves in Poland. Before Passover we succeeded in tearing ourselves through and coming to France. My sister is still in Poland. She does not have the possibility of coming yet. She is still quite a young child. She is eighteen years old. And she couldn't travel with me.

More people were supposed to arrive after us, but we were informed on. They don't want to let us out of Poland.

Why not?

Because they understand that Jews are still quite useful to them. Because all Poland is being reconstructed. Jewish hands are doing the reconstruction. Without us they know they won't accomplish anything. The Jewish Committee in Poland stands on guard so as not to let a single Jew out. They say that you can live quite peacefully and well in Poland; you don't have to go to *Eretz Israel*. We didn't become legalized either, because they hindered us. We had to be on guard against the Jewish Committee with each and every transport that we smuggled out of Poland. They stand [against] us all the time and hinder us in that work.

And now the whole world should help us get to *Eretz Israel* so that there we should be able to live our life fully and at least feel at home. Because no matter where it should be, we won't be able to find peace. America is not for us. Belgium is not for us. The whole world is not for us, because there we won't feel secure. We don't demand much happiness from life anymore, because we had too much unhappiness. But still, now we want a peaceful life and for once to feel what it means to be in one's homeland.

10   Benjamin P.

Boder experimented in some of the interviews by focusing on special episodes rather than trying to tell the subject's whole story. Benjamin P.'s membership in the Jewish Fighting Organization that revolted against the Germans in the Warsaw ghetto made it natural to begin there, although it was done at the expense of background information. We know only that he was a native of Warsaw, had studied German in high school, and that his father had been deported in 1941 and never heard from again. P.'s account of the ghetto uprising is brief but introduces several interesting elements, including the Germans' use of Jewish turncoats to ferret out Jews in hiding in the ghetto ruins during the last day of the revolt. It also mentions the inspirational figure of a woman who died in the first battle of the uprising, who, whatever the facts about her may have been, evidently served the cause of ghetto martyrology. Captured and tortured by the Germans, P. carried the marks of his own martyrdom plainly on his face.

Benjamin P. was one of the few Jews sent to Treblinka to be selected there for work elsewhere. He was sent to Majdanek and then to the Buna works at Monowitz (Auschwitz III). There he was taken under the wing of the camp's orchestra conductor and given the privileged job of cleaning the musicians' block. P. recalls spending two years there, but it could not have been more than eighteen months. He was evacuated on foot and by train to Dora-Mittelbau, a subcamp of Buchenwald, from which he escaped during a bombing raid. During the last chaotic months of Hitler's Reich P. succeeded in disguising himself as a wounded SS man with a medical discharge and ended up as overseer on a farm in the Sudetenland. Luckily, the Soviet officer who came to shoot him as a captured war criminal was Jewish and allowed himself to be convinced of P.'s true identity.

Benjamin P. faces up to one of the neglected aspects of the survivors' experiences, namely the rage and drive for revenge felt by some of them. He admits to committing atrocities against German civilians after his liberation, and his description of returning to Auschwitz to torment his old tormentors provides rare evidence that the Russians put captured SS men to work at the scene of their crimes. After a close call with the law in British-occupied Austria, Benjamin P. married, moved to Italy to prepare for emigration to Palestine, and at the time of his interview at

Tradate DP camp had just become a father. His very first words plunge into the story of Jewish resistance in Warsaw.

My name is Benjamin P. I was born in Warsaw, and that which I am going to tell you I have lived through and seen with my own eyes and felt with my own body. I will begin right away when a few transports of Jews had already been sent away, and we began to organize the Jewish Fighter Troops. These were called the ZPB.[1] In Polish these initials stand for Jewish Fighting Organization, which had as its aim the fight against the extermination of the Jews going on in Poland. The procurement of weapons was very difficult because the financial position of the organization was very weak. It was scarcely enough to buy a few pistols.

From whom did you buy the pistols?
The comrades who worked in various places for German troops, for instance the SS [and] in veterans homes, in the ammunition factory. These comrades bought from older people [veterans of World War I] who remembered what Jews had done for them; these people aided us very much with bringing food into the ghetto and with arms. This wasn't all. For this we needed finances. We went [out] at night, dressed in black, masks on our faces and revolvers in our hand. We went from door to door to rich Jews, and we demanded money from them. We didn't always get it. But when we threatened death or other things, then we got the money. And every time when we took a sum of money from anybody, we left receipts so that after the war that particular person should be able to claim [restitution] either from the surviving contingents of the ghetto, from the fighters, or from other institutions which would be created after the war. Not all Jews agreed to this. But against threats there was no way out, and they aided with something. But in the meantime [another] organization was created which also went under the name of ZPB which was composed of thieves and people of the Warsaw underworld, also of Jews who went around to procure money in our name. This money went into their pockets.

A few days before Passover in 1943 [the Germans] prepared to remove the Jews from Warsaw. The panic in the ghetto was very great. People went around like poisoned mice, one can say. People prepared themselves, made various hideouts, bought edibles, and hid. Because according to what was heard from the Germans, from Hitler's speeches, should the war end at 12:00, [then at] five minutes to 12:00 all the Jews in Poland would be exterminated. The organization also prepared itself [for] battle. The organization numbered about 170 people, and in the

1. The underground "Jewish Fighting Organization" in Warsaw is usually referred to with the abbreviation "ZOB." Either P. misspoke or he refers to another Jewish resistance group.

last two days the number came up close to 200. All were provided in the way of weapons, ammunition, clothes.

What kind of clothes?
SS clothing, because deep inside the ghetto, there was a shop, a factory [making] German clothing. The factory was named Brauer.

Wasn't it dangerous to walk around in an SS uniform? Couldn't another Jew take one for a real SS man?
No, no. That wasn't so, because when the battle occurred, an SS man didn't dare to walk around among Jews, because he knew what awaited him.

It happened on Monday morning, the day which is on the first Seder night. All around the ghetto a brick wall had been erected which had three tiers of barbed wire on top. Underneath [on the other side of] that fence were machine guns and also sentries of Ukrainians, of Polish police, and gendarmerie. That night the guard had been tripled; not just doubled, but tripled. And when the comrades from the organization noticed that the guard was reinforced, we prepared ourselves. We knew that something was happening in the ghetto. And so the comrades immediately [went] from house to house [and] notified all Jews that they should hide themselves because a raid would take place tomorrow. Only young people hid themselves. The older people could not be taken down to the cellar because it was already too late for that.

The next morning at six o'clock German troops entered, SS with tanks, artillery, cannons, machine guns. There was a Jewish woman, a comrade of our organization who lived near the entrance gate to the ghetto, and she had a box with grenades. The gendarmerie and the German troops were pelted. When the Germans noticed that they were being attacked by the Jews, they surrounded the house in which the comrade was. The comrade died as heroically as she had begun [the attack]. The Germans made use of dum-dum bullets, which tear up the body. And this girl was hit by such a bullet [and] torn up so that she couldn't move her arm anymore. When she saw that these were her last moments, she took a revolver and shot herself. And later, comrades who were supposed to go on a patrol to see where the Germans were, what they were doing—not everyone had the desire to go, because they knew they were going to certain death, but when the name of this comrade was mentioned, he went.

At night we went out and ambushed German patrols at close range. And when we killed them, we took off their weapons and their uniforms and put them on. The ghetto was bombarded with incendiary bombs, with tear gas, in order to get the people out of the hideouts. The ghetto was completely burned. People saw that the battle would not last longer. And so a proposal was made to escape. But how? It was decided to blow up one wall of the ghetto and a few hundred people should pass through, and only at the end should the organization, the comrades, escape. And this plan was indeed executed. A wall was blown up on Platz Mura-now. A few hundred people, women with children and older people, were sent through. A part of these people were killed by the Ukrainians who were standing near the fences. The lucky ones remained alive.

In the fourth week of the battle the comrades decided that one could not go on fighting anymore, that the rest of the comrades should escape. In the hideout I had my mother [and] a cousin [whom] I couldn't leave behind. So I proposed [that they] all escape, and I would remain with my mother because my mother looked like a dark, Jewish woman. She had a Semitic face, so it wasn't possible [for her] to escape to the Aryan side. One heard about the people who did es-cape. They were caught. They looked like Jews. They didn't have any documents, so they were killed in the Gestapo [headquarters]. Death either way.

After this, thirty or forty comrades escaped through the sewers to the Aryan side, and [from] there to Lublin, the center of the partisans. I stayed with my mother, hidden with distant relatives. People walked around at night and searched. "Where is my mother? Where is my father? Where are my brothers and sisters?" [And also] to get a little fresh air. We lay in the cellars where we were covered by an entire five story house. The bricks became heated from the fire that was burning, so that the ceiling of the cellar had become very hot and we couldn't breathe, so that at night we *had* to get out a little to catch fresh air. And indeed, on the 6th of May when we went out, we met a young man who asked about his father, about an entire family. And he mentioned the name. We said that we didn't know him, and that same "comrade" noticed where we were hiding, and next morning he came in again with gendarmerie and betrayed us. When I came out of the cellar, the gendarmerie immediately had me. The Jews who were hid-den with me all had to come out.

Do you know who he was?

I didn't know him, because he was not a Jew from Warsaw. And even from Warsaw one can't know all the Jews. You could tell from his accent that he was a Galician; Galician Jews have such a [peculiar] Yiddish pronunciation. That Jew persuaded us to come out [and that] we were going to work and nothing would be done to us. He [offered the] excuse that he was caught and had to show where the Jews were hidden. If not, he was going to be shot. But as we knew from be-fore, all people who talked that way were really Gestapo employees.

When I came out of the cellar, I hid the gun that I had and the ammunition in a water barrel. I was immediately taken to the side, and my hands were manacled.

You were in the SS uniform?

Yes. Then the Ukrainians built a huge fire of charcoal and began asking questions. Where was my family? I didn't want to disclose that I had family there; [I said] that my mother was a stranger. But my mother spoke up. She thought that she would save me, that if I still had a mother they wouldn't do anything to me. And so my mother was tied with a few other people, that cousin among them, and they were burned alive. I was standing before the fire, approximately twelve to fifteen meters away. I felt myself completely losing consciousness. I didn't know what to do. All around me SS men stood and guarded me with their weapons. If I took one step forward, I would immediately be shot. Should I throw myself on the fire? I just stood there. I sank into the ground. I saw that my mother was fainting in the fire, she did not know what she was doing, and the last cry from my mother: "My child, stay alive. I will watch over you. I will keep you in my hand."

After that I was thrown on a truck by the SS men and driven away to headquarters. I was tortured so that I should tell how many comrades [there were]. Where are the comrades? Where are the arms that we had bought? Where are the ammunition magazines? Where are the foodstuffs, and where are the partisans hidden? I didn't want to tell them. A few times a day I was hung on a hook in a wall. My hands were tied in the back, and I was hung up by the hands fifteen to twenty minutes. Afterward I was taken down unconscious, doused with water, and hung up again. I was kept there for six days. When the Germans saw they couldn't do a thing with me, they decided that maybe I would tell if they tortured me differently. They took me into a tiny room with a tiny window. It frightened me very badly. On the table I found hammers, pliers, pieces of flesh with hair torn off from [someone's] head, nails torn off fingers, and a lot of blood on the floor. On the table very large steel nails also lay. A drunken SS man told me to stick out my tongue, and my tongue was pierced. [P. opened his mouth for Boder, who noted that the whole tongue was scarred.] And also my nose was torn up. Later on, in the camp, [it] was sewn together by a doctor I knew.

After that I was released. They saw that I wouldn't tell a thing after such things. They decided to send me away to the transfer terminal from which a train would leave. Thousands of people were lying there without food, without water, in terrible conditions. It was very dirty, because all the transports which had been sent out from Warsaw went through the transfer terminal. And all the manure that the people had left there had been accumulating for four, five months. I met many friends [there], and I stayed two days with a swollen tongue and a beaten nose which already had stopped bleeding, because it had been tied up with a handkerchief. On the second day a freight train arrived, and they packed us in, 130, 140 people in one car.

How did you know how many there were?

Well, they counted. Three SS men stood at each wagon, and the people were thrown into the cars. And also they threw in corpses so that afterward the SS men should not have to deal with the dead people. During the ride I was terribly thirsty. There was an acquaintance of mine there whom I begged—I don't know how to say it—he urinated into my mouth, straight into my mouth, because of the terrible thirst. This wasn't the first case, because all the people drank this way. For me the relief was great, because the urine absorbed the heat of the tongue, and the swelling went down.

I was sent to Treblinka. A selection was made. They looked for people who could speak German. I had learned German at home, in a business school. And so I reported as one who could speak German. And so from approximately 6,000 people who were there, 320 were picked out. I was among them. And so these [other] people went, surely, to be burned. But the 320 were sent to Majdanek.

It was very bad in Majdanek. People were beaten, tormented. There was one of the authorities, the camp leader Thumann,[2] who could demonstrate that he could ride on a horse within a crowd of people and trample the people with the horse.[3] And also in the morning while going to work, if he would meet a group of workers, he would order them to line up in two rows, and let go with the auto at great speed and run over the whole group. This was his pleasure. Without this it seems he was unable to sit down to eat.

Did you see it yourself?

Saw it myself. Because I had a job street cleaning, to clean up the manure after the horses that worked in the camp, the straw which was strewn around, or such other things. So that I was able to see all these events.

After two and a half months in Majdanek, I was sent away to Auschwitz. In Auschwitz I was immediately sent away to the Buna works as a locksmith. That is three kilometers from Auschwitz. There I met a certain Bronislaw Staszak, an orchestra conductor of our camp. He was also from Warsaw, a Pole who had already been in Palestine six or seven years. And he could speak perfect Yiddish [because] he had been in Eretz Israel as an orchestra conductor. And later on he returned to Poland. I was in Auschwitz about two years. Towards the end I didn't have it so bad in camp, because I had enough to eat; that orchestra conductor

2. SS First Lieutenant Anton Thumann headed the prisoners' division at Majdanek from February 1943–May 1944.

3. Boder noted: "From experience with the Russian Kazaks [*sic*] it appears that in riding at a slow pace horses step aside from people whether they are standing or lying on the ground. It took special and diligent training to make them trample or push people in a crowd."

supplied me well. He always got more to eat than an ordinary worker. He was a political prisoner, one of the first people who came to Auschwitz.

On the 18th of January [1945] we were evacuated from Auschwitz because the Russians had taken Warsaw, and they were expected to come to that region any day. The journey took fourteen days. We marched on foot in the severest frost, because that is a mountainous region. We marched in the snow without food, without warm coffee or water. And people ate snow from thirst, and people ate grass that was lying on the road. Also, people dried horse manure in their pockets and smoked it [rolled] in paper. Because we *needed* cigarettes. Another thing about these cigarettes—they took away my hunger.

How many people were you?

Fourteen thousand people. I really don't know how people endured it. I don't know whether it was just the will to live, whether also the will to take revenge, to remain alive and be united with families and relatives, and marching together with friends with whom one had left one's home town kept a man alive. Very many died on the way, but the majority did endure it.

On the fourteenth day we arrived in Gleiwitz. From Gleiwitz we were sent away by train five days [via] Dachau, Buchenwald, and from Buchenwald we were driven away to Dora, a transit camp and also near the camp that built VI and V2 [rockets]. Skilled people were left [there], and the rest of the people were sent to coal mines and other such camps. I had been assigned to Nordhausen. Every day at dawn we drove away by train, an hour and a half, to Dora. And one time, when we were returning at night, there was an air-raid alarm so that we had to stay in the train a whole night in the middle of the way. And in the morning again the train turned around to work again, so that one didn't sleep, didn't eat, and again worked. The suffering in this camp was terrible.

In this short time there was a bombing of the camp. During the bombing I decided that I must escape. I had prepared myself beforehand. [I had been given] old, torn civilian clothing because toward the end in Germany one didn't wear the striped uniforms, but civilian clothing, and in the back a little window was cut out in which red stripes had been sewn to inscribe "KL"—that means "Concentration Camp." This was the badge of a prisoner. So on the day of the bombing raid I escaped in these clothes. Later on, at night when I had to find a place to sleep, I went into a railroad car. I had not noticed what kind of wagon it was. And so when I got up in the morning, I saw that I was lying in a Red Cross wagon, and old bloody clothes were lying in it. SS clothes, and also bandages. And I put these clothes on, and I took the bandages and tied [them] around my head so that my head was wider than my shoulders. Because only my eyes could be seen, the nose, the mouth, and the left ear. The rest was covered. I traveled around like this three months.

[Still disguised as a wounded and discharged SS man, P. was assigned to supervise a farm in the Sudetenland of occupied northern Czechoslovakia.]

I was sent for work to Neuland, a village two kilometers from Aussig. In that village was a large estate with seventeen people, and I was sent out there as an overseer. These seventeen people were Ukrainians and Poles, not prisoners but civilian workers who had reported in Poland as volunteers for labor in Germany. I worked there for a month. I harassed the Poles terribly just out of hate which I still had for them from Warsaw. Because they are big anti-Semites, and [so are] the Ukrainians. So they suffered a lot at work. I didn't allow them to have a free hour there. I shortened the dinner [hour] to half and hour. And the German peasant woman was on my side because I was a military man. And I also made the acquaintance there of a German girl. I went around with her, had fun, carried on a kind of love affair with her.

On the 3rd of May they said that Hitler had died. People hung out black flags. People cried. They said that should the Jews return, they [the Germans] would all be killed [or] the Russians would send them away to Siberia. And so they were terribly afraid. I wasn't paying any attention. On the 8th of May the Russians entered Aussig.

What did you wear, an SS uniform?
Still a uniform, because I was afraid to take if off so that the Poles shouldn't give me away. And so I waited. When the Russians would enter I would report who I was. So these seventeen people went down into town, and they brought Russian soldiers to me. And among them was a lieutenant leading the detail. He was a Jew from Baranowicz, from Poland, who in 1939 had escaped to Russia and had volunteered for the [Red] Army. To him was given the honor of shooting the SS man. He came in, told me to go out in the yard, and wanted to shoot me. [He spoke] to me in Yiddish so I should understand [it as] German. So I said, "Listen, brother, I am a Jew the same as you." He was very surprised, and I showed him the [tattooed] number. I showed him my tongue. He had with him a little Siddur [prayer book] in town. He specially sent down a Russian soldier to fetch [it], and I prayed. And I spoke Hebrew words to him, and I spoke to him in Yiddish, and I also showed him on the body [his circumcision] that I am a Jew. In the end he saw that I am a Jew. I was there two weeks. I lived well. I became an interpreter, from German into Russian.

After he believed you, didn't he ask about the SS uniform?
I told him everything. I told him all the experiences which I had lived through.
I understood and spoke German well, and so I took a bit of revenge on the Germans, and later on I left.

What does "revenge" mean?

For instance, I struck down a few people. Yes, killed dead. I, too, tortured a few people. And I also did the same things with the German children as the SS men did in Majdanek with the Jewish children. For instance, they took small children by the little legs and beat the head against the wall until the head cracked.

Did you do the same thing?

I did the same to the German children, because the hate in me was so great. Maybe I would have in time forgotten all of this, if not [for the fact] that the Germans themselves had reminded me that when the Russians would enter, they would be killed and sent to Siberia and the same things would be done to them as [they did] to the Jews. And the Germans still worried at the same time why Hitler didn't exterminate all the Jews so there shouldn't be anybody left to take revenge on them.

In two weeks I received two horses and a little carriage from that officer and left for home, for Poland. And when I arrived on the Czech border, in Ostrava, the Czech partisans took the horses away and took me to Krakow by car. In Krakow I went to the Polish Committee and received help and aid, but first of all I wanted to return to Auschwitz. I [did so and] kept an eye on the people who were there, on the SS men. I knew very many [of them] because during the time when I cleaned up in the music block they always dropped in to listen. So I knew them all well, and they knew me.

Well, did you talk with them?

I talked, and I also harassed them a little. The Russians in the camp didn't permit that they be killed or beaten, but at work one was able to harass them. The Russians dismantled the Buna factory; the railroad tracks had to be carried away. And whatever three or four people once carried, now two had to carry, so that the work was very hard. Returning after a day's work, there were very few of them who could make the two or three kilometers home.

What did they say? Did they try to talk to you?

What could they say to me? They knew that I hated them, because once they had harassed me, too. So they didn't talk to me at all. They were speechless.

Didn't they try to explain to you that they had to obey orders?

No, because they knew that they did it on their own. Nobody told them to do it.

And after three weeks I returned home to Warsaw. In Warsaw I met perhaps twenty or so friends from the camp who had escaped on the road in the middle of the journey when we walked for fourteen days. And also among them were maybe ten people [who] worked on the Warsaw [Jewish] Council. They knew me very well. They did help me. They gave me money, a room in which to stay, enough to eat, and some clothes, too. I was there in Warsaw for a week. I looked around. I saw the place where my mother was burned. I reminded myself of the old times so that it was driving me out of Poland. I decided to take to the road, to leave.

[P. then traveled to Austria by way of Hungary and Roumania.]

I was in Austria two months. In Judenburg.[4] And there I even spent [time] in prison.

Why?

Because I am a very nervous person, almost crazy-nervous. I had received dry provisions from a distribution center. There was a little stove in the room, and I wanted to cook something. I went down to the carpentry shop, and I gathered wood shavings that were discarded and wanted to make a fire. In the meantime a camp policeman, a Ukrainian, came in and said it was not permitted to build a fire. I said that I would soon put it out. He did not listen to me, but brought up an Englishman [who] turned out to be a very great anti-Semite, and he began to beat me. And so I was taken to the major, and the major ordered me arrested. I was taken down to a cellar. But I did not submit. I began to fight with them. I beat the Englishman up really good. I nearly beat him bloody. The major saw this. He ordered two more Austrian policemen with guns, and chains were brought. I was chained and led away to prison.

I sat there thirteen days and then I had a trial, a military trial. And here I still have the trial document, written in English, [about] why I was imprisoned and what happened. The judge was an English general. And also a newspaper reporter was there. I don't know his name. And the general freed me. Because I told him that I was nervous. I told him the whole story at the trial. I showed him the tongue. I showed him the number. I presented various facts; how can I be normal in such a moment when I have only been liberated for five months? And so he freed me.

During the trial six people testified against me, that I broke a bed, that I beat up an Englishman, and such things. The general freed me, and he also asked that I should come to his house privately; he would give a report of everything I went through. He took everything down, and he also photographed me. He attached the photograph to the papers. He made a little newspaper article of everything that I had told him.

4. A city in the English occupation zone of southeastern Austria, the site of a DP camp.

I still worked in an English kitchen there. The major later on found me a job in the kitchen.

The same major?
The same major. We became the best of friends. Afterward he helped me. And he also fixed me up with a wedding. I got married in Judenburg to a girl from Poland, from Upper Silesia.

Where did you meet her?
In Budapest. I knew this girl five months before the wedding. We came to the camp in Austria together.

Did you get married in the camp?
Yes. The major himself arranged the wedding. A very nice wedding! The way things were in the camp there was nothing to eat. On my wedding there *was* enough to eat. I got cigarettes for the wedding. I got clothing from the UNRRA. So that the wedding was a really nice wedding given conditions after the war. And for a boy like me without funds, without anything, this wedding was a *nice* wedding.

Where are the parents of the girl?
The parents were killed in Auschwitz. And she is now up in the hospital. We have a little baby, five days old. A girl. And I have named her after my mother. Sara.

How did you come over to Italy? When did you attach yourself to a kibbutz?
I was in a kibbutz all the time while I was in Austria—twelve months. Kibbutz Dror Habonim.

The camp there [Judenburg] was liquidated for certain reasons. They made investigations. Englishmen came with Austrian police. Raids were carried out. People were stealing there. The Austrian police came to search if we didn't have many English cigarettes or such things, whether people didn't do business. In the meantime they took away felt boots, gloves, things we had received from the UNRRA, for themselves. They said it was forbidden to own them.

[P. seemed reluctant to talk about his move to Italy, which was probably done illegally, and the interview quickly turned to the hardships of life at Tradate DP camp.]

I have family in Argentina. They sent me something like ten pounds through a bank, but here it is very hard even with the ten pounds. We don't receive enough aid for the baby, and I came without clothes. I arrived with just a handbag, a piece of soap, a toothbrush, toothpaste, things that one needs for the road. So I had nothing to wear. When I received the ten pounds, I had to buy a suit and a shirt. I had to buy some clothes for my wife.

Do you have a room for yourself?

Now I have a room for myself. Before we were in a camp in Cremona with seventy people, men and women together in one room because there was no possibility of living in any other way. It was a kibbutz that lived *collectively*. None of us had any funds.

And how are conditions here? How long have you been here?

Three months. People eat in two, three [shifts], so that sometimes, toward the end, there is a shortage of food. Because Tradate is a collective. Everybody comes over to the table and finds his food on the table. And when he finishes eating, he leaves and makes room for someone else. And occasionally one who has eaten and is still hungry goes to eat again. Nothing can be done about that, because they are hungry. For a man who has returned from the woods, a partisan, or a man who has returned from a concentration camp starved, should he now have to live on this? It is very little.

So what does one do?

Whatever one can to get something. If he has some things that he had brought from Germany, he sells them and eats. He goes to Milan. There are people who need such things for themselves, so they buy them.

When the baby arrived, did you get anything extra for . . .

For the baby I received a package given by the Joint. And to this package I have to buy another ten such. Because a child uses things up. When we lived in [the camp at Cremona] we had to buy additional food. So the major portion that was spent was spent for food. Not for clothes, but for food. Here maybe it is [more] stable. A person gets adjusted.

11   Rachel G.

Rachel G. was a committed woman of the political left, and that made a world of difference in determining her fate. She avoided stipulating her politics in the interview, but internal evidence suggests that she was at least close to the Polish Communist party, in which Jews were disproportionately represented. This gave her intimate contacts among non-Jewish Poles in Warsaw, friends who saved her life by spiriting her out of the ghetto on the eve of the 1943 revolt, after which she "passed" as a non-Jew. Previous to that she had avoided deportation by making herself useful to the Warsaw ghetto administration and, indirectly, the Germans. Since 1921 she had been secretary of the Polish ORT, the vocational training organization founded in Russia in 1880. Since the Germans needed skilled Jewish workers, the ORT was one of the few prewar Jewish institutions preserved under German rule. And yet, her position was no absolute shield from deportation as her description of a close call makes plain. Trapped by chance in a public square during a raid, Rachel G. exploited confusion and a ruse thrown out by a friend to melt into the crowd of onlookers.

Beyond providing valuable information about the ORT's work in the ghetto, Rachel G. intelligently comments on several other aspects of ghetto life: the work she was forced to do for the German Trusteeship Office, which collected and organized the movable property of Jews who had been deported or killed; Nazi manipulation of the Jews' psychological vulnerability; and the courthouse forming part of the ghetto wall in which Jews and non-Jews might still make precarious contacts. She also makes it clear that without official corruption and the money to exploit it, her story would have ended quite differently.

Rachel G. exposed her personal grief reluctantly and only after gentle prodding. Apparently she lost most of her family, including her mother and her son; she never mentioned her husband. Unable to begin again in Warsaw after the war, she moved to Lodz and threw herself into rebuilding the ORT. Technically G. was not a displaced person. She was visiting Paris as a delegate to a world ORT convention when interviewed in August 1946, and she was clearly determined to return to Poland and reestablish Jewish life there. We begin with her recollections of the sealing off of the Warsaw ghetto in November 1940.

ORT was located outside the ghetto. Jaszunski[1] was given a permit so that those belonging to the ORT could remain outside the ghetto. The Gestapo ordered [ORT] to present a list of all students and teaching [and] administrative personnel, and they would issue permits. But already on Saturday morning, the 15th, I was not permitted to enter the building, and nothing came of it. Afterward they gave us permission [for ORT to move] all its belongings into the ghetto, and the courses continued. I only want to say that ORT was the only institution which was given permission to proceed with its school and courses. ORT developed a very great activity and it had a very great sphere of action, because working people were maintaining [tolerable] living conditions. Those who worked in the ORT had work certificates and had the right to live. Temporarily.

Of course, afterward everything went to naught. The ghetto remained within these confines until the 22nd of June 1942. During that time terrible things happened. For instance, there was a certain Kott.[2] The Gestapo found out that he was in Warsaw, and they came to arrest him. So he drew a revolver, killed two Gestapo men, and ran away. For this they took 305 intellectuals—physicians, lawyers, engineers; they were shot at the citadel on the shore of the Vistula, and they were all thrown into the water. There was another instance in the ghetto when a hoodlum, some thief, was running. A policeman ran after him, and he shot the policeman. And for that all the men were taken from the building, fifty-eight men, and they were shot.

Where? Right there in the ghetto?

In Pawiak, a famous prison in the ghetto on Pawia Street. Every day at two o'clock there was a change of the guard. The Germans used to arrive in vehicles, [and] they would beat up every Jew who happened to pass by. And then the Jews started watching out. Between 1:00 and half past 2:00 a Jew could not be seen on Pawia Street and in that general direction.

Of course, to enter and to take people out of their homes, that was an everyday occurrence. This was of no consequence. The situation of the Jews was terrible. They were driven together from the whole Warsaw district into this small ghetto. On the 22nd of July 1942 we learned that there would be a deportation from Warsaw. A half a million [Jews] were congregated in this small area; they lived

1. Joseph Jaszunski, director of the ORT in Poland and Warsaw Jewish Council member.

2. Andrzej Kott, one of the founders of a Polish nationalist resistance movement. Although he was Jewish, he had no contacts with Jews or Judaism. His escape from arrest in January 1940 prompted the Germans to impose collective punishment by executing more than 200 Jewish hostages.

in overcrowded rooms, packed in with kit and caboodle. There was such a strong stench coming out from there that one could not pass by on the sidewalk.

On what sidewalk?
Where the refugees lived. The unfortunate deportees from the little towns, from the whole Warsaw district. The deportation started with the newcomers. They were the first. Unemployed. The Germans said that they brought in disease. There was a terrible typhus epidemic; as many as 300 people died a day.

Where were they buried?
In mass graves in the Jewish cemetery in the ghetto. They excavated enormous ditches, and they would throw them in quite naked.

Did they let them say Kadesh [the Prayer for the Dead]?
Yes, they did not begrudge it. [Later] the cemetery was also excluded from the ghetto. Those who worked for the Jewish Council had a special uniform and special permits to take the dead out to the Aryan side.

And they started the deportation with these unfortunates. And then came the psychological moment. Everybody thought that they would send a part away and [let] the rest remain. Sure, they [the deportees] were human beings and wanted to live, too, but nobody could be concerned about that. But then the chairman of the Jewish Council came to the conviction that they were being led away for extermination, and he poisoned himself. He could not stand it anymore.

Did he have to select the people for the deportation?
No, no. The people were selected by the [Jewish] police. But still he was the chairman of the Jewish Council. And on that account he carried the responsibility for them.

Afterward they went further and further. One section would be surrounded and cleaned out. Then a second section. They started taking people who had certificates attesting that they were working. "Oh bunk!" [they would say], tear it up, and send him away. People started to wonder where they were being sent.

Were they [the perpetrators] all Germans?
No, they used large numbers of Ukrainians and Latvians. In August 1942 they again proceeded to reduce the size of the ghetto, pushing it together. It was made smaller.

What was done with the other houses?

They were occupied by Aryan people; Poles occupied all the dwellings. And by September it appeared that things had quieted down a bit. The leader, the director of the Extermination Command of the Warsaw region was called Brandt.[3]

Was it called that openly?

Of course. So Brandt came to the Jewish Council and said, "All is quiet. From now on the Jews may live in peace. There were too many Jews, an element that did not work. We are unable to provide for so many. But those who have remained may work unconcerned, and there will be no more 'actions.' You should take special care of the children." We were supposed to arrange a children's home, and the Jews were so naive that they believed him. A children's home was fixed up. All the abandoned little children were assembled, people readily gave money for it, and it was believed that we would survive those terrible times.

But it lasted a very short time, and they started making "actions" again. First [people were taken] from the streets, and then right in the workshops. They would take away a number of people and then promise [that] they wouldn't molest again. Once they went to the [offices of] the Jewish Council itself. They ordered everybody to come out in the yard, and Brandt himself stood there; everyone had to pass by, and whoever he pleased he sent away—550 people that day.

Did the Jewish Council have so many people?

Of course. The Jewish Council felt an obligation to occupy as many people as possible. Because if you had a card from the council, that meant that you worked, and that meant that you would remain alive.

There were also people who were there by accident, those who came there to transact all kinds of business. I, too, happened to be there. But I got away. There were three squares. He, Brandt, stood in front; facing him were the vice-chairman . . . Czerniakow was no longer alive at that time. The chairman was the engineer [Marek] Lichtenbaum; the vice chairman [was Dr. Wielikowski?].[4] When I came over, I told him [Wielikowski?] that I was working for the community, occupied in the organization. He did not even want to listen. He grabbed me by the hand

---

3. SS Second Lieutenant Karl Brandt, overseer of Jewish affairs in the Warsaw ghetto. G.'s recollection of him heading an "Extermination Command," if correct, had to be a term used by the Jews; it was not Brandt's official title.

4. G. actually said "Dr. Gelikowski," but no one by that name was a member of the Jewish Council. She almost certainly refers to Dr. Gustav Wielikowski, a prominent Warsaw attorney and head of social services in the ghetto. He was widely disliked for his officious behavior.

and said, "You are going!" And Brandt then simply ordered me to go along. I was already far in the square, and I heard somebody calling, and there stood a woman, a Jewish writer: "G., someone is calling you." And I looked around, and I asked them, "Me?" So [Wielikowski?] yelled to me, "Yes, you! Go!" And we were then set free. Then they took 550 people away, and again Brandt said they would take no more. But in spite of what he promised, they always made new arrests.

Tell me, how did you live in the ghetto? Where did one live? In homes? What kind of rooms did you have?

When they reduced the size of the ghetto, the crowding became terrible. And toward the end there were fifteen people to a room. Men and women, all together. But there were people who lived very well because people could get out to [work stations] on the Aryan side. [The] Germans used to take them out for trustee details. In all the buildings which the Jews had abandoned, the task of these Jews was to search for all the things that remained. You know German efficiency. Everything to sort out, everything to classify. And above all they were interested in silverware [and] furniture. At 13 Leszno [Street] there was an enormous building, a storehouse for furniture. They classified it all. On the first floor were buffets, on the second were beds, on the third were mattresses, on the fourth were wardrobes, and so on. So often Jews who used to go over to the other side to work in these storehouses were earning very, very well. Because they used to find [steal] things. Many Jews did not have anything to live on, so they used to sell things on the Aryan side. And excellent profits were made on that. At night they would return to the ghetto [with] food. And so this category lived very well.

But how were their living quarters?

They too had to live among the rest in very crowded conditions. And so the ghetto became more and more constricted. But one could get everything if one just had the money.

And the money was not taken away?

If an inspection was made, and money was found, it was taken away. So people would hide it; there were ways. With money everything was possible. But that was no way to live. For instance, there were [she names two men, evidently self-declared ethnic Germans from Poland], and we knew that when they came into the ghetto, a lot [of people] would die. Every Jew they would encounter they would shoot. Without any reason. I myself saw him [she did not specify which one] shooting a Jew. Just came over and shot him. A panic would start, and the word would be passed, "The shooters have come." So they would come to a dwelling. "Why are you home? Why are you not at work?" "I am sick!" "So don't be sick," and there and then he was put down and shot.

What kind of business did they have there? Did they have anything to do with work, were they . . .

Absolutely nothing. They were Germans, and that was sufficient. The Jews were outside the law. The Jews could complain to no one.

I must tell you that while the Jews were led to the transfer terminal, nobody was chased; they marched along quite at ease. If there were older people or sick, they supplied a rickshaw and carted [them] away.

The Germans [then] started something different. They said that Warsaw must be made free of Jews. And so those Jews who worked in workshops and industries were to be transferred with the workshops to smaller towns. And so a transfer was made to Poniatowa, and to some other little town, the name slips me for a moment. The machinery was loaded with them. They were ordered to sing. I can still hear this singing in my ears. It gave me shudders.

What were they singing?

Anything; they were to make merry. Jews were standing on the balconies, and they knew that these people were being led to death. They worked there for a short time, and afterward one fine day they were led out. . . . [G. then gave a description of the shooting of these workers as they had been described to her by another Holocaust survivor.]

Now I have to turn back. In September 1942 it was announced that at dawn all people who worked had to appear at their workplaces. They should take food for two days; there would be a selection.

Why a selection?

Because there were too many Jews. Only the ones needed were to remain, and a part must get out. It was already known what "getting out" meant. And they also made a selection of those [who worked for] the Jewish Council. I also belonged to the Jewish Council because there was no longer something called ORT then, but we had to call ourselves the "Division of Jewish Professional Education." ORT was already banned. We were detained for two days in the building of the Jewish Council. We were lying on the floor. Then everybody was ordered out into the yard. The Jewish Council was ordered to make a list of all those people. They issued numbers, and all were led out, about 5,000 [of us], and they led us in formation; where we did not know. But not all were led out. [Those on] the right side were sent away the next day to Treblinka.

They led us out under guard, so that each one should go into his own home. For two days soldiers stood around with rifles. Nobody was permitted in or out. People gradually recuperated [from the experience]. People gradually appeared on the streets, and life went on. We did not know why it happened; one thing was clear, that in time there would be an end to the Jews. Every few days there were "actions," until the tragic day came, the 19th of April, the eve of Passover. A day before a delegation of rabbis visited the Gestapo and inquired whether they could have prayer meetings on Passover. The reply was, "Yes, if you wish, only don't pray too loud, do not yell. But you may hold prayer meeting as much as you want." The Jewish Council gave matzoth to everybody. People already knew [that] if something was distributed in the ghetto, a bit more food, that meant that there would be an "action." They gave a bit more food before every "action." There was a time during the deportations when it was laid out on tables. [The Germans said that] because there were so many people in Warsaw, those who presented themselves voluntarily would get 2 kilograms [4.4 pounds] of bread with a kilogram of honey. And therefore thousands of people presented themselves voluntarily. In part it was the influence of those who wanted to talk themselves into [believing] that they were going away to work. There were, for instance, the Warsaw coachmen who were healthy and strong.

Were there hackneys in the ghetto? With horses?

Yes. They took their horse and carriage, led them away with wife and children. And people told them, "You brutes! What are you doing?" [And they answered], "We are going to work, we will tough it out; they won't kill you as long as you work." Such was the psychology. [The Germans] said that the people were going to Smolensk. So some Jews went to the transfer terminal and jotted down the numbers of the railroad cars, and these same cars returned within six hours. Their destination was very near, right? They had been taken away and annihilated, but nobody believed it.

[Boder wanted to know if Rachel G. was still in Warsaw during the ghetto uprising. She then explained how she managed to escape a few days before the fighting began.]

I worked with the ORT, and it gave us whatever help it could. Always, when they [the Jews] were herded together from all the little towns, ORT helped all the artisans. They were driven out of their homes in ten or fifteen minutes, and they could take nothing with them. So it was necessary to give a tailor not only a [sewing] machine but a flatiron, a table and a stool, and some thread and accessories just for a start. And all were provided. And I must tell you they earned a living—tailors, cobblers, glazers, carpenters. But since the housing situation was catastrophic, they had nowhere to install their shops, so the ORT assembled crates, and these came to be itinerant "shops" for carpenters and cobblers. Each had his relatives from his hometown. So he would come into a home and fix shoes there. And highly moving scenes occurred. Artisans would come and say: "Today I don't go begging for soup. Here, see, I have earned, and my wife cooks our own dinner. I am through with begging." These were joyful moments. And the other joyful moments were the courses where young people were taught; and afterward they established themselves and earned. And this was going on until the last moment. And I was with it and kept up with my work.

But then something happened. I had a woman friend, a teacher, who made a living with great hardship. [The friend's apartment was requisitioned for use by Jewish workers at a nearby factory, and she was obliged to move in with her brother.]

Now imagine that in that dwelling she found somewhere inside a wall a hiding place [containing] a colossal amount of money, gold, and diamonds. This apparently was hidden by a Jew who had lived there, and when he was taken away it remained. So, when it came to so much money, they started thinking about getting over to the Aryan side to save themselves. Everyone who had money went across, and so . . .

With Aryan papers?

If people went across, they procured papers, and for that one had to have colossal sums. She [G.'s friend] had a woman friend, also a teacher, a Christian [who] had communicated with her often. Zelazna Street was still in the ghetto. On Leszno Street were all the courts [of justice], a very large building. On one side it faced [onto the ghetto], and on the other side it faced Ogrodowa Street. The Christians used to enter from the Ogrodowa Street side, and Jews would enter from Leszno, and they would meet there inside. In this manner my women friends also would come to see each other.

Irene [the Christian friend] obtained false papers for herself because she was an artisan, and on these she rented an apartment for them on the Aryan side.[5] In case something happened she would just not be there [slip back to her own apartment]. A double wall was installed in this apartment, and a tiny little door was made in the wall. And in front of it was a cupboard to cover it up. We used to sit in the room. As soon as there was a knock at the door we all got in there [behind the double wall], the cupboard was shoved back, and that was all. They had registered [as residents of] the apartment: Irene on false papers; a sister-in-law of my woman friend with a child; and one more woman, a Christian, a servant. Eight of us lived there unregistered.

After they moved in there in the second half of February 1943, this friend started to plead with me persistently that I go with them. And I hesitated to abandon the ORT. And the 15th of April, I was still sitting in the shops at the ORT, working normally. Somebody had to sit as usual by the window and watch

5. Irene needed false papers to rent a separate apartment for her friends. As a working woman she would draw official attention if she rented a second apartment in her own name.

whether somebody was coming. So I was sitting at the window, and in order that the work proceed calmly in the shops, I used to read to them the letter of Manachem Mendel to Sheine Sheindel by Sholem Aleichem so they could forget themselves [and their] woes. And there came the brother of my woman friend and told me, "Listen, G., Jeannie made me come. I plead with you to leave." So I answered, "You know that the Jewish Council will distribute Passover packages to all working people. But there are two kinds of packages, larger and smaller ones. I am afraid that if I leave not all our [apprentices] will get equal packages. I shall wait until Monday; everybody will get their packages, and then I shall get out."

So he went away and came back. Jeannie had sent another note; I should come without fail. So I said to him, "You know what, I am a bit religious. I shall go to the Jewish Council. If they promise me that all our coworkers will get equally large packages. . . ." [Using an excuse, she secured the council's assurances.] On Friday morning the 16th of April I left. I came to Jeannie, and Sunday night the ghetto was encircled for the last time. If the ghetto had been surrounded on the 19th, I would have been there, because by Monday I would have gone back. I was missing it [the ghetto].

I must tell you however about the perfidy of the Germans. They knew that there were some Jews on the Aryan side. For about two months before the destruction of the ghetto they posted an announcement that permits had arrived for a number of Jews to leave for abroad. And since these Jews were not there anymore, others might leave instead. With a good passport, of course. There was no shortage of money. There were rich Jews. And they paid several hundred thousand zlotys per person. They went to Pawiak prison. They were there for a certain length of time; they were permitted to receive food that was brought to them. And then they were led away to a beautiful region in Poland and wonderful letters arrived from there [saying] that the people there were expecting to leave the country, that they were well clothed, that they were given courses in various languages and were being told that they would soon depart for America. The end was that they were all taken to Auschwitz and gassed.

In May the destruction of the ghetto was completed—absolutely. And again they made an announcement that the Jews who were living on the Aryan side might register and come out and leave, and [that] those who had money were certainly permitted to leave. And then my woman friend fell victim to her money; she paid and departed. I just remained in that apartment.

And how about food and other things?

Well, there was the Christian woman, the servant. She would go out shopping. At that time I did not have any Aryan papers. I remained in hiding, along with eight [other] people.

That Christian woman—could you trust her?

Yes, that was a Christian one could trust. But here is the misfortune that happened in that dwelling. The sister-in-law of my woman friend was registered on Aryan papers, and she had a husband [who] did not speak very good Polish. She was a simple Jewish woman, and to make it brief, on the 19th of August 1943 at half past eleven at night the door opened, and the Germans came in and found the hideout open. And I [was there] among them. "All of you come with us." There was not far to go, because the police station was right near us. We used to have a lookout every night—not all of us slept, one would sit up—and we used to hear distinctly how people were shot there, five doors away from us. So they lined us all up face to the wall, hands up, searched us . . .

Well, your woman friend was already away.

No, no. All of us were there: my woman friend, her old mother, her brother with his wife and a child, two friends of the brother, and a few more people.

In how many rooms?

Three. But we were all in the [hidden] room. We had an agreement that the door should not be opened until there was a signal for us to hide, but stupidly the door was opened. They entered and found our hideout, and that was that. They started searching, and they took away a very large quantity of money and a heap of diamonds, and they left. They even told us, "You may go on living here." And we had to stay there because we had nowhere to go.

Who were they, Germans, Ukrainians?

Two Germans. [They took] money, watches, diamonds, brooches, a lot of things. Of course, when the Germans would search a home, they would take rings off fingers, that was commonplace. But they left. This was on a Thursday, the 19th of August 1943. And on the 21st, at half past six, they were there again. "It has become known that there are Jews here. You have seen that I wanted to leave you here, but I am unable to do so; we have to go, there's nothing we can do about it." We started pleading with him again, and they let us off again. Again money was given, not so much this time, and they let us go. But they told us, "You must leave immediately."

And then, like a good angel, Irene appeared again. I must say, this was lucky! We had a kind of signal. There were curtains on the window tied up with a ribbon. When Irene wanted to come up, she would look to see if the *green* ribbon was there. While the Germans were there, I quietly took off the ribbon and [they] noticed nothing. And as soon as she saw that the ribbon was missing, she came up to us [later], and we told her what had happened. She said, "Don't get desperate. I will do something immediately." She went to a woman friend of hers who had a store, and since it was Saturday, she asked her, "I beg you, close up the store a bit earlier, and lock up my Jews." And so it was done.

And she was a Christian?
Of course. So she locked us up in this store and left for home. All was well. We stayed there until Monday morning, lying on the floor. And by Monday, a new apartment was found. The underground committee helped in this.

A Jewish [committee]?
Poles and Jews together. All parties had united and I was given some relief because we already had nothing to live on.

We had a small, bare little room not more than a quarter [the size] of this one.[6] Humid! If we put our shoes under our beds for the night, they were green with mold by morning. The Christian woman was the one who rented the room. The apartment consisted of three rooms with a kitchen. The owners of the apartment lived in two rooms, and that Christian woman lived in one room. We had a hideout. It was a ground floor apartment. There was a small cupboard in the wall like a little box [that] could be completely pulled out. A ditch had been excavated, and in case somebody knocked at the door, the little box was pulled out, we crawled out, the little box was put back in place, and we were no longer there.

How many people were able to get into that ditch?
Five.

And who had dug out that ditch?
The landlord of the apartment. He constructed it specially [for us]. But then my woman friend and her sister-in-law said that they could not live under such conditions. They would rather pay off [gamble on the German "ransom" offer]; they would go to work and that's all. And they paid one hundred and twenty thousand zlotys all together. That was a large amount, and one needed great pull to arrange it. Unfortunately I am unable to find this person [now]; I should like to square our accounts. She was the go-between.

A Christian person?
Unfortunately, I think she was a Jewish woman. They departed, and [G. and two other Jews] remained in the room. We had an agreement with the underground organization. People used to come to us who had nowhere to sleep. In

6. Boder noted that the interview room was about twelve feet by twelve feet.

general a lot of people would come. And how we managed to stay alive is a question. Afterward we found out that the owner of the building had known about that ditch, and he said nothing during all that time. And some [people] remained living there until the 1st of August 1944, up to the Bor insurrection.[7]

[Following the suppression of the insurrection, the Germans destroyed Warsaw and forced the Poles to flee. G., still using false papers, was sent to live with peasants in a village near Krakow.]

[The peasants] were very eager that I not leave; I was a good servant.

Did they pay you anything?
No. Nothing.

Did they give you food to eat?
Very little. Very bad food. When I was liberated, I weighed 47 kilos [103 pounds]. Before the war 72 kilos [158 pounds]. And I worked very hard. And the circumstances were so difficult that one needed a permit even to leave the village. [The Poles] would process it, and the Russian commandant had to approve it. It was necessary to get in line at five o'clock in the morning. And to get in line one had to stay overnight in the village. And then there was an order that no stranger could stay there overnight under penalty of death. And so I went there four times, fifteen kilometers there and back. I got sick and could not get a permit. My mistress took pity on me, and her sister [in the village] took me in for the night. I got my permit and departed for Warsaw.

Did you find anybody from the ORT?
No, absolutely nobody. I found myself with no place to live in Warsaw. I remained all alone. But I encountered Jaszunski's son, and he told me, "I live in Lodz. There are already a few Jews in Lodz. Working people are needed; you will soon find work. So come there." So I departed for Lodz. He helped me out a bit, because I was without money, [and] he was already working. He was the editor of a labor newspaper. And so I arrived in Lodz at eight o'clock in the morning, and at eleven o'clock I was already among Jews. And I started working; things went well. I started taking an interest in ORT. Now we already have 5,000 [pupils] in seven cities, and I have returned, so to speak, to my original life work.

7. The disastrous Warsaw uprising of the Polish underground in August 1944 led by Major General Tadeusz Komorowski, alias "General Bor."

[Boder ended the interview by inquiring about the status of the Jews in Poland in view of the recent Kielce pogrom.]

Always after a war it is understood that various things may happen. They hanged the people who were guilty.

And you think that things will become normal?
I think it will. Poland, where there were three and a half million Jews, will probably have Jews again.

12 Lena K.

Sometimes the best way to "pass" was to find refuge in some rural nook and hide behind a mask for the duration of the war. In 1942 Lena K. found that living outside the ghetto in Warsaw with false papers left her open to blackmail and, finally, arrest. How she got to Warsaw is unclear. We know only that the young (born in 1912) woman from Wieliczka, near Krakow, studied at the Jagiellonian University at Krakow and taught school before the war. She and her husband evidently sought to melt into the urban masses of Warsaw during the early phases of the German occupation. They lived apart then, and relations between them must already have been strained. After the war they divorced.

Following an escape from German captors in 1942, Lena found a position as nanny on an aristocratic estate at Olchowek in eastern Poland, not far from Treblinka. Carefully playing the role of a non-Jew, she was able to record the attitudes of her employers; unlike some Polish aristocrats, these were no friends of the Jews. Following liberation by the Russians in 1944, she stayed on and founded a school on the estate, taking particular pleasure in revealing her Jewishness to her former mistress, who was now dependent upon her.

Once Warsaw fell, Lena sought in vain for her sister and then buried her grief in study for an advanced degree in educational psychology. Her life was eased in those months by the high position occupied by her brother in the new Polish government. When she agreed to help rehabilitate child survivors of the Holocaust who were then roaming about in Poland, she expected it to be a summer project. In fact it became the defining moment in her life. The hostility she encountered when she established a Jewish children's home at a hill resort south of Krakow compelled her to lead her charges out toward Zion. This section of the interview is particularly interesting on the subject of Catholic attitudes toward Jewish orphans who had been sheltered in church institutions during the Holocaust. For the priests and the sisters they were souls won for Jesus. For Lena K. they belonged to their people in Palestine. Attempts by church officials to extract payment from Jews for sheltering the orphans during the war must be viewed compassionately in light of the desperate poverty of these institutions at the end of the fighting.

By the time of her interview in Bellevue, a suburb of Paris, in September 1946, Lena K. had brought sixty youngsters between the ages of three and fifteen with her to France where they awaited certificates for emigration to Palestine. In Bellevue she directed a home for displaced Jewish orphans funded by French and American Jewish charities. Two years later K. and her charges would sail for Israel. We join her interview in 1942 at the time of her discovery and arrest by the Germans.

It was at night. I was walking in the middle. Two fat Gestapo men were walking in front and two behind, all with bayonets ready. I was thinking, "What shall I do? What shall I do?" If I had a revolver I would shoot all of them. Let them shoot me then. It was all the same to me. Then we came to the Allee Szucha [Gestapo headquarters]. The two policemen in front entered the gate. All of a sudden I turned around and began to run. The two ran after me, shooting every which way. I do not remember anything more. It was a miracle that they did not hit me. The bullets flew by me but did not touch me. And then in a moment I went around the corner and ran and ran. The Gestapo men did not take too much trouble with me. They were so fat that they did not want to run after me. But they were shooting. They believed that I had perhaps been killed. And then they left. And that is how I remained alive.

It was already quite clear to me that I could not remain in Warsaw anymore. I read advertisements in various papers, and I found someone looking for a governess for children in the country rather far from Warsaw. I said to myself, "I shall go to a small place where I will not be noticed. I will be alone there, just with children, until things develop further." I went to this address, and I reported to this woman. She liked me very much. The only thing was—she told me that she had very many candidates for this position, but she did not like these women. In two cases, she said, the women looked to her like Jewesses, so she did not take them. And me she took. It was unpleasant for me that I had to lie to her, but yet I wanted to go on living.

That is how I found a position there. I was a nurse to a small, seven-month-old baby. I slept with that child. I then became very fond of that child. I loved that child very much. And I was there with those people for one year.

Now tell me, living like that as a Polish woman in a Polish family, didn't you have to understand the religion?
It was very hard for me. The people kept on observing me all the time. I had to be so watchful of everything—of my Polish language so that expressions used by Jews should not appear. That I not talk with my hands [gesticulate]. And not only that, but at every turn I had to wear a "mask," all day and all night. And in addition to all that the people were not sure. I did not quite resemble a Polish woman, but neither did I resemble a Jewess. They always had a very bad opinion of Jews, that they do not work, that they do not want to work, that they are

dirty, and that they have a bad appearance, that they are not very intelligent, and so forth. Actually I was the best worker they had. That saved me.

As for religion, I did not want to go to church. During all that time I never once went to church. In a village if one does not go to church, it is always said that he certainly is an atheist. I said I was irreligious. And there are Polish women, too, who are irreligious. Some held it against me, but my mistress understood, and she did not force me. She said, "Well, yes, Miss Lena"—that was what I was called there—"she is a good worker. It would be better if she were more religious, but, well, there is nothing to be done about it."

But did they not talk now and then among themselves about Jews? Did they not ask your opinion about Jews?

Yes. Those people talked about Jews very often. And there were various opinions about Jews. It was actually very interesting from a psychological standpoint. The village in which I lived was not far from a famous death camp. I lived perhaps twenty kilometers from Treblinka. And we met Jews who were already completely insane. Such poor people. I suffered so much on account of that; I did not want to go on living. But with them [the Poles] it varied. They did have a little pity. They said, "Those poor Jews." But then someone else got up and said, "Well yes, but one cannot get rid of the Jews in any other way. They must be shot. Either they must be given complete freedom, or they must be shot." "And I," said the young squire, "am of the opinion that it is better that the entire people be exterminated. It will save us the trouble." His sister, my mistress, was actually a friend of Jews. She said she felt sorry for the Jews. She was always sympathetic toward the Jews, but in spite of all that she said, "The Jews are not worth our sympathy. They are an ungrateful element. Should we help them now, then after the war they will all turn against us." And so they had various opinions of the Jews. On the whole they were all great anti-Semites. Not once did I think what would happen if they discovered that I am Jewish.

I was with these people until the end of the war, until the Russians arrived. Then their whole estate was parceled out. I was still there. The count ran away, but his sister remained with four children. Everything was taken away from her. She was not even given a potato, nothing. I am by profession a teacher, so I founded a school in that village. I went to the commissar. None of them knew yet that I was Jewish. I asked him to help in founding a school there in the castle for the peasant children. And I asked that the woman and the four children should be permitted to live together with me in one room. And I supported these people on my pay as teacher six months. They did not have anything to live on. The Russians paid me, and also the children and the parents always brought something. The peasants liked me very much. And the children were progressing very well in school. There had been no school there for a few years. The children could neither read nor write. The older people neither. I worked very hard. And all over the village they liked me very much.

But they did not know that you are Jewish.

Until the end they did not know, because in spite of everything, these people were anti-Semites, and it would have been very, very difficult for me. I waited. I had to stay there until I could go to Warsaw, because my husband and my sister had remained [there], and I wanted to go back and search for [them]. But I have lost them. With my sister it was a terrible tragedy. I searched and searched for her until I found out that toward the end she had left Warsaw, run away. She was living in Lowicz[1] with a Polish family. And the husband suspected that she was Jewish, so he went to the Gestapo. This Pole then got 2 kilos of sugar for her head. That was the Gestapo's reward. They came and shot her seven days before the liberation. I found out the man's name. I went to the Polish police, the present one, and I made out an affidavit. I do not know how it ended because in the meantime I had to leave.

[K. then returned to Krakow and resumed her university studies.]

The work that I was doing in the field of creative ability was designated as a doctoral project. I would have completed the work, but they came to me from the Jewish Committee with an appeal to take care of the children who were then returning from various camps, whom people were bringing to the committee. Many Jewish children had remained alive and were roaming [around without] a roof over their heads. I [was asked to] organize a home for children, one of the first homes in Poland. I decided to organize just the [one] children's home, work through the vacation, June and July, and return to my research at the university in August. And I made such an agreement with the president of the Jewish Committee in Krakow, Dr. Kupferberg. And then as soon as I began the work with these children I could not tear myself away from them. My presence was indispensable in order to maintain the home, because we were struggling against tremendous difficulties.

The children were in a terrible state, terrible. They were so starved, so sickly, so covered with lice, so neglected morally, physically, and intellectually, that a truly tremendous job arose before us. Moreover, we had absolutely no financial means. We had no budget for all that. The Jewish Committee had barely any financial means at its disposal, and it was surrounded every day by crowds of people who were returning from camps. What could be done for these people? Barely a little

1. A city located between Warsaw and Lodz. Its Jews had been sent to the Warsaw ghetto in June 1941, and thereafter no Jew was permitted to reside there.

soup. And these people cursed us all, and we really did not have anything to give them. The Joint was not yet working in Poland. And the means which we did receive from the impoverished Polish government were minimal, completely out of proportion to the needs.

We decided to organize a home in Zakopane,[2] a resort for tubercular children. Zakopane is a place situated amid mountains, a very beautiful spot, but known from before the war for its anti-Semitism. There we rented a very beautiful villa, and we renovated it, because it had been ruined [by] the Germans. And I went there with the first group of children. The home had a capacity of a hundred children, and I always had the full number, even more. There were times when I had a hundred and seven, a hundred and ten. In addition, they sent me older youths with sick lungs, people who had survived camps who had to be saved. These I placed in Polish sanatoria because being seriously ill they could not live with the children. But frightful hunger raged in those sanatoria, and therefore we would also carry food to them every day. I brought them underwear, medicines, visited them, and I can say that I saved the lives of several people from among those youths.

Besides that, we had an enormous job with our children. It was very difficult for me to get personnel. There were absolutely no [suitable] people. I picked out a certain group of women who had returned from Auschwitz. These women had lost everybody. I told them that if they did not have their own children to take to their hearts, we should become true mothers to these children who did not have their parents; not work at it like at a trade, [but] truly consecrate ourselves to these children. Our home was not a boarding home. It was not even a children's home. It was one big family. We worked from morning till night. We were under terrible stress.

I was traveling constantly. I did not have the means to support these children. The committee was in constant financial predicaments. I called on various private people, begging them for money to maintain the children. I traveled to Warsaw to the Joint, [but] they were not allowed to give us money. And in spite of everything, the director, Guzik,[3] always helped me, even though "illegally," so as not to throw these children out in the street. Every week, every few days I was faced with an alternative of closing down the home.

Moreover, we were surrounded by such a wave of anti-Semitism that it is impossible to describe. The children could not go out on the street at all. They were hit on the head with stones. When I sent three boys to movies, other Polish boys sitting behind them were threatening all the time to stick a knife in their backs.

2. A town south of Krakow on the Czechoslovakian border.

3. Daniel David Guzik, a director of the JOINT in Poland until his death in an airplane accident in March 1946.

I could not send the children to Polish schools, because there they were *so* persecuted and insulted. The clerks, the officials of the supply service, did not want to give us any rations. They constantly tried to cut them down to the utmost. I really did not have anything to give the children to eat. I had to fight on all sides. Wherever I went I heard only anti-Semitic jeers. I was hated by the Poles in Zakopane because I was constantly defending our rights.

There was a second children's home in Wrotka, about thirty kilometers from us. That home was shot up three times. Bandits, Polish reactionaries, NSZ, with the aid of the entire population . . .

What is NSZ?

That is a Polish organization which fights against the Polish government and treads on Jewish orphans, shooting at us.[4] They attacked us and threw grenades through the windows. At that time we pulled all the children into the corridor, and they lay there all night. Three times, week after week, raids were made on this home. We had to close it down. We could not endanger the lives of the children. We foresaw that this wave would shift to Zakopane, and therefore I decided to be ready for it and prepare a defense. I applied to the security authorities and to the Polish police. I received ten people for defense with a machine gun mounted on the roof, and besides that I had an alarm siren, search lights . . .

Like a concentration camp.

Exactly like a concentration camp. And everybody had grenades and various weapons in order to defend ourselves. There were two groups [who] were supposed to defend us, some from the militia and some from the public security police. They tossed grenades at each other [horsed around] in my home, with the children present. Such was the defense I had. Seeing all this, I understood that they were not people on whom one could rely, and I decided to find Jews who would defend us, and I myself obtained a permit for weapons. I knew how to handle a revolver, and I would guard and defend the home. And, in fact, there was an attack on us which we repulsed. They were shooting at us, coming gradually closer. We fired from all sides. We received aid. We created a lot of noise so that all of them withdrew.

But similar things were happening after this victory, too. I myself was assaulted, too. But I do not know exactly what the motive was, whether it was of a political nature or robbery. Coming home at six o'clock in the evening not far

4. *Narodowe Siły Zbrojne*, or "National Armed Forces," the extreme nationalist and anti-Semitic underground army that refused to participate in the official Polish Home Army during World War II. It continued to fight against Communists and Jews following liberation.

from our home—it was beginning to get dark—two persons with guns attacked and robbed me. They took several thousand Zlotys away from me, and they beat me up severely. I was bruised all over my body and wounded. They tied me up, threw me on the ground, and beat me up. I had no weapon on me then, or I would have defended myself. And those two people were armed. I suppose, however, that this attack had, like all attacks in Poland, a twofold motive, politics and robbery. They knew exactly who I was; if it were just motivated by robbery, they would not have beaten me up so severely.

[K. abruptly turned to describing her charges in the children's home.]

The children whom I have collected come from various parts. A great many come from forests, mostly the older boys and girls, fourteen and fifteen years old. The main center of the partisans was in eastern Poland. These boys, naturally, starved the same as all the soldiers. They have gone through an awful lot. Some had lived [hidden] among peasants. The peasants did not know that they were Jewish children. These children worked very hard [as] shepherds, farm hands, tenders of cattle and horses, and did all sorts of farm jobs. They starved a great deal. A part of the children were hidden in various hiding places. I have children here who sat in wardrobes. I have a little girl here who sat two and a half years in a wardrobe. A tiny child three years old; [she] was completely unable to walk or talk when he came out. She was completely emaciated, covered with lice. The woman who kept her in that wardrobe—it was in Warsaw—had left the dwelling, locked the door, and did not return anymore. And this child had been there already two days without food. And then by some miracle we found out about it, and we pulled this child out through the window. I have children who sat in hiding places for a year or two with their legs doubled up, so that when they eventually left these hiding places, they had complete atrophy of the leg muscles. They were completely unable to walk.

A part of the children were hidden in Polish cloisters. But in the cloisters the children were converted, and later on the priests did not want to return these children. Only from a few orphanages where they could not feed the children, even the Polish children, would they bring them to the committee. At first children were brought to us disinterestedly, because they just wanted to get rid of these children. Later on they hit upon the idea that they ought to demand money for it—[ironically] the Jews, of course, have a lot of money. Subsequently larger and larger payments were demanded. And then the children were even sent to extort money from us; [they] would demand money for their Polish guardians.

Tell me, were these cloisters convents or monasteries?

It varied. Mostly the younger children were in cloisters. For instance I can tell the story of five children whom we call the "Bobols." They are marvelous children from a cloister named for St. Andrew Bobol.[5] While in Warsaw I found out by accident that a certain doctor had found some small circumcised children in a certain cloister supposedly in the vicinity of Zakopane. However, I could not find out who the doctor was and where it [the cloister] is. I began to search for these children on my own. I went to the deacon of the church and tried to find an institution or cloister named after St. Andrew Bobol. But the deacon did not tell me anything. He said he did not know. I do not know if he did not want to tell me or really did not know. In spite of that, I began to go around to all the cloisters [and] to all the children's homes in and near Zakopane and tried to find out where there might be such an institution. And in the end I found the track.

I went there. Although I did not know any details, I told them that I had found out that Jewish children were there. At first these people did not want to admit it, but finally I was told, "Yes, there may be two or three small boys here who had come from the Jewish ghetto." I was told that when the [Warsaw] ghetto was being liquidated, when the ghetto was burning, these children were found on the street. They were tiny children, infants in a swaddle, and these children were carried out of the ghetto in a knapsack by policemen and handed over to the Budlen Institution. That was a foundlings' home named after Father Budlen in Warsaw. And there these children were raised. Later on, when Warsaw was being bombed, the home was evacuated and these children were distributed all over the countryside. And these children were placed in [this] cloister.

This institution made a terrible impression on me. Dirty! A crowd of tiny children, all shaven to the skin, all in striped suits, all dressed the same. When I came, I brought pastries and candy with me. The mother superior permitted me to distribute the candy myself. These children threw themselves at me with such violence, and screamed so frightfully, and trampled and pushed me right against the wall, and the mother superior had to rescue me. They were completely wild from hunger.

I begged the mother superior to show me the Jewish children. At first she showed me only three boys. I noticed that they were much smaller [and] looked even worse than the other children. The sister herself told me that she was very much surprised but the Jewish children were doubtlessly faring still worse than the others. Then she told me that she would not give me these children without a special permit from the Warsaw city authorities. In view of that, I sent a certain lady to Warsaw. I did not go myself, because I was supposed to leave for France

5. K. has the name almost right. She refers to St. Andrew Bobola, a sixteenth-century Polish Jesuit missionary and martyr.

in three days with all the children. We had very little time. But I gave her the address of some very good friends of mine who were to take care of securing the permit for the release of the children. The journey took her twenty-two hours there and twenty-two hours back under terrible conditions. Two days she went without sleep, and she brought me the permit.

Then I scraped together some money from privates sources, and I loaded as many provisions as I could from my larder and drove over to them with money, provisions, and this permit. The nuns were very surprised that it took so little time. They had not expected that I would get the permit, because it was not so easy to get these things. I arranged it because I had many friends in the Polish government in Warsaw. And then they started to find objections. They argued that they would return them to me later, that the priest was against it seeing that these children were converted, that they were already Catholic children, that we would again make Jews out of them—they resisted as much as they could. Then they told me that the children were dirty, that they would wash them first, that they would comb them first. I, however, implored them to release these children immediately. I had brought so many gifts, so much food and money, and the permit. In the face of all that they could not resist anymore and finally returned the children to me. There were three boys and two girls.

Then on sleds I brought the five children in my own arms. When I showed these children to *my* children, all the children cried. These children were barefoot, and this was in February, at the height of winter, and winter in Zakopane is very severe. None had coats. They were bundled up in rags. The children all had colds. All were wetting themselves. Emaciated, just skin and bones. They constantly cried. Besides that, they had scrofula. I feared that they would not thrive, that at least two or three would die on me.

All of us surrounded these children with utmost care. My children brought them everything they had—apples, chocolate, all their food. Immediately we named them the "Bobols." They amused them, danced, sang to them, rocked them, carried them. Unfortunately we had very little time to give these children the proper care, because we had at once to prepare for the journey to France. And the journey was very difficult and took three weeks, because we crossed the Polish border illegally.

Now these children are chubby. One of the boys weighed 7 kilos [just over 15 pounds] when he came to me. Now he weighs 15 kilos. They are very intelligent children, very clever, and very beautiful. Everyone who comes here wants to take them from me [adopt them], but I cannot give these children up. They belong to the entire Jewish people. I believe that their place is in Palestine. These children are my entire family. Among themselves the children are very close. The older children pamper and play with the younger children. For instance, once when we went on an excursion to the beach and had to walk several kilometers, the children begged that these tots, the "Bobols," be taken along, too, so they should not remain home alone, so they should not cry. They would carry them. And each older boy and girl took a small child on the back. And such a procession passed through the streets of a small French town. People saw it and laughed. This is very moving, because it shows how close the older children are to the young, how very much they love them.

Each and every one of our children has such a tragic story. Every one of them has gone through all of hell. One could write volumes to write the full story of the children.

13 Lena K.'s Children

Short interviews with three of Lena K.'s orphan charges at Bellevue
grant us something like a child's eye view of the Holocaust. The first,
with thirteen-year-old RAISEL M., is understandably fragmentary.
Boder disagreed with the judgment of supervisory personnel at the
home that she was somewhat mentally retarded, believing rather that
she was deeply disturbed. He cut the interview short, possibly to save
her from further stress, and did not take it up again. Her parents,
natives of southeastern Poland, an area of mixed Polish and Ukrainian
population, hid their family from the Germans in a bunker, and then
in the forests, alternately helped and looted by the local Ukrainians.
Her father allowed himself to be persuaded by Jews from his own community that it was safest to return to the ghetto, whereas her mother
insisted on chancing fugitive survival for herself and her two children.
Raisel was spared having to go into the details of her mother's death.
Judging from the fact that the child spoke better Polish than Yiddish,
she may have come through the Holocaust by being taken in by Polish
peasants.

NATHAN S. was no more than twelve when he ran away from a deportation in his home town of Lvov and went to work for a peasant. In
1943 he joined a Russian partisan unit operating nearby and worked as
a scout. When his unit was trapped between the advancing Red Army
and the Germans in summer 1944, Nathan was severely wounded by an
exploding mine. Two years later he still carried the scars, and part of one
ear was missing. Lena K. found him in a children's home in Krakow and
took him to Zakopane, and thence to France.

Unlike her classmates, fifteen-year-old EDITH Z. could not elude the
Germans. Her parents fled to Lvov in eastern Poland from their native
Katowice in 1939, but conditions in the Soviet zone of occupation must
have been very poor, for they moved to German-occupied Krakow in
1940. Her mother's attempt to "pass" with forged Aryan papers failed
when a local ethnic German recognized her and informed the authorities. Edith and her younger sister fled to the Krakow ghetto and joined
their father shortly before all three were sent to a nearby labor camp.
When the two children were literally tossed out for being too young,
Edith managed for a time to provide her sister with a hiding place on
a Polish farm. But when all the Jews in the region seemed about to be

swept into Plaszow concentration camp just outside Krakow, she saw to it that the three of them would go there together, yet another example of powerful Jewish family bonds. Ultimately Edith was selected for work in the ammunition plants at Skarzysko and Czestochowa. Her knowledge of German doubtless played a role in getting good work assignments. She searched in vain for her family after liberation and was sent by Jewish authorities to Lena K.'s home in Zakopane.

RAISEL M.

Where were you when the war broke out?

At home still, in Busk,[1] with mother and father. When the Germans were there, my father worked for the Jewish Council. Before that my father made a hole where I, my mother, my father, and my little brother three years old . . . we hid there around two weeks.

Why did you have to hide?

Because the Germans wanted to kill us. There we lay. It was—can I tell where the hole was?

Yes, naturally.

It was a hole there where the horses stood. A stable. And we had that hole under the stable. On top was an attic, and the Germans were walking in the attic. My brother—he was not even three years old then—began to cry. My mother gave him [something] to drink. He refused. He cried so we thought that the Germans would kill us, but they did not hear. We had enough money. My father was a horse trader. We were not poor. A Gentile woman brought us food. Not much, because we had been robbed, too. Gold and such. The Ukrainians robbed us, at night. And my father paid the Gentiles to bring us food. And she [the woman] brought us a little cold soup. It was not good. Well, it is better than nothing. Then the woman said that the Germans were coming with dogs. The Germans had dogs which only had to sniff to know where we were, and we ran away in the morning. All of us.

We were in a grove. We got so scared. There were many Jews lying, not yet buried, but they just lay about. Dead people.

---

1. A town in Eastern Galicia, a few miles east of Lvov. In 1939 it was part of Poland and home to nearly 2,000 Jews. Today it belongs to Ukraine.

Did you yourself see that?

Yes, I saw that. And we got away. It was so muddy. It was going on winter. And we still had enough money, but the Ukrainians looted us. The shepherds took everything away from us. We were left with just one shirt. We only had what we had on us.

But you wore more than a shirt. You wore a dress, a coat.

We had only one dress, two dresses left, just what we wore. And we went on. Afterward we sat in the forest. It was raining. We made a shack out of sticks and out of hay and other such things. Later two other Jews arrived, a girl and a boy from Busk, our hometown. And they dragged my father away, and he went. He did not want to go, but they dragged him away.

How could the girl and the boy drag him away?

They took him aside and persuaded my father. [Imitating the conversation:] Why should he remain here? If he does this, he will be killed, and if he does something else, he will be killed.

Oh, they persuaded him to go.

Yes, yes, that he should go to a camp. My father said, "Shh, Rachel,"—my mother's name is Rachel—"if you want to come, you and Raisel, you must take the little brother and set him under a tree, or else you must throw him into . . . whichever . . . whichever you want, as long as you do not take him along." My mother said, "No. I will not leave the brother behind. Whatever will happen to me will happen to the children." And father said, "Yes. Stay if you want to. I am going." And my father was eating a piece of bread, and he leaned over. He started . . . he threw away the bread he was eating. He could not eat anymore and started to cry, just like a little child. Ah, he went away. And he went away. He did not want to remain with us.

Afterward the Ukrainians, the police, caught us and started to beat us, me and my mother. They began to beat and kick my mother. She cried so. She did not know what was happening to her. She fell down. They began to kick and beat me. I was thrown into some kind of a ditch. They began to beat me with a horsewhip. Afterward my mother got up and pulled me out. The brother, she left him standing on the street. And I cried so. My mother asked me why. I was still a small child, so I did not know. "Why is he doing this to me? Did I deserve it, or what?" I surely did not deserve it. I did not know. And my brother cried so.

After that, what else? I have already forgotten quite a bit. Such a long time. Aha! After that we went away. We went to a small town, Antolowka. There were ethnic Germans there. They spoke German. They were very kind, very kind. They gave us food. They brought food to us in the forest. I was there with my mother. Afterward the police caught us there in the forest. We were asked where we were from and what we were doing there and what business we had there. So we said simply, "We are Jews, and we have nobody." Mother talked to them. I was sitting like a fool. I did not know what to say. And he [the policeman] said, "Come." So we went. Mother pleaded so, she cried, to let us go. We gave him something, so he let us go.

After that we went to Huta Olejska, a Polish village. The Gentiles were also very kind. We slept in barns. Here a day, there a day. I helped a little. My mother helped a little. We worked in the garden. I had a cow I tended all day. After that we went back there [where] we had been, with the Germans. I have already forgotten what the name of it is. There my brother died.

What did he die from?

My brother had such a large stomach. He told my mother that his stomach hurt him, everything hurt him, and he could not walk. And my mother set him down, and I and my mother went for bottles. There were bottles there with which I could go to the Gentiles and bring water or a little milk. I always used to say, "I do not need any more." I said this because we were not supposed to be there in the forest, because the Gentiles had said that we should not come, that the police were around. And my mother took the bottles and went to the village. And when I came back my brother was already dead. And my mother cried so much. She began to do it *so* with her head [she demonstrated her mother beating her head against a tree]. She had such bumps. She screamed. She could not bear it.

After my brother died, we buried him in the forest, mother and I. Just dug a tiny grave. He was only three years old. He was very small. My mother cried very much. My mother was badly emaciated. My mother did not get better, because my mother cried very much. She was as thin as a stick. I was with my mother another two months. And my mother died.

Where? In the forest?

Yes, in the forest. Everything in the forest, because I was in the forest three years. Two and a half, not three. [Whispers.]

You must go? We shall talk again later, yes?

Yes.

NATHAN S.

In 1941, when my mother and father were taken away at night by the Germans, I didn't have anywhere to stay, so I ran away from Lemberg.[2]

How many people were in your family?
Two brothers and a sister. One brother was older than I, the other one was younger.

And the sister?
Older.

And where are they now?
I don't know. They took me, too, along with my brothers and sister, but I ran away from the truck. They told me to run away, so I ran away.

Who told you to run away?
My mother. She was taken away separately with my father, on another truck. And I remained with my brothers and sister. I told them to escape, too. They did not want to. They were afraid. So I escaped by myself.

All right. And where did you go?
I went to a Gentile. I did not have anywhere to stay there, so I went to a Gentile to work in the field. I worked everywhere, whatever he asked me to do. I worked in the forest. And then the Gentile did not want to hide me. I had nothing to give him. He wanted me to give him something for hiding me. I had nothing. I had no papers to show whether I was a Pole or a Russian. He did not want to keep me, so I left. I ran away into the forest. I went to the partisans.

Did the Gentile know that you were a Jew?
He did not know. If I had told him that I am a Jew he would have handed me over to the police.

Yes, but you had no papers.
He told me that if I had no papers he would not keep me. He was afraid. So I ran away to the partisans. When I came there, I did not see anybody, but one night I saw them there. I walked toward the river, about two kilometers. I noticed a Russian partisan. He asked me where I was going. So I said, "I am going to earn something. I have no place to go." He asked me who I was and questioned

2. He uses the German name for Lvov.

me about everything. And then he took me to the captain. He introduced me. He accepted me. He gave me food, everything. I was there eighteen months.

A year and a half. And how old were you?
I was then eleven years old.

Did the partisans like you?
Of course. I had food, clothing, everything.

Were these partisans also Gentiles?
Yes.

And Jews?
Jews, yes.

And what did you do there with the partisans?
I went scouting. I went to the Gentiles for food. I went with other Russians, not by myself.

Did you pay for the food?
No. We had nothing to eat, so we went and took. They [the peasants] could do nothing. We would take everything. But one day, on the 21st of July [1944] the Germans made an offensive on the Russians there in the forest. They bombed the forest terribly so that the trees flew in the air. We could hardly stand it. And in thirteen days the Soviets made an offensive. It was the same way. They [the Germans] mined the whole forest. We had nothing to eat anymore. So I and two other Russians went for food. We jumped over the German trenches. There were mines there. I was wounded. The other two were killed.

Tell me, how many partisans were with you in that forest?
There were a thousand men, an entire company. We made mines. Put mines under trains. Put mines under everything we could. The front lines were not far from our forest.
Afterward, when I was already wounded, the Russians came and handed me over to a doctor. I lay in a hospital eight months. I still have a piece of shrapnel here in my side. Then I left the hospital [and went] to a home in Krakow.

The Russians let you?
They did not want to let me. But Jews came there and took me away. [They said,] "Sure, just go back there [to the war]. Do you need more shrapnel fragments?" So I was in Poland, in a children's home in Krakow. Then the woman

director who is here brought me to Zakopane to the children's home. She just came for the children.

Tell me, what happened in Zakopane?
It was all right there, but we could not stay there anymore. The house had to be guarded by soldiers. Bandits came at night. They killed Jews there. So we could not stay. We went to France.

How did you travel from Zakopane? Did you go by train or by truck?
We went by truck as far as Czechoslovakia and then [by bus] to France. To Barbizon. We could not stay. The house was too small. So we came here to Bellevue.

And what do you do here all day?
Well, we are divided into groups here. One group works in the kitchen, another in the house. And groups keep the yard clean. We [all] study here.

Do they feed you well?
Yes

And do you know anything about your brothers, sister?
No. They were all taken away.

EDITH Z.

When the war started, I went from Katowice to Krakow, then, together with my parents, to Lemberg.

You were nine years old. And of whom did your family consist?
My father, my mother, and one sister, a younger sister.

About how old was you father then?
Forty-one years old. He had a big leather store in Katowice. Leather and rugs. All kinds of merchandise.

Do you know where your father is? Where your mother is?
No. They went away with a transport in '42. Father first.

Aha. Now then, will you please tell me the whole story. What happened, as you remember it, when the Germans arrived in Katowice?
Katowice is near the German border, and there were a lot of troops.

So you simply left.

Yes, a few days [before the Germans arrived]. We were in Lemberg one whole year. There was very little food. Everything was scarce. We ate very badly. And then we returned to Krakow. That was still when the Russians and Germans were not at war. There was more to eat [in Krakow]. We had relatives there. They helped us.

And then in 1941 the ghetto was established in Krakow, so we left for Wieliczka, fifteen kilometers from Krakow. We stayed there for a year and a half. And again an expulsion, a *real* expulsion, and we left on foot for Krakow. There was a ghetto [there], but we went to the Aryan side. Mother had Aryan papers. We were still very small [so] we did not need any. Father was hiding. He had a very Semitic appearance, so he had to hide. We were in Krakow a few days, on the Aryan side, and then somebody reported on my mama. He knew her, and he reported on her, and she was taken to the police. We remained in the city, all alone.

How did that come about?

We had stayed home, and mama went out on the street, and she did not return. We knew nothing [about what had happened to her.] After four weeks we learned that she was held in a German prison. Then we went to the ghetto ourselves, because we had no other way out. And we found father in the ghetto, and together with him we went to Bierzanow, because resettlement [expulsion of Jews] was starting in Krakow. And we left.

Now then, you say your father had hid himself.

Yes, but he returned to the ghetto because he could not remain where he was for long.

So he returned to the ghetto. How did you find him?

[Laughing:] On the street. The ghetto was very small, only a few streets. I came into the ghetto, and there stood father on the corner. He was very glad, but when he heard that mama was gone, then he . . .

[Her voice faded to silence. After a long pause Boder prompted her to go on.]

Then we went to a camp, Bedzin near Krakow. We went by ourselves because it was a work camp.

And what work could you do?

I could not work. They wanted to throw me out of the camp because they accepted only those from the age of fifteen and up for work. So we were thrown out, I and my sister. They did not tell us [why]. We were thrown out over the fence.

They lifted you up and threw you out?

Yes. Father did not happen to be present at the moment. He was at work, and we were alone in the camp. And so we went to a Pole, to a peasant, and we stayed there for some time. She [the peasant's wife] wanted to get some pay, so my sister remained, and I went to Krakow to the ghetto and brought back some money to pay up for my sister. And I myself remained in the ghetto, because I found a job there.

And then a deportation occurred from the camp to a large concentration camp, so I fetched my sister. Papa himself wanted that we should all be together. So we all went together to a large concentration camp in Plaszow.

Was that permitted, men and children in one . . . ?

No. That was a separate [part of the] camp, but people saw each other every day. There was a children's home, but I did not want to be there, because I wanted to do some work so that I could help out papa, because papa was very weak. My sister was in a children's home.

A children's home in the camp?

Yes, yes. The Germans permitted it at first. After five weeks I, all alone, was take to Skarzysko-Kamienna, to an ammunition factory. There was a selection at night. I did not want to tell my father and my sister anything—to say goodbye. There were a hundred people to a wagon. Men and women separately. We got a slice of bread [and] drank a little water. We did not know that we traveled to Skarzysko. We thought that we were going to Auschwitz.

Did you know what was going on in Auschwitz?

Yes. And then we were disembarked at Skarzysko, 900 people. They took 70. There were three workshops in Skarzysko. A better shop, a bad one, and one very bad where one just could die at once. I was taken to the best, and since I knew German I got work. They did not consider that I was a child, [simply placing] a box under my feet, because I was too small. And I worked at munitions. Shells. Toward me they behaved very well. Because I was small. But still it depended on his [the foreman's] moods. He was a good man. Then he left and other foremen came in his place. And then it was already very bad. I went hungry. I worked a lot. Three times as much of the same work had to be done. And so they beat us.

Who beat you? The foremen themselves, or were there capos?

No, there were no capos. There was continuous inspection. If you made a smelt,[3] you would get twenty [blows] with a rubber cudgel.

Where did you sleep?

There were long barracks. The beds were mounted. One hundred fifty people were in a long barracks. The women were separate.

Was you hair shorn?

Well, only from the head. Otherwise not.

Were you able to keep clean there? Did they provide soap?

Very little. There is a lot of soda in a munitions factory to wash the shells, so we washed ourselves with that. It was not permitted to take it. You got beaten for it, but sometimes you would get it from the foreman, when he was in a good mood.

Then, in 1943, we went away to the fourth camp, to Czestochowa for a year and a half, and there the Russians [liberated her]. Then I returned to Katowice along with the Russians, because I thought that my parents were there. I did not find anybody. My parents were no longer there. The house was sealed with lead, and I could not get in at all. When the Germans left, they plumbed it.

Couldn't you tear off the plumb?

Yes, but the Russians did not permit it, because I was not yet eighteen years old. That is what I was told, see? When I become eighteen years old, I will get the apartment back. Because nobody else from the family was left, and I was too young to have my own apartment. An officer entered the apartment. Nothing was there anymore. I spent a few weeks [in a shelter], and then a Jewish woman took me in, and I had it very good with her. And then I was sent to Zakopane [by] the Jewish Committee in Katowice. I had it very good there. I studied, and then we left for France.

Why did you leave for France? What happened there?

The Poles. The Poles beat us up. We were going to school, and they beat us up, and . . .

Who beat you? The children at school?

Yes. There were very many Jews in Zakopane, and they did not want any Jews. They could not look at the Jews.

3. A rejected shell that had to be remelted.

And what did the teachers say? The police?

The teachers, nothing. The director intervened some, hollered at them. But they paid no heed. So we left with Mrs. K. First to Prague, and then to France by bus. Two buses.

What are you doing here now?

I attend the second year of *Gymnasium*, and we study Hebrew, French, geography, history, and [so forth].

Do you work? Do you help with the chores?

Yes, every child helps here. Every week a different child has duty in the kitchen or in the house [or] the garden.

Could you tell me, if I ask you about all this time, which was the hardest moment in your life?

The hardest moment was when they took my mama away. I remained all alone with my sister on the Aryan side. Without a penny. And we did not know where father was. And then when I left without my parents, without my sister, for Skarzysko.

14   Israel U.

This interview returns us to the large urban ghettos of Poland. Israel U. was only a few years older than Lena K.'s three orphans. Had he been a bit younger, he probably would not have survived. His initiative and native intelligence helped, but without the ability to work in ghetto and camp his chances were slim. He was just eleven when the Germans overran his hometown of Kalisz in western Poland. His mother had died when he was three, and his father had abandoned him and an older brother four years later. Raised in a religious orphanage for Jewish boys aged five to thirteen, the two brothers and thirty other orphans fled from the Germans toward what they hoped would be the comparative safety of the nearest big Polish city, Lodz. They made it shortly after the Germans took Lodz on September 8, 1939, and threw themselves on the mercy of the local Jewish community. Israel U. would manage to stay there until the end of the ghetto almost five years later.

The morally ambiguous figure of ghetto leader Chaim Rumkowski presents itself almost at the beginning of Israel U.'s tale. Rumkowski, who headed the Lodz Jewish orphanages at the time of Poland's downfall, at first seemed to despair of aiding his additional charges but later saw to their needs. One can hardly blame U. for hating the man who later tried to deport him and the rest of the ghetto children to death camps, but even U. acknowledges Rumkowski's goal of saving at least some of the Jews through work and supplying them with rations that were fairly and efficiently distributed. This interview also introduces us to the far more shadowy figure of David Gertler, head of the ghetto police and second most powerful Jewish administrator in Lodz. Israel U. clearly shared the opinion of many ghetto inhabitants that Gertler was a more attractive figure than Rumkowski for his smuggling of food into and people out of the ghetto. U. does not mention that none of this could have been done without the connivance of corrupt German officials and that it led to Gertler's arrest and deportation in July 1943. Evidently Gertler survived the war. The precise nature of his role in Lodz and his subsequent fate have never been fully clarified.

Israel U.'s narrow escape from the massive deportations from Lodz in September 1942 is one of the more remarkable episodes in this collection. However, he could not evade being rounded up during the liquidation of the ghetto in 1944. He was sent to Auschwitz where he was healthy enough and lucky enough to be selected for work on a nearby farm that produced food for the camp. His luck held at Buchenwald, too. Sent there in January 1945, he was among those assigned to the youth block, most of whom survived. His account shows that at least some liberated concentration camp inmates subjected German civilians to revenge attacks before leaving the country. U. moved to France where he was studying dental technology at the time of his interview at the ORT home at Chateau de Boucicaut. He expressed no particular plans for the future, however. For him the lesson of the Holocaust was that "thinking about tomorrow won't do."

We begin with Israel U.'s account of the orphans' arrival in Lodz shortly after the city fell to the Germans.

We found the Jewish Council with great difficulty. They let us enter. We were received by an old man, completely gray. We showed him a document from the Kalisz [Jewish] Community that asked that the Lodz Community take care of us. The old man, who was later known as President Rumkowski, stopped us, read the petition, and answered us, "Dear children, I have nothing with which to help you." He took us through all the rooms. The bureaus were overturned, a mess. And he gave us back the paper. "You can't stay here with me. You will die from hunger." We left the paper in his hand and went downstairs. He threw the paper down after us, and we returned. The children asked us all about it, and we said that it was very bad. And so we waited a few hours. About five o'clock Rumkowski came. He asked, "Who here is from Kalisz?" We stood up, and he said, "Dear children, don't worry. You will have something to eat and drink." And he said that we would remain there. So we came to live on Pomorska Street for two months.

On Passover [1940] an order came [that] the ghetto was being closed. Every Jew encountered in the city would get the death penalty. In the meantime wire fences were installed all around the ghetto. Every fifty meters stood a German guard. There were large signs: "Entrance Prohibited!" And it was impossible. Some time passed. There were Jews who smuggled food into the ghetto. Hospitals were created in the ghetto for consumptives. Schools were created for the children to learn.

For the children to learn? Not to pray? [1]

At that time it was forbidden to pray. Right when the Nazis entered there were huge placards: "Every Jew caught praying gets the death penalty." There were Jews who were caught praying; they were paraded around town in their prayer shawls and phylacteries, and they were mocked and so forth. Jews caught

1. The Yiddish word for "school" can mean either that or a house of prayer.

praying during Yom Kippur were taken out dressed in their cassocks and prayer shawls, and they had to fill in ditches dug by the Poles during the bombardments. The Jews had to fill in these [ditches] with their bare hands. A fourteen-year-old Hitler Youth passed by, took a bayonet, and cut off the beard of an old Jew. They [the Germans] were allowed to do anything they wanted with a Jew.

It became steadily worse. I was then still in an orphanage in the ghetto. One can't say we were badly treated there. It was better than in [the rest of] the ghetto. Rumkowski became the president of the Lodz ghetto. He wasn't just president, he was an emperor, one might say. He had Jewish police under him. A jail, hospitals, schools. Us [children] he treated very well. But the town, that was terrible. One can say that 95 percent of the ghetto hated him terribly. A few times attempts on his life were made. They wanted to kill him. But he had German might with him, and nothing happened to him.

The worst thing for which he was blamed was this. A lot of potatoes were brought into the ghetto. And when Rumkowski was asked why he didn't distribute them, he answered, "You have no business to meddle in my affairs. I'll distribute the potatoes when I want." Frosts came and the potatoes became rotten, and they had to be thrown away. They were buried. And afterward for three years people still searched for potatoes at this spot where they lay buried. Moreover, the people talked themselves into believing that they tasted better that way, because the water had evaporated from the potatoes.

Time passed like this in the ghetto. Terrible epidemics began. The first was dysentery; people died like flies. They began to organize hospitals. People began to leave [escape from] the ghetto. There was a man by the name of Gertler. I believe he is still living today in Germany. He began to take people out of the ghetto illegally. It cost two or three hundred marks per person.[2] He would take them to Warsaw. Then an order came out from the German authorities [that] if any [Jew] came near to the wire fence, any German could shoot him. Hundreds and hundreds of people perished in the ghetto in this way.

The worst thing in the ghetto was the state of distress. We began to receive very little food. An allotment for fourteen days consisted of 30 grams [1.05 ounces] of turnips, 400 grams [.9 pounds] of flour, 100 grams [.22 pounds] of oat flakes, 200 grams [.44 pounds] of brown sugar, and 250 grams [.55 pounds] of white sugar. This was the ration for fourteen days.

Did you have to buy this, or what?

No. This came from the supply center. This was organized, one can say, very well. Because in the beginning it was much worse. In the beginning a committee

2. Given U.'s recollection of the prices of bread and sugar in the ghetto, this appears to be a mistake. He may have meant two or three *thousand* marks per person.

was organized in every [apartment] house, received the allotment for the entire house, and distributed it to all the people. This was very bad. They stole. But Rumkowski remedied this. There were forty-three district warehouses arranged according to streets. And everybody had a card for bread, a card for vegetables, and so forth. Today, for instance, bread comes out for such and such card numbers. One went to the warehouse, the card was clipped, [and the transaction was] entered in the book.

Didn't one pay for it?

. Certainly. In the ghetto we didn't walk around idle. We worked and earned from the age of ten. Large factories were organized. One simply can't imagine the factories that were organized in the ghetto. Nothing went to waste. For instance, I worked in a tailor factory. Materials came to the ghetto from [which] we made tunics for the German soldiers. From the scraps of the tunics rugs were made. The scraps from the carpets, the very small, tiny pieces, entered a factory that had machines to tear them apart. From this threads were made. From the threads materials were made. Nothing went to waste. Munitions were also manufactured in the ghetto. There were huge factories!

The hunger, the need, and the epidemics still were not able to break the ghetto. The worst things in the ghetto were the deportations. In 1942 they began to send thousands and thousands of people away. Where to we didn't know.

How were they chosen?

This is THE question. Without doubt this is Rumkowski's greatest offense. People who were sick, weak, and old were taken. People who couldn't walk. Jews didn't want to believe that people went to their death. Right after this, after 40,000 Jews were deported, thousands and thousands of kilos of tiny red radishes came into the ghetto. The leaves had been cut off of every radish. So people interpreted it in this way. How is it possible to cut the leaves from so many pounds of radishes? The only people who could have done this were the children and the old people from the Lodz ghetto [the deported ones]. And that is how we deceived ourselves and made believe that the people didn't go to their death.

Talk a little more about the deportations. What happened? They came and said what?

A document was sent to such and such family: On this particular day you have to report to the general prison. And when the man reported, he was sent away. If he didn't report, Rumkowski had a good remedy. A note was sent to the store where he received his food rations [saying] "So and so does not receive bread anymore." And this man did not get anything more to eat. Not the least little thing! And this man was doomed to death. There were people who went into hiding.

And many times they were found dead. There were cases of murder where people killed one another to take away ration cards [and] food. There were people who stole from others at night. There was a case when a girl was killed. She was seen leaving the store with two loaves of bread. A Jew followed her and killed [her and her mother] with an iron bar in the house.

When the ghetto was closed there were 130,000 Jews in the ghetto. By '42 there were 70,000. Then people from Vienna, Berlin, Krakow, from all over Europe began to be sent into the ghetto. If there were again too many people, another deportation began. I remember when the Viennese entered the ghetto. They came in from [conditions of] utter abundance. There were among them Jews who even had served in the German army.[3] When we asked them why they were sent to the ghetto, they said that the Germans wanted to protect them from the bombs, because where they were [from] there were severe bombings, and here there were no bombings. You *know* the German Jews! That is how people were deceived. In short, a field was allotted to them in God's acre. Thousands and thousands of them died. Because we, the Polish Jews, had become adapted to it little by little, [but] they who entered Gehenna directly from affluence were strewn over the field.

But all this wasn't the worst yet. The most terrible event in the ghetto happened in August of 1942. This was the general curfew.[4] We weren't expecting anything. We went to work one day [and] placards appeared: "Starting tomorrow at a certain hour, it is forbidden to walk on the streets of the ghetto!" Everybody understood what was going on. A day later Germans began to enter the ghetto. This deportation was for children. On the same day [that the placards appeared] Rumkowski made a speech on the square in front of the fire department, the most infamous speech in the history of the ghetto. He began with these words: "Mothers, bring your sacrifices." Then he spoke to the conscience of the mothers [to] bring and deliver the children. [Otherwise] "The ghetto will not survive. I want at least a small part to survive." And who should survive? Naturally his people. Those who stood in his good graces.

Naturally, there was screaming, wailing. "You lunatic, get down from the platform!" Instantly people began to build bunkers—places to hide, holes in cellars, up in attics. People hid wherever they could. The Germans started to go from house to house searching for children. Because the Jewish police on this occasion didn't want to cooperate.

3. U. may be referring to refugee German Jews who had fled to Vienna before 1938. But it is more likely that he means Austrian Jews who had served in the Habsburg Army during World War I.

4. The correct dates for this are September 5–12, 1942.

Who were called children? From what age?

Children up to fifteen, up to fourteen years. I was about thirteen or thirteen and a half. But the thing is that the Germans were aware that they didn't have too many children, because mothers had hidden them. So they began to take people who in the ghetto were called derelicts, people who looked bad. One had swollen legs, one's face looked bad. All these were taken away. One cannot imagine how the people were sent away. They [the Germans] were accompanied by trucks. When they entered a courtyard, they fired a revolver. "Everybody down!" People came out. They were lined up. The Germans looked them over. Hans Biebow was the boss then. His trial is going on in Poland today.[5]

This lasted four days. But the Germans saw that they had too few children. And Rumkowski, who as always never refused, took and handed over the orphanage where I was. We came out on the square and lined up. We waited for an hour. Hans Biebow and another German arrived. They began to go out on the square to look us over. He came over to a small boy of ten. "Ah, little one. Do you know what is about to happen to you? You are all going to be shot." The boy didn't answer him anything. He went over to the woman leader of the orphanages: "Genia, how many children are there here?" "One thousand two hundred." He called over the chief of the Jewish police. "Look here, if one of them is missing you forfeit your head!" When he finished saying that, we were surrounded on all sides! Jewish police, firefighters, chimney sweepers, whoever wore a hat and a uniform surrounded us. Trucks began to arrive. We began to run away, but it wasn't possible because there were police all around. Luckily, we were surrounded from three sides, and on one side there was a wooden fence. On the side where the fence was there were no police because no one thought that we could get through the fence, because it was very tall. Over the fence there was some kind of dump of different things [from] a factory. When they surrounded us from three sides, when we saw the trucks arriving, five or six of us got together and ran over to the fence. There was a frightful squall on the square. Everyone cried. Everyone screamed, so they didn't notice [us]. We began to tear away a board. We didn't hurry. I got out. How many got out after me I don't know. I only know one thing, that when I was quite far, I heard a policeman calling after me, "Hey, you, stop!"

I came to the tall wall of the cemetery. Near the wall was a pile of coal. I got between the tombstones. There I was safe for the moment. I heard screams of the children at night. We hid out. In the morning they came and searched the cemetery. The Germans went around with machine-guns.

5. This was in August 1946. Lodz ghetto administrator Biebow was found guilty and sentenced to death by a Polish court.

And what about the other children?

They were sent away. [Only a hundred saved themselves.] Some were freed, some through connections [political pull]. Of the rest [the deported] we received no more word.

A few more days passed; it rained on those days. We were in the Tohorah chamber.[6] We were five persons. We stayed there overnight. The Germans searched there, too. We hid in an attic.

Were there no funerals during the few days in the cemetery?

No. There were enough dead, but one wasn't permitted to walk in the street. There was terrible starvation because no food was issued. Thousands and thousands of people perished there. Just in the ghetto alone.

We were there for three days. Later the deportation stopped. We returned to that orphanage. Nobody was there. So we—myself, my brother, and another boy—got together and rented a room in the ghetto, a private lodging, and we went back to work. I was working at a band saw, and we manufactured toys for German children. Until the year 1944 things were quiet because after the deportation of the children, Gertler came to power in the ghetto.[7]

What had become of the other one, Rumkowski?

He was also around, but Gertler had a lot of power, too. A lot of potatoes had been sent into the ghetto. People recovered a little. A few good months passed. At the beginning of 1944 there was another deportation. It was carried out with another system. Every factory had to surrender 50 percent of the people who worked there to be sent away. Besides the deportation at that time there were terrible epidemics of lung disease in the ghetto. Tuberculosis. I can say that 60 or 70 percent of the people in the ghetto were sick with tuberculosis. The hospitals were full! At that time my brother, too, became sick. And sure enough he died in the ghetto.

I came to the hospital every day. One can't imagine what a hospital looked like in the ghetto! There were enough doctors, but there was nothing with which to heal. There were no injections. Every person knew that he wouldn't pull through. One consolation for the people was that *nobody* would survive.

This is consolation? What sort of consolation is this?

One would say, "Sure, I will die, but we will all die. One will die a little earlier, one will die a little later."

6. The *Bet Tohorah*, or cleansing house for corpses prior to burial.

7. U. is mistaken on this point. Gertler's powers increased until his arrest in 1943, but they never exceeded Rumkowski's.

And then the deportation came, too. Fifty percent from every factory. First on the lists were persons who had no family. At that time I was unfortunately also a single person and was also on the list to be sent away.

Did you bury your brother?
Yes. In the ghetto one was buried normally like before the war.

Was one allowed to say "El Moleh Rachamen" [a prayer for the dead]?
Yes. One was not allowed to pray, but there were not too many Germans in the ghetto. Nobody was there.

My friend, the one who roomed with me in the ghetto, was also on this [deportation] list. We already knew then that under the Germans to be sent away is not being sent to pick radishes or leaves, but death. We began to hide out. We slept in one attic after another, never in the same place twice, moving by night. We were not permitted to stay till morning. We had no [ration] cards because an order had come right away to the store not to issue [us] any food. We lived on what we stole from the fields, the leaves, radishes, and beets. This we cooked; we ate, till this deportation, too, ceased.

Then came the deportation of August 1944, the general deportation of the ghetto. They started to send [away] 5,000 persons a day. It became gradually worse and worse. There was no more order. There was no way out. The Germans surrounded whole streets and took people. I and my friend and another family with whom we lived hid out, but an order was issued that our side of the ghetto had to present itself. The ghetto was divided into three parts. There was a bridge to cross from one side to the other side. They closed the passage. The whole side had to go out. And we reported.

We traveled for twenty hours, and we arrived in Birkenau. We got off the train. The train was surrounded. A prisoner arrived, a Jew. He said, "Jews, know that you are now going to make a life and death decision." I knew what it meant. Then he said to us, "Say that you are older." To the old people he said, "Say that you are younger." We started to march in one row. The women were immediately detached. A German stood there, half drunk. "You *here*, you *there*." There were Germans who immediately separated [the two groups]. We didn't know where the others were going. Later we found out that they went to death.

I and my friend went into the camp. We were in Birkenau twelve days. There were about 6,000 [adolescents], Hungarians, Polish, Czechs. SS men arrived. They came over to us and selected 232 persons. It was said that we were going to an estate to work. It is interesting how we were selected. They watched that a brother should not remain with a brother, or an acquaintance with an acquaintance. We were taken into a barrack, told to undress the way our mothers had born us, and if one had the smallest spot on his body, he was immediately sent back.

I was chosen for Budy,[8] eight kilometers from Auschwitz. I worked in a cattle barn taking care of horses. This was an estate for the SS men. We weren't fed badly there, but one was beaten a lot. I was there six months till the evacuation came. The Russians began to approach. They took the whole camp, and half past three in the afternoon we marched out. We walked on foot a hundred and fifty kilometers. Thousands and thousands of people perished on the way. People were weak from walking. Whoever lagged behind a few steps, they immediately shot him.

Did you see it yourself?

What a question! Every ten meters there was a corpse. I remember a woman from our camp, a Russian girl. She carried a rucksack with bread. She wept to the SS man that she couldn't walk anymore, so he told her, "Throw away the bread." So she said, "But this is bread!" He took off his rifle and shot her. For nothing. She was still able to walk, quite healthy.

What happened to the bread?

It was left lying. They followed with dogs. Bloodhounds. When one ran away, the dogs were released after him, and they would find him. We left behind a few thousand dead on the road.

[At the German border U. and his mates were loaded on open railroad cars and sent to Buchenwald, where he was eventually assigned to the youth block.]

Did you work in Buchenwald?

We didn't. People worked, but when we arrived there were already so many thousands of people in Buchenwald that they couldn't employ the people anymore. One lay on top of another. We organized block theaters, in secret from the SS, naturally. Lectures were organized, schools of geography, of grammar. There, one can say, one spent the day very nicely. Besides the hunger, we didn't feel the terrible conditions of the camp.

[U. recalled the SS guards fleeing as the Americans approached Buchenwald.]

We began chasing. We caught many, brought them back, beat them.

8. An agricultural camp just south of Auschwitz where mainly women did forced farm labor producing food for the main camp.

You didn't shoot any of them?

No shooting was done because the political prisoners said no. We were not the ones to shoot. If we caught a prisoner [we were] to turn him over to the American army. They didn't allow shooting.[9] Perhaps it is a crime that we didn't take revenge, but they, the German political [prisoners], Communists, were in the majority; they took care that the camp should be orderly, not become wild.

We got out and went to meet them. To our great joy, in one of the first three tanks that came in was a Jew, an American soldier. Right away he gave us cakes to eat. We simply couldn't imagine, a Jew, an American soldier! We were liberated! The joy, I can't picture it in words.

Oh yes, half an hour after we were liberated, a telephone call came to the SS offices. The camp commandant [ordered] that the camp be blown up, to set off the mines. But it was already too late. The call was taken by an inmate [who] answered, "Yes, everything is in perfect order." But [he told the commandant] to come to Buchenwald. He didn't tell him that the Americans were already there. He didn't come. I don't know why. Possibly on the way he found out that the Germans were running away.

We left the camp right away. We went into the beautiful quarters of the SS. We were there four weeks. The first days there was still a lot of hunger, because everything was still far away. The tracks were out, Weimar hadn't yet surrendered, the American army still consisted of only the first line troops. Three days later food and all good things began to arrive. UNRRA [officials] began to arrive.

We began to travel. Where we passed we did some damage. We broke everything in the gardens, the houses. If we met a German on the road, a young one, we also *told* him *a bit*. The important thing is, we arrived in France!

9. This was hardly the rule at Buchenwald. Nearly eighty guards and camp officials were lynched by liberated prisoners, sometimes with encouragement from American soldiers. See Abzug, *Inside the Vicious Heart*, p. 52.

15   Julian W.

Julian W., forty-nine years old at the time of the German conquest of Poland in 1939, was managing director of the electric power plant in Lodz, a post he resumed after liberation in 1944. Evidently he was visiting Paris at the time of his interview and planned to return to Poland. For some unexplained reason he was prepared to grant only half an hour for his interview. When a spool ran out as his story neared its end, there was no follow-up. This is a pity, because W. experienced the entire span of the Lodz ghetto and was one of only a few hundred Jews who escaped its liquidation in August 1944.

Short though it is, Julian W.'s story offers some glimpses into the fate of Lodz Jewry, including its terrorization by ethnic Germans in the first months of Nazi rule and the frantic rush of Jews to escape the terror by moving into the ghetto created in April 1940. Evidently the Germans had succeeded in making it look attractive to at least some inhabitants of Lodz, because W. had to prove that his son was who he said he was and not some Polish orphan seeking a "free ride" to the ghetto. The interview also reveals how the Nazis skillfully lied to the Jews to secure their cooperation at various points, including their final removal from the ghetto, ostensibly to workplaces in Germany, but actually to the gas at Chelmno and Auschwitz.

Julian recalls work in the ghetto as being "a kind of silent sabotage" of the Germans as well as of the Jewish Council, widely viewed as corrupt by the mass of Jews. His job in the furniture shop explains why he was one of some 800 Jews exempted from the final evacuation of the ghetto to clear it of valuables, including furniture in need of repair. As the Russian army approached he was among those with the wit to go to ground and evade German death squads that combed the ghetto. We begin the interview as Boder quizzes W. about his status as manager of the Lodz power station under German rule.

How long did you continue working after the arrival of the Germans?
Two months, and then our plant was taken over by an SS man. And I, as a Jew, had to leave my post. Then an order came that all Jews were to move to the ghetto. Even before we moved to the ghetto we received such marks of discrimination as the yellow armband so that we would be recognized on the streets as Jews. And

then that appeared not enough to them, so they pasted yellow stars on our front and back, so that from all sides it would be recognizable that a Jew walked there.

Naturally going about town was almost impossible for the Jews because they were seized by the Germans on the streets [and] taken for common labor. Regardless of who it was, whether he was a laborer or an intellectual, he had to perform the hardest forms of labor. I, for example, was compelled one day to scrub floors. I also had an experience when my mother had died on the 5th of March and I had to bury her. I was the only one at the cemetery. Nobody [else] was permitted to accompany the body to the grave, and when I was returning from the cemetery, I was grabbed on the street by a young ethnic German, dragged through a gate, and compelled to carry coal from a cart to the cellar. In general, it was dangerous for the Jews in the streets, because everybody could do with us as he pleased. That was but a small episode which I experienced shortly before my entrance into the ghetto.

It was decided that we should go to the ghetto in an organized manner. For instance, every day a certain section of the city was to be resettled. Where I lived was to go first. That was a better section. And at 5:00 P.M. sharp our home was surrounded by the SS men, and all the Jews had to abandon the house. The SS men entered the apartments directly [and] gave us only five minutes time to leave. And so everyone could take only the least trifle of his possessions with him in a knapsack and then step out into the yard. I had a peculiar incident happen with my son. He has a kind of an "Aryan" look. So he was struck with a whip because he wanted to go with his father. The SS man did not believe that he was Jewish, and he thought that he wanted to smuggle himself away with the Jews. I had first to prove that he was my son, and so he was taken with us.

Now, that was in the winter. It was freezing. All the Jews from the various houses of this sector were assembled in a yard, and we did not know exactly where they would take us. The SS men, if they were not instantly admitted to an apartment would break down the doors, and where there were sick who could not go with them, they shot the sick people. After we learned that they intended to drive people to the ghetto by such means, the following days all the Jews went to the ghetto on their own. So, although it [ghettoization] was to last a week, all the Jews left the town on their own, because they had seen the inhuman methods with which the Jews were treated.

And so we were taken to the ghetto on foot; among us were many young girls, old women in bed slippers. Some were even running barefoot in the snow. En route we had to throw away the rucksacks because the burden was too heavy to carry. And so we arrived in the ghetto. The Lodz ghetto was completely isolated from the city. There was absolutely no communication. They selected the suburb, the worst section of the city. It was surrounded with barbed wire and strictly guarded by police guards so that nobody could leave. Afterward a so-called ghetto administration was formed, actually a creation of the [German] City Council. At the head of the ghetto administration stood the famous Biebow,[1] a German businessman from Bremen. He took over the whole management.

Then it was proclaimed that the Jews in the ghetto had to work; otherwise they would be unable to live. They were to earn their existence. Well, then various workshops were created where the Jews were compelled to work. A clothing shop, let us say, where all kinds of clothing was produced, metal details, electrical details, a rug detail. The people who had no trade had to reeducate themselves in order to do something. Naturally the Jews did not wish to work for the Germans. They were doing only a little bit in order to give an impression that they were working. Otherwise we would have gotten no provisions from the Germans. It was a kind of silent sabotage against the Germans. However, the ghetto council did good business in spite of that, because they were selling the products that were manufactured in the ghetto on the "left" [black] market. For instance our wood detail constructed very many pieces of furniture and little beds for children. They could sell [some of] them without certificates, and that is why it was worthwhile for me to manage these works. To be sure, we were not getting any money, but only provisions, and very little. The best proof of it is that thousands of people were compelled to starve. In excess of 200,000 people passed through the Lodz ghetto. These were mostly Polish Jews. But there were also Jews from Germany, Austria, and Czechoslovakia, and these were precisely the ones who were unable to adjust rapidly to the hard living conditions in the ghetto.

There were many deportations [from the ghetto]. It simply was said that the Germans were in need of people for various kinds of work, and so many people who were feeling bad in our ghetto applied. Other deportations were managed by the Gestapo. One fine day they established a total curfew in our ghetto.[2] All Jews had to assemble. They made a selection—women and men who looked bad were embarked on carts and trucks and taken to assembly points. Then big, heavy freight trucks with trailers came, and all the Jews were crowded into these vehicles and removed. Also the hospitals were cleared of the gravely ill. The children were removed from the hospitals and the children's homes. Some of them were actually thrown into the trucks.

Did you see it yourself?

Yes. It is interesting that afterward the clothes of these unfortunate people who were shipped away—these same old clothes—were returned to the ghetto to

1. Hans Biebow's ghetto administration consisted of 250 German officials. The Jewish Council in the Lodz ghetto was, of course, responsible to it.

2. Again these are the events of September 5–12, 1942, that are also described by Israel U.

be used by the Jews who still remained. These old pieces of clothing [and] shoes came back torn because they [the Germans] were searching for various valuable [hidden] objects. The better things were repaired in our ghetto and then partly distributed among the remaining population and partly shipped out by the Germans for the bombed-out German population.

Did you participate in community affairs?
I participated but little because we had an elder of the Jews, very much a man unto himself. Rumkowski. He received orders directly from the ghetto management [i.e., the Germans] and then executed the order as far as was in his power. I did not want to participate in these things directly because I was opposed to all that politics.

And so the last evacuation took place in the month of August 1944. At that time the mayor of the city came and also the functionaries of the ghetto. They made speeches, told us that the whole trend of politics had changed in Germany. Germany needed workers by the hundreds; Germany was bombarded, [and] many German cities had been leveled. These cities had to be rebuilt, and therefore Jewish labor must be made use of. Then there was a commission of generals [that] had decided that it would not be right to keep so many Jews near the front. They wanted to help the Jews, so they had arranged for us to leave and have better working and living conditions. But what actually happened: all the Jews were evacuated, not to the bombed-out cities, but through Auschwitz [where] the people were again subjected to a selection, and most of them were compelled to pass through the crematoria.

I remained among 860 people who were compelled to stay in the ghetto. That was a detail assembled by the Germans [that was] supposed to assemble the pieces of furniture that remained, all the pieces of clothing, pillows, and bedding. . . . That lasted a few months. As the last 70,000 people were taken to Auschwitz. We were housed in two factory buildings, the men in one factory, the women in another.

Where was your son?
My son was with me, and my wife [and] daughter were on the other side [in the other factory building]. These two buildings became some kind of a [concentration] camp, and from that instant we were regarded as a camp like Auschwitz or Dachau. They assigned the people to various labor tasks. This business dragged on until the 19th of January 1945, on which date our city was liberated by the Russians and the Polish armies. We had a concealed radio in the camp, so we knew approximately how things stood. Three days before the liberation of the city we all abandoned our camp and hid ourselves in various bunkers, in various buildings, in cellars, and in the attics of buildings. I personally hid myself in a trans-

former station. That was a high tension room, where I had my family. Altogether I hid thirteen persons there. And that is how I stayed alive. The Germans, as we learned later, had come into our yard and found, instead of 860 persons, only 23. They made a big commotion: "Where are the others?" The people were unable to give a reply, and they did not shoot them, only arrested them. And they decided to drag the rest of [us] out of the apartments and then proceed with a general execution. [We know that] because they had dug nine mass graves in the cemetery with Jewish labor. They intended to annihilate us in these mass graves.

There were about 120 SS men. The first day they were able to find about 70 persons. They did not shoot them yet, just arrested them, like the first 23. The next day they came to find the rest. This time they brought dogs with them. Again they found a few people; all were arrested again. Another night went by, and then they were compelled to abandon the city on the sly. And so that is how the people who stayed over in the ghetto saved themselves. The people who had been arrested were later set free by us.

16 Mendel H.

Mendel H., the son of Lodz shopkeepers, was twelve years old when
the Germans attacked Poland in 1939. He and a younger sister tried to
flee their native city but were forced to return when the invaders overtook them. In the Lodz ghetto he learned metal-working skills that
would save his life. Rather than being deported to a death camp, in 1943
he was sent to the ammunition plants at Czestochowa and Skarzysko-
Kamienna. H.'s description of conditions there shows that work was
arduous and punishments draconian. At the same time it shows that
tenuous contacts with Polish workers in the factories ameliorated the
Jews' position to some degree. Note the items confiscated from him
and his fellow workers upon their arrival at Buchenwald. Mendel H.
also shows that the Jews in Czestochowa retained some power to influence events by bribing German officials, as they did to save one of two
transports of Jewish children evacuated from Skarzysko.

Not long after dumping Mendel H. in Buchenwald, the Nazis tried
to move him yet again as the American Third Army approached the
camp in April 1945. Indeed, the Germans gave Jews priority in these
marches that often ended in the prisoners' death. Mendel was im-
mensely proud of eluding the guards and finding a place with the minority of prisoners who remained to be liberated. If he embellishes his
tale of evasion and concealment a bit, we can forgive him; the outline of
his experiences is perfectly credible, and, by any standard, remarkable.
His description of the final, ecstatic contact with his liberators should
touch the most jaded reader.

The interview took place at the home for young Jewish survivors
at Chateau de Boucicaut just outside of Paris. There Mendel H. was
studying to become a furrier. When kidded that there would be little
call for that trade in Palestine, he expressed no interest in leaving France
for kibbutz life. He had had enough, he said, of communal living. We
join the interview at the point where he told of being separated from
his family and sent by train to Czestochowa along with 3,500 other Jews
in 1943.

This journey ought to have taken a few hours; it took maybe a day and a half,
and we were treated like prisoners. Beaten . . . thrashed . . . everything taken
away from us. There was an ammunition camp in Czestochowa. There only rifle

bullets were manufactured. They let us rest a week. Afterward we were assigned to factories, everyone by trade, and we worked until they saw that the work didn't go [right]. Ninety men were selected from the factory, among whom I was [included], and sent to Skarzysko-Kamienna, one of the largest ammunition factories in Poland. There not only rifle bullets but artillery ammunition is manufactured. I was selected because I was an artisan. We were taken there to learn a completely different job and return [to Czestochowa] to install the machinery so that it would do the other work.

Were you paid for the work?

We were paid nothing. Only the food. That was 20 dekas [about 7 ounces] of bread and a [bowl of] soup per day and sleeping quarters. We slept on bare boards, four stories high. Before the war somebody had a stable for horses there. For clothing we wore a jacket, a shirt, a pair of trousers, and a pair of shoes. We got up around six o'clock. We washed up. Later we went out and arranged ourselves, everyone according to his job. A German came and counted [us]. Afterward we went to the factory which was a few steps from the barracks. And there we were counted again by every job foreman.

And the foreman was who, German or Jewish?

The foremen were only Germans. There were [Jewish] overseers—very few—who knew the job well, really well. They walked around to watch that we were working, and if something special broke that the inexperienced worker couldn't fix, they fixed it. And if it happened that maybe a worker broke something that had to be worked on for a half a day or maybe a few hours until it was fixed, one was taken upstairs. Two Germans walked upstairs, and that person was stretched out on a bench, and he was administered twenty-five to one hundred [blows]. One person could take it, but another could not. He could get sick and die from it.

If somebody became sick, what was done?

There was a hospital. There was medical care. There were Jewish doctors in Czestochowa.

How long were you in Czestochowa?

Maybe four or five months. Later I was sent to Skarzysko, as I told you, for nine weeks. To learn working on a new machine.

And who taught you that?

Old workers, Jewish, who already had worked on that machine, and there were specialists who told us how the machine works. [They] spoke German to us. We

[also] worked together with Poles, and they were, of course, free. With them, of course, Polish was spoken. They lived in the town, at home.

And how did the Poles behave themselves toward the Jews?
This depended on the person. But not especially good. If they could betray a Jew so that he should fall into German hands, they did it gladly. There were cases that a Jew was sold for a kilo of sugar. A Jew came to a Pole to hide. So the Pole first of all would take away from him all his valuables. When he saw that the Jew didn't have anything more, he would go to the Gestapo, report that a Jew is hiding out with him, and the Jew was taken out and shot. The Pole received either a liter of schnapps or a kilo of sugar for it.

In the meantime we heard the way the political facts were developing. We also heard that the Russians were beginning to approach, and on the other side the Americans and the English were moving forward. And three weeks before the liquidation of the camp of Skarzysko we were sent back to Czestochowa, and here we began to work on those machines that we had learned there. Three thousand people were sent to Czestochowa. Among them were forty small children up to twelve years old. They were in the first transport that was brought from Skarzysko to Czestochowa. They were taken away and brought out to the Jewish cemetery, and the children were slain [by] the Germans. After this there was a second transport. The Jews of Czestochowa had money, and they bribed the Germans, and the children were let into the camp so that one can say the children have remained to this day. The children were liberated.

Two, three months later [January 1945], when the Russians began to go forward, a list was made of 900 Jews, and they were supposed to be sent to Buchenwald, I among them. Suddenly one morning there was a roll call. The 900 people were taken outside the city, put on trains, and driven four days in succession until we arrived in Buchenwald. In Buchenwald we were stripped of everything that we had. We had traded with the Poles. So everybody had something. One had bread. One had dollars, another had gold. All this we had taken away. We were given prison clothes. That meant jackets and pants, blue and white stripes. And we were distributed to barracks. We lived there two, three thousand men in one block.

Only Jews?
Only Jews. This transport was of Jews only. The treatment was very bad. We didn't receive anything to cover ourselves. We had to sleep in our clothes. The soup that we received was water. Furthermore, the bread that we received had more [potato] peels than flour like sawdust. One couldn't call it flour. Furthermore, at night we slept fifteen men on boards two meters in width, knocked together, over four stories in height. No man can understand it who didn't go

through all this, but we had to sleep like this. It actually was impossible, but in the winter it was warmer because of it. Heat was not provided. There were barracks that were, maybe fifty, sixty meters in length and thirty meters in width.

In the beginning we were in quarantine four weeks. And in those four weeks one was given eight injections against all the diseases that a man can easily catch under such filthy conditions in which we lived. After four weeks we began to be distributed to work. In the beginning we carried bricks to build a bomb shelter. Later, I remember, on a Friday Russian planes bombed the first city near Buchenwald, Weimar. Saturday morning we were put on trains, and we were driven to this city, to work at the houses that had been bombed there. Naturally a lot of people had been killed. And later to carry out the things that still could be repaired.

Were you allowed to take the things which you found?
If there was, let's say, a bombed house. If one could find food or other things, one took it. If one could take it with him, he took it with him. If not, he ate it on the spot, so that we made out a little. [German] money had absolutely no interest for us, because we couldn't get anything for the money. [In the] camp it was different. There was special canteen money.[1] We received two marks a week, and for this one could get one [bowl of] soup with a liter of beer. This we could get on Sunday. Gold or dollars did interest us, because we traded among ourselves. And there were those who traded with the Germans. With the SS.

Wasn't it dangerous, the SS?
It was dangerous, but if it was in their interest, they [brought prisoners] 'out of danger.' [The SS were] putting away for after the war.

I want you to tell me which moment of that whole time was the worst moment.
I did not have any particularly bad moments. I was hungry, but only a small percentage of the whole time. A bad moment that I did have has to be combined with the liberation. One day, suddenly—this could have been on the 7th of April—in the evening, about four o'clock there came an announcement over the loudspeaker. "All Jews in the camp fall in on the roll call square. The block seniors will see to it that the Jews shall march out." A terror gripped the Jews who were in camp. [We knew] that they didn't want to isolate us in order to keep us alive. So, we didn't go. On that particular day we didn't go. In the meantime there was another [announcement] that the Jews should be let back into the camps and that tomorrow morning around 6:00 there would be roll call of the whole camp. We were let back into the camps. In the meantime one can imagine the panic that had

1. Camp scrip based on the valuables prisoners had brought with them to the camp.

reigned till we heard that we could go back into the camp. We ran around, and there were prisoners of other nations, not Jews, who were for us, who also cried that we should not go. I personally came into a block of Frenchmen. There was one there who recognized that I was a Jew. He came over to me and gave me a triangle, a red one with a 'P'. This denoted a Pole. I sat there till 11:00 at night. [We were let] into the camp, and we slept through the whole night.

About 5:00 in the morning we were awakened. We received 25 deka of bread with 2 deka of margarine. This we ate with coffee, and we went out on the roll call square. A counting took place with a lot of SS men. And they began to put the Jews separately. Jews saw what was in store. They began to run away. The SS men ran after them. They fired twice. He who could hid himself, and all the rest were taken. Near Buchenwald were barracks which were called DAW.[2] These had been factories around Buchenwald which by that time had been bombed and were in ruins. There the Jews were gathered separately, and we sat there two days. In the barracks. We were 4,000 men to a barrack.

And how many were taken from Buchenwald?

There could have been around 8,000 Jews. The floor was made out of stone, so we built a fire. We tore off boards that lay there. And so we sat around and told stories [about] various things. Suddenly, around 5:00 in the morning, SS men came in and told everybody to go outside. So I looked for a place to hide myself. There was a boiler for steam. For heating the hall. I searched for an entry into it. I couldn't find it. But yet, I was able to squeeze myself behind where the coal was put in. I barely made it in there. I went in feet first [so] that the head should stick out so that I should be able to look out every so often. I wore an overcoat so I put it underneath, where the ashes come out. I lay there twenty-four hours. I ate absolutely nothing. I didn't feel hungry. So great was the fright.

After twenty-four hours I went out. It was early morning; that barrack was already free of guards because nobody was supposed to have been in there anymore. I went out and was going to go over to the second barrack which was still full of Jews who were supposed to have been sent on another day. On the way a German sentry met me. "Why are you out here?" So I answer him as if nothing ever happened. "I was in the latrine and now I am going back to the barrack." So I went into that block and stayed there. There were Jews and Russians in the block. They already began to add from other nations because the entire camp was supposed to be evacuated. There we stayed for three days.

Next morning there was [an announcement] that an evacuation of the whole camp was to take place, block-wise. I prepared myself. I dressed, took what was necessary for the road, and went downstairs to the courtyard, and there I stood

2. German Armament Works.

and waited for the departure. I already had told myself, "We are lost. What will happen to everybody will happen to me also. I will go." So after the small [camp] was taken on the journey, a German came over and called out that the forty-seventh barrack, in which I was, was to go. It came out that I had to stand in the first 'row of five.' So I said [to myself], "No, first of all I do not want to stand in the first row. I will go down." I joined another one and with him I began to edge myself toward the back. I looked for a way up the stairs to the second floor. Lined up there were prisoners who were old timers who were supposed to remain, who took care of the block. They stood with clubs and chased down all the people from upstairs who had hidden themselves.

[Boder wanted to know the identity of the "old timers."]

Gypsies who had lived in Germany. They were helping the SS.[3] I do not know myself how I got upstairs. On the opposite side was a storeroom with all kinds of old clothing. Next to me stood a Russian. So I said to him, "I am going inside. You shut me in." So he said to me, "Foolish child, you will be found in here." So I said, "Want to bet? Either do it or not." And so he shut me in, and I stayed inside. The whole block was taken away, and I myself remained in the block. All the caretakers of the block who had remained inside did not know about this. After three hours I heard steps in the corridor. Somebody was approaching and opened the door and threw something in and went away. [A few minutes later men from the block came in and surrounded him.] I began to cry and beg to let me go, "I was left by myself. Nobody is here. Nobody will know about it. The Russians are coming any day now. Will it do you any harm?" They didn't want to hear it. They led me out. They took me by the collar properly, and they led me out on the road where everybody was being executed.

Were they SS men?

These people were those faithful henchmen of the Germans who were also prisoners. And there stood other prisoners who were called "camp police." They were prisoners organized by the SS. They guarded inside the camp. I was coming out on the road. So I stopped and looked over what sort of sick people I was going with. I wasn't especially weakened. The nerves still carried me, which made me strong. Quickly I thought to myself: "Am I going on the road? No! I'll see that I don't!" I had a blanket, a plate and pot. These I threw away. All of a sudden I began to walk with a firm step into the first street between two blocks. I walked as if it [being executed] did not mean me. I only walked about ten steps.

3. This seems unlikely. The only privileged positions Gypsies were normally allowed to hold were as musicians in the camp orchestra.

I thought that I had already succeeded, that I was not going to be noticed, and suddenly someone called after me, "Hey! Come back!" I saw that I was cornered.

I was led out on the road again. I came out on the roll call square and went over to someone who was standing there who guarded the road so nobody should straggle away. I told him, "I am fifteen years old. How can I go on the road? I have no strength." Says he, "That is none of my business. If you were brought out here you have to go." I was pushed till I was already half way across the square. I stopped and said, "No! I am not going any farther!" And I looked around. I saw there were sick people lying. Whether they were really sick or were doing the same trick that I was going to do, I do not know. Suddenly, I threw myself down! I threw myself on the ground in the square. I am dead. I have died. This is the end. I can't go any farther.

Suddenly, I heard that they were beginning to gather the sick, the dead. Suddenly a German came over to me and gives me a kick. "Damn you. Will you get up?" I didn't say anything. I pretended that I had died, but yet, with one eye I looked at him like this. With one hand I had covered the face and with one eye I looked out at him. He gave me another kick, "Are you getting up or not? If not I pop you." I didn't say anything again, but I saw he was taking out the pistol and pointing it at me. "For the last time, I am telling you," says he, "if you don't get up I will pop you." Right then another SS man comes over and grabbed him by the hand and told him, "But, man, it is a waste of the bullet that you are going to give him. You can see that he is already dead." Then he gave a stronger kick. I lay there as if I were dead, and he said to him, "Now see, he is already dead." And they picked themselves up and went away. They had already gathered nearly everybody. I got up and went over to one of those who guarded the road and told him, the same story: "I am fifteen years old, and how can I go on the road?" Suddenly, I noticed youths of twelve, thirteen, fourteen, fifteen, sixteen years setting along the side. There was a block which was especially for youths.

[H. then explained that earlier he had lied about his age in order to get a job and thereby maximize his chances of survival.]

I was fifteen, but I [had] reported that I was over eighteen. I do not know where I got the strength. I quickly ran over to the children. And I sat down in a way that I was not noticed. In the meantime people were going on the road. One block after another was led through, hundreds and thousands [of people]. And so it continued until about one or two [o'clock]. There was an air raid. American planes. And everybody was ordered to return to the blocks. [The next morning there was an alarm and the SS fled.] Our joy became very great, but we could not believe that this was possible. It lasted an hour's time. We already heard shooting from the Americans, and the Germans returned it. We began to stream out on the road from which we heard tanks rolling. At first we thought that they were German. But a block senior had field glasses. We looked. From far away we could already see the American star, the white one. So that we already knew that they were American. We surged out on the road with our last strength. We ran three or four kilometers through a forest, a field, [and] broke through the wires, which were electrified. We brought wooden beams and with the beams we tore up the wires. We got out.

We came out on the road. The Americans didn't know who we were. They started to point the machine guns at us. They didn't shoot. We put our hands up. And a tank drove over with a machine gun ready to shoot. And he asked us in English who we were. We couldn't answer him so we asked him if he doesn't speak German, so he said, "Yes," he speaks German. We began to talk to him in German. He stuck out a pair of eyes. He did not know where he was. Yet, we saw that his joy was great, that a camp has been liberated. And so, he started to question us, and he gave us cigarettes and chocolate and other things, which really gladdened his heart.

I ran on farther. "Let me be by myself near a tank. Let me talk to one by myself." So I chanced upon a tank; [the soldier] pointed the machine gun at me. He didn't know who I was. And I went over to him. I told him that I was from Buchenwald. He gave such a shudder. He didn't know what to think about this. And asked me in German whether any Jews were there. I said "Jews? I too am a Jew!" His machine gun fell down from the tank, and he jumped down to me and began to kiss me so that I didn't have the strength to hold out from the kisses that he gave me! And his ears couldn't comprehend the words that I spoke to him! And he began to give me different things. He gave me all kinds of clothes, and he said in a few days he would come there to me.

And it really was so. In a few days he came into the camp driving the tank. And purposely searched me out. And I didn't . . . he has . . . he has treated me . . . I have no words! And after that time I didn't see him anymore because, naturally, he went on. I don't know who he was. I went back to the camp. I wasn't hungry anymore. I already had stuffed myself with chocolate, with other things. There were a lot of sick who alas couldn't walk by themselves, who waited for somebody to bring them something. I had a lot of things. I distributed cigarettes to them. This in our camp was an especially important article. It was very seldom that one came across cigarettes. If one did come across cigarettes, they were [made of] dried leaves from trees.

And then the Americans began to come into the camp. After two days we began to receive dinner. A day before I got up, and I knew that bread could be had from a German who was in the camp. He was a prisoner too. That Gypsy who had pulled me out of the storeroom. I stopped before him and began to look at him so. I asked him, "Do you recognize me?" He said, "No, I do not recognize you." So I said, "You don't know me? Now I am going to settle with you. I am the one whom you took from the storeroom." He became shocked and pale, and he did not know what to answer. He was just in the middle of eating, so he gave me bread. So I said, "No, I don't mean the bread. Now I want to settle with you because you took me out from the storeroom. I begged you like a child a year old, that you should let me go." He says, "What do you want to do to me? Do what you want with me." And so, first of all I was hungry, so I took the bread from him. So I said, "Now I am letting you go, but, in a few days I shall find you." I should have settled with him then and there because I searched for him later. In a few days he was not in the camp anymore. That I could not help.

17 Pinkus R.

Anti-Semitism in depression-era Poland impelled some Jews to leave for healthier homes. Naturally that was always easier for persons of means, and Pinkus R.'s family, owners of a successful textile factory in Lodz, had already purchased a residence in Palestine preparatory to emigration. Hitler intervened.

With more resources than the average Jewish resident of Lodz, some of R.'s family attempted to escape the worst of the occupation by moving to Warsaw, only to find conditions there become as bad as those at home. In the end this divided the family between the two cities. Pinkus's parents, brothers, and two daughters, separated from him in Warsaw, disappeared into the machinery of destruction. Pinkus, his wife, and two sons remained in Lodz until its ghetto was liquidated in August 1944. Although in the interview he took pains to distance himself from the Rumkowski administration, there can be little doubt that it required pull to get and keep the coveted job of food distributor, one of the few ways of getting enough nourishment to stay alive.

In 1944 Pinkus R. was separated from his wife and two young cousins at Auschwitz and never saw them again. He and his teenage sons, however, managed to stay together, and they were healthy enough to be selected for work in Germany. There they were comparatively well treated. Marched into the Sudetenland as the Reich collapsed, they were simply abandoned by their SS guards and, after the fighting ended, recuperated in Prague. Although they contemplated smuggling themselves into Palestine in 1945, health considerations persuaded them otherwise. When interviewed at the ORT school near Paris in September 1946, the forty-three-year old Pinkus R. was understandably impatient that he and his sons had not yet been granted entry to Palestine, indignant that his ownership of property there had not opened all doors. We begin the interview with his story of the family's abortive flight from Lodz as the Germans descended on the city in September 1939.

On the night of the 5th of September we heard that the Germans were coming, and fear immediately brought great panic, so we ran. We did not know where, what, or when. We took along a little money in our pocket. The rest we left, everything unguarded, and we ran. Finally we saw that the Germans had come ahead of us on the road, and we began to reflect that running was totally useless, so we turned around and went back to Lodz. In Lodz we were stopped by the local ethnic Germans and were at once cleaned out. They took away everything we had. Afterward Lodz was incorporated by the Germans into the Reich. And all the calamities began to happen—being dragged away for work and the summons of the Gestapo—so that my father, an elderly man, decided that he would leave Lodz. Where should he go? Seeing that Warsaw was [declared a] protectorate at that time, an exodus [to Warsaw] began. [He] assumed that being a protectorate, it would have some sort of independence; he would have, so to speak, some kind of a chance. We might be able to save ourselves there.

So my father and my mother and a brother and I sent my two children ahead, and we journeyed to Warsaw. [But we found] no chance of living in Warsaw; our money was running out, and in Lodz we still had a little Polish money buried. I and my mother went back to Lodz to take out the money and get back to Warsaw.

What sort of money was it, gold, silver, paper money, Polish money?
We had all sorts of currency buried in the ghetto. We came back before Passover [1940]. There was already a ghetto, with all the trappings. And on April 30th the ghetto was to be closed, and about five days before Passover we tried to get out of the ghetto. People were then still stealing across the *Beth Hahayim* [the cemetery] at night. We did not succeed. We were shot at. I had already sent my two girls to Warsaw. The two boys had remained in Lodz.

Where did you live in Lodz? Was your house where the ghetto was later made?
No, it was not inside the ghetto. [When the ghetto was formed] the Germans thought that the Jews were moving somehow too slowly. They wanted it to go faster, and they simply attacked the streets and the houses and shot at everybody in the neighboring streets. Then we did not wait for the plan anymore—every day a certain street was supposed to go—we just ran by ourselves into the ghetto. We, twenty-odd people, were pushed into a room about four meters by four meters. Some sort of self-government was created in the ghetto, with [its] own currency. We were working for the Germans in all the shops and in every trade. And for that the Germans sent in the most minimal food supplies for us.

The elder of the Jews was Mordechai Chaim Rumkowski. He was known in Lodz; the man was a Jewish community worker. I can say, alas with regret, [he was] also a Zionist; he took part in Zionist Congresses. A man who was child-less, who had done much for orphans. He had collected money and founded an orphanage together with the greatest citizens. At the time the Germans marched in, he was one of the Jewish civic leaders, and because of his patriarchal appearance [the Germans] made him remain. They sent all the rest of the civic leaders away to Dachau where they perished. In this way he took over complete leadership. He alone remained out of the fifty from the [old Jewish] Community Council.

Take some typical incidents which happened to you and your family. Did you build a bunker?
No, because as a rule it did not happen that people in the ghetto built bunkers. Perhaps in the last moments when the time was already very short. They started to take our street among the first, so that we were not able to do it.

You say that people began working for the Germans. What did you do?
I was, accidently, the head of a point for provision supply which served a certain area with provisions which were rationed [and] issued every two weeks. It is altogether unbelievable that when the rations were issued it consisted to 30 grams [a little over an ounce] of turnips for two weeks; bread, 2 kilos [4.4 pounds] for eight days. That was it.

Butter?
None whatever! No fats were given. I was working where the rations were issued, so that I must admit that this stroke of luck made it possible for me to eat something when keeping watch at night in the store. That gave me the chance to survive. And so we went on suffering. Four years we were in the ghetto—no clothing, no heating, and wearing wooden shoes. My children were working very hard. When they got in the ghetto one was thirteen and one was in the fifteenth year. The Germans considered such [children] workers already. This was fortunate. In the beginning it was believed that whoever was willing to work would not be deported, and we already knew the odor of deportation, so that even eight-year-old children were sent to work. I can say that my children, who weighed as much as 60 kilos [132 pounds] lost 15 kilos [33 pounds] each. Before the war I weighed 96 kilos [211 pounds], and then, in the last days of the ghetto, I weighed 62 kilos [136 pounds]. We had virtually become skeletons.

Did you work in the administration during the entire four years?
I worked in the administration of supplies. That helped me so that I was not sent away.

How was the ghetto gradually reduced? Describe to me, let us say, the last six months of the ghetto.
When the Germans saw that the Russians were not far from Warsaw, only about 120 kilometers from Lodz, they began step by step to liquidate the ghetto. And so, first of all those who had sinned at one time were sent out. What do I

mean by "sinned"? If one had once stolen a piece of wood from an old fence [to use for fuel], or if a cart passed on the street and a child of five ran after it and grabbed a raw potato, this constituted one of the worst crimes for which they were in the first line, and these were sent away.

The parents of the child, or what?
The parents together with the whole family were sent away.

Who reported that a child grabbed a potato?
For that, alas, there were Jewish police who also had to cling to life. If, by chance, he [the Jewish policeman] let such a thing pass, kept silent about it, he would be deported. There were men who watched them.

So who made the list for the deportation?
At first the Jewish police made it.
And so, the so-called criminals having been sent away, they sent away single people, people who had come from the provinces and had already been deported previously. Their wives and children had already been taken away. Because insofar as possible we saw to it that whole families should remain. Then, when this was already finished, a decree came out to hand over all the children up to the age of twelve.[1] They would be taken to Germany [where they] would be raised and fed.

Children how small? Six months?
It made no difference how old it was. From a day to twelve years. All these children had to be reported, and all of them had to be handed over to be sent to Germany. Exceptions were made at that time for the [families of] the Jewish police and the so-called elite, those who were then in the service of Rumkowski's kingdom. Eighteen thousand children were sent away from the 5th to the 12th of September 1942. The police went around grabbing people, and the entire ghetto was locked up. Nobody could go out, but they simply went around from house to house, and all the children were taken out. They were assembled at certain points and then sent away in trucks.

Did you see it?
Yes, indeed, not only I, but thousands of people saw it.

Now, where were they sent? Did people know—did anyone find out?
All the time we did not know where they were sent. We did think somehow

1. Acting on orders from the Germans, Rumkowski called for the deportation of 20,000 children under ten, old people over sixty-five, and the sick.

that the children would perhaps be taken to Germany. It went under the pretext that the parents should be able to work, that they not be burdened with raising children. Although it could have been arranged in the ghetto as well, but we wanted to fool ourselves. We had no choice.

Tell me, were there any placards, any announcements to bring the children?
Rumkowski put out placards to come and assemble outside on the square, and we could already feel that the air was somehow not clean; another edict against the Jews was coming. And so there Rumkowski came out, with a broken spirit, it seemed. How much truth there lay in it we did not know, because we already knew that he had sold out to the Germans. It is not believable that he wanted so much for himself [or] that he foresaw that he would have to serve the Germans so much. But then he found that he had to. And so he issued the order for all the children to be handed over. I remember that he gave us to understand that we had to save *ourselves*, that [by handing] over the small children we would be saved. [He said:] "It is to be hoped that this is the last sacrifice." And we were so desperate. We just could not understand how a Jewish mother could give away her child. There were cases where the children were taken and hidden in ovens [or] plastered over [in walls]. A friend of mine took a child and gave it narcotics because he figured that the police would go through the house in two hours, and he put it in a hole in a far corner of the courtyard and strewed a little sand on top so it should not be known. And he saved his child that way. The great majority could not find a way to help themselves. There were cases that mothers went with their children. The Germans did such "favors."

Now, how long were you in the Lodz ghetto, until liberation?
No. Until the 25th of August 1944. From Lodz we were sent away to Auschwitz, myself, my wife, [and] two cousins who were living with us. They were girls. My wife and the girls went separately, and I [went] with the two boys.

What happened in Auschwitz at the station?
We did not know anything. That whole secret had been so well kept that we were still thinking that we were being sent to work. The Germans had persuaded us that fierce battles would rage and all of us might die at Lodz; it would be highly desirable for us to go to Germany to work. We took everything that we still possessed in the way of clothing along with us. And the moment we came near Auschwitz we saw our ruin at once. We saw the huge barracks, the guards, and we saw that we were already lost. The moment we got off in Auschwitz an SS man stood on the spot and at once carried out the selection. First of all men and women [were placed] separately, old ones and young ones separately, those who

appeared sickly and those healthier separately. My wife and the two girls were immediately taken away from me so that I did not see them anymore.

Could a husband discover whether his wife was in a block there or not?
No. Possibly in a few cases, but [in general] one could not find out. I do not know whether they perished in Auschwitz or were taken to the women's block and later on went to Stutthof.[2]

What happened to you in Auschwitz?
I was in Auschwitz twelve days, always together with the two boys. With the help of God, praised be His Name, although we were in separate blocks we still took pains just to keep together. And we were together. Life in Auschwitz is indescribable. The particular group with which we went to an Auto-Union plant in the vicinity of Chemnitz[3] was not tattooed. I went together with my two sons. It was more luck than brains, I must tell you. The children were already somewhat like grown-ups. In Auschwitz people registered who wanted to go to work. We had decided that if something happened that we had to go away, we all should register together in order to be together again. And we succeeded. I registered myself, and naturally there was a doctor, too. We were all checked, and thus we were all sent to the vicinity of Chemnitz.

After that we were in another place. This factory was burned down by the bombing. And we worked there until the 13th of April 1945. I have to say that until the 15th of February conditions were not so bad yet in comparison with Auschwitz and the ghetto. We had comparatively tolerable conditions. We got a loaf of bread [weighing] a kilo and a half [3.3 pounds] for eight persons, and soup every day. We got no clothing except for the one shirt which we had received in Auschwitz. We wore it until liberation.

Who liberated you?
The Americans began approaching, and the factory was in danger. So as not to be surrounded, we started to march out. We were not able to march very far, fifteen [to] thirty kilometers daily, to the vicinity of Marienbad, Karlsbad.[4] We got six potatoes a day, not always cooked. If we stopped for a day, they would be boiled there. If we marched on, they would not be cooked. We were 450 in

2. The concentration camp near Danzig to which large numbers of women prisoners were evacuated in the last phase of the war.

3. A large industrial city in eastern Germany.

4. Marianske Lazne and Karlovy Vary in the Sudetenland of Czechoslovakia, south of Chemnitz.

the factory. Only 8 persons had died in the entire eight months. But when we marched from the 13th of April to the 7th of May, 150 persons died.

How does one know these [exact] numbers?
Because there was a scribe there in the office as long as we were there in the factory. Naturally there had to be entries [in the books] for everything. He kept all the files. We still figured, if we should be liberated, then everybody must be informed: "Your mother died." "Your brother died."

On the road we were just marching, and at night we were given a barn where we could go in to sleep. Where normally 60 or 70 people could go in they put all 450 persons. And during the day we marched again, and people would drop like flies. Without food, just marching.

And what would be done with the people who fell?
There were cases that they were shot. In other cases they would tell us to carry the people. The SS man in our group was not yet the greatest enemy of Israel. The weak who had to be taken in carts—he requisitioned carts there, and they were transported. With horses.

So then he was a kind enough SS man.
According to what we hear about others, one must admit [that he was] a kind one. We talked with some [of the SS men], and they would say, "You should know that you will not suffer too much longer." That meant that the war was coming to an end. Those were the same [men] who also guarded us in the factory. And they would also explain to us that there were Communists among them, but they were a very small percentage.

Then where did you arrive?
We arrived in the vicinity of Marienbad. There we saw that we were already surrounded. Somehow we could feel that the skin was already burning on the SS men, so we sat down and said we were not going any farther. And he [the SS officer] said, "Well, I am setting you free. Go home." And they scattered and left us. Because they themselves already saw that it was all over for them. We went around the villages there and begged. We got something to eat. The Czechs treated us very decently.

And then where did you go when you were liberated? Did you go back to Lodz?
The majority of us went back. I myself did not. We knew that we had property in *Eretz Israel*, and we knew that the family was no more. We considered it purposeless. And we did not want to go and build in Poland anymore. When we arrived in Prague, both of my children fell sick and lay in the hospital three

months. With difficulty I got them out. I got in touch with an unofficial *Aliyah* [an underground Zionist group] to "black myself across" [cross the border illegally] and go on foot to Italy, and from there get to Israel. [But] I saw it was impossible; our strength was not up to it. The children were very run down. They were skin and bones. And seeing that I have a home of my own in Tel Aviv, my children and I figured that we would surely have the right to enter *Eretz Israel*. But in the end we were not.

Who is responsible [for that]? Every month fifteen hundred certificates are available.

I do not know anyone who did go on the fifteen hundred certificates. I only know it is one great cry to heaven that I am sitting here with my children, undernourished, and do not eat meat all week, and not wearing adequate clothing, and not having adequate shoes, and cannot enter *Eretz Israel*. This is a crime which should awaken the conscience of the world!

18 Anna K.

The Jews of eastern Poland were under Soviet rule for the first twenty-one months of the war and hence were spared Nazi persecution until Hitler turned eastward in June 1941. Anna K. never made it clear where in Poland she and her husband lived before the war, although it is probable that it was in or near his parents' hometown of Grodno in the northeast part of the country.[1] Evidently he was in the Polish army, and she was visiting her hometown of Kielce when the Germans attacked in 1939. Shortly after Poland surrendered, she made the 300-kilometer trip from Kielce to Grodno in the Soviet zone; such travel was still possible in the weeks immediately following the capitulation. In Grodno she was reunited with her husband, and there they experienced the second German onslaught in 1941.

Grodno sits on the ethnic border between Poland and Belorussia in an area of mixed languages and cultures. It had been part of Poland from 1919 to 1939 and then of the USSR until 1941, when the Germans annexed it to their province of East Prussia. At the beginning of November 1941 its 25,000 Jews were herded into two ghettos, one for able workers in the synagogue quarter and the other for "nonproductive" Jews in the suburb of Slobodka. Shortly after the birth of their daughter, Anna and her husband managed to slip from Slobodka to the central ghetto and then to escape deportation, but someone denounced them to the Germans as they attempted to reach the partisans in the forest. They were separated, and Anna never saw her husband again. After surviving slave labor at Auschwitz and in Germany, she learned the tragic fate of her only child.

Anna K.'s interview is striking for what it says about Gentile willingness to help Jews in Grodno and its surrounding area. A woman she scarcely knew took in her baby and raised it as her own. Complete strangers gave her and her husband shelter as they fled the city. And yet, various other Gentiles turned them over to the Germans and later identified her baby as Jewish. One could never know. Although Anna probably could have passed as a Pole once she escaped from the Grodno ghetto, and had Gentile friends to boot, ties to her family and her com-

---

1. This interview appears in Boder's *I Did Not Interview the Dead*, under her real name, Anna Kovitzka.

munity brought her back even when she had grounds to fear the worst from the Germans. Once in German hands, she was virtually forced to take on an "Aryan" identity, and actually did so for a while. But this time despair and perhaps even the wish to die compelled her to reassert her Jewishness. The long-term prospects of "passing" successfully were not good, but in Anna's case the will to try was all but absent.

At Auschwitz Anna had the supreme good fortune of being assigned to a block run by a Polish political prisoner, probably arrested for resistance activity, who knew how to please the SS while helping her charges. The woman probably saved Anna's life. While Anna was in Auschwitz the famous Sonderkommando revolt of October 7, 1944, occurred. Her vivid recollection of the rising is mistaken in several respects. Just one SS man was burned alive, and two more were killed in the ensuing struggle, along with 450 prisoners. Nor did any of the inmates escape. What is significant is the iconographic quality of Anna's telling of the event. The very fact that Jews had at last turned on their tormentors took on dimensions in the minds of the victims that can scarcely be imagined today.

Anna K. was thirty-four years old when she was interviewed on the afternoon of September 26, 1946, in the rehabilitated synagogue of Wiesbaden, Germany. Described by Boder as "a woman of fair complexion with naturally light hair," it is understandable that she could, and for a time did, pass as a Gentile, although the idea was not always her own. During the interview she frequently fell into episodes of sobbing that obscured parts of her story. Boder observed: "These paroxysms were obviously nurtured by depressing memory associations, justifiable self-pity before a sympathetic listener, and a sense of 'guilt' at having survived. It might be said that Mrs. K. feels as if her own redemption from the fate which befell her near and dear ones and her concentration camp associates was a betrayal of the bonds of love and solidarity."

We begin as K. speaks of the founding of the Grodno ghettos in 1941.

They arranged two ghettos, one in Slobodka and one in the yard of the synagogue. When we came, the fences were not ready, and it did not make such a terrible impression. But the next day everything was fenced up, and there was an inscription on the gate: "From here one does not return." I was in my ninth month. We used to live like affluent citizens, my father-in-law, my husband, and my sister-in-law. Now we were given a [single] room. And there I was to give birth to my child. One day they opened the ghetto, and every Jew was permitted to go into his home to fetch some things. Then my father-in-law went back to his home, and he saw the destruction of the home for which he had been working for thirty years, and he returned gravely ill. He saw how it was ransacked and ruined.

Who ransacked and ruined it?

We had left the house just as it was, with only the clothes on our body and a few bundles in our hands. Everything else had to be left. And the people, of course, who lived around—what did they care about the Jews? They just waited for such a moment. They went inside. The things of value the Gestapo themselves hauled away. My father-in-law had been working hard all his life, and when he saw what had become of his home, he took badly sick and remained sick up until the end.

The 26th of November I gave birth to my child, a little girl, in my room in the ghetto because there was not yet a Jewish hospital. The doctor and everybody tried to comfort me. At the end of the summer [1942], people [Jews] began to arrive from everywhere, from Brest-Litovsk, from Lvov. . . . On a day when my husband was working, we had hope to survive. But when people came to the gates of the ghetto and said, "No more work required," that was a dark day. We knew it was coming. November 1, 1942, the ghetto was surrounded. We knew what that meant. And nearby were Russians, Poles. Not all, but many were waiting for what they could "inherit" from the Jews. Possibly they had waited so that in case the Germans themselves would not put an end to us, they could step in.

Step in for what?

So they could consummate the terrible deed. [But the Germans] had their mission. Herr Ehrlich, the Gestapo chief, said to the Jewish Council, "Mass murder? Oh, no, that is out of the question. So is deportation! It [the Grodno ghetto] will be converted into a work camp. No more loafing. And believe me, my word of honor." His word of honor! In two weeks it [the deportations] started.

[Thinking that the other ghetto would be less likely to be liquidated, K. and her family sneaked inside. But it, too, was subjected to deportations.]

Within a week they [the Germans] started [to liquidate] the ghetto in the yard of the synagogue. The most horrible thing was that the Jewish police—in the beginning we were not told about the horrible role they would have to play—came and led us to the slaughter. Every few nights we would sit up, my husband and I, all dressed—the child was asleep—and expected the police to come for us. Every night we said a Vida [prayer of those who expect to die] of our own composition, and forgave each other, but they did not come. My husband worked as a carpenter then; he is a lumber sorter by trade, and this kept us there.

Once my husband said, "I can't make peace with them. Our child must be saved even if the two of us die. We have nobody anymore. You look like a Christian.

Get out with the child. Put it at the door of a Christian orphanage. I don't want her to die." It snowed that night. It was twenty-six degrees below zero [−13°F]. Sixteen Jews fell at the gate in the first attempt to escape. I went over the wires in the second attempt. My husband set up a chair for me, raised one wire, and I crawled through.

Weren't those electric wires?

No, they had no electric wires then. He handed me the child. I removed the yellow patch [star] and went down the street. It was eight o'clock. Curfew was at nine o'clock. I did not know where to go. All at once I remembered a Christian woman whom I happened to know, whom I had possibly seen only twice before, and I went to her and said, "This is all that I have got. Take the child and carry it to an orphanage. Say you found her in the street. I am returning to my husband, and we shall perish together."

She started to wring her hands. The Poles were threatened with death for such things. And she said, "I am afraid. Put her in the street. I will come out of the house with a neighbor woman. We shall come out as if by accident. I will pick up the child and take her to the orphanage tomorrow, but you go away immediately." I went with her down to the door and stood there across the street, hidden in the gate, and I saw how my child was lying on the snow. And I could not pick her up! The child that I had brought into the world! [Here she broke into sobs.]

In a few minutes she [the Christian woman] came out of the house and picked up the child. I ran away through the streets of Grodno, and I didn't think of the curfew—that I might be caught—and I didn't know how to get back into the ghetto as it was such a late hour. There was another Christian woman in the city with whom I had once worked during the time of the Soviets. I stepped into her house, and a girl friend of mine was hiding there. I said, "Panuvka, I don't have my child anymore. How light my hands feel!" Then she said, "Twenty-six hours you suffered to bring her into the world, and now you will suffer as long as you live."

I didn't ask her for much—just to keep me overnight. She couldn't help me for much longer, because on Sunday no one could show himself in the city. The Germans were grabbing the people and dragging them to work in Germany. I wanted to return to the ghetto. Ten thousand Jews were deported that day. The ghetto was surrounded. One couldn't get in or out. I ran into a Christian, a working man. I told him, "I am a Jewess—I can't get into the ghetto." And he said, "Get out of the city. You do not look Jewish. Go wherever you can, but don't remain here. You see it's *hot* here!"

And so I departed alone, without papers, into the woods. I did not know the roads. Through the woods, into a Russian village. I entered. "Give me some water." If one is alive, one has to drink water. And sometimes one has to eat. Everybody gave me something. I did not look Jewish, but they knew—what else could be driving me in the snow through the woods? Everyone kept me for one night.

The Christians?
The Christians—I can't complain. Everybody gave me warm water to wash myself. They gave me food, so that I should have strength to wander farther. And there was a priest, a Catholic. He hid me for eight days to regain my strength. But I felt compelled to go back to Grodno to find out what was going on. The priest encountered some Jews that were going to work. So he asked them, "Do you know whether Jack K. is there?" They said, "He is there. He has remained alive." Three thousand Jews were still in Grodno.

So the priest said, "Tell K. that his wife is alive, that she does not want to remain among us. She wants to go back in a few days." The next week the priest took me out part of the way in a cart. He was afraid to go farther. And I went alone toward Grodno—

[K. returned to the ghetto with the help of other Poles. She and her husband were almost immediately swept up in the next deportation.]

At two o'clock in the morning we were driven out to the train. My husband said, "No, you are not going to die. Should you perish because you returned to me?" And I said, "I am tired. Maybe I shall rest in the grave." But he did not want to understand, and just one street away from the train he pushed me into a gateway, in spite of the guards, because it was still dark. We remained standing in the gateway until morning. We both took off our patches [stars].

What to do now? Where to go? A city where everybody knew my husband. Again I went to the suburb to an acquaintance, a Christian woman. We washed and got ready to start out at night. We rested up, then wandered on. No arms, no money, nothing. If only we could reach the partisans—at least sell our lives dearly! But where are the partisans? They told us one hundred fifty kilometers away, and one had to go in the direction of Szczuczyn.[2]

One night in Niemce we went into a little house. There lived a widow, a Christian—I don't know her name—with her son. It was dangerous for them, but they took us in and gave us a place to sleep and watched all night in case the Germans might come. She had a son whom they wanted to drag away to work. And in the morning they gave my husband shaving things, and they gave me plenty of food. At night we slept in an open shack, and in the morning we marched on. Not all Russians were that way. Another, after giving us food, reported us, and we were taken to the Gestapo. [Again she breaks down.]

2. A town in a wooded area between Grodno and Bialystok.

In the Gestapo [offices] — I don't know what happened there. When I saw my husband receiving the first blow, something tore apart in me. "My wife is Polish — you are making a mistake. She wants to die along with me. But she is not a Jewess." And then he [the German officer] asked me, "Are you a Jewess?"

"Yes, I am Jewish."

"That is nonsense, you do not look Jewish."

"Still, I am Jewish."

But my husband continued repeating that I was a Christian until they were taken by doubts. There was a Polish policeman present and White Russians in dark blue uniforms. "Oh, so you are a Jew lover?" And I replied, "I am Jewish, I am not ashamed." The whole night they kept us locked up, calling us out separately, then both of us together. My husband whispered to me, "I plead with you, go try to live. Go back to Grodno. You will be a mother to the child. Maybe you will tell her someday that she had a father." And I yielded, and I went out to live. Then before they led me away, the Gestapo man said, "I give you my word, you will live, and your husband will live." Could one believe them? Still it was a ray of hope. [Prolonged weeping.]

[K. was then sent to a work camp for Gentiles and for a time posed as a non-Jew. When she could no longer continue the ruse, she confessed that she was Jewish, and this time she was believed. The Germans sent her to Auschwitz.]

In Auschwitz I was a complete so-called Moslem, a kind of person who wouldn't eat. There was food, but I could not eat. I was sick. I was sick at my mouth — I don't know what they called that sickness. A kind of eruption, then my tongue became completely hard. My legs were covered with boils. Then my illness from before — gallstones — returned. In Auschwitz not to appear for roll call meant death, and still the supervisors of the barracks had pity on me and let me remain on the cot up to the last moment when the SS men had come for roll call. Then they would drag me off the cot and lead me out.

In Auschwitz I met a girl friend from Kielce, and she told me that the oldest daughter of my brother was alive as [was] the wife of my youngest brother. Both were in a work camp. Then I was taken by hope that I would see them. And that gave me some courage. I decided to live. One day a distant cousin of mine appeared in my block, Nelly K., a seventeen-year-old girl. Her face was that of my little girl. And I was overcome with hope that I should return. Maybe she was alive. And I started to fight again, to struggle for life in Auschwitz. I became a . . . I was cleaning the block, a block that housed 1,300 people. I cleaned it, I scrubbed it, and for that I would get an extra helping of soup, and at times a little piece of bread that the block senior would leave uneaten. I dressed [better]. There was enough to wear in Auschwitz. There was the clothing of the dead. They were burning people every day. The whole night the ovens would flame, and the skies red, dark red, just like . . .

One night I was standing in front of the block. A Christian block senior stood nearby. That night they were burning [people] from the Gypsy camp. And I was standing there, and I mumbled to myself, "Dante was just a dog. They [the Germans] know it much better." The Christian woman heard it and said to me [imitating a voice of extreme surprise], "You know about Dante? How do you come to know anything about Dante?" She thought that I always must have looked like [I did] in Auschwitz. And from that night we became friends.

She was a block senior, and she had say over life and death, but she was a human being. Only afterward did I realize [that]. She would beat us, and in spite of all that she was fighting for the life of every prisoner. For the Christians she did not have to fight. Christians normally did not go to the ovens, only those who had died. But for the Jews she had to fight. Just two years ago on Rosh Hashana there was to be a selection, so she took all the weak and the sick, including myself, and sent them away outside the camp for work [in an] external detail so they should not be present for the selection. However, there was no selection after all at that time. But I became convinced that she was really human, that if she mistreated and beat us, it was only because she herself wanted to survive and wanted us to survive. She wanted to earn the confidence of the SS men. She was a political prisoner, a very intelligent woman from Warsaw, a nobleman's daughter. I stayed on in the camp for part of a year. I was gravely ill with gallstones, so she herself cooked me some food that I could stand, and she shielded me and reported that I was working for her and I did not have to go [outside] to work.

Once [this] Christian block senior reproached me: "Why are they going to their death with such indifference? Why don't they fight? Why don't they kill somebody?" So I replied, "How can you say that? You haven't been in a ghetto. You have not seen how Jews went away in transports with congealed nerves. A human being can cry himself dry. A human being clings to life, and up to the last moment there is a ray of hope. And they are defenseless. They have no arms. Maybe you just want to soothe your conscience talking that way."

And the same day a miracle happened. The Jews seized the oven. They first threw in some forty SS men; 150 [Jews] lost their lives, and 150 more ran away into the woods to the partisans.

Do you really know that for sure?

I was then assigned to outside work, and I saw it myself, just as I shall see the delivery of all the Jews. [I] was a few kilometers from our camp, Birkenau. [We] were about fifty people guarded by SS men, and then I just heard the explosion, and when I came out I saw the oven in flames. And then we heard shooting.

The result was that the SS men were caught unaware, and they [the Jews] threw them into the burning pits. And afterward they blasted the oven. And I thought, maybe we shall still survive. An answer had come to what she [the block senior] had said about the Jews. If others had said it, I wouldn't care. But if such a Christian, who was so valuable to us and respected, should think that way—*that* we cared about. Why should she say the Jews have no courage? That hurt. And then this happened.

In October they began to assemble transports from Auschwitz. I had no hope of getting away with a transport because I looked very sick, but I dressed and painted my face for each roll call so they would not see how terribly pale I was.

Where did you get it [the cosmetics]?

Well, transports of Jews would come from all over the world, and they did not know what their fate would be. So every woman still had these things. And they would be taken and thrown on the dumps, and those [prisoners] who had access to the dumps would collect it and give it to everyone who looked bad to help them cover up. And so I was heavily painted.

One day they came to our block and told us that we were going to be led to a transport block. And I, too, was selected during roll call. We were sent to block thirty-one, the transit block [and] remained for eight days. Then there was a selection, and we were sent to the shower bath [to] bathe. Afterward everyone was looked over. For me that was very dangerous, so a woman, a block orderly, told me, "Don't go in there. Simply sneak out through the other side and stand up with those on the right side, because externally you look well enough."

And so I mingled in with 300 other women, and I went away with a transport to Lippstadt.[3] In Lippstadt there was work. In Auschwitz there was *no* work. They manufactured ammunition in Lippstadt, and there the strength to live returned to me. Such work! I had to stamp cartridges for machine guns with which the Germans would shoot the Americans who came to liberate us! And because I looked *so* decrepit, they thought that I was a fool! In a few days I learned the mechanism of my machine and started to work very ardently. The assigned quota was twelve thousand, but I would produce fifteen thousand pieces. But fifteen thousand smaller [or] larger ones, never the caliber that was required. When they discovered it, there were eighty thousand rejected pieces.

My foreman came over to me and said, "If you do it once more, I shall chop off your hand." So I said, "You can report that I am doing sabotage, then they will just do me in." [He replied], "Oh, for that you are much too dumb!" I don't know, maybe he had noticed what I was doing, but it may have been too late,

3. A manufacturing town in Westphalia, between Dortmund and Paderborn.

and he already was responsible along with me. I can't be so naive as to assume that the Germans wanted to cooperate with me against Hitler. Such [Germans] do not exist. Their faith held to the last moment.

On the faces of the Germans I read [defeat] just like in a newspaper. They were very sad the last days. It was already March 1945. They still drove us to work, and they would beat us at every air-raid alarm. But, thank God, the air raids would last for twenty-four hours. They would run into the air-raid shelter, and we would run right out into the yard and laugh, and the SS men would say to us, "Aren't you afraid? Do you think that your friends will spare you?" [I told them], "*You* are afraid! Why aren't you in the battlefield? All you are fighting with is 800 defenseless and weak women. That is the kind of heroes you are!" The girls thought that I was insane again, like I had been at first in Auschwitz. But it was all the same to me. To die in such a fashion might have been well worth while.

The 27th of March we were driven out of Lippstadt at night. We were to go to Bergen-Belsen. They didn't know it, but they couldn't take us to Bergen-Belsen anymore. They drove us at night and during the day locked us up in warehouses. They had everything ready to finish us off, but there was no more time.

What do you mean, finish you off?

They had orders not to release us alive. On the third day at dawn we were standing in a little lane, deep in mud, and the top [officer] was frothing at the mouth. We heard the rumbling American tanks, and we were led into the woods. I don't know how they happened not to hit us. He said—he still yelled even then—"You band of Jew-pigs!" And he left us alone with all the SS men, and he himself ran away. So I said to one of the girls, "You know, I don't know whether or not we are going to survive, but he won't make it." She said, "I have half a loaf of bread that is yours if it happens the way you say." And I still thought that I would have a chance to eat that bread.

The American fired three times, and then a silence came over us. An airplane came down at low altitude, and the Germans raised a white flag. And here we were, almost crazy. We didn't have a strip of something white. Somebody had a bandage around a wounded leg, and that bandage was raised at an approaching American tank, and the women prostrated themselves on the ground, kissing the wheels. The Americans thought we were from a lunatic asylum. They looked at us. And how we looked! All in tatters! And we were all speechless. And then [an American soldier] understood, and two tears rolled down his face. And until the others arrived, he wept with us. Not a Jew—a Christian!

And then the tanks began to arrive. It was Passover, the last day, and matzoth fell from the tanks. And chocolate! And cigarettes! And they would jump off the tanks, and they were kissing us. Us dirty and lousy ones! "Don't cry," they would say, but we kept on weeping. The Ninth Army had not seen any Jews in Germany, and we thought that we were the only Jewish survivors, and we did not want to live. But they consoled us. They were telling us that there were many other armies that had reached other camps.

We were all dead sick. I was half swollen. Immediately the American army led us into homes. They burned everything we had on, although we wanted to save the clothing. But it was all infected, and we were afraid to keep it. We could take things, good things, from the Germans now. They gave it to us themselves. They were afraid now. We dressed! We washed ourselves! Soap, warm water, a clean towel, clean underwear. Oh! The Americans themselves were crazy with joy. That army hadn't seen liberated people before. We were the first ones, and they were rejoicing with us like little children. And in the evening one American put a hat on his head, a German hat, a woman's hat, and another one played some kind of instrument, and he danced with a little girl from our camp. I will never forget it.

[Boder inquired about the fate of Anna's relatives.]

I have been in Wiesbaden a year and I have searched. I don't have my child. Last year, about the end of the year, I went to Poland with the hope of finding my child. I arrived in Lodz, and the wife of a doctor there told me the child was not alive, that the Christian woman had been thrown in jail because she had been reported. An investigation [had been] made, and it was found out that she had picked up the child on the street. They established then that she was a Jewish child and they . . .

How could the Germans establish that the girl was Jewish?
I don't know how they established it. Possibly somebody reported to them, because the child looked very much like my husband. The K.s were a well-known family, and they all resembled each other very much. It was also suspicious because the woman was childless, and she had not given the child to an orphanage.

Why didn't she place your child in an orphanage?
Because she loved the child, she kept the child like her own. And she left a present for me—a few pictures. They buried the child three weeks before the Red Army marched in. When the Red Army arrived, the woman interfered, requesting a permit to bury the child. It was said that I apparently was not alive anymore, but they wanted to remove the child from the Christian cemetery. The Jewish cemetery was entirely desecrated.

Then there was a rumor that my husband was alive. Somebody wrote from Kovno, but I don't know where he is, and a year has passed. I have been unable to find him. Maybe he went to Russia, but so far there is nothing from him. Now I am working in Pfalzheim, in a kindergarten. There are twenty little Jewish children, and I play with them, and then I forget about all *that*. Again I have Jewish children around me.

But after work, to come to my room alone. . . . Today is a holiday. Where are all mine, who used to celebrate the holidays with me? Thank God! There are Jews staying with me on this holiday. There was never a holiday in Auschwitz. But my own people are no more. I am alone.

Roma T.

Roma T. lost both her husband and her legs in the Holocaust. A Polish Jew married to a Jewish physician in Kielce, she accompanied him as a nurse's aid when he was called up by the Polish army at the time of the German invasion. They ended up at Lvov in the Soviet zone of occupation and encountered the Germans for the first time when Lvov fell in June 1941. There they lived through the devastating pogroms carried out by local anti-Semites, both Polish and Ukrainian, who believed a Nazi story that bodies found at the city's NKVD (the Soviet secret police) jail were the victims of "Jewish Bolsheviks." Evidently both she and her husband managed to escape from a forced labor camp at Lvov, but Roma's husband fades from her story until their final separation in 1943, when she was sent to Majdanek. Quite possibly the painful memory of his loss explains her self-centered narrative; later she affirms that until 1943 they were always together.

Polish friends warned Roma T. that the Germans were sending the Jews to crematoria, prompting her to seek the anonymity of Warsaw, passing as an "Aryan" with forged papers. Like so many Jews in her situation, she was betrayed by hostile Poles and sent into the ghetto, where she worked gathering Jewish belongings for delivery to the Germans. At this point in her story Boder asked her to skip ahead to her time in the camps. He was pressed for time and had heard about the Warsaw ghetto from other survivors.

Roma T. was deported to Majdanek from Warsaw shortly before the ghetto rose in revolt. She has some instructive things to say about women's physiological responses to overwork and undernourishment and about the disposal of bodies at Majdanek. Without a doubt her most moving anecdote is of the Majdanek women's standing tribute to a comrade hanged by the Germans, an act of courage and defiance in the face of SS guards. At some point late in 1943 Roma was sent to work in munitions factories in western Poland and then, as the Russians drew near, to the infamous women's concentration camp Ravensbrück, north of Berlin. Her feet became frozen just prior to the final evacuation to Bavaria at the end of the Third Reich, and her American liberators had to amputate both legs below the knee.

The German Museum in Munich, where Roma T. gave her interview, was then the site of a UNRRA college where she was studying pharmacy and waiting for permission to enter the United States. Cheerful and feisty, the thirty-year-old refugee had mastered new artificial limbs. We join her narrative in late 1942 when she was denounced by Poles and forced into the Warsaw ghetto.

The Warsaw ghetto was already very small then. According to statistics it had only 50,000 Jews. But some were still hiding, and there probably were more. Then there was the so-called Appraisal Office that occupied itself with sorting out all the things that remained after the Jews [left]. Jews were compelled to work there; it so happened that I worked in this office.

And what were they doing there?
Sorting bed linen and clothes from the ghetto proper. There was a big storehouse of all the things that remained behind. There I went through the second deportation. During the actual deportation, troops were taken from us "for work." [1] That means I entered a room where an old woman was lying on a bed. She held a card in her hand; she apparently [had] wanted to show that she was working somewhere. And with this card in her hand and her mouth open she was shot. The cry of death was still staring out from her face, and her last cry [had come] from the open mouth—one should not forget it.

Then we came, we saw the most varied scenes, which are completely indescribable, because this could go on for hours. The Jewish police had gathered the bodies together. The streets were full of blood [and] bodies because they were shooting during the march. All the columns were led to the square, [the transfer terminal where there] was a siding that led to the railroad. And from there all transports were sent to Treblinka.

Then we had the first attempts at resistance in the Warsaw ghetto. There were cases of shootings, but not yet coordinated. The organizations worked, but the work was not yet coordinated, and the help from outside was very small. Second, we knew only one thing, that the struggle was lost. We were a last platoon that must die. At that time they took the children [from] the children's home. The SS entered and gave the children chocolate, so that the children [would] be willing to go. The management of the home went with them. There were even attempts to demand the release of a few [managers]. But they [the Germans] would not accept the demand.

Many, however, still remained. We were still needed for work. Not everything was yet in order. And so we continued working for a couple of months. In March came the last deportation. That was the day of Passover. Before Passover we were

1. Presumably she means that she and some of her coworkers were forced to take furnishings from the homes of Jews being deported.

given a large food allotment so that we should be more calm. At night, at two o'clock, the signals were passed: "Yes, another deportation is coming." The ghetto was surrounded with various collaborators of the German SS. The deportation started.

And the collaborators, who were they?
Ukrainians, Lithuanians.

[At this point Boder asked T. to skip over the story of her deportation and pick up again with her experiences at Majdanek.]

The first transports went to Treblinka. The last—I was in the last—went to Majdanek.

And where was your husband?
Always with me; [we went] to Majdanek together. First we were taken to the Lashkevich airfield near Lublin. There the men were taken in one direction and we in another. It was then that I lost my husband.

Did you ever hear from him?
No. Later I received word that he was sent to Trawniki, and Trawniki was annihilated so that not a single witness remained.
Then the next day we were taken to Majdanek. We were led two kilometers under SS guard; for every five women, four SS were marching along. Of course we did not know where we were going. Straight into the ovens, we thought.

How come? Did you already know that such things were happening?
Yes, we knew that it happened because many had already escaped from Treblinka.
So then we arrived there, first to the bathing installation. Then in the bathing installation they proceeded with a selection. An SS man came—women also, men with dogs—we were completely naked, and they simply looked us over, like animals. Looked into our teeth, tested our muscles with their hands. And the dogs barked, and then some of the older women and the sick were pushed to one side. These did not come out of the bathhouse anymore. Afterward we were bathed, and we were . . .

In the same bathhouse?
Yes. But the bathhouse was divided into two parts. This was the old crematorium. The new one that we ourselves constructed was not yet ready.
We had our turn in the bath; then we were given other clothes. Everything was

taken away. In addition we were told that we should conceal nothing, because we would be examined gynecologically.

Men did that?

Yes. Some women, out of excitement, standing for the first time stark naked in front of men, became hysterical. They cried terribly. But among us were those who said: "If they are not ashamed, why should we be ashamed?"

Did they cut off your hair?

No. We were given other clothes, rags of course, and sent off to sector five. That is [next to] the renowned extermination field.

In what year was that?

March 1943. In this extermination camp, the first days everything was almost excellent. We were told everything would be all right. We were told propaganda that we were going, not into the ovens, but to work. They even brought in women with children. There were two barracks for the women and children, which represented the so-called quarantine. Then we were naturally assigned boards [to sleep on]. Then it began. They had received orders to beat more, because too few of us were dying. Then very many died of diarrhea. Why? The Jewesses were not permitted to go to the hospital. For the Jewesses it was either healthy or dead. No hospital, no help for the sick. There were also Polish women, political prisoners from Warsaw. They brought us medicines, which were simply stolen from the hospital. Later there started to be a selection every week.

[There was a break in the wire. When the interview resumed T. was apparently responding to a question about menstruation in the camp.]

Right after we arrived in the camp we all stopped menstruating. The German physicians explained it was due to excitement and also due to absence of men.[2] We were unable to detect whether there was something in the food or not. Of course we were too exhausted to be able to notice what was going on. At any rate, up to 90 percent stopped menstruating.

And how long did it last?

For some it was forever, for some, for quite a few it returned nine or ten months after liberation.

Each week began with a selection. We spent sixteen hours in the open air. We were not permitted to enter the barracks during the day. That means even if

2. Boder noted that this was one of many legends in the camps and the DP centers.

it rained or anything we had to stay outside. We could not enter for fully eighteen hours.

What kind of work were you doing?

No—I must tell you about the climate. It was windy, and then again sun. And it burned very hot so that the legs would swell, and at that time during selection he [the SS doctor] looked only at our legs [to see] whether they were swollen or not. So that many completely healthy and strong women were compelled to go into the oven solely because their feet were swollen. And then exactly every week, a whole transport went into the oven. The SS man stood there eating candy bonbons. And, with the bonbon in his mouth, he pointed, this one to the right, and this one to the left. We already knew what that meant.

The crematoria were not yet completed. For that reason they gassed them in the bathhouse, and then they laid the bodies out in the field. There was a big ditch in the field, and there they were burned. Every week right after the selection we observed a large square fire, and then we sensed the smoke of burned flesh. And then a few days later we would go to that place as a working crew and carried the ashes into the fields. The fields of Majdanek are now fruitful from the ashes of the burned.

These selections were insufficient. They had to present us with another spectacle, and that was a hanging. It was supposedly as punishment for escape; allegedly some had attempted to escape. That was also not true, because it was impossible to imagine that such a thing could be attempted there.[3] In May a woman was brought in. She must have. . . . All at once we noticed something standing in the middle of the field. We really did not know what it meant. They had erected a gallows. We all had to stand for roll call, forming a square, facing the gallows, and then the woman was compelled to fetch the chair herself. She stood upon the chair, and then the SS man asked what her last wish was. I stood very near then. She said she had no wish to make of the Germans. So he asked her whether she regretted her deed. She said she was not attempting to escape, because that was absurd. But if she only had a chance, she would have done it. She regretted nothing at all, because life at any rate had no worth, and she died readily. But she probably was too weak to slap him in the face. She died calmly without a single outcry. That woman was twenty-three years old. Then we had to stand as punishment and look at the dead woman for three hours. When the roll call was over we all remained standing without having planned it. We all remained standing for several minutes. The SS even thought [giggling] that we had attempted a revolt. We only remained standing to honor the dead woman. Every last one of us. There

3. Actually there were a number of successful escapes from Majdanek, although mostly by non-Jews.

were Russian women, Polish women, and Jewesses. And all remained standing as if dead after the end of the roll call.

Did she suffer much?

No. He [the SS man] only swung the noose around her neck and pushed the chair away with his foot. She died with open eyes. I stood directly in front of her at a distance of about ten meters. Her hands were stretched downward and folded, looking downward and perfectly calm as if she slept. There were 20,000 women at that time . . .

[Boder wanted to know how she could be sure of that figure, and T. became irritated.]

We carried numbers! Every day each block was counted. I know exactly!

Did you not have a clergyman, a rabbi there to give the woman the last rites?

Oh God, the SS did not recognize any clergy. They had torn all the medallions and all such objects from the Polish women; they said, "Here one needs no God anymore. God won't help you anyway!"

The quarantine is interesting, a chapter by itself. There were women with children there. There were no multilevel plank beds, because the children could not climb up. All children were lying on the floor. We were not permitted there, but we wanted to see what that really was. So at times we would enter with a cleaning detail to sprinkle chlorine around. The children were lying on the floor, and it was full of excrement, because the children could not step out at night. And a child does not look out. In hell one does not see such sights as one has seen there. Dirty, hungry children, like animals. And then one fine morning, all the children were taken out with their mothers in a vehicle, taken to the crematorium, and that was all.

Then they brought Greek Jewesses into the quarantine, 200 women from Salonika. These were brought from Auschwitz. We could hardly understand each other because they spoke only Greek. Some of them understood Hebrew, and with these one could communicate a bit. After a month these, too, disappeared from the camp, killed at Majdanek. The quarantine had come to an end. Then they brought in Russian women from Smolensk.

Russian Christian women?

Yes. This was only a part [of those] who had come out of the battle of Smolensk alive. They, too, went "to the smelter." Later the strongest from among the 20,000 women were sent away in several transports. I was in the first transport, which was sent to a factory. This selection was also terrible. We were looked at like horses, the muscles tested, the teeth, all that inspected.

Did they make a gynecological examination in search of coins, money, or the like?
Yes, for money. A few of the women were picked out at that time and examined [by] a German physician in uniform.

And then I was off to a labor camp, to Skarzysko, a camp for Jews only who worked in an ammunition factory. The guards of the camp were SS and Ukrainians, but as workshop police we had Ukrainians, and there were German foremen, not SS. That was characteristic of the German psyche, that all of this was perpetrated not just by the SS but German foremen [civilians] as well. There was a German foreman by the name of Krause, the most terrible in the factory. When Krause would go by, even the machinery would run differently. Sometimes he would get drunk, pick a few women and rape them, and later they were shot so that there be no "race pollution." There was a well known SS [officer who] did the same thing. And one more interesting thing: the so-called yellow labor at [which] the factory people perished in a few months. When they were already badly sick, they were led into the woods and exterminated.

In general, to what extent did women suffer from attempts of rape or other advances by the guards?
Officially it was prohibited. But it only appeared that way. For instance the most beautiful girls disappeared from Majdanek.

[T. did not appear eager to continue with the subject. After a pause Boder encouraged her to return to her own story.]

From Skarzysko we were taken to Czestochowa, also a munitions factory [where] there was a repetition of the beatings at work. The provisions were such that several died from hunger. The people from Majdanek suffered most. Of the 1,200 women who came from Majdanek, very few remained. Then we were transported from Czestochowa to Germany when the Russians approached. I was in the first transport. The others remained behind because they [the Germans] were unable to drive them out.

I went to Ravensbrück. The conditions were terrible. Four persons on one plank bed. Lice, and the food, terrible. My work was chopping wood. My feet became frozen doing this. The SS woman saw that I was walking without stockings. And when I once reported to her that I was unable to work in the woods, I was given twenty-five blows on my bare back [by] the same SS woman. I still have a very large scar from it.

What were you beaten with?

With a horse whip. By that time I was already sick, but I continued to go to work in the woods for several months. When the Americans approached, we were sent from Ravensbrück in the direction of Dachau in locked box cars. For eight days we were given nothing. Not even water.

Now tell me, how does one live eight days without water?

[With hostile irony:] That is interesting. Of course *you* are unable to imagine how much a human being can stand. But *we* know. *Eight days without water!* At the end, near Bayreuth, many were already dead from hunger and of course from exhaustion. We decided to knock. Let them shoot! And we knocked so that they were afraid we would break up, smash up the whole boxcar. They threatened, "We are going to shoot." And we said, "Shoot!," so then they [the SS] brought us [something] from the Red Cross.

And then we continued traveling. We arrived in Burgau, a branch of Dachau. It was still very cold; [we were] in white overalls, without underwear. No stockings. And when we arrived, we looked so terrible that when the foremen of the Messerschmidt factory arrived to look us over and to take some of us for work, they openly stated: "That is an outrage!" There were to be 500 persons in Burgau, but they sent in another transport so there were a thousand women. And spotted fever [typhus] started. Very many women died. The Hungarian Jewesses suffered most, from spotted fever and from diarrhea. The lice were so widespread that one could not stand it. Then I came down with spotted fever, and my legs [gave out]. I was unable to get up anymore. From Burgau we were sent to Kirkheim.

And how did they send you?

I was carried. The prisoners carried me. I was completely sick, my legs were already black, so I was sent to the camp infirmary—Camp Four near Landsberg, the famous camp infirmary in which thousands died from spotted fever. There it [her legs?] started to fester, and they could not help me anymore. The physicians came, of course. They told me nothing, but I saw it was the end. Then evacuation from the camp. Whoever could still walk was chased away. I, of course, could not get up anymore. The SS came and brought a horse cart. I told him then, "Shoot me!" He said, "No, child, now you will live; it is *I* who will be hanged." He already knew that the Americans were approaching. It is interesting about the SS. If somebody came forward and pleaded to die, you had to live. But if you wished to live, then you had to die.

Then I was taken to another camp, Camp One, [where] I was liberated by the Americans. The last day before liberation the SS had run away, and we remained. The front passed through our camp. The Germans were on one side, the Americans on the other, and they were shooting at each other. Those who could get out got out. I had to lie there. Then the SS barracks which stood nearby happened to catch on fire, and I thought then that the barracks was set on fire by us. Everybody who could still drag his legs ran out. I did not know what to do, because I did not want to burn to death. I threw off all the blankets, threw myself down from the plank bed, and slid out. It had just rained. I did not have a good bandage, but only a paper dressing, and the dirt and all that got in and everything came to an end and went kaput [she lost consciousness].

Two days after liberation the Americans took me to a German hospital, and the physicians said I would live only ten days. But I told them that I would stand ten operations. And I did stand it. I went through three operations, three amputations. I weighed 32 kilos [70 pounds]. After liberation very many still died. From diarrhea. Because they started eating. It was terrible. People saw food for the first time.

[At the end of the interview Boder asked Roma if she wanted to convey any message to American students.]

I want to say that we have learned a lot. Still we are not pessimists. We have come to learn that there is only one reality, the reality of *evil*. But in spite of that we are not pessimists. We have also learned that the potentiality of the human soul is very great. One can stand a great deal. [Laughing]: And that is told by a person who runs around on false limbs.

20 Rabbi Solomon H.

Jews could sometimes run away from the Germans and live in the forests of eastern Europe, but their chances of survival were slim. Rabbi H., the spiritual leader of 1,400 Jews in the Polish town of Potok, led a portion of his flock into the woods. Less than a year later nearly all of them were dead.

Potok is in Galicia, the easternmost reaches of prewar Poland that fell to the Germans only in June 1941. The thirty-two-year-old Rabbi H. at first attempted to placate the Nazis when they looted his people and removed them to the ghetto in nearby Buczacz. Later he encouraged them to hide from deportations that occurred in October and November 1942 and from the massacres at Fedor Hill in February and March 1943. His story shows once again that the Germans unhesitatingly resorted to mass shootings once the Jews learned about the death camps and began to resist deportations. It also suggests that by then the Germans were treating the existence of death camps as an open secret, in Buczacz at least. On the other hand, the rabbi's assertion that he personally witnessed the Fedor Hill massacres should, perhaps, not be taken literally. This was a man who was both determined to convince a foreign observer of Nazi atrocities and unused to having his words questioned. That the mass shootings did occur, of course, is not disputed.

Discovered in their hiding place in Buczacz while trying to aid a family of homeless Jews, Rabbi H. and his elder son slipped away from a large group of prisoners and made it to the forest with several hundred Jews. There they established a "family camp" of men, women, and children of all ages organized for survival rather than partisan action against the Germans. But how could they survive without reliable sources of food and shelter, in constant danger of being discovered by unfriendly peasants, and with only minimal aid from Soviet partisans operating far from their front lines? The rabbi provides a profoundly depressing sketch of the destruction of the camp during the last months of 1943. He and a handful of fellow fugitives lived to experience liberation by the Red Army in March 1944 by bribing a peasant to hide them under his barn. In Warsaw following its liberation, Rabbi H. personally experienced the anti-Semitic climate that made a revival of Jewish Orthodoxy in the Polish capital all but impossible.

Boder interviewed the rabbi at the once grand but then run-down chateau at Henonville near Paris, home of an orthodox kibbutz run jointly by the ORT and the Agudah. Note near the end the rabbi's expression of Orthodox Jewry's changed view of Zionism in the wake of the Holocaust. We begin the interview with the German entry into Potok in 1941.

The Germans immediately organized a kind of a Jewish Council. They took a few people and demanded that they put at their disposal a registration of each Jew [and] of all the possessions on hand.

How many Jews were there in your town?
Fourteen hundred persons. There were three times as many Christians. Then it was ordered that in fourteen days not a Jew should be found in that little town. Where did the Jews have to go? To a larger town eighteen kilometers away, Buczacz, the county seat. Sixteen thousand Jews from the entire region were concentrated in Buczacz. A ghetto was created. It was ordered that all the Jews had to be in such and such a street. It was indeed terrible. Jews were lying in the street.

What time of the year was it, Rabbi?
In the middle of winter, in blizzards. Jews froze on the carts. And another Jewish Council was created in Buczacz and ordered to gather together all the gold and silver. I, too, was one who went to collect all the gold in the Jews' possession. With that gold we thought we might save ourselves for a certain time and be allowed to live.

So did you give the gold or . . . ?
Everything. Not a scrap was left. I myself went along in order that it should be handled honestly, because those members of the Jewish Council were scum. Because usually he [the German], when he had to take people to go and rob his [own] brothers, took the scum, low elements. In spite of that I went along so that the gold should be delivered. We thought that with this we would save ourselves for a certain time.

Were you on the Jewish Council?
No, but [it] usually summoned me as an individual, as a religious dignitary. I was of the opinion that we should give them the gold and silver. As soon as they collected the gold and silver—it took about fourteen days—the Gestapo came again from Czortkow and demanded a contingent of people. It was ordered that as we had no more possessions, 1,200 [people] should be handed over to be killed. It was said openly! The first transports it was said [were] for deportation. They were [really] taken to Belzec, a burial ground of millions of people. There was a

factory where people were destroyed electrically, and later [the Germans] made fats out of them.

Tell me, who has seen that? Who knows it?
It is known! It is known exactly, because people jumped off the trains during the journey to Belzec. They were undressed already a few kilometers before Belzec. But there were only three transports from Buczacz to Belzec because later on [the Germans] begrudged the trains. [They] saw that people were jumping off. So [they] didn't come with transports anymore. But [they] arrived and took out a few hundred Jewish workers to dig a grave six kilometers in length.[1] Later on Jews were led out. [The Germans] asked to be given a contingent of 500 or 1,000 people for slaughter. Naturally the Jewish Council did not want to. They said, "Who should be handed over, and who should remain? Go and do it yourself!" So the Germans went around from house to house with militia and took people out to be killed. Then we began digging bunkers underneath the floors in every house to hide ourselves. [The Germans] entered a house. They went around and knocked and dug until they found. Instead of the 1,000 burned offerings they had originally asked for, they gathered 3,000. All were shot. They left only twenty or thirty Jews and [ordered them to] bury the dead.

Did you see that yourself?
Yes! Later on these twenty or thirty were, alas, shot. What does "saw" mean? I have just put up a gravestone on that large and holy place, on that mass grave. There lie all my relatives, all my brothers and sister, and everybody. Six thousand Jews lie there in one grave. It is a fact! Some question! It happened that way every time. Every three or four weeks an "action" would take place until only 2,000 Jews remained in Buczacz.

And where were you during all that time?
In all I went through thirteen "actions" and remained alive under the ground in my house. As soon as the Germans raided, everybody would hide in any kind of hiding place he had. But people were found. Whoever succeeded, succeeded. I lost my family in the eleventh "action."

Where had your family been?
My family was in a pit with me. Eighty persons. We made a gigantic underground cellar [in the house] the Jewish Council gave me to live in, extremely well

1. Either the rabbi misspoke or he referred to a ditch made for some other purpose, such as a drainage ditch.

camouflaged. And I took in eighty people there because there were people who were shelterless, who didn't have any bunker, so I told them they should come to me and hide. This perhaps brought about the tragedy, because that is how it was discovered.

I can describe the night of the catastrophe to you. During the eleventh "action" we heard that the Gestapo had arrived, [so] we bunkered ourselves around twelve o'clock at night. Around two o'clock I heard voices from the outside: "We are six persons, a Hungarian family. We are standing outside. The murderers are not yet on this street. Have compassion, Jews, and let us in because we are standing unprotected, in danger of being killed." I said to myself, "I don't want to have six burned offerings on my conscience." I unscrewed the cover of the bunker and ran out to the gate of the house and took in that family. And then, at that moment when I took them in, a few of the Gestapo already on the street sensed that something was going on.

That family really was a Jewish family?

Yes. And two hours later [the Germans] overran the house. Everybody was taken out and shot. At the last moment I and my fifteen-year-old son lay down among sacks and featherbeds on the ground—eighty persons had a lot of baggage. Because of the great noise and the tumult and the screams, they left [us] behind. I was trod under feet. And I wasn't noticed. I gave my whole family advice. They scattered in small groups. Unfortunately, they were seen; they were all picked up and led away. I had eleven persons in my family. And I remained in the cellar with my boy.

And the others from your family were . . . ?

My wife, [her] five sisters, my father, may his memory be blessed, and a boy of nine years who showed abilities of becoming one of the world's great . . . He had a terrific memory. He remembered half of the Book of Psalms by heart. When he went to be slaughtered, he was saying the Psalms from memory. He said, "I am still going to pray to God. Maybe in the last moment we will still be saved."

How did you find out about that?

One escaped from that transport and told me how they were killed. After that, when I saw that the last 2,000 Jews remained in Buczacz, I said, "Let us run to the forests!" I gathered 350 Jews and brought them out. I told them that they should come in groups to such and such woods, in such and such direction. There we would plan how we would support ourselves and which peasant we could trust to bring food. There we would plan how to hide underground. Maybe we would live through Hitlerism there in the woods.

Can you describe what people did all day in the forest? Where did one sleep? Describe the life.

Life in the forest was a constant terror. One was afraid every second that a group of Gentiles might come and kill us all. People looked only for thicker trees [in which] to hide. Entire days passed in which one neither ate nor slept. Once it rained constantly for three days. And it became so muddy that afterward, when we got up, people got lost. We couldn't find one another. We were submerged, covered with mud. That is how we slept in a forest. And at the beginning the food consisted of mushrooms from the trees, around the trees, on the ground. Dark mushrooms. Like bark. It is a disgusting food. One peeled it and boiled it thoroughly in water, and one ate it and drank the water in which it was boiled.

Were there only men, or were there . . . ?

Oh, women and children too. There were engineers and doctors and rabbis, all sorts of people. And the engineers began planning how to make underground bunkers. In an area of five kilometers we made forty bunkers. There were a few people in each, in fives, sixes, tens. In the daytime we lay underground the whole day, and we were afraid that should a peasant get lost there, a Gentile with a cow, it would soon be known that there were Jews in the forest. In the evening we let ourselves go outside to take a bit of fresh air, because at night we weren't afraid of a raid. It was a dense forest, so at night we used to come together from all the bunkers to one assembly point around me. And we used to make a campfire. We baked potatoes and sat and talked about what would become of us.

While we were in the forest, thirty Russian partisans arrived. That was very interesting. Parachutes descended in an open place. They knew that the Germans were there, so they ran into the forest to hide. And they came to us, and they were hiding with us for six weeks. Our spirit rose. Now we already had a few arms. If an attack came, we had something with which to defend ourselves. During their stay we lived well because these partisans would raid. At night they would go into the villages and attack the peasants and burn the crops. They would spread damage. In the meantime, they would bring provisions from the peasants.

Then on one occasion they brought a radio to the forest. They had taken an ordinary radio away from a Ukrainian, and an engineer bunkered it. It was tied with wires to a tree, and it was powered with fifteen simple [flashlight?] batteries. We had it every night. People risked their lives disguised as Gentiles [to go] into the towns to buy batteries so that we should get some news every evening of what was going on in the world. We got all 350 Jews together. The radio began to inform us when the Soviets made the Germans pull back. It brought us a bit of hope. I used to sit all day long with a map to try and figure out how many kilometers they covered in a day, how long it had to take till they came to us.

And then came the catastrophe. The forest was attacked. [Somebody told] the

Gestapo that thousands of Jews were located in the woods with ammunition, a secret radio, and with partisans. Imagine what was sent out against us. Whole [German] divisions were sent to surround the woods, and a gigantic raid began on the forest. The moment the partisans sensed that the woods were being raided, they were recalled, and they created only a little Jewish partisan group. They organized fifteen young men, gave them arms, and the Jewish partisan group got ready to protect us at least against common bandits who went around robbing.

They [the Germans] were raiding the woods constantly. Already they had found the radio, and Jews were being killed. During the whole summertime we were able to hide in the forest because the leaves [hid] the bunkers. The moment the snow fell, since we had to go out on the snow occasionally, we left a trail. They tracked them down to each bunker. The few Jews remaining in the forest came to be annihilated. Out of the 350, no more than 15 remained.

Might not some have run away to other places?

No. We were constantly on the run. As soon as we were discovered in this little piece of forest, we had to leave it and escape to another [and] build new bunkers. How was one able to build a bunker in the forest? It had to be propped up underground. Trees had to be cut in a quite different part [of the forest] because if somebody should come, he shouldn't be able to notice that trees had been cut there. And later on when the ground was dug up, the earth, too, had to be carried away a few kilometers. It should not be noticed that the earth had been dug up there. And the engineers made a bunker of five stories.[2] And twigs were kind of braided. And so we slept, one on top of the other, like on plank beds. And when the Germans found that bunker they were astonished! They brought down a photographer to photograph it. I heard the voices: "Look what the Jews can do! A subterranean little Paris." Because it was so artistically constructed. It was such a masterpiece.

All that didn't help. Winter brought catastrophe, and very few were left. We escaped into the villages and persuaded a Gentile [that] he should make a hole in a stable. We laid there, four persons, for four months in a stable underneath the cattle.

Who was with you? Your boy?

The boy and two other persons who had more money to give to that Gentile for my share. The Gentile took exorbitant sums for every day, and I didn't have it. The Soviets arrived in our parts before Passover in the year 1944. So when we heard that the Soviets were there, we left the bunkers and walked into the town. And then eight days later the Soviets executed a retreat again, and we remained.

2. This seems unlikely. He may mean "five rooms."

When we left for the woods, I took a count, and I had forty-nine people. [The others came from] a few groups also hidden in other forests.

When I saw that a retreat was in process, I knew that we were again in mortal danger. I got in touch with a Jewish captain in the Russian army [and] asked what was going on. He said [they] had besieged a city with sixteen German divisions, and the main army went on. [The Germans] had broken out and would regain control of the entire region of Galicia.[3] So I begged him, "Take these forty-nine people back [with you]." He granted me this favor. We ran with the army to the Dniester [River], twenty-two kilometers, at night. It was something terrible. There was chaos in the retreat. At the beginning he had promised us that he would put the women and children on the vehicles, but when the moment of the retreat came, there was such a tumult that we couldn't do it. Each soldier packed up and ran, and we civilians had to walk. At [one point] we thought we were again surrounded by the Germans, [but] we ran to the Dniester and crossed over to Horodenka and went as far as Czernowitz.[4] We were saved, we were in Soviet hands.

We found 23,000 Jews in Czernowitz who received us very nicely. I distributed the forty-nine people among [them]. There had been 80,000 Jews in Czernowitz; [the Germans] deported sixty [thousand]. We got settled, and I became the Czernowitz rabbi. I was [there] a year. In 1945 the repatriation to Poland started. I as a Polish citizen had documents made out in Czernowitz and went to Poland. I was in Warsaw for six months as rabbi of Warsaw. I began organizing a Jewish life. It cost me a lot of effort. I saw that I was again in great danger, that danger lurked at every pace and step. In Warsaw a Jew couldn't show up on the street.

After the liberation of Poland?

Today there are pogroms! I will tell you why. The poison of Hitlerism has remained. There it did more damage than any place else. There Hitlerism took such deep roots that Hitlerism exists today like an epidemic. The extermination of Jews is still advocated, and they are doing [it]. True, the government is very well disposed, but they are unable to control this situation. In Warsaw with every step I took outside I was in danger. I was beaten. I had to walk every step [because] I couldn't ride on a streetcar. I concealed my beard with a kerchief. Thus I saw that it was impossible for me to carry out my Jewish life. I got out of Poland and came to France.

3. A reference to the encirclement of the German First Panzer Army and its breakout, aided by two SS divisions, on March 30, 1944.

4. In 1945 the two cities became part of the USSR (more recently of Ukraine), and their names were transliterated as Gorodenka and Chernovtsy.

With whom did you get out of Poland?
With a transport [of] 200 [members] of the Agudah Israel, an organization which endeavors to mold life according to the letter of the Torah. Now [it] is endeavoring to build the Land of Israel. Once they believed that the important thing is to see that Jewish life be according to the Torah. And it can even be in the Diaspora. But today, since they see that there is no place for a Jew in Europe, they endeavor to rebuild the Land of Israel in the spirit of the Torah.

How did the Agudah Israel gather the 200 people, and how did you get in touch with them?
After the catastrophe, after the liberation of Poland, five or six people got together who had remained Jewish religious comrades. They went out in the street, and they searched, simply searched for children. Many [Jewish] children were hidden in Christian homes. They took each child and clothed it and fed it. And they said, "You should know you don't have your parents. You have no family. But you are a child of Jews, and you have to be a Jewish child, and you should believe in God." Gradually these six or seven people gathered hundreds of children together. They bought them from the Gentiles. A lot of money was paid.

Why did they have to be bought back?
Because the Gentile woman didn't want to surrender them. The Gentile woman knew that it was a deal. If she has saved a Jewish child, she demands money. People got in touch with the Joint, with the Americans, and up to thirty thousand zlotys was paid for a child, even up to fifty thousand. Quite a sum— hundreds of dollars.

Then a *Benoss* was created—separate quarters for women, since there cannot be a mixing of men and women. The older women instructed the younger women about the spirit of the Torah. Nowadays there are forty-odd kibbutzim in Poland created by the Agudah. And we were brought over by train to Prague with a transport of the Agudah.

How did you cross the border?
We crossed somewhat legally. It was said the border guards had been bribed a little. It was quite an undertaking. And from Prague to Paris by train.

Who provided the food? Who provided the . . . ?
Who provided all the things? There is an Agudah in Prague, and there is an Agudah in France. And there is the *Va'ad Hazzalah* from America. [It] is now spread over the whole of Europe. Their mission is to rescue the *Sha'arith Hap-latim*, the survivors, and to take them out of the dangerous countries and bring

them, for the time being, where a Jew can more or less move freely. We live under hard conditions here in Henonville. And still we are in a country where we can move about freely. The Jew is a man equal to all men in France.

You should know that all the Jews have one aim, to go to Israel. All of them from Agudah Israel and from other parties aim simply to have a little piece of home, a little piece of land as their own. Some people who have relatives in America are struggling to get to America, because, for the time being, the road to the Land of Israel is complicated. But the majority consists of idealists who, in spite of the situation there being difficult, want solely to get to *Eretz Israel*, legally or illegally. To us *Eretz Israel* is always legal. Our journey to *Eretz Israel* is legal because it is our country, and we are going there as to our own. This is our hope.

Rabbi H., would you please tell me a little about Henonville. How many people are here? What does one do here, and how did they come, and so forth.

Here in Henonville we are in a kind of *Hachsharah*, a preparation for *Eretz Israel*. We want to go to *Eretz Israel* as active people. We want to prepare ourselves, build up our bodies physically so we will be able actively to build the land; not go there as people who have to be assured an existence, but capable of building and creating. There is a kibbutz here in Henonville. People work at gardening, in the fields, at carpentry, at tailoring, as painters, at shoe making. Everyone learns according to his trade [and] his abilities [so] he can enter *Eretz Israel* as a trades-man [and] be able to help in building the land. We need to be able to conduct all the branches of life by ourselves. We shouldn't need any protectorate over us.

How many people are there here in Henonville?

Now more are arriving. There were already over 200. Now there could be about 300. A Yeshiva will be installed, too. I as the spiritual leader see to it that all these labors should be carried out in the spirit of the Torah. That means, for instance, in the morning when we get up, everything is punctual. At six o'clock there is a bell. Everybody has to stand on the square. Up and about. The people are taught punctuality. Until eight o'clock there is prayer and breakfast. Prayer first. After breakfast I give a lecture to the men studying the Torah. They are taught for an hour or two. Then people go to work until dinner. At nine every-body has to be at work. People work eight hours a day. [At] twelve or half past the bell rings. Everybody leaves work and goes to eat dinner. After dinner, at two o'clock the bell rings again. People go to work again until six.

Saturday no work is done, but the whole day is spent in songs, with dances, and we eat together, and lectures about the Torah are given. And every Saturday thirty or forty strangers come to us, [Jews] living in Paris, to take part in our Sabbath. We spend a Sabbath from beginning to end full of Godliness, with diffidence, with lectures, with study. The whole Sabbath is to us a spiritual day, free of labor.

I want to add something about life here: people really strive that there be a brotherly life. One would walk into fire for another. The love of one for another becomes forged together here. All of us are constantly together. One treasury, one food, one treatment. When one gets married here, it is a joyful event for everyone. Everyone joins in the happiness the same as if his own brother were getting married. And this life creates in the people a great love of one for another. This is almost the most important asset of the life in a kibbutz, that it creates a bond. Everyone is taken by love of one for another, with loyalty because one loses the individual problems, the individual endeavors, and everything ties into one collective endeavor. We all have one aim and one endeavor.

21   Isaac W.

Conditions for Holocaust survivors in DP camps after the war often seemed little better than enslavement by the Germans. Isaac W., who managed to elude the Germans, doubtless articulates the feelings of many of his fellow DPs who were not so fortunate. In the immediate aftermath of events, it was easy for them to forget that the rest of Europe was bleeding, too.

Isaac W., twenty-three years old at war's start and a Zionist in Lvov (he calls it by its German name, Lemberg), was drafted into the Polish army and slightly wounded in fighting with the Germans in 1939. The Russians were awarded his hometown a short time later and taught him to be a railroad mechanic; Isaac fled with them when the Germans attacked in 1941. After a close call or two, he managed to reach safety and avenged his fellow Jews by volunteering to fight in the Red Army. By 1945 he was a decorated veteran of numerous battles, including Stalingrad and the liberation of his hometown, Lemberg.

Isaac sensed that there was no future for him in Poland—he had lost everyone in the Holocaust—and decided to travel west on his way to Palestine. He spent almost a year after the end of hostilities in various DP camps in southern Austria, the British zone of occupation, and he leaves no doubt about his impression that the English were much less sympathetic to the Jews than were the Americans. His interview documents the impatience of the would-be emigrants with restrictions on their activities. It also highlights tensions with the Austrians, whom the refugees found hard to distinguish from Germans, and with Ukrainians, who were suspected of crimes against the Jews. Crossing illegally into the American occupation zone and then making their way to Italy, Isaac and a band of followers (including his pregnant wife) found no satisfactory refuge until they reached the camp at Castle Tradate, between Milan and Como, where members of several kibbutzim enjoyed self-government under the general sponsorship of the UNRRA. As a member of the camp's elected governing committee, Isaac W. was well situated to comment on the situation there. His position gave him, his wife, and their new baby the luxury of a single private room. One can imagine life there for the average displaced person.

We begin the interview with W.'s description of his flight from
Lemberg to escape capture by the Germans in June 1941.

When the German fliers were already bombing Lemberg, I still worked on the
railroad. Up to two days before the Germans entered, under the bombs, under
everything. And then I ran away with the Russian army as far as Woloczysk. And
there, near Kiev, we were surrounded by the Germans. We organized as partisans,
by ourselves, on our own, because we knew what he [Hitler] does with the Jews
because we had read the book *Mein Kampf*. We knew the meaning of the "Jewish
question." We knew that we would not go to death voluntarily.

*You said that you went with the partisans. Why didn't you go with the
regular army?*
They didn't want to accept us then. We were told that we should go farther
into Russia, and then we would be accepted. We ourselves saw how bad the situation was. And we had nothing in our hands. We couldn't protect our lives. And
we took to the forest. We took weapons from the dead Russian soldiers. I lived
eight days in the trees. With straps that I kept till this day as a souvenir, I tied myself, one strap around the legs, one entirely around the body, so that I wouldn't
fall down. I had perhaps a half a kilo [1.1 pounds] of bread in my pocket. A friend
had about 2 kilos of dry bread. We throwing it from one tree to another.
And on this we lived a few days.

Why did you have to be in a tree?
Because the Germans were walking around. They were calling, "Jews and Russians are around here." And we were afraid, because they were walking around
looking for us in the forest. Then we saw death before our eyes. You understand?
We had nothing to lose. We also killed many Germans, because they came after
us. We kept a pistol in our hand this way. [Apparently demonstrating.] He [the
German] shouldn't notice. And when he came close [and] said that we should
hold our hands up, we killed him. We killed fifteen Germans at that time. Before
they could get ready to kill us, to search us, we killed them right away, and we
went on.

At that time we met a Russian patrol, and the Russians stopped us [and] asked
us who we were. We showed that we had papers that we were Russian railroad
workers and Jews. They let us live. They didn't say anything. They believed us.
And then they asked where we wanted to go. We said that to us it was all the same.
We wanted to go into the Russian army or join the partisans, because we didn't
want to go to death voluntarily. And we were taken into the Russian army. I
fought at Stalingrad, and I still have decorations from the Russian army. I fought

till the last day of the war. For my own sake, for vengeance, because they took and killed my parents [and] sisters. I took a lot of revenge on these Germans.

The Ukrainian partisans were there, those "Banderovtzi"[1] who were helping the Germans. The Ukrainians were indeed much worse than the Germans. When they met a Jew on the street, they killed him. As soon as we entered a village or town the Ukrainians ran away, and the blood of the Jews whom they had killed was still warm. There were some Jews who had hidden themselves with Christians. They had given gold, all their possessions to the Christian so that he should hide them. So he took the gold and said, "I will hide you." [But then] he told the Ukrainians. The Ukrainians themselves have killed many more Jews than the Germans. The Russian partisans always walked into the town or villages dressed in civilian clothes [to] signal so that the Russians should enter. And the Ukrainians were caught in the act of trying to kill the Jews. I was present. I saw [it] with my own eyes.

And then I [returned] to Lemberg. I had come home. And strangers were in the dwelling where I had lived. I stopped still. My heart turned to stone so that I couldn't speak. I fell down, I was simply without strength. And I revived [and] went on. Where should I go to look? I went to the cemetery. There I met an old man who told me, "Here lies your mother. She was killed, and here I have buried her." And then I returned to the Russian army.

I was in Budapest when we heard that the war was over. I was told that I could go home. Whom would I find there? Nobody. And it might come to it that I would commit suicide. We had seen the Jewish homes [in Lemberg]. They had thrown bombs into them; they shouldn't even exist. And we saw the Jewish blood that was still not dried in the streets. And there was still a cemetery where the people had been burned when I was there. I still saw how the earth was still quivering—people had just been put in.[2] I said, "I can't go there. Lemberg is a Jewish cemetery." I couldn't go home to that house, after six years, and not find my parents. Then I would have to commit suicide.

From Hungary I went to Austria. I myself was in a camp at Judenburg, where the English were. It was very bad. They did not sympathize that much with the Jews. There was even one Englishman—we knew that he was a Jew, but he did not want to admit [it]. He took us into the forest to work. We were still sick. He didn't care about that. The English caught us [and treated us] just like the Germans, the SS. We were kept by the English under Austrian guards, police.

And at the same time the English took the Ukrainians—they didn't want

1. Followers of Stefan Bandera, the pro-Nazi Ukrainian nationalist leader. In 1942 they formed the Ukrainian Insurgent Army to fight with the Germans against the Red Army.

2. W. evidently believed that Jews had just been buried alive in the cemetery. There is no evidence confirming this.

to return home because they knew that the Poles and the Russians would kill them because they were bandits—and appointed them police guards. They [the Ukrainians] didn't let the Jews eat. When a Jew came over hungry [wanting] to eat a second time, they chased him away. Because he wanted another piece of bread! Under the mantle of the English, who had given them police authority, they were taking revenge. Then they took stones and threw [them] at the Jews. [Ukrainians] were made chauffeurs, and the Jews were not admitted to any jobs.

And then we went to Trofaiach[3] in November or December 1945. That was a Jewish camp, too, not far from Judenburg. There we had a UNRRA director, an American Jew. He sympathized with the Jews. He did a lot for the Jews. He taught Jews to be chauffeurs. He clothed them. He erected a Jewish synagogue. He made a cinema for the Jews in the camp. Immediately we recognized that he was not an English Jew, but an American. He couldn't see them cold. He brought doctors, medicines, [and] sick Jews were saved. [But the English] did not permit a Jew to leave the camp without a permit. One wasn't permitted to travel. So we said, "What, are we going to just sit here? The war is over, and we are in a concentration camp again." We hit the road to Italy.

How many went?

A hundred and thirty people had gathered together. Kibbutz Dror Habonim. I myself gathered my friends who were with me in the army and such.

We were caught [by] the English. Other Jews went [with us], so 300 people were led back. The Austrians had said that Jews were passing, so the English brought us back with automatics. We were led on foot like criminals to the railroad, not far away. We were taken by train, and we jumped out of the train again. While the train was moving I pushed everybody out. The English guards in [another] wagon came out [and] caught a few Jews, [but] we went on, because we didn't want to go [back] to a concentration camp. We ran away, on foot, to Kolbnitz, a camp that was newly established. There was a Jewish camp leader, Mr. Katz, an American. He was a father, one can say, for the Jews there, and whatever he could do he did for us. He gave us shoes. He clothed us. We were immediately given something to eat, and the sick [were] put into the hospital.

[Later Isaac W. was sent to a DP camp at Villach, Austria.]

Then [the camp] began to be liquidated, because the Austrians had attacked the Jews. I myself stood [watching] when a Jew went over to take some wood. There was a sawmill where boards were sawed to make barracks for the Jews. The Germans [Austrians] came over and beat up the Jews. [One of the Jews] re-

3. A town about twenty miles northwest of Graz, Austria.

mained lying. Eight days he lay sick. And we took that German, and we said to the English, "If you don't put his man in jail, then we will consider the English the same as the Germans." Then that Mr. Katz turned him over to the English police. What they did with him I don't know, but eight days later we saw him in town. He had been released. I didn't know how to understand that. Either they had an understanding that the Jews should be beaten or what. . . .

Then there were always more people [coming into the camp]. The camp was transferred to another place, into a forest between mountains. The Jews were to be separated from the city.

[W. then took his wife and sixteen other Jews, illegally and on foot, to Salzburg and then across the mountains to Italy.]

Didn't you have anybody to lead you?
A Greek! One took a watch off his wrist, one had a ring, whatever people had they gave him, and he led us over the mountains. My wife was pregnant. We took nothing along. It was cold; snow was in the mountains. [Then] we were afraid to ride [the train] because police were asking questions. In Merano, eighty kilometers from the border, we boarded the train for Milan. [There] the Jewish committee began to give us aid. We were put into the Cremona camp, eighty kilometers from Milan. Before it had been an armory for soldiers. [It was] like a stable, without doors, without windows, the floor [made] of stone. We lived in one room, eighty people. My entire kibbutz was there. [W. then took his group to Tradate.]

In America we know nothing about these kibbutzim. How do people live here? How is it all organized?
We get three thousand liras a month [per person] from the UNRRA.[4] On this we have to live. And we have a committee here [that] takes care of whatever we need. We can't permit more than eighty liras a day to be spent for provisions.

What is done with the rest?
Something is given to a sick person, to someone without shoes. Because now we don't have any shoes. Many need them.

And how long do you think people will sit around here?
That does not depend on us. We can [go] today if they let us; we would even go on foot. Because we are impeded by the English, by the Italians . . .

4. At the time the dollar was worth about 700 liras.

Where would you go?

To Palestine. We have no other home. Where can we go? Who can give us a guarantee that in a year or half a year the same won't happen again, like here? Maybe you heard. Ukrainians were here in Italy, too, in a concentration [DP] camp. There were Jews and Ukrainians; they attacked them, and four Jews were beaten to death. Those were Ukrainians who don't want to return home because they are afraid. They had beaten, killed, robbed the Jews. They are hiding here, and the English don't send them home. The Russians have already demanded many times that they should return home, and the English won't send them. And they are free. They have many more conveniences than the Jews. Because when Jews want to go some place, they don't permit it. You know how it is with a Jew. He doesn't ask; he [just] goes. And they attacked the Jewish camp. The English police also got inside to aid the Jews; they arrested the Jews, and they drove the Ukrainians away by truck so that the Jews shouldn't be able to avenge themselves for the four dead.

Then we saw that it is impossible for the Jew to be together with the Ukrainians. The American Joint intervened and *Hachsharahs*[5] were established. The UNRRA did not want to allow [them] at first, but then *Hachsharahs* were established so that the Jews should learn to work. One teaches the other field labor.

Tell me, why do you have roll calls twice a day, just like in a concentration camp?
We assign work for the next day.

Can't that be done in the dining hall?

No, we don't have a big enough dining hall for all the people that we have here. Now we are about six or seven hundred people. You see how it is here. One shift finishes eating [and] then the others go in. And that is why we have roll call twice daily. People are given instructions, and for discipline, too.

This morning I saw that in one section you have many married couples sleeping in the same room. How does that influence morale?

It is very bad. If it were for a short time, the husband and wife could be put separately, but when it is for a long period—we don't know how long we might stay here—one can't separate [them].

I am going to ask you frank questions. A husband and wife have relations. The other people must hear it.

I can tell the truth about myself. Now I have a small baby. I have a separate room, but until [recently] I also lived with a pregnant wife. I can tell you that

5. Zionist training centers that prepared DPs for life in Palestine.

we were living like strangers, one bed near the other, and we were embarrassed one of another. You understand? Because to have relations amid strangers is not moral. As a friend told me, "I have a wife, but only as a picture [in my imagination]." People had a saying, "I have a wife, but we have no relations." It is very terrible, such a life, but what can one do?

And the UNRRA knows about it?

I will tell you. The UNRRA [people come] for ten minutes. They look around only [to see] if things are clean. They came in this week [and] saw that we had no water, no lavatory, because the toilets are all plugged up. So I said, "Maybe you want that we should all get sick of malaria or typhus. Give us some help so that we should have water. The only way out is to go on a hunger strike in two or three days." I went to the Joint, and yesterday they brought the pump. Thanks to the American Joint, we have water today.

What will be done in the winter?

That I don't know. There are some comrades who receive dollars in letters [and give] it to the kibbutz. We [as individuals] have no money. People who are in a kibbutz say that another comrade is to him the same as himself. Let us say a comrade has received chocolate; he says it should be distributed among the children. We have religious people here, so we have a kosher kitchen, too. Everyone lives collectively, because if not collectively, we cannot exist.

Lithuania

22 Ephraim G.

Lithuanian Jewry, like its counterpart in eastern Poland, encountered
the Germans for the first time in June 1941. The principal difference was
that Lithuanian nationalists, embittered by Soviet rule in 1940 and 1941,
viewed the Germans as a lesser evil and the Jews as supportive of Communism. Ephraim G. had been born in 1917 in Ukraine, but he lived
most of his life up to 1944 in the Lithuanian capital of Kaunas (which
G. calls by its Russian name, Kovno). He experienced the birth, life, and
death of the Kovno ghetto. On the day of his interview at Henonville
Displaced Persons Home near Paris in September 1946 he was one of
only about 2,000 survivors of a Jewish community that had numbered
40,000 before the war.

 This interview documents poor relations between Lithuanians
and Jews in 1941. Although Lithuanian contempt for the Jews is well
known, Ephraim G.'s sentiments suggest that it was heartily recipro-
cated by at least some Jews, who sneered at their neighbors as primitive
"Lithuanian Klumpes," named for the peasants' wooden shoes. Far
more graphic, however, are his descriptions of Lithuanian nationalists lashing out at the Jews at the moment of German conquest. These
extremists were exacting revenge for what they regarded as Jewish
sympathy with the USSR during its brief occupation of their country. The Soviets had restricted Jewish religious and economic life but
opened the doors to Jewish participation in higher education and politics, thereby attracting a following among young Jews. This association
by Lithuanian nationalists of Jews with Communism had catastrophic
consequences in the form of pogroms during the interval between the
flight of the Red Army and the arrival of the Germans. G. and his family
were spared only by the intervention of a sympathetic Lithuanian acquaintance. His recollections also show how the Germans subsequently
were able to draw ordinary Lithuanians into measures against the Jews
by permitting them to share booty taken from the victims. Lithuanian
volunteers would continue to assist the Germans in actions against the
Jews throughout the war, both in Kovno and elsewhere.

 Ephraim G. is most intent upon describing the initial acts of Nazi
violence against the Jews in the first months of the Kovno ghetto, as
well as the last, heartbreaking deportation of children and old people
in March 1944. But he also shows how the Germans gradually whittled

down the population of the ghetto to around 18,000 with executions and deportations. A close reading of G.'s interview reveals that he and most others who survived in Kovno had, or were related to someone who had, a "Jordan card" attesting to the status of a skilled laborer working for the Germans in the ghetto. These were issued by SA captain Fritz Jordan, the superintendent of Jewish affairs in Kovno and from all accounts a thoroughly sinister figure. In September 1941 he delivered 5,000 of these "Certificates for Jewish Artisans" to the Jewish Council, led by Dr. Elchanan Elkes. Elkes and his fellow Jewish elders were divided over the wisdom of distributing the certificates, but they finally bowed to demands from the Jewish workers themselves, who hoped that possession of a "Jordan card" might enhance their chances of survival. G., an electrician, had one of them.

Among the most interesting passages of G.'s account are those regarding the involvement of at least a part of the Kovno ghetto's Jewish police force in preparations for resistance and establishing bunkers in which Jews planned to hide from future deportations. Sadly, the Nazis succeeded in turning the lower ranks of the Jewish police against their officers, resulting in reprisals and the discovery of many bunkers. Nor did such hiding places save many Jews when the ghetto was liquidated in July 1944. Using dogs and grenades, the Germans flushed out and killed or deported virtually all the survivors. Fewer than one hundred Jews were still in Kovno when the Red Army returned at the beginning of August, following which G. recovered the hidden ghetto archives that he had helped to organize.

Ephraim G. abruptly terminated the interview before describing the ghetto's liquidation. Boder was perplexed. Was G. called away by a legitimate emergency, or was he unable or unwilling to go on for some personal reason? The interview begins with the panic that accompanied the German breakthrough on June 23, 1941, and the abortive attempt of G.'s family to flee to the interior of the Soviet Union.

About 90 percent of the Jews wanted to run away with the Red Army into Russia. Unfortunately, only a small part managed to run with the Russians; the rest had to turn around. I, too, was among the Jews who attempted to run, and we [made it] to the hamlet of Ynovo, about thirty kilometers from Kovno. We observed that the Germans were already at the town of Vilkomir; the Germans got ahold of the [town] because the Lithuanians [had already] overthrown the Soviet authorities. Seeing that we were unable to get to Russia, we waited a few days until a semblance of order appeared in Kovno, and then we returned. And on the roads along which the Jews had to return to Kovno stood Lithuanian partisans, hirelings in the service of the Gestapo, and they were catching the Jews and leading them to the seventh fortress, not far from Kovno, and there they were shot en masse. And we were stopped immediately by the so-called partisans, and they wanted to lead us to the seventh fort, too.

Whom do you mean by "us"?
Myself, my mother, and nine brothers and sisters. I am the tenth, and I am, unfortunately, the only one who remained of our whole clan.

And where was your father?
My father was a rabbi in Kovno, and he was fortunate to die in 1940.

The Lithuanians wanted to drag us to the seventh fortress, too, but fortunately among them was a Lithuanian, an acquaintance of ours; he also wore the band on his arm with the swastika, that is, he was also a partisan; recognizing us, he felt embarrassed and requested his comrades that they let us go because this was the family of the Kovno rabbi. And so we returned to Kovno. The mood was terrible; they were seizing people in the streets and taking them to the forts to be shot. Those are the old fortifications which the czar had erected around Kovno. And they led all the Jews there to be shot.

And then General Pohl,[1] the general who took Kovno, started to negotiate with the Kovno rabbi, Rabbi Shapiro;[2] he was to take steps to form a Jewish Council consisting of several Jews who enjoyed the confidence of the rabbi, who should take steps toward the creation of a ghetto near Kovno, in Slobodka.[3] He gave as his reasons that since the Jews had been suffering mostly from the Lithuanians—and that was correct—it was his advice that we Jews should better be separated from the Lithuanians, and better go into the ghetto. And on the second Saturday an order was issued that Jews had to wear yellow patches, that is the Star of David, *only* on their chests, and so . . .

What do you mean, just on the chest?
Because later on, when we were in the ghetto, the orders were that we had to wear [it] on our back as well, while at the start only on our chest.

Before there was a ghetto an order was issued that the Jews may not walk on the sidewalk; the Jews were permitted to go only in the middle of the street,

1. Major General Pohl, the German military governor of Lithuania. Not to be confused with SS Lieutenant General Oswald Pohl of the "Economic-Administrative Main Office" of the SS.

2. Abraham Duber Kahana-Shapiro, chief rabbi in Kovno. He died in the ghetto in 1943.

3. A suburb of Kovno, across the Vilija River from the city, where many Jewish artisans already made their homes.

just like dogs. And many Jews, forgetting that they were already disqualified as humans, would get on the sidewalk—such a thing happened to me, too—and then we would be beaten up, not by the Germans, but, alas, by the Lithuanians with whom we had lived for hundreds of years. Thanks to [us] they had come to learn what a pair of shoes are. Because before [that] they were called "Lithuanian clodhoppers" ["Klumpes"], that means "wooden shoes." They were unable to achieve more than that in their lives.

And why was it "thanks to us"?

Thanks to Jewish progress, Jewish industry, Jewish culture, they also began to develop into human beings, and they started wearing shoes. Not only in Lithuania but generally abroad it is known that the Lithuanian is called the "Lithuanian Klumpe," "wooden shoe," because they never had anything more.

[We skip over G.'s description of the establishment of the Kovno ghetto in August 1941 during which the Germans systematically looted the Jews.]

Soon after, within a week, came [Willy] Koslovski—he was the German commandant of the ghetto and lived across the street from the ghetto—and he said that, since last night shots had been fired at his residence, he demanded that Dr. Elkes as head Jew surrender 500 Jews to him to be shot. Dr. Elkes told him in reply that among Jews there is no such thing as delivering people to be shot. It was clearly stated in the Jewish religion. [He said] that in spite [of the fact that he] wasn't a particularly pious Jew, still he was a Zionist. Even in case they are all being threatened, they all should submit to being shot rather than deliver one Jew. And then Koslovski told Dr. Elkes: "If you will not deliver 500, I shall take more than 500." And Dr. Elkes replied, "It may cost [the lives of] all 45,000 Jews in the ghetto, but I shall not deliver any Jews to you to be shot." Half an hour after the conversation took place, many Lithuanians—the same Lithuanians who were in the service of the Gestapo—and Germans marched into the ghetto; one block of the ghetto was cut off, and all the Jews [who were there] were led out to a square. Whoever had a "Jordan card," a card of an artisan which was issued a month earlier, remained alive, and all those who did not were led away to the ninth fort across from the ghetto, a kind of a hill, and there all of them were shot.

Could you see that?

The fort was visible only on the way to the ghetto, because the ghetto was in a valley and the fort was on a hill. And standing in the ghetto, one could see how the people were led up the hill. That day I was in the city working for the Lithuanians, doing compulsory labor. I didn't know a thing about it. By about four o'clock I saw the Lithuanians coming drunk carrying Jewish things. I recognized that these were Jewish things because there was a whole truckload of [clothing] with the yellow patches. And I asked the Lithuanians, "How did you get these Jewish clothes and overcoats?" So they replied that there was an "action" in the ghetto; that meant an event when the Jews were taken to be shot.

I want to note that there were two ghettos, a little ghetto and a large ghetto, because a [major road] cut through between the two ghettos, and the Germans, reserving the by-pass for themselves, made a bridge for the Jews to cross from one ghetto to the other. [On the 4th of September 1941 the Germans] came to the ghetto, and they put up a guard on the bridge, and the word was passed that no Jew could [cross], and they led the whole little ghetto away. The hospital of the ghetto was there; first they set fire to the hospital with the people and the doctors all together. Also, early the same morning, they set fire to the Jewish children's home which [the previous authorities] were unable to evacuate to Russia. They burned the children alive and all the sick in the hospital. And then they led out the Jews from the small ghetto to a square and again sorted them. Whoever had a "Jordan card" remained alive. This time [they] did not permit the Jews who remained alive to return to the little ghetto but drove them across to the large ghetto. The Germans took all the property of the little ghetto for themselves, but they left the place fenced around, and nobody was permitted to live there, neither Lithuanian nor Jew. From the beginning all that was incomprehensible, but later it became clear that that was preparation for the great "action."

So now we turn to the third "action." We don't count what happened in between, lesser shootings and so on. The 27th of October 1941, in the evening, it was announced on the streets that all Jews, men and women, children, and the old and sick, had to report the next day to the big square, the Square of Democracy, at six o'clock in the morning. This order read that the German police would later go searching the homes, and whoever remained at home would be shot. The order instructed that only sick people unable to get up from bed should remain in the house, but there should be a sign on the door saying that upstairs in such and such a room there was a sick person. And the order also said that everything had to remain open, the doors, the wardrobes, the valises, everything.

By six o'clock the next morning the Jews started to assemble, and an hour later, even though the square was located within the ghetto, [it] was again surrounded by German guards and with Lithuanians, and it was ordered that people should assemble each according to his place of work. The Jewish Council [members had to] stand up separately [in one place]; Jewish artisans, carpenters, tailors who worked for the Gestapo separately; the Jordan brigade separately; the airfield [construction brigade] separately; and so on. Each one should have his whole family with him. [Jordan then appeared and separated the assembled Jews into two groups.]

Who was Jordan?

Jordan was an SS captain.[4] He himself was a *Shaygets*,[5] about twenty-one years old, a teacher of physical education, and as it appears, he possessed but a low sense of human values, and that is what they wanted.

What happened to him afterward?

He had appropriated large quantities of Jewish property when the order which I mentioned before was issued to surrender Jewish gold and diamonds. He used to take the better things for himself. The other Germans could not fail to begrudge him [this loot], so they reported him, and in punishment he was sent to the front, and later we read in a newspaper—the German newspaper, which we were not free to buy but which we bought anyway—an obituary that [Jordan] had died in action for Führer and Fatherland—cursed be his name and memory!

And so let us continue. The Jews who were taken to the right were led away to the little ghetto. The Jews who were taken to the left—I was among these fortunates—were led back to the ghetto and ordered to disperse to their homes. The weeping and wailing in the ghetto was great. People returning to their homes would not find their father, their children, and in general people didn't know what the fate of those 12,000 Jews in the little ghetto would be.

How do you know this number?

The next morning a census was taken [which] showed that 12,000 Jews were missing in the ghetto. And the people were kept in the little ghetto until early next morning, and even [they] could not imagine they would be shot. They were squabbling over housing accommodations, firewood, [and] things that the Germans had not managed to cart away yet. And the next morning at seven o'clock they were aroused, ordered to step forward four abreast, and all taken to the fort. We standing in the ghetto again saw how a queue moved toward the fort for hours, and then a short while later we heard the German machine guns. The next morning Dr. Elkes asked Jordan what had happened to the 12,000 Jews, so he replied, "Do not speak anymore about it. Those Jews are not alive anymore. But such things will not happen again in the ghetto; that was the last of the 'actions.' Now you all shall remain alive."

4. Jordan in fact was an officer in the SA, the Storm Troopers, used as auxiliary police in the occupied Eastern territories.

5. Yiddish for a "Gentile boy," a term of contempt implying ignorance and arrogance.

Who buried those 12,000?

Gigantic ditches had been prepared. Russian prisoners would first prepare the ditches, and there they [the Germans] would line up the people, naked or in their underwear, and shoot them with machine guns. Afterward they would cover them with lime to prevent an epidemic, and the ditches were kept ready for those whose turn was to come later.

Little "actions" continued to happen in the ghetto, but not large ones. One of the greater "actions" occurred the day when the Germans lost at Stalingrad. To give vent to their wrath—they had to pacify their blood in some way—an order came to the Lithuanian police in Kovno that should Jews step out a bit from their places of work, they should be arrested immediately and brought to the Gestapo. And at night the Gestapo would come to the ghetto and take the families of those people away to the ninth fort and shoot them.

And they were taken for not working?

Only because they stepped out a bit from their place of work. For example, there was a famous [Jewish] mechanic in Kovno, Sadowski. He stepped out of line to ask for a piece of bread from a Christian, a Lithuanian woman. The Lithuanian guard noticed it and arrested him. And at night they came and took away his wife and daughter, and they sent them away the next morning and shot them.

Later on in 1943, before the high holy days, early one fine morning a German arrived and said that from then on it was no longer to be called a ghetto but "Concentration Camp Kovno" and that he would be the camp commandant. His name was [SS Lieutenant Colonel Wilhelm] Göcke. From the beginning he revealed himself as an intelligent person. He inquired about the state of nutrition in the ghetto, so Dr. Elkes reported [that it consisted] of 50 grams [less than 2 ounces] of bread. So he [Göcke] said that of course the ghetto couldn't live on this, the people must get more, and they must get other things. And they started giving butter, but unfortunately there was a price for it . . .

What do you mean, real butter?

Real butter! They started giving some marmalade. And in the ghetto a saying appeared: "If you get butter today, there will be an 'action' tomorrow." And so on the 28th of October 1943 the ghetto was surrounded again, and they transported 3,500 Jews to Estonia. To various places of labor.[6] First, a few days before the 28th, he [Göcke] announced that he needed 2,000 Jews for work twenty kilometers away from Kovno. And it came out afterward that he had told a lie and

6. Boder noted: "It is obvious that the improvement in rations was intended to permit them to gather some strength for the journey and for the impending hard labor."

that he had sent them away to Estonia. The women, all of them, were driven to the airfield and separated [from their] children. The smaller children were shot right in Kovno. The women and men together were driven away to Estonia, and it is understood that unfortunately [only] a small part of them survived. Two of my brothers were dragged away to Estonia, and one was shot and the second perished later in Auschwitz.

Events in the ghetto [corrects himself] — the concentration camp — proceeded. No more mass "actions" took place [until] the 27th and 28th of March 1944 [when] an "action" against children and old people occurred. I want to state that this man Göcke was very cunning. He seemingly had experience from other ghettos and camps, because [before his arrival] people always had a presentiment that something was going to happen before all the "actions." This time there was no premonition whatsoever. On the evening of the 26th Göcke came to the chief of the Jewish police and ordered that [the next] morning the Jewish police should assemble at the office of the German commandant for instructions. The police arrived at eight o'clock, rather cleanly dressed, and as soon as they arrived at the German commandant's office, White Russians appeared from the hallways of the offices. In Russia they were called *Vlasovzi*,[7] the Ukrainian traitors who fought on the side of Germans, and they appeared with rifles in their hands and ordered the Jewish police to lie down with their faces toward the ground. Then large trucks arrived, and they were all driven away to the ninth fort. This all was an overture to the play to come.

And the police were executed?
No, unfortunately many of the police remained alive. I want to repeat, *unfortunately*!

At the same time [that the police] were led out of the ghetto, a little vehicle, a taxi, arrived in the ghetto with a loudspeaker, and in it sat a man, whether a German or a Jew we wouldn't know. And this little vehicle ran all through the ghetto and called out: "Attention! Attention! All Jews should retire to their homes. Otherwise they will be shot." That meant that all Jews had to abandon their places of work, since there were many workshops in the ghetto itself. Right in the ghetto there were what they called the big workshops where several thousand Jews were working. There were [also] little workshops. At any rate there were many installations, and all these instantaneously had to come to a dead stop, and everybody was compelled to return to his home. People understood that something was about the happen. People had prepared hideouts in the ghetto called *malines* . . .

7. Russian units organized by General Andrei Vlasov, a former Soviet officer captured at Leningrad in 1942 who then volunteered to fight on the German side against the Allies.

[Boder was unfamiliar with the word and asked for an explanation.]

Malines originates from the Hebrew word *malon*, which means a hideout. In the ghetto they were called *malines*. Possibly the word originated with thieves, because when thieves would steal something, they would say that the thing had to be "malinated." That means to hide it.

Jewish thieves?

Yes. The Jews who had prepared *malines* beforehand were running to hide, and a short while later when the vehicle had run through the whole ghetto, large cargo trucks rolled into the ghetto with *Vlasovzi*, Germans, and also Lithuanians with their rifles; they went from house to house, and where they saw a little child the child was taken away; or they forced the mother herself to lead [her child] out on the street where a truck stood on the corner and throw him in, or *they* would throw him there. And so they worked all day. The Jewish police, meanwhile, were still in the ninth fort and not yet shot. The "action" dragged itself out until seven o'clock in the evening. Then . . .

How many people were there in the Jewish police? Did they wear a uniform?

There were more than 300 men in the Jewish police. They were wearing only a cap, a special cap with the Star of David [and] "JGP"—that means "Jewish Ghetto Police," or as it was later called the camp police—and on their left arm a band with a blue Star of David and inside "JGP" was inscribed with a number. Each policeman had his number, first of all a serial number and second a number of the sector to whose militia he belonged. They had no arms, only cold weapons, that is only a little club or a whip.

I want to remark that on that day the people who [worked outside the ghetto] were driven out to work in order that the ghetto should not suspect what was going to happen. And in the evening when the people came back from work and did not find father or mother or children, the wailing was boundless. The old ones and the little ones went together the first day. People thought that that was the end of the "action," because it was customary that "actions" in the ghetto lasted only one day. Unfortunately it was noticed that the guard—the ghetto was especially guarded so that the Jews should be unable to escape during an "action"—the German police were not removed from around the fence. And it was understood that something was in the offing again. It was assumed that tomorrow they would stage a general "action." That meant adults as well.

But the next morning, early, at five o'clock, the drama was to repeat itself, only in a special manner, in a different form. They went searching for the *malines*, and they [used] the Jewish police. Kittel, the Gestapo chief for Jewish affairs, came up to the ninth fort where the Jewish police were held under arrest and informed them: They were all doomed to be shot, but they could ransom their lives only by pointing out the *malines* in the ghetto, the places where the Jews had hidden. Unfortunately many Jewish policemen could not resist the temptation to remain alive, and they mounted a truck along with Kittel and arrived at the ghetto and pointed out where the *malines* were.

What number do you imply by "many"? You said there were 300 [policemen altogether].

It is known that 60 drove into the ghetto and pointed out the whereabouts of the *malines*. I want to note that the trick was not only to show that there was a *maline* in such and such a building; they had to show how one could get into the *maline*, because the main trick was to camouflage the entrance so that it could not be found. And they [the Jewish police] showed them how to get in, and they took out the old ones and the little children, and all were led away to the fort and shot. They discovered and ransacked all, literally all *malines* of the ghetto. [And yet] 40 percent of the children remained hidden after all; the children hidden in the *malines* did not remain alive, while children who were hidden in lesser places, under a bed or tucked in a bed, remained alive against expectations. And in the evening the "action" was over, and the results of the second day were much worse than the first; there were many more victims.

When the children were found, many mothers wanted to go along with the children because it was announced that the children would be shot, but the Germans would not grant it to the Jewish mothers. For instance, they took a child away from one of my sisters, and she pleaded to be allowed to go along with the child, so he [the German] said, "Your turn will come, but for the time being you still must work." I want to emphasize that the "action" against the children made the strongest impression in the ghetto, much more than the great "action" against the 12,000 Jews on the 28th of October 1941. Because seeing the children being taken away, and the old people, was interpreted as preparation for the total destruction of the ghetto, or "camp" as they then called it.

The "action" against the children was over. The hidden children were taboo from the start; one could not take them out on the street, but again a few weeks passed, and the children began to show themselves. Now what had become of the police? The police who betrayed the hideouts were returned to the ghetto [along with] a part of the police who had not betrayed. They shot all the higher officials of the Jewish police because during their stay in the fort all the secrets of the ghetto were revealed. The ones of lower rank betrayed [the fact] that people in the ghetto were joining the Red partisans and that arms were [concealed] in the ghetto, and so on and so forth, so that the blame fell upon the higher [ranks] of the Jewish police. All were shot, up to the chief of police. Moshe Levin, the chief of the Jewish police in the camp, did not distinguish himself intensely by his kindness or nobility toward the Jews, but one has to give him credit that from the moment he was brought to the fort he was among those who preached to the Jewish police that they not betray anything about the ghetto to the Germans because they would be shot anyway, and they should not stain the Jewish name.

Germany

23 Jürgen B.

Boder described Jürgen B. as "a young man of twenty-two who looks much younger than his age due to undernourishment and somewhat stunted physical development caused by the concentration camp regime."[1] Born into a middle-class Jewish family in northwestern Germany, Jürgen recalled his physician father breaking up Nazi meetings before 1933 by threatening Jewish boycotts of local farmers. This oversimplified complicated local conditions and exaggerated the economic power of Germany's Jews. It correctly pointed out, however, that they were not passive during Hitler's rise to power.

Like most small-town Jews, Jürgen's family reacted to Nazi persecution by moving to bigger towns and cities, seeking the shelter of large Jewish communities with their own schools and other social services. He and his mother were put to work at slave labor in a Berlin munitions factory during the war, and the importance of that labor to the German economy accounts for the fact that they were among the last Jews to be deported from the German capital to Poland in 1943. Since Jürgen had been removed from the ammunition factory to work on the rail lines, he and his mother were deported separately. He never learned exactly what happened to her. Jürgen's confidence in the Berlin Jewish Community Council, which organized the deportations for the Nazis, remained unshaken at the time of his interview. Although the question of just how much Jewish leaders knew about genocide at the time remains open, recent research suggests that German Jewish institutions probably did as much as was possible under the circumstances to make life bearable for the Jews.

Jürgen tells us that he saved his life in Auschwitz by playing a trick on the Germans. And so he did, although it could easily have backfired. What is most interesting about this episode is that it succeeded with the help of his capo, a non-Jew and, in fact, one of the professional criminals who as a group were notable for barbaric mistreatment of fellow inmates. Unfortunately Jürgen does not elaborate much on the capo's motives.

Like so many other survivors of Auschwitz, Jürgen recalls that the

1. A version of this interview appears in Boder's *I Did Not Interview the Dead*, under the pseudonym "Joern Gastfreund." It contains several translation errors.

worst happened to him *after* he was evacuated from the giant concentration camp. He as sent to Dachau, near Munich, and then farmed out to work on a new airfield in southern Bavaria in the last months of the war. Jürgen was half dead with typhus when the Americans approached in April 1945, which may have saved him from the worse fate that befell some of his healthier fellow workers who were evacuated by the SS at the last minute.

Following his recovery in an American hospital, Jürgen moved to Fürth in northern Bavaria where he lived on his own in a German home, worked in a movie house, and learned English. When he gave his interview he was living in the "Funkenkasernen," a former German signal corps center near Munich, then a huge DP camp. One of the few refugees fortunate enough to have all his papers in perfect order and a relative in America prepared to sponsor him, he was just days away from his departure for New York.

I was born on the 30th of September 1923 in Bernkastel on the Mosel River. My father was a physician, and my father died a year before Hitler came to power, that is, in the year 1932. My mother had no profession. We lived from the money that my father had earned—our inheritance. And in the year 1933 we moved to Trier, about forty kilometers from Bernkastel. I was then admitted as the only Jewish child to the gymnasium [classical high school] in Trier. And even then a certain military routine was adopted by the teachers in dealing with the children. When the teacher would enter in the morning, he would greet the children at the door with "Heil Hitler!," and the children had to respond with "Heil Hitler!" Of course, I as a Jew did not do it.

I knew from my father that Hitler was coming to power. My father himself broke up quite a few [Nazi] meetings. He threatened those Christians with boycott, that the Jews would not trade with them, and since that region lives mainly from the sale of wine, many were impressed by his threats and would not permit the meetings to take place. My father told them that the Jews would not trade with them. And since all these people trade in wine and the Jews were trading with these farmers a great deal, he threatened that he would advise the Jews not to trade with them anymore if they should tolerate Nazi influence and propaganda in their midst. After 1933 that was impossible. One knew that if he permitted himself to say one word, he would get into a concentration camp or would be detained on some other way. Everybody was very much afraid, and at any rate, one could not dare to be conspicuous.

And so your family went to Trier. How was it that you were accepted in the gymnasium?

Well, in those times a certain Jewish quota was still allowed, and a few could still be admitted to the gymnasium. The regulations were such that if one had graduated from the elementary school one could be admitted directly to the gymnasium. Since my mother had in mind that I should become a physician, I had to choose a curriculum in the humanities such as Latin and other subjects, you know. Things were very bad. One constantly was driven into conflicts with the Germans because the anti-Semitic propaganda was very intense, and, of course, life became very hard. After a year I did not want to go to such a school any more, and so I started pleading with my mother to send me to a Jewish school. My mother moved to Cologne [where] there was still a Jewish semi-classical gymnasium [from] before Hitler's time. I continued at the gymnasium in Cologne until 1936. I went through to the fourth year, and from there I found myself in Coburg, in a Jewish boarding school.

Why did you leave Cologne?

In Cologne we studied only French and English, and I wanted very much to study Latin as well. In Cologne one could not do that, and besides, a Jewish boarding school had much more to offer. There we led a Jewish life, and in general it was better there.

How many children did your parents have?

Well, besides me I have a sister who also went to the same school in Cologne, a coeducational school for girls and boys. And afterward my sister was transferred to a school of domestic science, a Jewish school.

Did you complete the course of the gymnasium?

No. At that time one could not graduate anymore. At least, it was very difficult. And since my mother was very apprehensive because Coburg was noted for its anti-Semitic mood, she took me out. We moved to Berlin, and I started to attend a commercial school supported by the Jewish Community of Berlin. Since I had always been interested in photography, at the same time I took a course in photography which was also operated by the Jewish Community in Berlin. In 1941 I was forcibly taken from school and compelled to work in a factory. That was the military labor service into which the Jews were taken. I was assigned to a factory where I was working at shells, and my mother was also working there punching shells. In those times one could not escape such work. It was compulsory, and if one would try to avoid it, it was considered sabotage and one was consequently arrested, or, as happened to many, just disappeared.

JÜRGEN B. : 259

What happened to your sister? Was she, too, working at the factory? And where is your mother?

Fortunately my sister managed to get over to England in 1939. That was arranged by my mother, who wrote to England to a children's hospital, and my sister was accepted as a baby nurse. My sister is two years older than I. My mother apparently is not alive anymore. On the 27th of February 1943 we were taken away from work. I worked at that time on the railroad, and the *Leibstandarte Adolf Hitler*[2] packed us into a truck, and we were all driven to a distribution camp.

We will come to that later. Did they pay you for the work?

Yes, a little. The women were getting forty pfennig an hour, and I—I was still considered a juvenile—got something like forty-three or forty-four pfennig an hour. I still lived at home. We had an apartment of three rooms and a kitchen. The situation became more and more acute, and it started with the order to wear the Jewish star.[3] It became dangerous to walk on the streets. Nazi agents, Gestapo agents would arrest Jews on the streets. For instance, I had a friend who worked with me. His father was arrested one evening. It was said that an assault had been made on a Nazi installation, and these Jews, I think there were 500 as far as I can remember, were all shot at the SS armory in Lichterfelde.[4] And the relatives of these people were forcibly dragged away. They called it "evacuation" that time. Only later we got to know what that really meant.

Didn't you know the truth at that time?

No. And I have the impression that even the Jewish Council did not know because, even later when I was arrested, they supplied us with soap and pieces of clothing, since we were taken from work and had nothing with us except the things on our person. I think that if they had known *where* we were going, they wouldn't have done that for us. In Berlin nearly all Jews were arrested at once. Some fifty Jews who worked nearby in the station were taken. We just didn't know what was happening to us. All at once we were surrounded by [the SS]. We were trampled, kicked, and loaded into trucks. We were taken to a distribution camp, which was just a building of the Jewish Community. They had mattresses, and we had to spend three or four days under guard there. And again the trucks came, and again the guard took us to a remote railroad depot. We were shoved

2. Hitler's personal SS bodyguard regiments.

3. This order came into force in September 1941.

4. B. refers to the torching of an anti-Soviet exhibition in Berlin on May 18, 1942, by the "Baum Group" of Jewish resisters. Half of the 500 Jews taken hostage in reprisal were shot, and the remainder perished in Sachsenhausen concentration camp.

into railroad cars. The cars were locked, and we were forewarned that if anyone should escape from the car, the whole carload would be shot.

Did your mother know when you were arrested?
I don't know. I haven't seen my mother since that time.
At that time we were about fifty people to a car. Women, men, and children [were] all together. The doors were locked. We left at about 5:00 in the afternoon and next evening about half past ten we arrived in Auschwitz. The Jewish Community Council had supplied us with six slices of bread, margarine, and cheese. In each car they had placed a can with water, a large vessel.

What kind of cars were they?
The usual cars for transport, freight cars. We had no toilet, and during the day it became a very acute problem, because due to the excitement many people had to use the toilet, but there wasn't any. We had a kind of a dishpan in the car, and it was very uncomfortable, and the air became bad.

Were all the people in the car from the same place where you worked?
No, by that time there were all kinds of people in the cars. The men were compelled to give the addresses of their wives because they presumably had to know where they were going, and then the women were brought from their homes by the police. And now, I remember, I have forgotten something that I consider very important. Before being sent away, we had to sign affidavits that we had to leave Germany on account of our disloyalty and hostility to Germany.

What happened when you arrived in Auschwitz?
We were driven out of the cars by SS men who in addition to their firearms were armed with walking sticks. They just started clubbing us, and the women were compelled to go over to one side and the men to the other side, and we were separated. There were screams and wails which were terrible to listen to and which one cannot describe. I shall never forget those screams.

Why did they start screaming? Were these women the wives of the men?
Oh, certainly. There were many couples, and in some cases the men had the children in their arms, and the women were compelled to take the children from the men. In the crowd and in the dark they were unable to find their wives, and that is why the screams were so terrible, and possibly the people had a premonition of what was going to happen to them. Well, I was among the men, and an SS man asked me whether I was in good health, and I replied "Yes," so he told me that I must go to the right side. And on the left side stood old and feeble men

and mostly women and children and all kinds of elderly people. Much later we learned that these women and elderly people were taken to be gassed.

It appeared strange to me. I couldn't understand what it all meant. I looked around and saw the turrets all manned by SS guards with machine guns, and at a distance I saw great fires. I didn't know what that was. Only later I learned that these were the crematoria of Auschwitz, and all these masses of people were gassed and burned.

Then we were loaded on big trucks and taken to Buna. When we arrived, we were again beaten, and then we had to stand there until 5:00 in the morning.

Why were you beaten?

Why? Most people didn't know why. There was a so-called camp senior who was one of the first prisoners of the camp. He was a professional criminal. He was not a Jew. And he beat the people indiscriminately. For example, I still remember that the father of one of my friends was pushed by his trusty toward an open stove and burned a big hole into his legs.

Then we were led to the bathing room. There we had to bathe with ice cold water, and they cut our hair from the entire body. That was done by prisoners. We were submitted to what they called a delousing process. We were rubbed with kerosene. We had to walk naked across the yard and take another cold shower, and again we went naked across the yard, and then we were given a damp shirt that had just come from the laundry, the prisoner's coat and pants, and a pullover.

A warm one? Were the things new?

Some of them were thin, some were heavy. That depended on how lucky a fellow was. The things had all been worn, taken from the previous transport as was customary in Auschwitz. The things had belonged to those who were taken to the gas chambers and the like. You see, we had to leave all our things at the station.

When I was sent to the camp, we had to register. We were tattooed with the Auschwitz numbers. I was given the number 106377; the triangle was added three months later, and that means a Jew. The Polish prisoners and the foreign workers were also tattooed, and so they wanted to mark the Jews distinctly. And then we were sent to work the next morning. Many attempted to commit suicide. They would run out of formation and would be shot. Their number was then written on their stomach, the same number they had on their arms, with an indelible pencil, and then they were loaded on trucks and transported to the crematoria. I was assigned to a detail that was in charge of carrying cement. We had to work without stopping even if somebody's pants would slide down and, of course, the pants did not fit well. In most cases people had pants that were too big for them. We couldn't pull up our pants, and there was always a capo who would beat us with an iron rod as soon as anyone would make an attempt to rest or to interrupt the work.

In June 1943 I was transferred to the Auschwitz main camp, [where] we were near everything. We knew what was going on, while in the auxiliary camp we knew nothing. We knew that people were taken away in trucks. We were told they were taken to other camps. But nobody knew exactly what was happening to them. I learned what was going on only later in Auschwitz [i.e., the main camp]. For instance, if people were sick, they were put in a special barracks. Their names were taken down, supposedly because they were to be given more bread on account of their poor health. The next day they would be loaded on trucks and taken to the gas chambers. There they were gassed, and the next day the clothing that these people were wearing was back in the laundry.

Seven people altogether were transferred by truck [from Buna to the main camp]. We were taken for the simple reason that they asserted that [we were] too weak. We were put into the so-called sick people's building, and we were told that we should try to get out of there as quickly as possible in order to escape from being gassed. Fortnightly transports were taken from Auschwitz [to Birkenau], sometimes even oftener. I immediately reported that I felt well again and that I wanted to return to work. And on the strength of that report they released me from the sick people's barracks, and I was assigned to a carpentry shop located between Auschwitz and Birkenau. In the beginning we worked nights and often at 12:00 at night my friend and I would climb up into the upper story of the shop, and from there we could see how the fires were burning.

[Evidently conversation continued during a break to change spools. Boder summarized:]

And so, Jürgen, at first you were doing construction work and then you were transferred to a fishery. Go ahead.

In September 1943, around the time when Italy capitulated and the Fascist system had broken down, the anger of the Nazis became very great, and immediately they assembled a large transport to be gassed, and I was also assigned to this transport. But I extricated myself by a trick. The transport had to leave after the daily roll call, which usually occurred in the evening, that is, after work when a count was taken daily to see whether anyone had gone astray or run away. And when these reports were transmitted to the commander of the camp, I simply marched off to work instead of the gassing to which I was assigned.

But how did you know you'd been assigned to the gas chambers? Who told you?

Well, they told me that a transport was being formed for weak people to go to another camp where there was lighter work. But that didn't seem right to me. At my bunk—we had three-level bunks—there was a cross mark made with chalk meaning that I was being assigned for this transport. I saved myself by going to work. When I returned to the camp next morning, this whole transport had been gassed, and their clothing was already back from the laundry, as was usual. I saved my life that way. I did it in collusion with the capo.

Was the capo a Jew?

No, a German. He was even a professional criminal, but at times he showed some very good traits.

Did you give him something for it?

No. I couldn't give him anything because I was not in a position to do so.

Now I want to tell you how afterward, when the Russians were approaching, we were transported to Dachau, and that is interesting because this was the greatest torture of all we had undergone in the camps. We were accustomed to a lot, but Dachau was the worst, and probably most of the people lost their lives. On the 18th of January 1945 we saw flare bombs going off at the front. Krakow was within sixty kilometers from us, and rumors trickled through that the Russians were already in Krakow. All at once we were all put to transport. One transport left in the morning, but we still had to go to work during that day. We returned to the camp in the evening, and we were the last ones to go.

It was very cold that day. We were given some food to take with us and then sent on the march. We marched through the night for hours and arrived in Ploetz. En route many, many people who could not keep up were shot. Those who stopped, everyone who fell on the road, was shot, no matter whether it was a man or a woman. You see, we left after the women, and we overtook them before Ploetz, and en route we saw many dead bodies of women lying on the ground. We marched at night, and we had to rest during the day, so that the people should not see us being led through. And evenings when it was dark, we marched on again.

[B.'s group then mounted freight cars for a trip to Gross-Rosen concentration camp where conditions were so bad that he and others volunteered to go to Dachau.]

We stepped forward, we were given a plate of soup, and we were sent to the station accompanied by SS men and loaded into wagons. Some were gondola cars, some closed cars. We thought that the closed cars were better, but later it turned out that we were worse off. We stood at the cars, and soon the SS men drove us into them, 120 people into each. The doors were shut.

We had no food with us, and then we tried to sit down. When 80 people sat down, the others had no place to stand, and there were many people who were very tired. We trampled on other people's fingers, and these people, of course, resisted, and were striking each other, and so a panic ensued. It was so terrible that people went crazy during the trip, and soon we had the first death among us. And we didn't know where to put the dead. They were taking up space on the floor. And then a way out occurred to us. We had a blanket with us, so we wrapped the first dead man into the blanket and tied him onto two iron bars above us in the car, like in a hammock. But soon we discovered that this wouldn't work, because we had more and more dead due to the heat in the car. And the bodies began to smell.

There were German troop transports retreating from the front, and we had to stand for days to let the troop transports through first, and at night one could not see a thing. And one was beaten and trampled. In my case it happened that my prisoner's trousers were torn lengthwise, and I couldn't wear my trousers any more. And I remained in my underpants. And so without any nourishment, without a drop of water—there was snow outside, [but] the SS men gave us nothing—there was a mass of insane and dead people in the car.

After five days we arrived in Regensburg. And it was night when the SS men opened the doors and said, "If you throw out the dead bodies, you will get some food." And so I myself, together with a friend, removed twenty-five dead bodies from this car and laid them outside in the snow. Then we were given a piece of bread and a little paper beaker of soup. The Red Cross had their feeding point there, so we had to line up before the cars, and each was given some, car after car.

Was that the German Red Cross?
Yes. After we had eaten, we had to get back into the cars. And so I was in my underpants in the snow. I had no socks on, and I don't know what the people there may have thought—those sisters and nurses, but at any rate, we traveled on.

Couldn't you get yourself another pair of pants?
No, that was impossible unless I would have taken them from a dead man. But I was so exhausted from the long trip, and I hadn't eaten anything for five days and nights. I had been standing all the way and I saved my life only because I had fastened a piece of rope to the car and held on tight. It was indeed utterly impossible. For instance, a friend of mine, who withstood all the years in Auschwitz, went insane during this trip and attempted to attack us with a knife. Four of us, even five, had to hold him, otherwise he would have killed somebody. It was decidedly a panic. We always were afraid of the night because [then] we couldn't see

when someone approached. The whole car was in a tumult, and we heard later when we arrived in Dachau that in the open cars it had been the same. At least there they had air, but many of the people froze to death. And when we arrived in Dachau, there were more dead bodies than survivors. It was the younger people who withstood it.

I was in Dachau altogether three weeks. A great epidemic of spotted typhus raged in Dachau, and entire barracks were dying out. In the morning the dead were put on hay carts and taken away for cremation. Today I myself don't know how the epidemic spared us, because in front and on the sides there were barracks with typhus—it was terrible. Most of the people tried to wash themselves as often as possible during the day to escape this epidemic because there were swarms of lice. And three weeks later, after we marched past the commandant, he made the selection [of] who went to transport and who remained in the invalid block.

I myself chose to go to transport, to a camp called Mühldorf, a locality near Rosenheim seventy-eight kilometers [southeast of] Munich in Upper Bavaria. When we arrived we saw a camp of the kind we had not seen in Auschwitz. It really was not a camp at all. There were only round paper tents—the so-called Finnish tents. And most of the blocks lay half underground. Water was available at this camp only every four or five days. We were guarded by SS men and at work by the Organization Todt.[5]

The Organization Todt? Who were they?

They were men in brown uniforms with swastika arm bands and did as much chicanery as the SS. There was no difference. We had to carry cement there. They intended to build an airport. The work was proceeding in three shifts. After the Russians had occupied large districts of Germany, naturally another reduction in rations came about. Then we were only given one loaf of bread for eight people, one slice of bread a day per person.

Where was that bread baked?

In Mühldorf, in part by [commercial] bakers. And I believe there was also a bakery in the camp. I remember that during an air attack this bread depot was set afire, and we didn't get any bread at all for four days, just three or four boiled potatoes. And the conditions in Mühldorf were catastrophic. People were covered with lice. We received no underwear to change. The people who arrived at the camp from as far away as Warsaw did not receive fresh laundry for months. There were no towels. If one wanted to wash himself, he had to dry himself with his

5. The Organization Todt performed essential building tasks during the war, often using conscripted and concentration camp labor. It was named for Fritz Todt, Hitler's first minister of arms and munitions.

only shirt. And it was very difficult to keep clean because in the lugging of cement one would get completely white, and it was very difficult to endure, since water was available only one in four or five days. Typhus began to rage on a large scale, and I was also struck.

We were lying in a round tent, and in this tent the beds were mounted in three levels one over the other. We were two in each bed, and it was very unpleasant. For example, if a man died, he would not be removed before twenty-four hours had elapsed because the block senior wanted the bread ration and soup allotted to this person. And so we had to lie all that time in bed with the dead person. That happened to me personally with a dead Frenchman. And he died from intestinal typhus, from diarrhea, and I had to lie with him a whole day.

On what level was your bunk?

We were on the middle level, and that was a very gruesome situation, especially at night. First of all, the dead men were badly emaciated, and they looked terrible. In most cases they would soil themselves at the moment of death, and that was not a very esthetic event. I saw such cases very frequently in the sick people's barracks. People who died from phlegmonous, suppurative wounds, with their beds overflowing with pus would be lying next to somebody whose illness was possibly more benign, who had possibly just a small wound which now would become infected.

Sometimes a physician happened to make his rounds in the morning. He would come without any drugs or instruments. With plain scissors, large suppurative wounds would be opened. With the same scissors, without previously cleaning them, he would attend another patient who had possibly just a small wound. Bandages were almost nonexistent. The bandages were of paper and they would last a maximum of an hour. There were no remedies at all against fever such as aspirin and the like at the end, and the more we were surrounded by the Allied troops the more catastrophic the situation became. At the end things became totally disorganized in the camp, so catastrophic that we were not given any more food. The SS men got busy with trying to escape before the Americans arrived. A special German police was put on the watch towers, and then, when the SS departed, but before the Americans arrived, the stores of supplies were looted by the prisoners. People were completely famished. But we, the sick, were unable to get up and so got nothing. It was ordered that the sick also be shot, but then the camp commander got scared, because at this late hour he was afraid to comply, and we simply remained lying there.

24 Hildegard F.

German Jews living in mixed marriages with German Christians were among the last to be taken away. Hildegard F.'s fate was sealed when her Christian husband died during the war. A little more than two months later she was sent to Theresienstadt.

Hildegard F.'s family lost its retail shop in Nuremberg to the Nazis in 1934, following which her two sons emigrated to the United States. She says nothing about her husband and herself trying to get out, although it seems probable that the elderly couple, already in their sixties, saw little hope of starting over someplace else. Her husband's failing health may also have slowed them down. Following his death in October 1943, Hildegard was deported to the "model ghetto" at Theresienstadt in the comparative luxury of a third-class passenger coach. She knows no good reason why she was spared subsequent transport to the killing fields of Poland. In the end her comment about being lucky is as good an explanation as any.

A particularly vivid memory of Theresienstadt was of SS attempts to intimidate F. into renouncing her husband's will, which evidently bene-fited his relatives. Had she agreed, the Nazis could have declared his estate Hildegard's and then confiscated it upon her death.[1] That she was able to resist their pressure demonstrates that the SS was not prepared to go too far where the property rights of purely German relatives were concerned. The facade of law and order had to be upheld.

F. returned to her bombed-out apartment after the war to find its remaining contents looted by the couple, also intermarried, who had subletted from her. However, other property that she had left for safe-keeping with a Christian friend was safely returned to her. Boder commented that he found many cases of Jews slated for deportation entrust-ing their valuables to Gentile friends and retrieving them satisfactorily after the war, especially in Czechoslovakia and Western Europe.

When interviewed at her temporary home in the Munich "Funken-kasernen" DP camp in September 1946, Hildegard F. had regained the weight she lost at Theresienstadt and looked younger than her seventy-five years. She was just days away from departure for Bremen and the sea

---

1. Under the terms of the Thirteenth Ordinance of the Reich Citizenship Law, July 1, 1943.

voyage that would take her to live with her sons in America. We begin with her description of the 1934 "Aryanization" of her family store.

I was in Nuremberg with my sons and my husband. We were working with *my* relatives in a "ready-to-wear" store. And in 1934 we were compelled to sell the business since we were Jews. Our employees were completely of National Socialist orientation and reported every customer who purchased from us to the "Brown House" [Nazi party headquarters], so people withdrew their patronage.

What kind of a business did you say it was?
A very large business of ladies' "ready-to-wear" [clothes]. You simply purchased them from the manufacturer and then sold them ready-made.

Ours was a mixed marriage. Because I was a Jewess, my husband [and] sons had to be discharged, simply put out on the street, so to speak. The sons then emigrated to America. [Now] I am all alone. My husband died. [He] was very, very ill due to all these harassments and the hardships that we endured. And due to the air raids which we lived through. For nearly a full half year I hardly got out of my clothes in order to be able to help my sick husband to the cellar when the [air] attacks would start.

Where were you during all that time?
In Nuremberg. In 1943 it became so frightful [that] I went to the country with my husband for a few weeks. There he became very, very sick. I had to return him to Nuremberg in order to submit him to an operation.

Now your husband was a Christian?
Yes, and he was German. And then he died in Nuremberg in October 1943. And on the 17th of January 1944, with two days notice, I had to vacate my apartment and was moved to the KZ where . . . [Here she broke down and wept bitterly.] Let me take hold of myself a bit.

At the age of seventy-three I was dragged away to Theresienstadt.

Now tell me, you say they gave you two days to liquidate your apartment?
Yes. I could not move from the apartment anymore. I was compelled to leave everything exactly as it was.

How many people went with you to Theresienstadt?
Fifteen people went with my transport. We were [sent] by train under guard of the SA of the Gestapo.[2] It was a third-class railroad car. [The other people] all

2. F. confuses two very different organizations. The guards were probably SS men.

were of mixed marriages. Only the Jews. [At Theresienstadt] they assigned us to an attic of a building where we had to sleep and live. Below was an infirmary for incurables. About thirty-five people were lodged in that attic, women and men together in the same room. We slept in a kind of box with a sack of straw.

A bed for each one separately?
Yes. I was permitted to take only the most indispensable things with me. A suitcase with clothes, which I had been using at the time, a little underwear, a blanket, and a pillow. I was allowed to keep it. I happened to be lucky, but many had it stolen, so that they had nothing.

How was it afterward in Theresienstadt? How long were you there?
A year and a half. Until the liberation by the Russians had come. For seven weeks I lay in the hospital. The "Grand Hotel," it was called.[3] And there I lay for seven weeks, because I lost weight so quickly. Within three months, four months, I had lost forty pounds. That was too much. So all my inner organs, heart and everything, were affected by it.

And what did they do for you there?
Oh, dear God! How much could they do? I was discharged too early, because this hospital was really used only for people with lung sickness. And so I was returned to my attic.

Who were the physicians in this hospital?
Jewish physicians. There were only Jews there.

Now tell me, as time passed and it came nearer to the defeat, did the conditions change a bit in Theresienstadt?
No. I mean at the end we did not believe anymore that we would ever be freed. We were completely cut off from the world. We did not get any news, nothing. No newspapers, no radio, not even a letter placed in a package. They took that away, too.

Did you get any packages? Didn't you have any friends left in Nuremberg?
Yes, but none of them sent me anything. I also did not request anything, because I did not want to embarrass those people. Because it was strictly prohibited that the Jews should have anything sent to them.[4]

3. A large, one-story building facetiously called the "Grand Hotel" even before Theresienstadt was turned into a ghetto.
4. This is not correct, although many Germans were reluctant to call attention to

Now tell me, did you still have any money?
No, not a penny. I was not permitted to take any money. But there was ghetto money in Theresienstadt—sorry, I don't have any with me. Every month we got fifty crowns so we could buy something. Now the food was less than paltry. We were fed from a central kitchen. We had to fetch the food, and we sat down on the bed and ate. We didn't know what a table was anymore. I had my own bed linen; these I had taken with me. And I washed them regularly. We got some soap paste. There was very little of that.

Did it not get a little better toward the end?
Commissions began to come from Sweden and from Switzerland, and it had to become a bit better for us. What the Nazis wanted to show was put in order. The rest remained as it was. Then once we would get a bit more food, and when the commissions left, they deducted if from us again—we got less.

Who were the Nazis with whom you had come in contact?
We had less contact with the Nazis. It was the Council of Elders who received the orders from the Nazis, and the council had to execute them.

Once I was summoned to the commandant's office where I was confronted with a will which I and my husband had made out in the year 1932. And they asked me if that was in the handwriting of my husband, and they told me to declare it void. I did not agree to that. I said to myself that I lived with my husband in a very happy marriage, a forty-three-year happy marriage, and that the family of my husband was sacred to me.

Was that a Jewish group that . . . ?
No. These were the SS! And if I somehow had voided it [the will], then *they* would have taken over everything. We had some property. The apartment and the furniture, everything that there was. And so they were very eagerly after it in order to distribute it among their Nazis. But they could not do that, because everything was in the name of my husband, and I did not agree to give it up.

Did they not threaten you?
No. I just told them that under no circumstances would I acquiesce to counteract the wishes of my husband, and the will should remain as is.

---

themselves by sending packages to Jewish friends and relatives. F. may be making excuses for them.

Tell me please, were there any selections in Theresienstadt?

You mean transports? Oh God in heaven! In my time many, many people were sent to Poland. So and so many people were simply ordered. And the transports came for them; partly for Auschwitz, partly for Belsen. They were kept in KZs, and almost all of these people perished. Then there was one transport, the last one, in October. Eighteen thousand people were dragged off to Poland. Germans and all possible nations were among them.

How did you succeed in remaining there?

That I don't know. I had luck.

Were there any in the transports who came with you from Nuremberg?

There were. And of them only a single one, a woman, has returned. She was a younger person. The others all perished.

[After liberation by the Russians, F. returned to Nuremberg in July 1945.]

We were fetched from Theresienstadt in cargo trucks by the Americans.

Now what did you find of your property in Nuremberg?

Nothing at all. The house was bombed out. Of my whole apartment I salvaged hardly anything. The people who had sublet from me had helped themselves rather well. There were only a few things, a few valuables that I had stored away with a Dr. Mombart.

A Christian?

Yes. He kept it for me wonderfully, while the intermarried couple who lived in my apartment did exactly the contrary. But I don't want to do anything against these people. It is over. I don't want to prosecute. They have deprived me of a lot. They left the apartment afterward. A bomb hit. It tore off one wall, but the things, the furniture remained standing. I got a few pieces back, but they said they had nothing more.

And your bank account? Did you get that back?

Yes. But of the furnishings of my apartment, I lost very, very much.

25 Friedrich S.

Friedrich S. was a retired Viennese civil servant, sixty-four years of age when Hitler annexed their native Austria to the Third Reich in March 1938. Born in Mistelbach in Lower Austria, S. was an architectural engineer by profession and a former ministerial counselor in the Austrian Railroad Ministry. As a former member of the Habsburg imperial bureaucracy, S. enjoyed a comfortable pension and the respect of his community. In retirement he divided his time between an old hobby studying the acoustical properties of wooden instruments and service to the Jewish community as head of a local B'nai B'rith chapter. S. describes initial Austrian Nazi measures against him and his associates, which were part of an anti-Jewish program that greatly impressed officials from Germany proper. He and his wife were able to send their daughter to England as a domestic servant at that time, but they themselves were unable to find a place of refuge before the Nazis banned emigration in October 1941.

Friedrich S.'s status as a former Habsburg civil servant and a leading figure in the Vienna Jewish community helped determine that he and his wife would be sent to the "old folks" ghetto at Theresienstadt in occupied Czechoslovakia. Initially placed in the fortress at the edge of town and then moved into Theresienstadt proper, they participated in plucky efforts to make the hideously overcrowded facilities capable of supporting at least some of the prisoners. While his wife worked as a nurse in the infirmary, Friedrich S. volunteered for the camp's technical services, using his engineering skills to pipe clean water into the town. He is obviously proud of an achievement that doubtless saved thousands of lives.

Was Friedrich S. one of the privileged Jews who survived by exploiting their prominent positions and contacts with the camp's Jewish leaders? S. takes pains to distance himself from Jewish Council chairman Rabbi Benjamin Murmelstein and other camp notables, but Boder's probing of this point implies that he entertained some doubts on the matter. Indeed, later in the interview S. reveals that on more than one occasion he was able to get his name removed from lists of prisoners scheduled for deportation to Polish death camps. That happened even when members of the important construction detail were losing their previous immunity to deportation. Moreover, S. and his wife enjoyed a "very lovely" private apartment that went with his administrative position in the technical services department during the last months of the ghetto. On the other hand, there is no direct evidence that S. was corrupted by power. Otherwise it seems unlikely that he would have been entrusted with important postliberation tasks on behalf of his former fellow captives.

When interviewed at the Paris offices of the American Jewish Joint Distribution Committee in August 1946, Friedrich S. was awaiting a telephone call from Lisbon with information on his ship to South Africa. There he hoped to join his son, who had emigrated before the war. We take up his interview with his arrest shortly after the German takeover of Austria.

[We were accused] of connections with Communist groups, above all with Moscow. They searched for our correspondence with Moscow, they searched all our archives, they incessantly inquired about our connections with New York, with the "Elders of Zion." We were beaten with rubber truncheons. We were thrown into those closed patrol wagons like cattle, and driven to the police jail where we spent the night. On the following morning we were distributed in separate rooms and placed like common offenders. I personally, with six others [who were] arrested with me, was placed in a cell for serious criminals that measured about three by three meters. My wife remained home, comparatively unmolested during that time. We [men] were regularly taken to the main police station for night interrogations, and in the morning we were returned to jail. That lasted two to three weeks. I shouldn't say every night, but a large part of the nights were spent in night interrogations.

Could you engage lawyers?
My wife had endeavored to engage a non-Jewish lawyer. And that was successful; a Nazi lawyer succeeded [in getting me] released by the end of March. This time being home was, of course, hardly bearable, because one was not safe for a single night against searches. On the pretext of searching for arms, they ransacked everything that could have looked like concealed objects of value. Valuables were simply taken away under assurance that these things could at any time be reclaimed from the Gestapo. But in fact a great deal of the jewelry simply disappeared. In apartments where the owners failed to show their possessions voluntarily, everything was searched, all the leather furniture coverings were cut, the upholstery searched in order to establish whether jewelry, pearls, diamonds, or valuables were concealed anywhere. That happened in my house [apartment building], while with me personally they contented themselves with taking whatever they found in the strongbox and some other valuables.

This was a frightful time because one never knew when one would be arrested. One was repeatedly arrested. It happened to me three times. However, twice I was released again in the same manner and lived in Vienna up to September 1941. However, I was unable to retain my apartment. We were compelled to sell our buildings. In one of my buildings I had my apartment, and I had, of course, to give that up too. We were compelled to retreat into furnished rooms, more and more crowded. During these three years I moved five times.

Did they pay for the buildings which you were compelled to sell?
About a fourth to a fifth of their real value. These buildings were purchased by people who had to have an affidavit, so to speak, that they had rendered services to the Party and therefore deserved to obtain Jewish property. We had prepared ourselves for emigration to South Africa before we abandoned our apartment. Unfortunately nothing came from this emigration, since I was unable to obtain the [entry] permit for South Africa, in spite of all efforts by my son, who by that time was not yet naturalized [there]. We then tried to emigrate to Australia, and again we were unable to obtain the [entry] permit. All attempts with the help of American lodges to obtain an affidavit for America dragged out so long that conditions for emigration became impossible. I tried to get to Cuba, but also that could not be realized, and in August of 1942 we were informed that we had to expect our deportation within the next few weeks.

Who informed you about that?
The Jewish Council had taken it upon itself to select the people and get them ready for transport. It was thought—I don't know whether that was correct—that if the Jews did it themselves, it would proceed in a more "humane" form. Otherwise the Gestapo themselves would do it. But it appeared that the Gestapo was not eager to undertake this matter and found it more comfortable to let the Jews make these selections. In fact, the council was compelled to devote its whole personnel to these selections. With some exceptions, most of them did so. I regret to say that they did it because they believed their own persons [would be] protected. And indeed they were protected until nearly the last moment—until the winter of 1942–43.

We did not possess much anymore. We had become poorer and poorer through the various moves. We packed the most indispensable items into our trunks and made ready for the voyage, and indeed we were sent off on the 7th or 8th of September with a transport from Vienna to Theresienstadt.

This transport proceeded in a comparatively humane manner, because I voluntarily entered into an agreement. I had been selected once before already. Arrangements had already been made and in a manner customary in Vienna. Our house would be taken over by the employees of the Deportation Service of the

Jewish Council. The house would be blocked off, [and] one of these "deporters" would be assigned to each floor. He then [would take charge] of the people in the separate apartments—the apartments were thickly populated, because two, often three or four persons lived in each room. Each family had one room, so that twenty persons lived in one apartment of four to five rooms. All these people were then assembled in one room. The Jewish Council had one functionary on each floor [who] made them wait until the arrival of a functionary of the Gestapo. He would then go through the whole building from bottom to top, would look over each and every one, and decide whether the particular person was to be deported or remain. On what basis such a decision was made I don't know.

The people [who] had to pack went to it immediately with the help of the functionaries of the Jewish Council; its Deportation Service would proceed to get their effects ready for the trip. They had to be ready by six o'clock in the morning. The people were not permitted to leave their apartments anymore. In the morning a truck appeared with an additional trailer, and the people with their bundles were loaded on them and taken to the assembly station to wait until the general transport was ready. The transports were usually about 2,000 strong.

These people were assembled at the assembly station, former homes or schools of the Jewish Council. Often the people had to remain in these homes eight days. They, of course, had no means to take proper care of themselves; they were sparsely fed . . .

Who took care of that?
The Jewish Council through its "feeding" units. And in a few days, when the organization of the transports was completed, they came again with the trucks, and again they traveled with their bundles to the embarkation.

Now tell me. You say you presented yourself voluntarily? Why was that?
Because I believed I had rendered such services to Jewish public life that I at least had the right to demand not to have to spend another five or six or eight days exposed to vermin and lice, unable to sleep. [I hoped] that they would arrange it in such a way that I should not have to go through too great hardships. That is why I was told, "You must hold yourself ready for such and such a day, present yourself on that day at such and such a home," and that is what I did.

And so you arrived there with you wife. How much baggage did you have?
Two large trunks, two small trunks, and two bedrolls. We hoped that we would really be able to take this baggage with us. Assurances were given that it would not be taken away. It turned out differently. On the 8th of September we were put on a train which departed from the East railroad station in Vienna and ar-

rived on the 9th in Theresienstadt via Prague. That didn't even take twenty-four hours. We were sent in a regular third-class passenger coach. Crowded!

The arrival at Theresienstadt was . . . very sad. We were disembarked and were compelled to carry our hand baggage. The large pieces were on a carriage brought into the city later. The railroad station is located about a half-hour walk from Theresienstadt. It is obvious that for such a distance, with all these old people, much more than a half an hour was required. It took us more than an hour and a quarter, and we did not present an especially beautiful sight, [but one] which we observed repeatedly in the following years during our stay in Theresienstadt.

We crowded in, we dragged ourselves in with the others. We were received by the Gestapo and the Czech gendarmerie. Our baggage was searched, and everything prohibited was taken away. Unfortunately, we were assigned to the worst armory. Theresienstadt is a city which owes its existence solely to military needs and is completely cut off from the outside by a system of deep trenches which could be flooded with water. These trenches were about eight or ten meters deep and thirty meters wide with adjoining mason walls on the outside facing the surrounding terrain. Some of these positions were artillery positions. The heavy artillery was located on the bastion, and the trenches were designed to make the city safe from every kind of attack. There were about eight large armories, and the rest of the city in between these armories consisted mostly of one-story structures in which everything was located that the military could use in their spare time, such as restaurants, cafés, small and large stores, artisan shops, and all that was required for a garrison of about 8,000 men.

By the time we arrived the Czech population was already evacuated. Of course, the place was not in any condition to offer human habitation to such a multitude. The population in normal times was about 8,000 military men and about 4,000 of the civilian population. I know that the population of this ghetto at one time reached over 65,000 people. That is in excess of five times the normal population. [Hence] in an average room of about twenty-five square meters, up to twelve or fifteen people had to be accommodated; which, of course, was not possible unless the wooden beds were put over each other up to three levels high.

From the beginning my wife and I endeavored to show ourselves useful to the commonweal. My wife immediately reported as a nurse for a hospital, and I undertook the "liberation" of about 100 of my comrades in transport, with whom we were lodged in the so-called Border Riflemen's armory. This was an ancient structure which consisted only of arched vaults covered high with a layer of earth, about four to five meters thick, on [which] the artillery positions of the fortress were originally located.

We were lodged in subterranean masonry structures, small, very dark rooms about five to six meters wide and about forty meters deep. On both of the narrow sides was a small double window. In each of these casemates 90 to 100 men were lodged, and we, too, had to live [there]. We did not know that a hospital was also located in this armory, that typhus and dysentery patients were located next to our casemates. And indeed, from the first few days cases of grave illness occurred. Every day a few died, and in the hospital where my wife rendered her services people [died] daily.

In the beginning we had nothing to lay down on. We covered the stone floors of the casemates with straw sacks which we obtained later on, put our clothes and the pieces of bedding we had brought with us on them, and managed to arrange a place for ourselves for the night.

Were men and women together?

Men and women were together. There were mostly old people, rarely with a son or a daughter. There were hardly any young people. And the old people were frequently in such a state that they perished during the first few weeks. Besides, after eight and fourteen days there were further selections, and a large part of my comrades were again sent away to Polish camps. Nobody ever knew where these transports went, and there were never letters from these people anymore.

The inhabitants of these casemates suffered badly, of course, from vermin and the danger of becoming louse infested. Nobody could properly undress or change clothes because nobody could properly wash himself. People in the casemates actually died amidst their own excrement. After two months my wife suffered a breakdown; she was not up to the strains of night watches. She had to give that up and took over another service.

Where was the latrine?

At the end of the casemate, in a precarious condition, so that one shuddered when one had to use it. The women had a toilet at the other end of the building. A toilet which with four or five sections was, of course, by far insufficient for the approximately 1,200 people who were housed in this armory, so that people would stand in line.

And how would the women change clothes or dress?

One had to hang up something, or the men looked away. It was . . . a special existence; people got accustomed to a great deal under these conditions.

What was done with the dead people, the ones who died?

These were put together in another casemate. The bodies were then called for a day or two later for interment. [When] we had an epidemic of dysentery and typhus, one night 220 or 240 people happened to die. My neighbor . . . in the morning he was dead.

Now tell me, were there any religious manifestations, did they permit the people to pray, a synagogue . . . ?

Yes. In a short time opportunities presented themselves. Regular prayer hours were held in prayer rooms, in synagogues. Premises were converted into synagogues, and the hours of prayer were normally maintained. There were always services, and there were always many Jews who participated in the services.

There was a large number of Jewish actors, pianists, violin virtuosos, singers; there were film people. There was no shortage of cultural life. [But] cultural life came to develop only when the whole management of Theresienstadt was steered into an organized course. It took the whole first year of my sojourn there. During the first year conditions had to be created so that people could live. We had no water system. With 65,000 people crowded together in such a small locality, and dependent on wells to obtain their water, a number of wells were contaminated in a short time with typhoid fever. That was the reason that we had to close a number of wells and undertake to extend the existing water pipe system. That was really a great piece of public works created under Jewish inventiveness and by Jewish labor. They expanded the water supply system, and not only produced good drinking water but also enabled the toilet installations to be flushed with water, so that these unhygienic conditions were removed. The Germans permitted it, and we even obtained the material from them.

The Border Riflemen's armory was abandoned in two months because of the need of a thorough disinfection, due to being infested with lice and other vermin. And we were distributed into other dwellings. We, ourselves, were assigned to a so-called block building. Those are the one-time private dwellings in Theresienstadt where we, my wife and twelve or fourteen other women, I and eleven other men, occupied one room [for each of the groups], in which we were housed the whole winter of '42 and '43. In view of the urgency to keep all rooms in strict darkness against air attacks, and the severe penalties that threatened for infractions against the black-out rules, it was impossible for the inhabitants of such rooms to maintain a supply of fresh air. The nights, therefore, were painful.

Afterward, in the spring of 1945, the inhabitants of Theresienstadt were screened. The Gestapo made a classification and took note of prominent individuals [who were] granted somewhat better living conditions. The people who were put in the class of the prominent were usually given a room for two, so that a family of husband and wife obtained a room and could live by themselves. The prominent were also, to some extent, protected against further deportations to the Polish camps. There were not too many, about one hundred and fifty, two hundred prominent persons.

You were not among them?

I was not among the prominent. Murmelstein was among the prominent, [along with] a few of his people whom he brought with him. Friedmann and Stricker[1] were also among the prominent but lived in a house that was not reserved for the prominent.

You were not among the prominent?

I was not among the prominent, and also I, too, was put into the transports, but twice, one must say due to the play of fate, or God's will, I was counted out again.

In November 1942 I placed myself at the disposal of the technical services. I have already mentioned that we had to build up the water supply, to make the existing water installation serviceable for the needs of the present large population, to lay new water lines through all the streets, to work on the installation of the large tubes. We had to do not only that; we had to put the houses into such condition that they would better fit the sanitary requirements. That kept us very busy. We also had to look out for fire hazards, since we had to occupy the attics of the buildings because the [regular] floors did not offer enough space to house [all] the people. We had to form a fire brigade among the Jews. The Gestapo supplied us with a motor pump and two other pumps, and so a real fire brigade was established under a fire chief, and we also had to organize a fire police, which always had to inspect that the dwellings be beyond reproach from a standpoint of fire [safety]. We had to create a procedure of fire fighting, and that kept us busy for a few months.

We had to proceed with an immense number of other technical tasks which are contingent upon the management of such a mass of buildings. Besides—and of course this greatly occupied the technical service—the Gestapo with its whole personnel placed great emphasis on their quarters being maintained under most perfect conditions. Something always had to be built, they always had some demands; nothing was good enough for them, because the "gentlemen" from the Gestapo lived in their own buildings [in] a special section of the city, separated for the Gestapo alone, [with] large park outlays, the beautiful, the modern, the best buildings of Theresienstadt. Marvelous accommodations had to be installed for the pastime of the Gestapo—cafés; restaurants; a cinema theater, a magnificent one; clubrooms—all that had to be created by us, and that took a large part of the efforts of the construction service.

1. Dr. Desider Friedmann and Robert Stricker, pre-Nazi Zionist leaders and Vienna Jewish Community administrators. Stricker also led the Austrian section of the World Jewish Congress.

These contacts with the Gestapo—were they friendly? Were they polite?

Most of the Jews had nothing to do with the Gestapo. One was glad not to see them. Naturally you had to be at attention and salute them on the streets. The same courtesy had to be shown to the [Czech] gendarmerie because they formed the guard service used by the Gestapo; the city was guarded by the Czech police. And so it was the duty of the inmates to salute every one of these people. They were not permitted to return the greeting, and they did not. One was glad not to have anything to do with them. Unfortunately, the chauffeurs of the Gestapo drove their automobiles in the most inconsiderate manner, and there were quite a few cases where people were run over because they were unable to get out of the way in time. It even was said that one of the chauffeurs made it his business to run over Jews.

The work demanded from the technical service was very large in scope. By the beginning of the year 1944, it appeared that the Gestapo got orders to convert Theresienstadt into a "model" camp that could be shown to visiting people and possibly to the Red Cross. And so all at once an order came to beautify the city. [Then] the technical service had an unspeakable amount of work. Everything was to be put in order, everything had to be shined up, painted up; the streets had to be kept meticulously clean. No scrap of paper could be thrown away. It became, indeed, a rather clean little town.

The armories had to be partially evacuated because the Gestapo had transferred a large central archive from somewhere in Germany to Theresienstadt, a whole card index of the members of the Party. And so a large armory had to be cleared out within a few days, and all the premises had to be adapted for this archive. In a few weeks this archive was indeed installed, and it was serviced by Gestapo personnel. The Jews did not have access to it anymore, except those who were doing maintenance work, the attendants, those who were tending the stoves, people who were doing some kind of chores . . .

But not office work.

No office work of any kind. That was blocked off from the Jews. The year '44 stood under the "sign" of beautification of the city. We had repeated visits by foreign representatives of the press, foreigners who were not involved in the war—Sweden, Switzerland. And it was customary not to give any answers except to what the Gestapo asked. One could not answer at all the questions which the representatives of the press happened to ask.

Could the representatives of the press see the people?

Yes, but of course they were shown only places determined beforehand, according to a most definite red line on the map, and they followed that route, and all the dwellings which were included in the plan of the tour had to be spick-and-span; they had to present an appearance that would be free of any objection. That occurred a few times, and in order to show something more to the press, provisions were made for shops, [and] ghetto currency was printed and earned by the working people. All those who rendered any kind of labor for the community were paid in ghetto dollars.[2]

And so, in order to present this village with [an aura of] complete reality, stores were opened and the inmates of the ghetto were able to buy all kinds of things that were allotted to these stores, predominantly merchandise which was taken away from the Jewish members of the transports. The people who came to Theresienstadt were rarely permitted to keep their "large baggage." The big trunks were simply kept under lock, and every week many hundreds of trunks were emptied by working women of the ghetto, sorted out, and all the underwear, clothing, or other gear that was found in the trunks was stored in one of the armories, the so-called warehouse armory.

I frequently had some business there because I had to build the shelves on which the goods were arranged and to reinforce them because they became overloaded. No clothing factory in Germany, I believe no clothing factory in the world had such a large inventory of men's shirts, women's shirts, or the like as I have seen in the warehouse armory. Without exaggeration, hundreds of thousands of pieces of clothing of every kind were in readiness. Not only was the baggage of the inmates there in that armory, but from all parts of Germany. The baggage taken away from the Jews was sent to Theresienstadt, and there it was packaged, sorted out in order to be sent out all over the country for the people who were bombed out and who suffered a shortage of underwear and clothing. It was an immense storehouse of objects of necessity of every kind.

Stores were fitted out, and the Jews were now able to buy the merchandise which was taken away from the Jews with their ghetto dollars. Naturally, there was often among the things very beautiful merchandise, but "pull" played a part here. With good connections one could get good merchandise, and those who had no connections only got bad merchandise.

And who worked in the stores?

Jews. And then, in order to complete the picture of a community, steps were taken toward organization of a social life. They created a café. Concerts were given on the premises. On orders of the Gestapo the ghetto was compelled to organize a Jewish orchestra. Enough musicians were found, the instruments obtained, and concerts were given in the café hall. Within the landscapes of the park, which were laid out on the grounds in order to embellish the city, an orchestral

2. S. uses the English word "dollars," but the ghetto currency was actually denominated in kronen, or crowns.

pavilion was erected where concerts were given nightly, which, by the way, were not at all bad—the Jewish musicians did very well indeed.

Also, all activities [were] directed toward an agreeable leisure time for the workers and the old people; and so arrangements were made for lectures, committees for the utilization of leisure time were formed, lecture societies, language courses were given, scientific lectures in all possible fields, technological, medical, religious. There was a quite active life in all these fields. Stage plays were given. Stages were erected in the attics, arrangements made for the audiences, and so a quite active spiritual life slowly got into motion. That was in the year '44, and by that time the life of the Jews in Theresienstadt, as seen from the surface, had become quite tolerable.

What made the stay at Theresienstadt so terrible was the anxiety about where one might find himself between today and tomorrow. Every week transports arrived, twelve, fifteen hundred, to two thousand people, often even more, but since the size and installations of Theresienstadt could not take beyond a certain number, equal numbers of people had continuously to be deported. Every week transports were sent away, with the exception of a short spell during Christmas time and Easter time. With the exception of these two periods, there were always transports sent to Poland. Nobody knew whether he would be put in one of the transports. One could only surmise from a certain activity in the offices of the management that transports were in the offing.

As a rule, the lists were compiled by the ghetto [administration] itself. The Jews were compelled to compile a list and name the people who were to depart with the next transport. Eventually the Gestapo itself designated certain people for the next transport; people who had committed, in [its] judgment, any kind of offense.

Now, according to what kind of criterion did they act?
For a time the first Czechoslovakian transports, the so-called *Aufbau Kommando* [Construction Detail], designated with the letters AK, were exempt from all transports; they considered themselves secure, and would surely remain in Theresienstadt.

Czechoslovakian Jews?
Czechoslovakian Jews who had arrived with the first construction detail, who so to speak inaugurated Theresienstadt and had taken care of the first installations. And this criterion was indeed adhered to until the autumn of 1944. [Then] this distinction was not made anymore; the Jews who had arrived with the construction detail were being deported to Poland.

Did they not consider age?

In the early period the overaged were sent to Poland. Take my transport, for instance—all who were over seventy-five were simply transported on to Poland where they probably perished or possibly were gassed within the shortest time. In the case of other transports, certain age groups were taken according to another principle. It was simply ordered that those over sixty or sixty-five not be taken. There was no protection against such deportations, and it was most fortunate for the poor people in Theresienstadt that almost up to the end they were completely ignorant of what would happen to these transports. It was said that they were simply being transferred to another camp and would live [there] no worse than they had lived in Theresienstadt. It was not known that the people were going to their death.

The fact that the people were permitted to receive packages from relatives or acquaintances also improved conditions during the last two years. The Czechs could receive one package every month; they were issued a stamp to that effect, and later on the German and Austrian Jews also could receive packages, although not of such large size. But by that time the Foreign Organization [the International Red Cross] had come to life and started sending small packages from Portugal, as well as some packages from Denmark and Sweden, without names [designated recipients, and others] with specific names. However, soon the packages got in the hands of the Gestapo [who] appropriated whatever they pleased. Later a Jewish postal service was organized, but the personnel were not entirely beyond reproach; the packages frequently arrived ransacked, so that the recipients did not really receive much. Nevertheless, these packages saved many people from death by starvation.

Now how could they be sent? Have, for instance, people abroad known about your family?

My family had known through information furnished by the [International] Red Cross. They knew in Vienna that we were deported to Theresienstadt. Of course, it took about three-quarters of a year until they received the communications.

The food provisions included, in the morning, a weak broth of chicory drips, a black broth which was sweetened as long as there was sugar and later was unsweetened.

Did you not get any saccharin?

No. But when those who worked were remunerated, they were given small boxes of sugar, and when the mortality became rampant, small rations of sugar and fat were issued to the nonworkers, too, so that [they] would receive 20 grams [0.7 ounces] of fat [and] 50 grams [1.8 ounces] of sugar per week. The working person received 80 [2.8 ounces] of sugar per week. Not very much, but it was something.

In the spring of 1944 I and my wife were nearly at the limit of our strength. My wife then worked in a war shop; there was a shop in Theresienstadt which was called the mica splitting shop; [it] had to be split so thinly that it could be used for purposes of insulation in telephones, radios, and the like. Between twelve and fifteen hundred women had to produce a certain quota, [and] those who could not were eventually assigned to deportation, or they were made to catch up—they were assigned longer hours. The work proceeded in two shifts, one from 6:00 A.M. until 2:00 in the afternoon, and the second from half-past two until eleven o'clock at night.

I worked in the technical service, and due to the shortage in nutrition we became so depleted that we could barely drag along. For me walking one flight up to my office in the armory had become almost impossible. Then I lay in bed for weeks, completely devoid of strength. Heart symptoms appeared, and in such circumstances the only thing that the physicians could prescribe was to tell you in confidence [to] save your strength. At this time one of our cousins who was with us was sent away to Auschwitz, but fortunately [she] had connections abroad and had received mercy packages from Portugal, Denmark, and Sweden. When she departed, she told my wife, "Look here Fany, I don't want the packages arriving here to get lost [or] that the Gestapo or other people simply should take them. I am leaving an endorsement here for you so that you will get the packages. Take [them]; unfortunately you cannot forward them to me . . ."

Did she know already where she was going?

She knew only that she was going to Birkenau. About Auschwitz, the gassings and the like, nothing was known. She took everything she needed with her since she expected to be relocated in another camp. She did not know that she was heading for death. But the packages which our cousin left behind with us kept us afloat during the next few months. The little bit of fat, sugar, and cheese, and whatever else we got literally saved us from starvation. In addition, by that time I began to receive "mercy gifts" from my Viennese relatives, my brother, who had remained in Vienna, and a woman friend—a Catholic woman—they could send us packages even if at times they consisted of only a few kilos of potatoes or 2 kilograms of bread. Even if it arrived hard it still was bread, isn't that true? And so we pulled through the worst period.

Potatoes. Where could you boil the potatoes?

In every room there was a stove, and we made fires; we gathered wood, or wood cuttings—purchased or searched for, in some way it was gathered together. Coal was stolen wherever it was possible to steal it. In Theresienstadt stealing was the order of the day. Yes, yes, I say it frankly, one appropriated whatever one could in order to get the room a bit warm. Unfortunately, thefts among comrades also occurred.

Was there not a tendency to share with the others what one would receive?
Unfortunately, no. I must say, frankly, that the solidarity among the Jews left a lot be desired. Because I know that especially the Czech Jews got quite a lot, and what they would not use they used to sell for dear money in order to obtain other things which they could use. One would [not] give things to others. With few exceptions—unfortunately, I know none—everybody did his best to use whatever he would get for himself.

And so the autumn of 1944 came. Very large transports were leaving. It was said that Theresienstadt was to be completely evacuated during the next few months. All the people were to go to Poland. In fact, during these summer and autumn months the population was reduced to 24,000 and [later] to 18,000 from a peak of 65,000.[3] All the others went to Poland, and with them went a large part of those people who believed themselves safe due to belonging to the construction detail. An exorbitant number of engineers from the technical service went to Poland. By that time I had received a different assignment, the management of a quadrant, that is a "quarter" of the city, and I had my own office with adjoining small service apartment, with my shops nearby—carpentry shop, machine shop, electrical and plumbing shops. And that gave me the advantage that I was able to live together with my wife from the late autumn of 1944. I had a small, very lovely service apartment which my predecessor had fixed up. He went to Poland.

We lived in this apartment up to the liberation by the Russians. This period [December 1944 to May 1945] was very disquieting. The Gestapo, due to efforts from abroad, appeared to be prevailed upon to send a part of the Theresienstadt Jews abroad. In February 1945 1,200 people were selected who were sent to Switzerland by the efforts of the International Red Cross. [They] actually reached Switzerland.

How were they selected?
One could register. Three or 4,000 registered. Some people deliberately did not, because they feared that the transport still might not go to Switzerland. These registrants were then called before the Gestapo, and the commander asked his questions and decided who was to go. Unfortunately, my wife and I were rejected because I possibly appeared suspicious to the man. He asked a few questions: "Where were you? What are you? An architect? Where did you live? In

3. Postwar research has shown that the population of Theresienstadt peaked at about 53,000 in September 1942 and fell to around 11,000 at the end of 1944.

Vienna? You were ministerial counselor in retirement?" It said so in my passport. "Where were you a ministerial counselor then?" [S. responded], "In the ministry of railroads." "That will be all." I think they picked people who were not dangerous, who could not do much harm. This transport was to be followed by several other[s] to which the eligible people from those who had registered were to be assigned. These did not materialize, however, for the simple reason that the Red Cross sent a representative to Theresienstadt.

At that time there were people who were spreading rumors about gassings, and it was also rumored that installations had been assembled in Theresienstadt, too. The Technical Service did get certain premises ready which could serve this purpose. We had to construct doors in places where we could not exactly imagine for what purpose they were installed. The doors were padded [with weather strips] as if for cold storage rooms. It was definitely thinkable that these premises which we built could be made use of for purposes of gassing. But in April the Red Cross sent a representative to Theresienstadt. This Monsieur Dunant countered the anxious rumors; nothing would happen that could be to the detriment of the inmates. He would keep his eyes on Theresienstadt. On the 21st of April Dunant definitely moved to Theresienstadt,[4] [and] placards were posted that for sure nothing would happen that could cause the people alarm.

There were already battles very close to Theresienstadt. Up to this time we had seen nothing of the war, except for the large American flying squadrons which now and then flew over, [although] it was not permitted to be on the streets, to look [at them]. We knew, of course, that the Americans knew not to drop any bombs on Theresienstadt. By that time the situation was well known, that the battles in the Rhineland were in the offing . . .

How did you know that?
Through the Czech gendarmes, [who] had radios set up so that the inmates could listen. Also sometimes people were getting out [on work details] and smuggling in some newspapers, and so one sketchily knew what was going on in the world. And by the end of April the battle contingents came nearer and nearer, the bombardments became more and more frequent. In the last days of April we heard about shooting encounters very close by, and indeed in these days exorbitant numbers of refugees began to appear, Jews from other camps which the Gestapo had emptied and crowded them into Theresienstadt. Unfortunately, all these were brought half dead. Lice-ridden, starvation-depleted, poor people who brought epidemics with them. We had an epidemic of spotted typhus of such di-

4. Paul Dunant of the International Red Cross in fact visited Theresienstadt on April 6 and April 21, 1945, but resided in Prague until May 2, when he took up residence in the ghetto.

mensions that 80, 90, 100, and more would die in one night. We then established a quarantine into which the inmates of the dissolved camps were placed. But too many arrived. It was impossible to hold such multitudes in the quarantine station; frequently they would break out and so increase the danger of the spread of epidemic. In spite of that the epidemic slowly subsided.

At the beginning of May the fighting reached Theresienstadt. The retreating German troops, specifically among the SS, repeatedly fired into the city; at times they even threw hand grenades which cost the lives of several people, but these incidents were soon over. At the end of April Russian troops actually entered Theresienstadt, received with joy by all inmates.[5] The Russians immediately furnished us with food supplies. We even got fresh butter, fresh meat from Czechoslovakia [and] Germany. In general the Russians took good care of us.

5. In fact the Germans turned the camp over to the International Red Cross on May 3, 1945, and the Red Army entered five days later.

26 David M.

David M.'s parents were among the 70,000 Polish Jews who had come to Germany before World War I in search of economic opportunities and refuge from Polish anti-Semitism.[1] Germany, like most European countries at that time, naturalized foreigners only in exceptional cases. Hence M. bore his parents' Polish citizenship even though he had been born in Wiesbaden in 1914.

In 1938 the Polish Jews in Germany were the first large group forcibly deported from the Third Reich, and David M. was among them. But family ties could not be so easily broken, and he did not stay in Poland. Determined to save his parents and get his family to a safe haven, he undertook the risky business of smuggling himself back to Wiesbaden where he witnessed the Crystal Night pogrom of November 9–10, 1938. This was the Nazi response to the act of another son of Polish Jews expelled from Germany. Hershel Grynszpan, who had been sent to Paris by his parents, heard of their harsh treatment by German and Polish officials at the border, and murdered a German diplomat in Paris as an act of revenge.

Although M.'s family succeeded in escaping to Belgium, Hitler's westward invasions overtook them in 1940. His aged mother died in Antwerp and hence was spared deportation and gassing, the usual fate of old people in the Holocaust. M. was trapped in France, and in 1941 he was included in the thousands of Jewish refugees handed over by the Vichy regime to the Germans. Then began a four-year trek through forced labor camps in Lower and Upper Silesia, beginning with several of the Organization Schmelt camps, continuing with the construction of satellite installations for the Gross-Rosen concentration camp empire, and ending in the Heinkel Aircraft factory near Wismar in northern Germany. M. reminds us once again of the important distinction between Jewish camp trusties and non-Jewish job foremen that marked life in several of the camps. Probably crucial to his survival was selection as a camp clerk, made possible by his business experience and his fluency in German. His father, a brother, and two sisters did not survive, however.

1. This interview appears in Boder's *I Did Not Interview the Dead*, under the pseudonym "Jack Matzner."

David M. was liberated by the Russians in May 1945 and, following his recovery from intestinal typhus in a Russian hospital, returned
to Wiesbaden. Far from rejecting the thought of a future for Jews in
Germany, M. appeared committed to staying. At the time he gave his
interview on Rosh Hashana 1946 in the rehabilitated Wiesbaden synagogue, he was actively working to restore the local Jewish community
with the support of the UNRRA. And yet, four years later he and his
wife emigrated to the United States. Later he penned a memoir of the
Holocaust that was published after his death in 1986.[2] From it we learn
several things about its author that he did not share with Boder, including the fact that he studied in Jerusalem in the 1930s, was ordained a
rabbi in 1938, and then returned to Wiesbaden to be with his parents.

David M. begins his interview with a few comments about the
impact of the Nazi advent in 1933 on his family's business.

First of all my business activities, which I pursued up to 1933 with complete freedom, were completely halted on the day of Hitler's ascent to power. I had a mail-
order business in textiles. Within Germany, especially greater Hessen, Rothen-
burg, Bavaria, and Baden, [customers] would order by mail, and we would ship
by mail.

In 1938 the Polish Jews were deported. One night the Gestapo arrived, and
within twenty minutes we had to leave our home. My brother, my two sisters,
the two children of one of my sisters, and myself were forcibly taken to the
police, leaving behind all our belongings, a comparatively large amount of cash,
and a quite large amount of jewelry. It all was taken away from us. We regarded
it as most fortunate that both of our old parents were not taken with us because
they had doctors' affidavits to the effect that they were completely unfit for transport. We were then deported to Poland in cattle cars, crowded together, sixty to
seventy people in one cattle car. We arrived on the morning of a Sabbath in Beu-
then at the Polish border. We were pushed over the Polish border and arrived on
a Sunday at the main depot in Katowice. The reception given to us by the Jews
in Poland, who had been informed about us, was so warm and marvelous that for
a moment we were able to forget the pain, the misery, and the want. The [Polish
Jews] sacrificed everything. Day and night they provided us with food, nourishment, clothing, and everything possible. Don't forget that we were not permitted
to take a thing with us.

2. David Matzner, *The Muselmann*.

Were you admitted to Poland?
Poland admitted us. However, the same night I had a telephone conversation with a rabbi, Dr. Ansbacher in Wiesbaden, trying to arrange that nothing should happen to my two old parents and to comfort them, telling them that we had arrived well and endeavoring to create the impression that we were all right. Shortly afterward, in about six weeks, I managed to return illegally from Poland to Wiesbaden, with the intention of taking care of my house and moving my parents to Holland.

I simply smuggled myself through. We were a group of thirty-one people. We were even shot at when we crossed the border, on which occasion a six-month-old baby of a young woman was killed. These were all people who lived formerly in Germany. Polish Jews who were deported that time to Poland. They decided to return in order to be able to salvage something of their belongings they had left behind.

And then to return to Poland?
Yes, and then to return to Poland. Or, there was also the illegal immigration to Belgium, Holland, France, and Italy. At any rate, for me the deciding reason was a wish to save my parents. I returned illegally to Wiesbaden and was a witness to the burning of synagogues, as a consequence of the shooting of Herr vom Rath[3] in the Paris embassy. The affair was represented by Minister of Propaganda Goebbels as a plot attributable to the Jews, and he put well-prepared pogroms against the Jewish synagogues and temples of Germany into effect by instructing members of the Nazi party to set fire to the synagogues. The Temple of Wiesbaden was counted among the six most beautiful synagogues of Germany.[4] The sacred scrolls were thrown on the streets, spread out and trampled on the pavement. My old father who came daily to this synagogue came that morning as usual to attend the services. There were still Jews in Wiesbaden who attended the services in the synagogue and worshipped their Lord. He was turned back. He recognized that there was danger and returned. My father himself saved one of the holy scrolls, which I later, with the help of my father, shipped away to Switzerland, where it still remains. With the help of the [American] chaplain now stationed here, Chaplain William Z. Dalin, we shall get this holy scroll back again to Wiesbaden. I hope that for the coming dedication of this synagogue, which is to be restored, we shall also have this holy scroll here.

In July 1939 we decided to leave the country and to go—that is, illegally—to

3. The German diplomat shot by Grynszpan in Paris on November 7, 1938. His assassination provided the Nazis with a pretext for their Crystal Night pogrom two days later.
4. The Michelsbergstrasse Synagogue.

Belgium. My father, my mother, and I. In the meantime my two sisters and the two children had returned from Poland, also illegally. So I arranged an illegal departure to Belgium for them, too. An outsider may not be able to comprehend what kind of difficulties such an undertaking presents, to leave the "German soil," as the Nazis called it, especially in secret. First of all, there was the enormous cost of it. Second, we could not take anything with us, because you actually had to crawl across the border. You had to creep on all fours. But at least you would save your life. We arrived in Antwerp about the 9th of July 1939. We were very well received by the Jewish Relief Committee then functioning in Belgium. We obtained an apartment, and we remained in peace in Antwerp until Easter 1940.

On the 10th of May 1940 Hitler executed his attack on Belgium. The first bombardment started at night, and my late mother pleaded with me to flee to France, so that I could at least prepare a further refuge for the rest of the family. And so, on the 14th of May I left for France. I bade good-bye to my father, my mother, to my two sisters, and to the two children, and I did not know that that was good-bye forever.

[M. escaped to France where he was arrested, interned, and in 1941 deported by train to Gogolin in far eastern Germany, near what was (and still is) the end of the autobahn.]

We had to disembark—not all of us, only the men between sixteen and forty-five. All men older than that and all the women had to remain in the cars. And I was among those who jumped out. To say "jumped out" is an exaggeration, because we could hardly move by then. I remember clearly that while I was getting out of the car an SS man came running by and said "We're going to break your balls." Soon we were lined up in groups, and immediately we had to get down on our knees. There was a total of about 900 persons lined up in the form of a little square. There were about twelve or fifteen such blocks of people. In mine there were about 900 men. We had immediately to get down on our knees, that is not standing and not sitting, but in a position with our knees bent, in a manner that the buttocks almost touched our heels. That's how we had to remain.

Not moving up and down, not like in calisthenics?
No, not like in calisthenics. That was expressly for the purpose of torturing us.[5] Some people tried to put some little piece of baggage that they had salvaged underneath, so that they could sit on it. Immediately these pieces of baggage were

5. Although it must have seemed torture to the victims, this was a method of crowd control and provides further evidence of the guards being undermanned.

pushed out from underneath them, and they were thrown to the ground and had to get back in the bended-knee posture.

We were sitting there for about forty minutes. An automobile arrived, and an SS man alighted, all decorated with plenty of gold around his neck and on his chest. We inferred from that, that he must have been a higher sort of animal. I myself had been in Germany during the [time of the] Nazis for about five years and was able to recognize the special insignia [of an] SS first lieutenant, a man whose name I learned years later. This Liepner put on his gloves and made some remark to his aide, which we of course couldn't hear, but we saw him make a gesture like throwing something away, kind of abruptly. And we were ordered to get up, loaded into trucks, and driven to a camp. There we were registered in the books, and the next day we were distributed into barracks. During the night we had to sleep in the yard. The barracks had a capacity for about thirty-five to forty people in military cots which were stacked up in threes, one over another. But they shoved eighty to ninety people into each room. Each group had to pick a room trustee, and these room trustees were subordinated to the camp senior. This was a system entirely unfamiliar to us at the time. The camp senior was also a Jew, a prisoner who had already spent some time in that camp. That morning, at roll call, he told us: "You have no business of any kind with the Germans and with the German supervisory personnel. Your supervisory personnel are the room trustee, the block senior, and the camp senior."

All these were Jews?

All these were Jews. "If you have some trouble, report to your room trustee. Don't report too often, and don't become conspicuous. Do not talk much, and do what you are told to do. Don't talk much to each other, and don't try to do anything which is against the order of things in the camp. Here you don't talk much. Here you don't say much. Something may happen to someone that he does not wish to happen to him." The next morning we were led to work for the first time. This was work on the Reich Autobahn. For five prisoners—at that time I did not yet consider myself a prisoner—for every five people there were two guards. These two guards were armed with rifles, with a revolver, with dagger, and with a watchdog for each one of them. These watchdogs are really the most terrible thing that I can imagine, trained [to attack] human beings, people *not* in uniforms. And it almost appeared to me—of course, it seems ridiculous to say it—that these watchdogs were trained against anything that was *Jewish*. And prisoners who would escape would have been followed by the dogs with their supervisors until they were found. During the fifty-five months of my imprisonment I never heard of a single case where a prisoner succeeded in escaping. He might have been away one day, even three or four days and nights, but he would always be brought back, dead or alive.

In about fourteen days we were transferred from Gogolin to camp Fürsten-grube,[6] near Katowice. There the task was to dry up a flooded mine, and at Fürstengrube the saddest chapter of my experience began. It was in November 1941 when we arrived there, and right from the start we had the feeling that the end had come to everything. The guard was very strict; it consisted of SA men. The camp commander, who was in charge of things, was a certain Mareck, and he had an assistant who was at one time a police sergeant, Lapke, to whom we gave the name "Messiah."

Every morning roll call started at about 3:00 and lasted until 5:00, and we had to stand outside in the yard at attention. During these one or two hours, this Sergeant Lapke was in the habit of making speeches in a horrible tone of voice. He walked from group to group. He yelled all over the yard, so that it was clearly audible, and you always had the impression that he was drunk. "What do you suppose, that you have come here for a rest? Soon you will see your Messiah. That's all you want, to see your Messiah? You will all land back in Jerusalem, but not back there in the Jerusalem that you hope to see. You will all remain here. Here is your Jerusalem. And soon you will all see your Messiah." And that was the reason we gave him the nickname, "Messiah." He was one of the most feared men that ever lived.

And sure enough, on the second day of our arrival, this Lapke shot a prisoner. He ordered him to bring something from the woods. Lapke went with him and shot him in the back. Afterward, that evening, it was said that [the prisoner] was shot in an attempt to escape. We saw then which way the wind was blowing. Then we had a camp trustee, a Jew. His name was Cohen, a very fine fellow. He himself was in despair over the situation of the people for whom he had taken responsibility.

And then winter came. Every day we had dead. People frozen, killed, or dead from starvation. We worked in a plant then. There was a chief engineer, Reichmann, who put on the appearance of being a decent person. He was the general work manager and was always ready to help, and so on, and so on. But in the meantime this man tortured the prisoners to death by means of work assignments. At night and in fog, day and night, we had to work outdoors. We had nothing to wear. Our overcoats had been taken away from us and were deposited in the storeroom of the camp, and we were not permitted to wear them.

Why?

Because we had to keep in action. They said that when a Jew is warm, he does not work, therefore he should not have any overcoat. He should generate warmth through motion and through work. And at work it was always demanded—"keep

6. One of the Organization Schmelt labor camps.

moving, moving, moving." Always in motion, "*davay, davay, davay*," give, give, give. These were mostly Polish foremen who constantly shouted the orders at us, and I still remember the horrible "davay, davay, davay." On with the work, on with the work.

Then there was a foreman—his name was Bielka. Daily this man killed people with his own hands. He killed them with shovels, not those long shovels, but the short spades. People most frequently died afterward from such injuries. This Bielka also got after me, and only through a fortunate accident I was transferred to another work division and got out from under Bielka's eyes. Otherwise he finally would have killed me, too.

Were you personally mistreated?

[Hesitantly] In this camp—since I showed myself very willing and presented myself for any kind of work, I was never beaten *inside* the camp. But, of course, you must remember that we had a Jewish trustee, and as Jews we still had a certain amount of solidarity. Inside the camp we were rarely beaten. Only in cases where disciplinary punishment was administered for disobedience, which may have happened to all of us. It was only at work that we were beaten regularly and that was by the SA and by the foreman. The foremen were mostly Polish and non-Jews.

I remember well how we got an order to dig holes for telegraph poles. They assigned a Dutch Jew and three other Jews from Poland and myself to this job. Now, to dig in December or January in clay soil that was frozen harder than granite, in the beastly cold. . . . And I must say we worked half naked to get it done. The sweat pored from us in torrents, but we had to do it, we had to do the job. So we got it done, but at what sacrifice! Of the five people who worked at the hole, two Polish Jews froze to death, and also that Dutch Jew. I myself had signs of frozen legs, and I myself was one of those who carried the dead from the place of work into the camp.

This camp had no crematorium, and so there was a special detail to dig graves in the nearby forest. [Every] five or six days ten or fifteen dead would be carried out [and] simply thrown into the pit! At the beginning we were still permitted to say Kadesh [prayer for the dead]. Later, an old *Schlomask* [scoundrel] appeared. *Schlomask* is what we called the foremen and guards. And so this old *Schlomask* prohibited it. "What are you mumbling there? Nonsense? Stop that nonsense. Do your work and go."

During the summer of 1942 this camp was evacuated. It was to be used for Russian war prisoners. And we came to Gräditz near Gleiwitz. Gräditz was an old mill which never was fit for people to live in, full of rats, mice. The floors were full of holes, and it had high ceilings, such as mills have. We were established there. We lay over each other in five tiers in stacked up bunks, lying next to each other like sardines in a can. At three o'clock in the morning we had to get up. At 4:00 was roll call. That lasted until 5:00. At 5:00 we marched out, and we had to march an hour and a half to the station. There we were put in box cars, which would take us to the place of work. We worked in the famous textile plant, Christian Dierig in Ober-Langenbielau. We also worked in Reichenbach, in various textile mills.

When we returned it was 9:00 in the evening. Then we had to struggle to get our food, because the people there were frozen stiff and starved, and had to stand in line until they got a little soup, watery soup with turnips. And when they had gulped down their soup, they had to get back into the halls to bed. There they handed out that little piece of bread. For eight, nine, or twelve people a two-pound loaf. And when everything had been passed around, it was already 11:00 or 12:00 at night. And at 3:00 we were waked again.

Every day we had dead. It was an intolerable situation. Only because I was on very friendly terms with the camp trustee, a certain Zehngut from Sosnowiec, he assigned me to a labor transport which was sent to Hirschberg in Upper Silesia. We arrived in Hirschberg, thirty-three people, in November 1943. There I worked in the Frick Industries making wool out of wood.

Was that really possible?

That was possible. Of course, I don't want to pass judgment as to the quality of such wool, but they really made wool out of wood, wool that was used to manufacture clothing. In Hirschberg I was awakened one night and was called to the office. And before me stood the commander of the camp, SS Technical Sergeant Weigel. Then he asked me, "You are German? Can you write? Can you type?" And I said, "Yes, Herr Technical Sergeant." "Well, sit down. We shall give you a trial." And he placed a typewriter before me, and I had to write something that he dictated.

And so I was found suitable to be assigned as a clerk. The camp foreman told me afterward, "That is a great opportunity for you. This may be your lucky moment." The same night I was given clean clothes. Up to then we were wearing sheer rags, and early in the morning at about four o'clock I had to depart, accompanied by the same technical sergeant, Weigel. Then we traveled as far as Strigau in Upper Silesia, and from there we marched on foot. On the way that technical sergeant told me in his Sudeten German dialect, "Don't you dare to disgrace me. Stand at attention. Don't ask any questions, and keep your mouth shut." All at once I noticed a sign "Gross-Rosen," and I got pale inside of me. I was checked in, and here are the subsequent events.

I was put in a prisoner's uniform, the blue-white uniform. I was given the number 30-201. Meanwhile twenty-four Jews were delivered from other camps, and a few days later we were assigned to Camp Girsdorf, also in Upper Silesia. In Girsdorf we were taken over by Lieutenant Colonel Lütkemeier who made a speech, telling us that we were now to erect the camps, to build them, and that any instance of misbehavior would be punished by death without delay. We were ordered to select from our midst a camp deputy, who was to be responsible for the whole camp, and we were sent to Camp Wolfsberg.

Wolfsberg was really an empty stretch of hills and valleys, bare terrain, and we were told to build a camp. We were given the material, and within the next day or two the first 8,000 Greek and Hungarian Jews arrived. They all had tattoos and came from Auschwitz. These Jews were immediately checked in and assigned to build the camp with the material at our disposal. And shortly the camp was ready.

It did not consist of "blocks" but of some type of round Eskimo tents. We called them Finnish tents. Within a short time we had a population of about 21,000 persons, all Jews. Rabbis, *shohets*,[7] scholars, *Hasidim*, artisans, judges, lawyers, workingmen—Poles, Hungarians, Rumanians, Germans, French, Greek—a wholly international conglomeration of men. Since we, the leaders, had decided to hold together and to help save everyone we could, we set up a hospital under the direction of the Hungarian physicians, Dr. Friek and Dr. Deutsch, and we put there all the rabbis, all scholars, all Hasidim, even if they were not sick, simply to protect those who had never done manual labor from the heavy work in the tunnel. You see, a tunnel of twenty-five to thirty kilometers was being constructed, and we were the ones to construct it. Every day we had deaths. Construction accidents, cave-ins, the excavating machines killed people daily. The foremen were clubbing people. Only because we had a good organization were we able to prevent occurrences contrary to our plans inside the camp itself.

We remained there until January 1945 [when] the camp was abandoned. We knew why. Our exploratory senses and our eyes were directed toward the outside world. We knew the Russians were on the march. Every night we saw how Breslau was bombed. We saw the allied flying fortresses over our camp, whose pilots knew for certain that the people there below in the blue-white uniforms were their own and that no bombs should be dropped on them.

People who were old and sick and weak and unable to stand the march would fall on the road. We had to drag them with us and bury them at night. Before burial we had orders from the SS to break out gold teeth. So we marched on and on. Piles of corpses and mountains of corpses rose, which were just buried anywhere or scarcely covered with sand. And then one night we arrived at Bergen-Belsen.

Bergen-Belsen! At first we did not see this camp in its true light. But the next day we understood. We saw the treatment given us—undress, give up everything, lie down, stand up, roll calls lasting for fifteen to twenty hours in mud, in snow, in ice, in water. Daily we found people in the barracks who had gone to bed in the evening and were dead the morning after. In darkness we were unable to see

7. Slaughterers of cattle and fowl according to Hebrew ritual.

what was going on in the pestilential and overcrowded blocks. One was killing the other. The population of the camp must have reached the 100,000 mark.[8] Gentiles and Jews, Catholics, Protestants, English parachutists, French volunteers, who were fighting on the side of the Allies, Jews, Maquis—all of them were here, and everyone knew it was merely a matter of minutes.

In Bergen-Belsen I saw for the first time how people were burned on open pyres. Apparently the gas or gas piping stopped functioning, so they piled the people in mounds and poured gasoline over them and burned them on open pyres. One got accustomed to such a sight as if it was something ordinary. It is terrible to say that. And even now I can't conceive how I was able to bear this stench which would stick to one's palate as though it were something palpable, this repugnant, pestilential stench that filled the air.

One day it was announced that a labor transport was being formed for some other camp. We all wanted to get away from Bergen-Belsen at any cost. We reported accordingly, and I had the good fortune to be among the 3,000 persons that were chosen. We marched to the railroad, and after a trip lasting a full day and a full night, we arrived at Messenthin, a small place near Frankfurt on Oder or Stettin. After all, we never really knew where we were. At any rate, we were working now in the industries in Poelitz,[9] a plant as big as a city.

There they manufactured benzine and fuel. A foreman under whom I worked told me that this plant had been producing four and one-half million liters of fuel daily until one night nearly two thousand English and American planes came in waves which within an hour or so demolished the whole plant. At any rate, it was our task to clean the place up. We had to remove the wreckage and mountains of rubble, for the work [of the camp] had to go on. However, we were already under the artillery fire of the Russians who were located on the opposite bank of the Oder. Our camp and the plant were on this side of the Oder, and Russians were then on the opposite side. One day we had as many as twenty-five or twenty-six dead and injured, among them guards who were also killed by the Russian artillery.

After we had cleared this camp, we were sent to Barth, a small city near Wismar.[10] And there we were located in the Heinkel Aviation Industries. The camp was very beautiful, but what occurred there defies any description. There for the first time I felt that I was beginning to weaken. I could not stand it anymore. And my friend, Fischel Wiener from Sosnowiec, with whom I had been together all the time, all those years, kept telling me, "M. hold out, brace up, keep up your

8. This figure is not too far off the mark. There were approximately 60,000 survivors when Bergen-Belsen was liberated in April.

9. A small town just north of Stettin, near the mouth of the Oder River.

10. Actually, a small Baltic port near Stralsund.

strength. It cannot last much longer. You have to hold out, you have stood it this long. Keep your strength." And meanwhile every day my best friends were dying. My best friends perished. I was together with a Hungarian landowner, Ludwig B., [a Jew] from Schatmar. His brother had perished there. And how did the people die? One of my best friends, Moshe R., hanged himself. A pious man who said, "I can't stand any more!" And so we had daily suicides, and daily more people were killed.

One "fine" morning I felt that I had fever. I had been having fever most of the time, but that morning it was especially high. I went to the hospital to have my temperature taken, and the attendant found a high fever. With the slip on which he had written my temperature, I went to the camp foreman and pleaded with him to let me remain in the camp since I had such a high temperature. He gave me a kick in the stomach.

And that was a Jew?

No, that was a Christian, a professional criminal. He said, "You Jew-pig, get out of here. It is high time that you croaked." And so I was lying there, and when I came to—you see, I had lost consciousness—I found myself in the cellar. The cellar was about chest high under water. This cellar was an invention of this BVer. At the time of my arrival about ninety or ninety-five people were lying or standing in the water.

They couldn't lie there!

Those who were lying there were already dead. And those who were standing had arranged the bodies of the dead in such a manner that they could stand or sit on them. Otherwise the ones who were still living would also have drowned. I did the same thing. I found myself a place at the wall. I dragged two bodies which were under the water and arranged them against the wall, and I sat on them. And so I remained in the water, counting from that morning, exactly two days and two nights. During this time my friend who stood next to me drowned. . . .

And then all at once it began to happen. I myself don't really know how. I was almost unconscious throughout these days and nights. I just breathed instinctively. I just lived instinctively. I had nothing to eat or to drink, but I was still alive. And all at once they were yelling, "Out! Out!" And people from upstairs came down, and all at once I found myself in a room and there was no water, and I was lying on the floor, and afterward on a table. And again my friend, Fischel W., stood before me, and he was saying to me, "M., you will live! You will live! The Russians are at the gate, the Russians are coming!" Then I knew I was lying in a real bed and everything was white.

27 Jacob M.

Jacob M. was born in 1907 in Zurich, Switzerland, to Polish Jewish parents. He was raised in an orphanage in Hamburg and always carried a stateless passport, which would make it difficult for him to emigrate once the Nazis came to power. Arrested at the time of the Crystal Night pogroms, he spent ten weeks in the camp he calls Oranienburg, the original name of the concentration camp better known as Sachsenhausen.

M.'s story jumps rather abruptly to October 1941 when he was deported to the Lodz ghetto. He remained there for nearly three years, becoming a member of the ghetto fire brigade that was so important to German authorities worried that a blaze in the dilapidated wooden ghetto structures might spread to the rest of the city. Boder drew M. out on the barter economy and social life of the ghetto. Equally interesting is M.'s account of his deportation with other Jews from Lodz to Birkenau (Auschwitz II) in August 1944. His description of a prisoner saving a mother's life by forcing her to give up her child during the initial selection suggests a degree of risk-taking and of prisoner control that is not always well understood. Likewise, M.'s account of newly arrived Lodz Jewish police being targeted for death by the veteran inmates of Auschwitz demonstrates the existence of a rough and effective system of justice within the camp. The corruption of the block seniors at Auschwitz gets further confirmation in M.'s description of his living conditions there.

Jacob M. was one of the lucky ones transferred to work in an ammunition plant in the German city of Görlitz, where conditions were much better. That lasted until the camp was evacuated in the last days of the war, when he and his fellow prisoners were sent on a westward death march. His release by the SS at the time of Germany's surrender was followed by a wild wagon ride across Czechoslovakia to Vienna.

Boder interviewed M. at the Paris headquarters of the American Jewish Joint Distribution Committee. M. recalled his experiences in disorganized episodes, which has required considerable reassembly. We begin with his incarceration at Oranienburg (Sachsenhausen) concentration camp in November 1938.

We were driven into Oranienburg by the SS at night, and there was a slope. We could not see that it was going downhill abruptly. The first ones fell down. You can well imagine if 2,000 people crowded forward, they [the first ones] could not get up so quickly. We trampled them, so that right from the start we brought the first dead into the camp. I was in Oranienburg about ten weeks.

We were [subjected to] "camp ripening." Upon arrival we had to stand about ten hours lined up before the barbed wire fences, motionless. [That was called] "camp ripening." It was unbearable. There were sentries in towers to watch you. Then various persons were strapped to the rack, a towerlike contraption, and they got about twenty-five [blows] on the behind with an ox tail. The skin on the buttocks would break. [Then] they were hanged on a pole by the hands tied behind [them]; the rope was pulled up so that only the tips of the toes touched the ground. You can imagine that when they cut him loose after two hours, he would collapse like a sack. That was terribly painful.

At that time the worst cold that could ever be remembered reigned in Oranienburg. I worked at the canal and had to shovel sand into lorries under quota. And I only remember that my portion of bread, which I had in the side pocket of my prisoner's suit, was frozen into ice. So you can imagine how cold it was. The wheels of the lorries would not turn anymore. We were four people assigned to a lorry, regardless of whether old or young. At times the old people could barely stand up, and we had to cart them in addition. And the camp commander at that time, Bugdala, an SS man, the boxing champion of the SS, an infamous scoundrel—he spoke little, but when he slapped you in the face you tumbled over twice.

I remember that I had to carry heavy rocks together with a colleague, and there was glazed ice [on the ground], and everything had to be done at running pace. And that, of course, is impossible. [Bugdala] caught us once carrying the stuff at a walking pace; so he took down our numbers, and we got three hours "at the wire." We had to stand three hours at the barbed wire fence. One could not touch it, because it was charged with ten thousand volts. Many threw themselves against it because they simply could not stand it anymore.

An SS man passed from one to the other and inquired, "What is your profession?" One would say, "Physician." [The reply:] "You have dishonored our women," and he would slap him, a pair right and left. To another, "What are you?" "A lawyer." "You have done in many of our people." So he, too, got his face slapped twice. I could not understand one thing. Next to this lawyer stood a state's attorney. Apparently he was so confused that he [actually told the SS man] that he was a state's attorney. So you can imagine what an effect it had. "You will be shot today with cat shit." I don't know what they did with him later.

At any rate, with people who were very stout they had special fun. They were ordered to stand like a stork [and] compelled to bend in order to pick something up. Of course a person with a big belly. . . . And the clothes did not fit them well either; they had to fasten the prisoners' garb with a rope so that the pants would hold.

It was strictly prohibited to leave the block at night to eliminate. Of course, at the beginning that was not known, and whoever would step out of the block was immediately shot down. They illuminated every block; and as soon as somebody somehow began to move in the yard he was shot. It also happened that the patrol which guarded us simply would attract a prisoner and tell him to come over. We were told that it was strictly prohibited to pass beyond the patrol line. Many prisoners, uninformed about this rule, unsuspectingly followed the call and were shot down.

In my time we were 10,000 people in Oranienburg. The camp senior was a [former] member of the Reichstag. Only on one day were we not compelled to work, Christmas; in its place we had to do "sports." Marching! I and a few others wanted to duck out and reported that we had sore feet. So one of the platoon leaders said, "Well, we shall march slowly." But then an SS man walked up and said, "What? They can't run? [Commands:] Run! Lie down!" You know, running and then stretching out full length.

We were always compelled to sing some songs after the end of work. They simply [named one], say "It sat a birdie in the tree." I didn't know it. You had to sing a song that you didn't know. So an SS man passed by and saw that I stood there, not participating. "Why don't you sing? What? You don't know the song?" So he slapped me over the snout and said, "You should at least tear open your snout." And in the evening there was practice in the block.

[M. chuckled as he recalled this episode, evidently tickled at the brutal stupidity of the SS. He must have been released from Oranienburg and allowed to return to Hamburg sometime in 1939.]

In October 1941 I received an order by way of a registered letter from the Gestapo to appear on a certain day at Mohrweiden Street with twenty-five pounds of baggage.

So for two years they left you alone?
For two years we could relatively . . . That is, we wore the Jewish star; we had to buy in designated stores. We had no right to go to theaters and other [public] places. To cover up the Jewish star was a severely punishable act. It was [considered] an act of camouflage.

We were assembled there in a large building, and that was the first transport for Lodz.

Why to Lodz? Were you considered a Pole?
One cannot say that there were exclusively Poles. There were all nationalities. There were also German Jews. There were about 1,200 Jews [sent in] relatively decent railroad cars. Not cattle cars. Wooden [third-class passenger] cars. He [an official of the Department of Emigration] said ironically to those assembled at the station, "Now you will go to the Promised Land." In two days we arrived in Lodz.

Were you fed on the way?
We got something from the [Hamburg] Jewish community. When we arrived in Lodz, we were assembled in a school. It was in a frightful condition. We, of course, were unable to imagine what that meant to live in a ghetto. There we had [to live] under the most frightful conditions, from a hygienic standpoint one would say under conditions worse than in a concentration camp. As far as I know at most three [persons] have survived from this single transport. Most of them either starved to death in the ghetto, died of typhus, or were immediately "re-settled." [That happened to] people who were idle, who did not accept a job. Most lived under the belief that the war would soon be over. Why then should they accept a job? And that was their misfortune. I don't know what moved me to accept a job. . . . [M. joined the Lodz fire brigade.]

[When I] speak about Lodz, I think especially about the terrible hunger. The hunger was so great that we collected rotten potato peelings in order to convert them into a kind of mush with saccharin. A goo just fit to clog up the stomach. And with it we got a few coffee grounds [from which were made] cutlets, you see? Dried on the skillet. Life was insanely expensive. We were getting one 2-kilo [4.4-pound] loaf of bread for the week. Sometimes it did not weigh two full kilos. We made a special effort to get really stale bread. Fresh bread stimulated the appetite, and that was dangerous. One pleaded for very stale bread so that one would not eat so much. I generally distributed it so that every day I would eat about two slices.

For a long time objects had no special value, while food had an unbelievable value. I remember, for instance, I had a new suit of clothes with me for which I had paid 350 marks in Hamburg. So you see, it was quite a piece of wealth. And I got 1 kilo [2.2 pounds] of flour for it. You could purchase a pair of shoes for 100 grams of margarine; and you see from these prices that objects other than food or cigarettes were worth nothing. Germans who would at times come into the ghetto with 1 pound of bread or margarine would leave with a trunkful of new things. For the sake of saving one's life, one was ready to sacrifice all these things. I, too, was at one time so run down from hunger that I barely could do my duties as fireman. I was twice brought home in a state of collapse. When I looked at myself in the mirror, at times I saw death before my eyes.

There were 165,000 Jews [in Lodz] at the beginning, and they came down to 40,000. Many were deported, but a large part died from typhus. They had selected the worst section of Lodz for the ghetto, where the worst scum had lived before. Those were mostly broken down dwellings; and people lived under the most frightful conditions. At times the people lived ten families in one flat. You can imagine what the results were under these most horrible hygienic conditions. For instance, when you needed something, say medicine, you had to get it on the black market. The price was prohibitive. For instance, as fireman I earned 3 ghetto marks per day. The cost of a loaf of bread on the black market [was] 1,300 marks. You can imagine how much bread I could buy.

We got soup for free. But, let us say someone had diarrhea or something else. He would sell [his soup]. Thus a kind of trader always stood before the kitchen who would buy up the soup tickets for a certain price in order [to resell it] to another. Say he had sold a piece of bread. There were people of a rather peculiar point of view. They would sell their own loaf of bread and bought soup in order to stuff their belly full. Of course from a health standpoint that was completely wrong. Thus, if they wanted to buy something equivalent to two or three hundred marks, they would sell a piece of bread. He weighed it as if he were weighing gold; and the bill was then settled with bread.

Will you permit me a question? Could you tell me anything about sex life in Lodz and afterward in the camp?

Well, that was, of course, an unhealthy situation since male and female were housed together [in the ghetto]; I would almost say the people were not embarrassed at all.

Now let us say, when one family lived together, how did they go about sexual intercourse?

I would almost say, completely without embarrassment. I remember when we came from Hamburg a certain group of us took lodging somewhere. We were eight people, among them one woman. And she did not show embarrassment at all. She undressed completely naked in order to wash. And the people became in time the same as in the camp. The life in the camp made the people, so to speak, hardened, completely devoid of feelings. One did not feel anything. Without any sex drive. You should not forget that when hunger is so intense, one does not think about it.

Of course, if one worked in a bread factory, he could always save himself a piece of bread. And you know, a piece of bread was a fortune. With a piece of bread he could buy anything. I know, at the beginning when I came into the ghetto, prostitution was so intense. On the street, for instance, girls would cling to you for a piece of bread.

Jewish girls?

Of course. We were in the ghetto. For a slice of bread they would go into a yard or somewhere. Possibly the mother was working, so the daughter would use the opportunity. Of course, later this led to misfortune; because the girls who were not working were in time deported.

Now let us return [to the original question]. Let us say a block senior in the camp who had enough to eat. Have you any idea how he satisfied his sex needs?

Many block seniors had boys with whom they amused themselves, children from ten to twelve years old. These, too, were prisoners. They were actually supposed to go to work, but they always found a pretext to retain them in the camp. A block senior could, of course, do that. He [the boy] would be registered as sick, and then the block senior would retain him.

In 1944, about in July, [the deportations] also reached the fire brigade. We were the last. Biebow[1] would tell you that we were going to Germany, to work, and that there were opportunities to be better fed. I decided there and then to join the transport. We were loaded into lead-sealed cattle cars; eighty [persons] in each car.

Men and women together?

Men, women, and children. I must say that at that moment I almost regretted that I had taken that decision. Because even if I did not know exactly that I was going to a concentration camp, I still had a peculiar presentiment that if we were traveling to work under the [favorable] conditions which were presented to us, then it appeared strange that we were sealed in cattle cars, without even being able to "step out" [to the toilet]. And no light. Fortunately one of us had a drill on him; he drilled a small hole in the floor. It had a diameter of about ten centimeters [four inches] so that we could throw "it" out. With the excitement that prevailed, everyone had to relieve himself. And so we were en route two days without the slightest possibility to move. You cannot imagine in what condition we arrived in Auschwitz.

Arrival in Auschwitz was also somewhat remarkable. At any rate, when the railroad car was opened, we saw the prisoners for the first time. Prisoners in striped suits. One of them turned to me and asked me to give him my wristwatch with the remark that, anyway, I was now going to Saint Peter. What that was to mean I found out later.

Was it not known in Lodz what was going on in these camps?

We were actually cut off from the outside world. That is why we knew much too little. We were not . . .

1. Hans Biebow, the German chief of the Lodz ghetto administration.

Well, he asked you for your watch. What did you say?

Nothing. I would not dream of giving him the watch. We were to get out of the cars and leave all the baggage there. And in addition, we had to get in formation, five in a row; and someone in uniform who revealed himself later as the physician of the camp indicated by gestures where each one had to go, right and left. Looking from where I stood, going to the left meant to go into the camp. Those people who were to stand to the right were going immediately into the crematoria. That, thanks to God, we did not know.

I noticed how a prisoner who worked at the railroad was tearing the child away from a young woman in order to force it on an older woman. This had the following meaning: an old person was to go to the crematorium under any circumstances while a young person, alone, not accompanied by children, had a chance to go into the camp. Of course, he could do that only at a moment when, by chance, the camp physician would not notice it.

Did she know that?

She, of course, did not surmise what that could signify. He took her child from her arms and transferred it to an older woman [who] would be burned anyhow. That was explained to us later.

The whole Lodz fire brigade marched into the camp, except the ones who departed before us. The [Lodz] Jewish police were present, too. Since the police had a very bad name among the population, and [since] many prisoners were already in the concentration camp who previously were in the Lodz ghetto, they came to an understanding with the supervisors.

What kind of supervisors? Jewish prisoners?

There were some who occupied a privileged position such as capo and the like. And it made no difference to them who they were burning, right?

Let me see whether I understand you correctly. The prisoners who had something against the Jewish policemen had them . . .

Made arrangements that these were immediately shoved into the oven. We were then assembled in a square and ordered to throw anything that we had in our pockets on the ground—watches, gold, everything that we still had. After this we had to undress in an open square that was closely fenced in. Then we were taken into a hall. Various prisoners sat there with razor blades, who shaved our whole bodies—shaved us completely with dry razor blades, without soap, wherever there was a single hair at all on the body. You can imagine how painful that is, when one is being shaved in a hurry and then being smattered with various tinctures.

Why?

I don't know. Possibly for disinfection. Then one had to run through under a shower. Then they threw us some prisoners' clothing, size estimated on sight. After [that] we camped outdoors the whole night—it was rather cold that time. We were led into the camp proper. We were then assigned to various blocks. They were kind of like horse stables. Barracks. We were taken into the Gypsy camp; that is, before us it was occupied by the Gypsies who were all burned.[2] We were assigned to the various blocks, crowded up to 1,000 people in a hall where normally about 300 people could possibly find room.

The block senior who gave the instructions—a Pole, not a Jew—said that he knew especially about the Jews of Lodz, that they had gold and diamonds in their possession, and that they, in order to hide them, were capable of swallowing them. They should surrender them voluntarily; otherwise they would do all kinds of things to us, and we would feel sorry later. Afterward, in order to give us an idea, so to speak, of what it meant to be in a camp, he picked one of us out and beat him up with a thick club. Frightfully. Over the face, on the back, and all over so that he could not move anymore. That made a terrible impression on us. And afterward he said that everyone should lay down whatever he still possessed. In order that it proceed unobserved we were driven to the other side and the people could then leave whatever they possessed. After he had established that what the people left there was too little, he again delivered a speech to us and said that we would be led out in the square right away and that there would be a much stronger check. If we had something, to surrender it.

Were there people who had swallowed some gold?

No. That is a ridiculous notion of that man. He wanted to bluff us.[3]

Well, I heard differently.

Well, I knew nothing about it. At any rate, [we] were then called to the roll call square. I still had comparatively decent shoes on me then, and I observed how somebody, also a prisoner, was sort of circling around me, eyeing my shoes. He ordered me to take off my shoes so he could try them on. They did not fit him well, but he liked them far too much to part with them. And he threw me a pair of old, tattered ones in return. I was told not to do anything about it since there is a frightful punishment for it.

Sleeping was the worst [thing] in such a block, on the floor, naturally. Since it was made of limestone squares, the floor was covered with boards. Every night

2. The Gypsy camp at Birkenau had been liquidated on August 2, 1944.
3. Cf. the interview with George K., chapter 33.

these boards were laid out; in the morning they were collected. One could not stretch out. Your legs had to be pulled up to your chest. One had to spend the whole night in this position. That meant until 4:00 in the morning . . .

From what time in the evening?

We entered the block at 7:00. Then the ration was handed out. The ration depended on the kindness of the particular block senior. [It] consisted of a piece of bread, a spoonful of canned meat, sometimes a spoon of honey that would be dispensed as a supplement to the ration. Since the block seniors liked to drink liquor, a certain black market existed in the camp. Prisoners who worked outside the camp, who consequently had some contact with the peasants, brought liquor into the camp in a concealed manner. And for this the block seniors paid with bread. A liter of liquor corresponded approximately to eighty bread rations.

Officially we received one [loaf of] army bread for four or five persons, [but] the block senior would distribute the rations so that ten or fifteen people [had to share it]. And the rest he used to obtain liquor for himself. If you dared to complain that your portion was too small, he would beat you up frightfully. And so one would accept what he got. We compared our portion among ourselves at times, going around from block to block.

At any rate, the sleeping was frightful. At times it was possible to stretch out, but then we were lying lengthwise just like herring. One was unable to move. Now imagine those many who had bladder trouble, who had to get out at night, had either to walk over the heads or the feet of the others, or inadvertently step on [them]. There was not enough light to see well, and so some individuals would begin to yell. The block senior who slept nearby would [punish the prisoners with] a "game"—for instance sitting in a squatting position with arms stretched out for about a half hour.

How did he sleep? Did he have a bed?

Yes. He had a little room for himself, and a couch, and food was no problem for him since they had contact with the kitchen most often, since they had deals among themselves. A block senior was like a king.

In the morning at about four o'clock, or half past four, we were driven out of the block. We were served cold coffee. It could rain or pour out and no chance for shelter, because the hall had to be straightened up.

And what kind of utensils were used?

The dishes were tin plates; of course there were never enough for all, so a part had always to wait. Everything was stuffed directly into the mouth in the most primitive way. At first we attempted to make some little wooden sticks to consume our food [laughing] in a Chinese way. This, naturally, was prohibited to us; and whenever such sticks were noticed, they were taken away.

No work was done in the [former] Gypsy camp; the major part were idle. That was also intolerable. All day one had to ramble. Even a pin had value, and for a cigarette one would give away his soup, which actually meant life. I never believed that I would get out alive. Imagine! As far as the eye could ever see, you see only barbed wire. So if you could overcome one barbed wire fence, which was hardly possible, you would have innumerable barbed wire fences to overcome.

I was exceptionally lucky; I got out of Auschwitz. One day there was a search for skilled workers, and someone from the Labor Division, also a senior prisoner, examined the people on their skills. My friend who came with me from Hamburg prevailed upon me to register with a group of 300 skilled workers. I had no trade whatsoever. I just told them that I was some kind of a specialist. At the last minute the block senior embezzled our bread, the complete allotment, because he knew we would depart the next day. A friend of mine, a dentist who is now in Lodz, had the courage to demand the rations. For that [the block senior] "befogged"[4] him terribly.

Then we traveled in open railroad cars, escorted by two SS men. The travel ration of bread [and] a little piece of sausage we consumed in half an hour because we did not have the ration of the evening before. And so we had a chance to breathe fresh air; and for us it was a certain comfort that we traveled. We knew that we were not going into the oven. We landed in Görlitz, in Silesia, about a hundred kilometers from Breslau. It is a peculiar feeling when after such a long time one sees a civilian again.

Görlitz was a work camp, a paradise in comparison with Auschwitz. We had to work outside the camp at an ammunition factory, as prisoners, always escorted by the SS. And evenings we were returned to the camp. We worked with civilian people. It was, of course, prohibited to talk to them. Still, now and then one exchanged a word with them. And since Frenchmen were also working there, and all possible nationalities, there was a chance to get some bread now and then from them by way of barter for cigarettes.

Where were you liberated?

I was liberated indirectly by the Russians. The Russians were entrenched for weeks about eleven kilometers from Görlitz. And strangely enough they did not advance further. An order was given to evacuate the camp since the Russians were bound to march in someday. [The Germans] did not want any evidence left against them. And so we found ourselves on the march; and unfortunately a great

---

4. The term used is *"vernebelt,"* literally "befogged" but suggesting "beat him senseless."

number of our prisoners were shot down because they could not walk, especially by the Ukrainian SS who hardly spoke a word of German.

I remember one day I was assigned to a detail of fifty people who had to dig graves in order to bury the dead from the journey. I remember an SS man, twenty-four years old, [who] gave the impression of an innocent youth. He was the champion marksman. Every day he used to shoot down about thirty or forty [people]; he himself helped to dig the grave. Probably for him that was a kind of sport. He was one of the people who were subsequently sent away at the last moment, apparently out of fear that they might fall into the hands of the Russians. The whole Ukrainian SS were sent away. They were frightful, they were the worst evil.

The Russians marched in about the 8th of August.[5] The camp leader explained to us that we were actually free. If we desired, we could go over to the Americans, and whoever wanted to remain with the Russians could remain.

Was the camp leader a prisoner?

No, he was an SS. I really must say that he behaved comparatively decently; that is, I never saw him touching a prisoner. [But] the camp senior was a super-gangster; a prisoner, but not a Jewish prisoner.

After that there was already such confusion that everybody did what he pleased. The [German] army was in retreat and en route—I was still with various colleagues, [and] we crossed all of Czechoslovakia, and in an SS vehicle at that.

In an SS auto?

No, no. With horse and wagon. We *took* it. It was still full of provisions, and with real SS boots and all sorts of things. And so we crossed the whole of Czechoslovakia until we arrived in Vienna.

And nobody stopped you?

Of course, en route we met the Russians. They saw that they were dealing with prisoners so they always let us pass. On the way we were very well received by the population. And you can imagine what a moment it was for us to enjoy freedom after we had given up the thought that we would ever get away.

---

5. M. obviously misspoke here. Görlitz fell on May 8, 1945, the day of the German surrender.

France

28 Edith S.

Edith S. taught in a Yiddish school in Paris when the Germans marched in in 1940. Born thirty years before in Bessarabia, she and a sister had moved to France some time in the 1930s. At the start of her interview she sketches out her efforts to place her charges in French Catholic homes to keep them from being deported by the Germans and their Vichy minions. The greater part of her account is devoted to the time following her arrest and deportation to Auschwitz in summer 1943. Set to draining swamps near the death camp, S. recalls the struggles of victims to help one another, which she recognizes as critical to survival. She also contributes to our understanding of camp iconography in lifting spirits and keeping hope alive. Once again we encounter the uprising of the Auschwitz Sonderkommando in October 1944, this time told with fewer exaggerations than usual. We also encounter the venerated Mala Zimetbaum, a Polish Jew who escaped from Auschwitz in a stolen SS uniform together with another inmate, Edek Galinski, in June 1944. Recaptured two weeks later, both were put to death on September 13. Her defiant execution scene clearly meant a great deal to S. and all who witnessed it in the women's camp at Birkenau.

Unlike the many Auschwitz prisoners who fixed their attention on daily survival, Edith S. wanted to know the details of the extermination process in the crematoria. A friend's fiance was a member of the Sonderkommando that disposed of the bodies at Birkenau. A letter from this doomed man smuggled to S. tells of his feelings when forced to assist in gassing an old and much loved teacher. It is one of the highlights of this interview.

S. withstood eighteen selections at Auschwitz, one of which was a close call. However, her closest brush with death occurred after having been evacuated to Ravensbrück concentration camp in the winter of 1944–45. Assigned to the gas, she managed to hide with the help of French prisoners. She was one of 2,500 truly fortunate women evacuated from Ravensbrück by the Swedish Red Cross in April 1945. Back in Paris, she found that her husband had deserted her for another woman. At the time of the interview Edith S. was awaiting permission to enter the United States and join her mother, who had moved there before the war. We begin with S.'s description of her resistance activities in Paris under German rule.

When the Germans came it was a duty to fight against Germany. We did everything to fight fascism, and I placed Jewish children with Catholic people in the villages. They [the Germans] did everything to take hold of Jewish children and Jewish families, so the task was to hide the children. I was also in the resistance.

Did the Catholic people know that they were Jewish children?
Yes. Quite a few knew—the majority knew that they were Jewish. I returned and found the children [to have been kept] very well.

Were they paid for keeping the children?
Yes. We had organizations which worked all the time, and the children were paid for all the time. And these organizations consisted of both Jews and Christians. I myself also hid my child. My child is now nine years old. And I also hid other children.

Now tell me what happened to you afterward.
I belonged to a resistance group. A child was arrested, a fourteen-year-old one, and the child was badly beaten. He was asked, "Who has hidden you?" So he said, "Such and such a woman has given me and my mother the chance to hide ourselves." The mother was already arrested. [She] did not want to betray me; but he, being a child, told. They found out my address and came and arrested me. I was severely beaten so that I would report the addresses of the children and the other people who were working on the same [project]. Of course, I did not tell; and for this reason I was deported to Drancy and from there to Birkenau. En route we were kept in locked cars. In twenty-four hours we were converted into beasts. People traveled with children, men, women. There was no air. In the middle of the car stood a large tub in which we had to satisfy our needs. And the air was very terrible. There were cases where people got deadly sick. We traveled this way three days and three nights. . . .

At the station there was a selection. I had three women friends, Russian Christians who were married to Jewish men. They were arrested [in France] with their children because the police had found out that their little boys were Jewish. We imagined that the camp was just a work camp. They took the children, and they were assigned to the "death truck" used to transport hundreds of people to the gas. The women with the three children were on the truck with older people, with sick people. They started yelling to me that I should come along with them. I started running. I did not know that *that was death.* [But] the German told me that I had to croak in the camp, and he put me in the line to go into the camp.

When we entered, we found ourselves only 360 out of 1,600 women. All the others went to the gas, and a part of them went for experiments. We were completely stripped. We remained completely naked for five days. Our heads were shaven. [We were] tattooed, not given any food, and beaten all the time without any reason. Afterward we were transferred to the blocks, where we remained in quarantine.

[After six weeks S. was assigned to a detail draining swamps. Boder noted that she showed him dog bites on her thigh inflicted by SS dogs on that detail.]

At seven o'clock we would come to dry the swamps. It was muddy and dirty there. There were leeches and little snakes. We were bitten by all the insects. In October we were still going barefooted, and the cold was very great, and we had to enter the water up to our neck. So we, a detail of fifteen or sixteen hundred women, would start walking gradually, just to get accustomed to the water. But the SS men set their dogs on us so that we would run. The women would start to run fast. They became demoralized, started yelling. A lot of women fell, and we, not knowing it, would kill the drowning ones with our feet because one was running over the other. There was not a day when there were no dead. And that is how we were bitten by the dogs. We did not even know that we were being bitten. We noticed that the mud would become red from our blood.

When we left work, we would take the bodies on our shoulders and carry them to the crematoria. The SS men beat us [demanding] that we carry them well. But we were so weak; we ourselves could not walk on our feet from such a day's work on a half liter of soup. And he [the guard] delivered lectures to us. "You dirty Jews, you who deprived us of bread for years, you have become rich, you have everything, [gorging yourselves with] food and drink. And now we have brought you here to punish you. The crematoria are too good for you. We shall make you croak little by little. You will plead for death, but death will not come so soon. Death would be too good a thing for you." We were beaten until twelve o'clock. The SS man who could prove that he had "produced" dead women in the detail was considered a good worker. He mastered his trade well.

On days when we helped each other morally, and there were no dead, he forced us to make genuflections [do calisthenics], and we would get demoralized. And in this way we would get sick from not eating and from the cold, and so they went to the crematoria anyhow. That was an extermination detail of a sort.

[S. recalled the arrival of large numbers of Hungarian Jews in 1944.] The crematoria burned through the nights. And the pits were [also] burning. There were four crematoria and four large pits.

Tell me about the pits.

There were very many [people] who say that very many were burned alive because there was no gas. In order to be killed by gas people needed a minimum of three quarters of an hour. But there was not [enough] time. The people were gassed every ten minutes. They were only put to sleep, and the bodies were pulled out, and from there they were thrown into the fire. And the people were not actually dead. That happened with the great transports from Hungary because in six weeks they burned twenties of thousands of people. They had no time for the people to be completely dead.

And they were burned in the ovens and in the pits?
Four pits and four crematoria. They worked day and night. [The pits were] large, rectangular ditches smeared with a kind of grease. And the people were thrown in and inflammable material thrown over them. These were burned out, and the [ashes were] taken out and come winter sprinkled over the fields to "fatten" the fields. My block was the twenty-seventh, across from the gas chamber. We heard the screams of the men and women being gassed.

And why was your block not taken?
A fixed contingent had remained in the camp. If that were surpassed, then people were also taken from the camp and gassed. They needed the camp to exist; they needed to show Berlin that they were doing some work.

See here. You went through eighteen selections. How did it happen that you were not taken?
It was fate. It was fate. Other women were also not taken. We were in a block of 2,000 women. They would take out people from the block to take baths. Of course, we did not bathe. But when it was necessary to go into the gas chamber, we were told that we would be going bathing. Then we would undress. A doctor would come and [Maria] Mandel, an SS woman who was a chief in Auschwitz, who with her own hands used to lead the children to the gas chamber. And so the selection proceeded of those who had to go, and when they happened to be chosen, they took the number [of the tattoo on the arm and] wrote it down.

Once my number was taken, too. But the doctor said, "She can still croak on for a few weeks. So have her marked down; *then* she will go into the gas." And the SS man gave me two big blows over the head, and called me a dirty sow, and ordered me to step aside as fast as possible, to go away.

[S. asked if she could read part of a letter written in the camp and sent to her via the unofficial camp postal service by a member of the Jewish Sonderkommando who was betrothed to one of her close friends. It appears that some of the material that follows is quoted from the letter, although it is not clear how much.]

I badly wanted to know how things happened in the crematorium—what they did, how they worked there, and why he worked there. For a long time he did not want to write. But when I wrote to him I knew that we [too] were extermination material in the camp, so I was entitled to know. So he wrote to me about how things proceeded there, how they gassed and burned. He later requested a working suit. I asked him, "Why must you have a blue work suit?" He replied that he dealt a lot with blood. We did not understand him, so he explained, "When people are being gassed, the people die very hard. People choke, they are being suffocated. Blood breaks out from the eyes, mouth, and ears. They are covered with blood."

He also told me about the work. The chief[1] was a wild beast. He was big and very strong. He beat us all most bitterly. When they were gassing the people he would stand and watch through a small window which was installed just for him. And he drank champagne when they choked. He writes: "Already I have worked on this job for three years. I am already transformed into an animal. I have already gassed my mother, my father, my sisters, and my brothers, and the whole Jewish people. I thought of myself as a scoundrel, as a criminal. I already thought that I no longer had a heart like other people when I have seen so many children and women and men perishing. But no, that is not the case. Today I have seen that I still have a bit of the human left in me. Because they led in my Rebbe [Hebrew teacher] from the Yeshiva, who had arrived with twenty or so students. And the Rebbe recognized me, and when I saw that, I cursed myself."

When he saw the Rebbe perishing with his bright students, then, he says, "I broke out crying. Today I have recognized that I have a human spirit in me like all people." Afterward he [the Sonderkommando member] was among those who blew up the two crematoria, and he perished.

We also had a very beautiful song about a woman who was a young girl in her early twenties, Mala from Belgium.[2] She worked for the SS men as a messenger runner. She was very smart and very beautiful. She used her intelligence and her niceness not for her own existence and her own selfish aims but for the good of the women who had come to the camp and who were to be killed. She was a political prisoner in Birkenau. Every Sunday she "organized" soup for us and gave everybody an additional liter to eat. Now where did she get that soup? The soup was ordered for the SS men, but they never ate that very good soup. She would bring it to us.

1. SS Captain Otto Moll, executed in 1946 by the Americans.

2. Mala Zimetbaum was born in Brzesko, Poland, in 1918, but was arrested by the Nazis in Belgium.

And why didn't they [the SS men] eat it?

Because they ate meat, butter, and much better things—they did not have to eat this. And she helped us a great deal with that. There were very many women who had become sick, who were lying in the hospital. One could not lay sick for long [or] their numbers would be taken, and they were sent to the gas chamber. But she [Mala] used to erase their numbers from the paper. And these women would not go to be gassed. She led such a work of solidarity among us that had she been caught at such work she could have been shot. But she did not stop. She did everything to help us. Early one morning Mala donned the clothes of an SS woman and escaped along with a man. She wanted contact with the free world to tell about our sufferings. We in the camp thought that we had been cut off from the whole world.

And when she was caught [along] with that man, the man was hanged in the men's camp, and she was supposed to be hanged in the women's camp. They held her several weeks. She was clubbed and beaten [so that] she should tell how she managed to escape, with whom she had connections on the outside. But she told them nothing. One day we all returned in the evening from work. We were lined up and in the middle of the camp a gallows was erected. And Mandel, the SS woman who mistreated the whole camp, said, "This Mala, in whom we had such great confidence, escaped. An order has come from Berlin that a Jewish woman who dares to escape from our camp must be hanged."

Mala had a razor [hidden] in her hand and at that moment cut several of her arteries. When the leader of the work service saw that she was cutting her arteries because she wanted to die her *own* death, he ran over to her, grabbed her and twisted her hands so that the blood should not run out. She stood up and slapped him twice, and she said, "I take on you the last vengeance for my sisters and brothers and children who have innocently perished." We heard it and we saw it. So the work service leader gave an order that she should be burned alive. She was taken to the crematorium in a little cart [where] she was shot to death by a prisoner who worked in the crematorium. Because he said, "Mala does not deserve to burn alive." When we heard that Mala was shot by one of our people, we were very happy.

How did he have a revolver?

The men who worked in the crematoria were organized so that one day they could fight the SS men. And they blew up [one of the crematoria]. And the SS men found out that Jewish women working in the Union armaments factory had stolen the explosive materials. They arrested six girls, who were betrayed. All six girls were beaten; but one did not behave well and betrayed the others. And all six girls were hanged in the camp.

You saw it?

I saw it. I had to carry their bodies. I then worked in the Auschwitz sick room. One sister was sick, and her sister had to be hanged that day. I had to take care of the sister and help her and comfort her. The whole camp had to look on at how they were being led to the [gallows]. When they were hanged, they stepped up with shouts and stamping feet. They were going like heroes, laughingly. They jumped on the board and shouted, "Vengeance!"

We [knew] that the camp was an extermination camp and that we would not come out of there alive. So we started to organize ourselves around the Bund.[3] Only political women who knew that they lived to fight against fascism and Hitlerism. So we started to organize resistance in the camp. We could not accomplish much with our work because we had nothing in our hands. When a woman would get sick in the winter—we were permitted to wear only one shirt and one dress—the healthier women would take off their underwear and give it to the sick one. And so we all kept up each other's spirit. When one would get sick, and we did not want her to die, we gave a little piece of bread. Everyone had to give a little piece. And thanks to such an organization we saw that we would be able to save ourselves. And we also started to organize ourselves and to make propaganda that we should defend ourselves. We would not permit them to take us to the gas chambers.

We formed an organization together with the men. We "organized" scissors to cut the wires of the camp. We "organized" knives. We dug big holes outside the block and hid a lot of things—clubs. . . . So if they should come to exterminate us, block by block, we should defend ourselves, tear the wires, cut the electricity, and blow up the crematoria. That happened in the winter of 1944. When they came to take a detail for gassing, our men blew up two gas chambers.[4] And from that day on they did not gas anymore.

What was done to the men who blew up the gas chambers?

They were all shot. The men had cut the wires so that the women could run away. We did not know about it because we were outside, ten kilometers from the camp.

In 1945 the great evacuation of the camp occurred. We were taken from all the camps around Auschwitz. We made one hundred twenty kilometers on foot in snow. We discarded everything because it was impossible to walk in snow with-

3. "League of Jewish Workers in Russia, Lithuania, and Poland," a Jewish Social Democratic movement popular in Poland before World War II.

4. Just one, crematorium IV, was destroyed in the Sonderkommando revolt of October 7, 1944.

out food [or] drink. Beside the roads mountains of people were lying shot, because they were unable to walk. Whoever went near the roadside was also shot. Those who could walk, walked. And those who remained behind were shot. The majority were shot. And that is how we arrived in Breslau. We were loaded into open railroad cars. That was the 18th of January. In the summer, the time of the great deportations, we were loaded into closed, stuffy cars. In the wintertime we were placed in open cars. It snowed all over us three days and three nights.

I found myself in an open car with sick women and children because I had the people from the sickroom. The five women gave birth to their babies.[5] That was a picture which I shall not be able to forget in my lifetime. They came down in labor, lying stretched out, half-naked, to give birth to their babies. They could not be active and so were not able to give birth. A woman when she is about to have a baby must be active, she must expel the child from her body. The woman had no strength; she was frozen. We took off our dresses and threw them over the sick woman so she could . . . she was frozen. . . . And we pleaded with the women, "Be active, deliver your child, gather strength." But the woman was so weakened and said, "I can't. We are cold."[6] We saw the baby emerging with a head half outside, and it goes back. The baby cannot come out. Finally, it lasted three days and three nights, and the women gave birth to their children—live children on the snow.

All five?

All five. All alive. And in a corner of the car little children were lying and saw how women have children. And in [another] corner of the car an SS man and an SS woman made love. They were not ashamed that women were lying there unable to deliver their babies; they were not ashamed that little children were present who saw things which they had not seen their parents do. They made love like a dog, like a beast. Right then we saw the baseness of the SS—what they are capable of. They did not see us. They acted at their pleasure, whenever they wanted.

When we arrived in Ravensbrück, we remained standing in the camp for twenty-four hours. It snowed all the time. They did not want to let us in. The camp was overcrowded with people. When we entered, we were put in a large tent. At night we were given one loaf of bread for ten people. We got no soup like [we got] in the other camps. We were not given water to wash. We had no toilet—just nothing. And they began to assign us, all the women who had come from Auschwitz, to transports. Very many women perished from hunger, and very many of them did not return. The [five] women arrived at Ravensbrück with

5. During her last days at Auschwitz S. had worked in the infirmary caring for, among others, five Yugoslavian women, non-Jewish partisans, who were about to give birth.

6. Boder commented: "There is a constant mixture of singular and plural. She speaks of one and the five pregnant women interchangeably."

their [babies, but they] did not live because the camps did not provide milk to maintain their existence. All the time I repeatedly saw that the women were sick, and when we were redeemed, I learned that three [of the five] had died. And the [other] two, sick like the others, possibly perished.

In Ravensbrück I also was once taken to be gassed, because although I was only thirty-four years old, I looked like a woman of fifty or fifty-five. We were all driven outside, and the camp senior selected the older women to go to the gas; the younger women were to remain for work in the front trenches. He asked me how old I was. I told him I was thirty-four, so he slapped me twice. He threw me to the ground; he trampled me with his feet; he beat me, and he said, "You dirty woman. You believe that you may present yourself as a young child. You shall go into the gas chamber with all the old women." And he put me among the old women. I made every effort to wiggle myself out. I was able to run away because there was a mass [air] raid. They put the older women aside and at night led them away to the gas chamber—to the "Jew camp" as it was called.

I went over to the sick ward. I joined the French women arrested for political reasons. I was badly beaten up and very sick from his blows, and they hid me so that I should not go for selections anymore. This lasted a few weeks, and then we were delivered. It was already the end of the war; that is why they were so set to exterminate us. They did everything so that not many people should get out of the camp.

And how did your liberation come about?
The SS men had become very downcast the last few days before liberation. They were no longer the great heroes as we imagined them to be. They were the great SS men when Jewish homes were being destroyed, when we had no weapons to fight against them. But when they saw Berlin being bombarded, the "great heroes" had become very little men, and they would not beat so badly anymore. They became very demoralized. Orders came from the [Swedish] Red Cross; they requested the release of French, Dutch, Belgian, and Finnish women. Afterward they were taking Polish women. I was considered a French woman. All women who were deported from France were considered French women. The SS men transferred us into the hands of the Swedes. We traveled in the busses of the Red Cross. There we were given proper first aid because we were all demoralized and sick. We knew that if the war would have lasted two weeks longer, not a single prisoner would have come to be liberated. There were women who weighed 33 kilos [72 pounds].

And what did the SS men say when you were taken?
They said that they wanted to release only Aryan women. On the first transports they sent exclusively Aryan and not Jewish [women], but the Red Cross

protested and said that they were an international organization. They wanted to take out all who had suffered. And at that instant they handed over the Jewish ones also. But unfortunately there were not many to be liberated because the majority were killed in the camp.

I was in Sweden two and a half months. We were given a very fine reception. They were very courteous and very concerned. When we arrived, the majority of the women were very sick. They gave us great care there. And the population did everything for us—we were their darlings . . .

29 Nelly B.

Sometimes a survivor's experiences of the camps arouse less interest than the events surrounding them. Nelly B. spent two years at Auschwitz and then in Ravensbrück and its satellite camps, but what happened to her during that time was exceptional only in that her knowledge of German and English qualified her for a comparatively protected job in the Political Department of the Auschwitz administration offices. Of that job she has little to say beyond her matter-of-fact report that she learned from the files of the death of her husband, who had been sent there long before her arrival.

Nelly B. has more to say about her frantic efforts between 1940 and 1943 to keep her family together and protect her children from the Germans. Born in Vienna around 1915, she had met and married her husband, a Czech Jew living in Paris, in the mid-1930s. When Paris came under German fire in 1940, she bicycled to the south of France to reunite with her husband, then serving in a Czech unit under French command, and her two children. Her husband was arrested in 1941, shortly after the birth of their third child, and Nelly B. smuggled all three of the children to safety in the unoccupied zone. She was arrested herself in March 1943 and after three months at Drancy was sent to Auschwitz.

Still more interesting is Nelly B.'s account of her escape from a Nazi death march at the end of the war. Evacuated from Auschwitz to Ravensbrück and then to a series of work camps south of Berlin, she simply walked away from her camp during an air raid and passed as a German refugee. Fluent in German, she had the wit to exploit the chaos of the collapsing Reich and secure the assistance of Nazi welfare agencies to stay alive in spite of her frostbitten feet. We will never know for certain if escaping saved her life, but it may have done so. SS men sometimes shot their charges at the last moment rather than let them go. In the last days of the war Nelly B. found herself in a German-held area surrounded by Russian and American forces, encountering little sympathy from the latter when she approached them for help.

Boder interviewed B. in a storage room of one of the Paris offices of the Joint Distribution Committee. We join B.'s story in July 1942 when she, her three children, and a governess left Paris with the intention of smuggling themselves to Lyon in the unoccupied zone of France.

We took the train to the demarcation line. And then we went on foot with two guides. I had to carry a bundle of clothing for us, and my governess carried the small one who was fourteen or fifteen months; and my little girl, who was five, had to walk. We walked all night. At that time we hadn't got the false papers. We had two guides, and we were crossing the woods.

Where do you get two guides? What kind of people were they? Did you pay them?
They were French. Yes, I paid; but not very much for they were good people, you see. Well, we walked from 11:00 in the night till 3:00 in the morning. And then we were led to another house. And there we could pass the night. We had to walk another two hours in order to reach the [bus line]. [There] they made an inspection. They wanted papers. Of course, I hadn't got any, but I had been a volunteer in the French [antiaircraft force]. And I had a kind of *sauf-conduit* from the *prefecture* [police pass] which didn't show anything. Just my name and address, and my name is very French. I showed them this paper, and it worked out all right. Well, in Nievre we did stay for two or three months, and then we left. And we lived in a small place till March 1943. Then I had no more money. And in March '43 the demarcation line was opened to French citizens. As I had a French identify card I went back quite openly with the train from Lyon to Paris.

With false papers?
Yes. I couldn't change my name because of the children. Because if somebody asked them . . . they couldn't . . . I couldn't teach them overnight that they had to change their names. So I thought, anyway it's French. And I came back to Paris. And I got arrested at the Gare de Lyon [train station] because I had two identity cards. I had my other one, too.

Oh, and from the other it was known that you were Jewish, or what?
Yes, of course. There was a stamp on it 'Jew.' Well, I was arrested, and I was sent to Drancy, that famous camp near Paris. And I stayed there for three months. The children remained in the [south] with their governess. And as soon as she knew that I had been arrested she moved them on to quite another part of France, and she left them there with a French lady who didn't know that they were Jewish children. And they have kept them all the time, and they are over there even now. I go to see them sometimes, but it's rather far from Paris. I wish to take them back, but my flat is occupied [by other people] now, and I can't get it back.

[Sent to Birkenau in June 1943, B. was dressed in an old Soviet army uniform and assigned to a work crew that demolished farm buildings to make way for expansion of the camp.]

We did that for a week or so; but personally I didn't remain there. When we had arrived, even before we were tattooed, there was a young Nazi. He was quite a boy. He came to ask for somebody who knew English. There were three of us, and he took down our names; and he chose me afterward. And so I was removed from there, and I came to Auschwitz to work in the office.

Yes. Why did they need English there?
One of the Nazis wanted to take English lessons. He never did afterward, but anyway I came to the office, and I have been working in the administration of the camp until Auschwitz was evacuated.

Did they give you other clothes?
Yes, I got better clothing. I got these striped clothes, you see. And then I was allowed to grow my hair a bit. Personally I had a relatively good time [of it] in Auschwitz, working in the office. I had a bed for myself. We had a shower room. We had warm showers twice a week. There was hot water to wash oneself with. Whereas in Birkenau there was no water at all. When we came home from the "outdoor" work, we were dirty and thirsty and everything; and there was no water, neither to drink nor to wash ourselves in.

Now tell me. You were in Auschwitz in the office. Did you know then at all these gassing procedures?
Yes, I did. Officially everything was kept secret. But of course, we knew because before selections were made we got the lists. We were taking out a file card on everybody and marking his death even before he was dead. I worked in the so-called Political Department, and I found [my husband's] file card, and I found that he had been killed by a guard in 1942, three months after his arrival.

By the by, they burned all these cards. My husband's file card was still there in July 1943, but it was no longer there in October '43.

They would pick out the cards and . . .
They would take out the cards by and by and burn them; officially they [the cards] were sent to Birkenau, but they were burned.

Tell me, in general how did the women fare who had to work with the Nazis? How did they behave toward women?
Well, they didn't behave very well, I'm sorry to say. That's to say, they made an exception for us who were working with them. They behaved fairly well. Of course, if they had an occasion, they got drunk even if we were there or not. That was a different kind of thing; but on a general scale they treated us like machines, like automatons. Some of the girls they called by their first names.

[After her time in Auschwitz and Ravensbrück, Nelly B. was taken to Tachau, a camp just northeast of Leipzig, in March 1945.]

Conditions were better. We had one bed for two [people], and even the food was better. It was cleanly cooked and after [the other camps], it seemed like paradise. We couldn't work. We were much too exhausted.

By the way, you wear glasses. Did you have your glasses with you in camp?
They took them away. I got other ones later on, as a special office worker.

We remained for only ten days. We had to leave Tachau one evening very quickly, and I had a lot of trouble because I couldn't walk. My foot had been frozen. I marched along with them for two days, but then I simply couldn't, and I knew I would be shot. So I escaped. We were then in a town called Oschatz, which is between Leipzig and Dresden. And they had moved us there to a kind of open-air stadium. It was outside of the town and a bit elevated, and so we had a view of the town. There were stairs leading downstairs, and they had a Nazi guard on every staircase.

And what kind of clothing were you wearing?
I had no more stripes on the back. In one of the camps I had been to the hospital because of my foot. They had taken away all my dresses, and when I got out from the hospital, I got a civilian dress with a big white cross on the back. I put the cross on the inside. Well, there was an airplane attack. These were American airplanes who were attacking the place, and there was a panic. And suddenly I saw that one of the staircases [was] not guarded, so I went downstairs quietly, and by chance I found an air-raid shelter. I didn't know what it was, and I went there, and I heard some voices, and I was rather afraid. But it was too late. The people were coming near so I couldn't do anything but just stay down there. Well, they took me for a civilian or they pretended about it.

When the attack was over, I marched out of the thing. There was a Nazi guard at the entrance; but he didn't pay any attention to me. So I went to the [Protestant] church. I had located the church from upstairs. I went in there, and I remained there for three days. I hid between benches downstairs. You see, I lay down on the floor. I slept a lot. I was absolutely exhausted. And I didn't even think of eating through the third day. Then I thought I was obliged to get something. Otherwise I would be sick, or I would be found or something. So I went to see the Protestant chaplain. I told him my story. I was quite open and asked him to help me. Well, he would have done, but he was terribly afraid of the Gestapo. So he just gave me some biscuits, and I even wanted to save some for later; he didn't allow me. He wanted me to eat them immediately because he was afraid if they were found on me, they would ask me where I had got them from.

Did you tell him you were Jewish?

I didn't. He asked, but I told him that I was Roman Catholic but that my husband had been a Jew—a French Jew. And that I was born in Vienna, which is a fact and which accounted for my good German, of course. And he said, "Well, if you are a Catholic we have a Roman Catholic priest here." I said, "Oh, that's fine. I didn't know, and I didn't want to ask so many people." So he gave me the address. And I went to see him. Well, this young priest was very kind, and I told him the same thing.

Do you know enough of the Catholic religion to take a chance on it?

Yes, I know something. He gave me some money, and his mother brought me some food, some sandwiches.

And you told him that you were running away from the camp?

Yes, I told him. He even told me, "You're not the first one. You are the second or the third." And he advised me to get to the country[side]. And I did, and I walked for an hour or two; but I didn't get very far because I couldn't walk. I fell down in the ditch near the road. Well, there I was, lying there for I don't know how long a time, till somebody came up to me and asked me what I was doing. So I told him that I was taking a rest. He was a refugee from Russian-occupied Germany. A civilian evacuated there by the government. And I asked him if he couldn't [give] me a room to sleep in this night. I explained to him that I had hurt my leg and that I couldn't walk; and he said, "You see, we are very crowded, and my wife and myself are just refugees, and we haven't got any room for ourselves. You just go and see the mayor." Of course that was the least of things I wanted to do. Then there came a friend of his with a bicycle, took me on the bicycle and led me to the mayor [of the nearby village].

The mayor wasn't there, but his wife was, and I told her that I [needed someplace to stay]. I couldn't walk. That I was a refugee myself from—I don't remember what I told her. And she advised me to go to [a particular] hotel and to get a room there. Well, I didn't get a room, but I was sent to a big dormitory where there were many other refugees. Well, they took me up very friendly and were very kind, and I told the landlord that I would go away the next morning. Later the landlord came and ask[ed] me for papers. Well, I didn't have any papers, and I told him that I had lost them all. So he said, "Well, if you have lost them, we'll call for the police, because you understand this is wartime, and there are a lot of spies getting around everywhere, and we'll see to that." And he told the others to take care that I shouldn't run away. Well, there was no danger for that because I had a high fever. I fell back on my straw, and I slept.

I was awakened by two policemen who asked me what I was doing here and how I had come here and so on. Well, I told them the same thing, that I had escaped from Leipzig because the Russians had taken Leipzig, and they asked for my name. I gave my maiden name.[1] And they asked for the address. Well, they asked what I was doing in Leipzig. I knew that there was a factory for munitions in Tachau where I had been in camp, because comrades of mine had been working there. And I knew, too, that the Americans are already there so he couldn't check. I invented a street according to the name of this station, you see, and it worked out all right. But he said "We'll leave you alone; you remain here without papers. Anyway, you can't roam the country without any papers." So I [decided] I'd get back to Oschatz and see the NSV.[2]

Next morning I [got] away to Oschatz in the milk van. They took me along, and I dropped into the Nazi welfare office and told them about the lost papers, and they said I should go to the town hall. Well, I did, and I signed a declaration that I had lost all my papers, and I invented all kinds of [things].

But didn't you have your tattoo?

Yes, but I had long sleeves. They didn't have the idea to ask for that. Then they sent me to the police. I went there, and he just told me, "Well, if you lose your papers, I can't help you now. You know very well that you can't get them back." I [replied], "I can't walk, and I haven't eaten, and I'm hungry, and I'm sleepy, and you must tell me where to go to sleep." So they indicated [to] me a kind of school, sort of a shelter for German civilians, and he told me, "I don't know if the director will take you in without papers, but you might try." I went there and saw the director, and the same thing, "I can't take you without papers." So I said, "Listen, I have been to see the police, and they told me to see you." So he said, "Well, I'll take you until tomorrow, but I'll ask for some identification for you from the police. [Remind] me this afternoon." I said, "O.K."

Well, he put me into a small schoolroom. There were mattresses, and I got two covers, and it was clean. Everything was all right. We were about fifteen people in this room. And in the afternoon there came a German sanitary officer, and he looked at me, and I must have a high fever, and I must have looked very flushed, because he came to me and said, "What's wrong with you? Anything wrong?" I said, "Yes, my foot." "Let me see that." Well, you see, I hadn't taken off my shoe for several days, and I was really most unhappy when I saw this foot. It was sore and swollen, and he told me, "We'll have to get you to the hospital." But I didn't want to [go] there because of this tattoo. I was afraid. If I had to take off my clothes, then everything would be . . . So I insisted on just remaining.

"If you just leave me alone on this mattress, and if I haven't got to walk for

1. Nelly B.'s maiden name sounded German, and not specifically Jewish.

2. *Nationalsozialistische Volkswohlfahrt*, the Nazi party agency responsible for welfare and social services.

miles and miles, it will be all right." Well, I succeeded, and he disinfected it and made me a good bandage and told me, "Now certainly don't move and just remain stretched out. Don't walk on this foot." He must have been a student of medicine, you see. Well, the director [returned], and I said to him "You wanted me to remind you of this paper for me for the police." He said, "Yes, that's all right. You just remain here, and I'll take care of that. You see, I didn't know your foot was as bad as that. Please forgive me."

Well, I remained there for a few days, but then they even opened a kind of hospital for me. There was another lady, too, who had something wrong with her foot, and we were put there. I was afraid to have to undress and they would see my tattoo, but this kind of hospital, a kind of nursery, was not much better than this big room except that there were nurses and [we didn't have to] go and fetch our food ourselves. I remained there for a week or so, and then the Russians were approaching, and we were told to evacuate the town. I tried to walk. I couldn't so I turned back. It was 4:00 in the morning. I turned back into my bed and remained there. A nurse found me at 5:00 in the morning and said, "But dear me, you can't stay. You must get away." I said, "I can't walk." So she told me there was a train leaving at 6:00.

The station was not very far away, and she said it would be better on the train if I would be able to walk to the station. I said yes. Well, I got on this train, and when we got off, we had to walk. I had heard on the train that the town of Grimma[3] was occupied by the Americans. So I made up my mind to go there; and when we got off the train, I asked where it was. So they told me, "It's this way, but you can't get there. It's occupied by the enemy." I went all the same. I took the direction, and once on the way I was stopped by some person in a uniform. He said, "You can't go there. It's occupied." I said, "But where should I go to? I've been turning around for weeks or months now. I've had quite enough of this stuff. Even if its occupied by the Americans, I don't mind, and I'll get there and settle down someplace." He said, "But you can't. It's verboten."

Well, then somebody else was arguing with him, and I slipped behind his back, and I went on all the same. I went on, and I came to a small place where there was a kind of a shelter again for civilians. A school which was turned into a shelter house [for] German civilians who were displaced. There was great disorder. Nobody was asking any questions, so I just took a bed which was free, and at noon I went to fetch some soup. At 10:00 the next morning somebody told us we have to get back to Oschatz where we came from because [the enemy was approaching]. I didn't want to go back, and I was afraid to go ahead because I was afraid that people who would join the enemy would be shot. I didn't want to be shot after two years of Auschwitz.

3. Southeast of Leipzig.

[I stood at a crossroad and] was just thinking it over when I saw a group of French prisoners of war who were taking this road. So I called to them, "Where are you going?" "Why, of course, to the Americans." I said, "Oh, I'll join you." "Well, come along if you want to." And they waited for me. They were a group of four men and two women. They took me along, but I saw that they would march much quicker without me. I said to them, "I don't want to bother you. You just walk ahead, and I'll follow you even if it's some distance. It's of no importance." But this group was nice. It was my good luck because they slipped through everywhere. There were German troops on the roads, and every time when I came [to] some such post, I said, "Well, I belong to this group. I'm a French prisoner," and that was all right, so I slipped through.

And how did they let the French go through?

Yes, the men wore uniforms, you see. They let them go, yes. Well, the war was more or less over. It was the end of April. They knew there was nothing to be done. Well, I had to walk a long way. I had to walk some twenty-five kilometers till I reached Grimma in Saxony, not very far from Leipzig. Well, there was a bridge which had been blown up by the Germans when they retreated. Part of the bridge was going down into the water, and the Americans had put ladders up there, and that was how people got over.

And there were American guards. I came to see them, and I spoke English and asked them if I could get over. "But who are you?" I said, "I'm a French political prisoner." "Well, I'll ask the captain for that. I haven't got any instructions for you. We just have instructions to pass over the prisoners of war." The captain came back and told me, "I'm extremely sorry for you, but so far I haven't got any instructions for political prisoners, just for prisoners of war." I said, "What shall I do? I haven't any money. I haven't got any papers. I have got nothing to eat. Couldn't you take me over? I have a bad foot, and I need a doctor." "I'm extremely sorry, I can't. Come back tomorrow. Perhaps I'll have such instructions by then." Next morning I came back.

[The Americans repeatedly refused to let her pass. Evidently they had orders not to advance but await the arrival of the Soviet army. Fed by passing prisoners of war, B. sheltered herself in an abandoned barn for several days.]

I had heard about a German nurse who could pass over to the American occupied zone. I went to see her, and I asked if she couldn't help [me get] an authorization from the American officers.

Was the war over?

No, not officially. It was the end of April. Well, the Germans knew that everything was lost anyway. Well, I went to find this nurse, and the first thing she did was to bandage my foot again; and she saw that I really needed a doctor. So she took the paper, and she went over. She crossed the bridge, and she obtained authorization to bring me over. Well, the next day she came to fetch me—it was in the afternoon—but in the morning the Russians had arrived there. And now there was a Russian guard on this side of the bridge. He told me that I needed a Russian authorization. I didn't pay any heed to him. I said I was ordered, was sick, and I had an American authorization. Well, I got over, and they immediately put me into a hospital; and three or four days [later] there was a French prisoner who was making lists for French people, and she took my name down, and a few days later I was sent to Leipzig and back to France.

30 Fania F.

Fania F. was born about 1910 in Augustow, Poland. Escaping Polish anti-Semitism, she, her husband, and four children came to Paris in 1937 by way of Luxembourg.[1] There they and other refugees encountered mounting resentment from a French nation worried about the lingering economic slump and possible war with Germany. On the eve of Hitler's successful blitz of France in 1940 there were approximately 200,000 Jewish refugees in France out of a total Jewish population of 350,000. The right-wing, collaborationist Vichy regime that ruled France for the next four years willingly complied with German demands to deliver the Jews, starting with the refugees. Only the initiative shown by some of the victims in finding hiding places and the willingness of some Frenchmen to help them kept the total number of deaths relatively low—about 78,000.

The fact that Fania's husband did work of military importance to the Germans saved her and her family from the early deportations, but it did not prevent some close calls. She and three of her children were included in the infamous roundup of nearly 13,000 Jewish refugees in Paris on July 16 and 17, 1942. Herded into a race track, the Vélodrome d'Hiver, held under hideous conditions, and then sent to the concentration camp at Pithiviers, they were saved from deportation only at the last moment. Something similar occurred a year later when she and her surviving family were taken to Drancy concentration camp. Only after that did they flee to a village and go into hiding until liberated by the Americans in 1944.

Boder observed that Fania F., a woman of little education and modest background, was far more bitter about the French than about the Germans, so much so that she could not wait to leave. Boder was rather critical of her attitude, noting generous postwar French assistance to the DPs at a time when food and housing were extremely scarce. Certainly Fania F.'s narrative is unbalanced. She underlines the participation of the French police in the deportations and the denunciation by an anonymous French neighbor of her daughter for appearing in public without the yellow star. On the other hand she has nothing to say about the Frenchmen who must have helped her and her family hide in the

1. A longer version of this interview appears in Boder's *I Did Not Interview the Dead.*

countryside during the last year of the occupation. And yet, modern scholarship has revealed just how thinly stretched German forces were in France and how crucial the cooperation of local police forces was to the success of deportations from France. Although Vichy leaders claimed after the war that they had done only as much to the Jews as the Germans forced them to do, we now know that those leaders actually seized the initiative in order to impress Berlin with their qualifications as long-term allies of the Third Reich. Fania F. sensed the essence of the truth and told it forcefully the day she told her story to David Boder in Paris in August 1946. We pick up the story in 1942 when she and three of her children were arrested.

They led us away to the commissariat for registration. In a large shop the gendarmes, the police, the inspectors were "working" very efficiently. They did their work even better than the Germans had told them. Loyally. French men and women stood all around. All were rejoicing. The Jews are being taken away. They have our apartments.

What do you mean—"they"?
(Impatiently) French Gentiles! Gentiles! Gentiles! "The Jews will be taken away. We will take their apartments! We will take their things! The Jews are all rich, and we have nothing! We shall have more to eat!" They patted their bellies. They were rejoicing. The Jews were marching. Blood was flowing from their eyes. Two o'clock at night with no sleep, with sleepy children in their arms.

[Then] they led us to the Vélodrome d'Hiver, a place where they race on motorcycles. They could pack in 100,000 people, but when I arrived with my children, there wasn't even room enough to set down a bundle. I was not exactly in the best of health because I suffer from [diseased] gall bladder. And the daughter of mine had a lot of courage. She dragged the bundles. She got hold of some straw that was lying around on the sides prepared for the people, and she fixed a place to lay down.

"Here, mother," she said, "here we will lie down and sleep overnight." It was very hard to find some room. People were jammed together like herring. That night was—hell,—hell! Children cried, women fainted, and we lived to see the day. When day came, they brought a bit of black coffee.

For 100,000 people?
We were about 50,000 people,[2] but the bundles that everybody had with them —we needed room for that. Some food was cooked and distributed afterward

2. In fact there were about 13,000 Jews packed into the stadium.

for midday. The children got something thrown—to them. The Frenchmen pretended to be kind. [Mocking:] It was not their fault! They would throw a cookie to a child, a bonbon, saying over and over, "It is not we who are doing it, it is the Germans." We understood well that it was not done by the Germans. If they hadn't helped the Germans, the Germans would not have done it. Alors! I was at the Vélodrome d'Hiver four days with the children. The place was a battlefield. They carried away about 500 dead, people who just died. The aged, the sick, the chronically ill—couldn't stand it for more than a day or two. In that whole place they had altogether two physicians who were ministering to 50,000 people.

What kind of physicians were they?

Frenchmen! Murderers! I, too, was under them—murderers! They would deal with the people just as if these people had no business to be alive anymore. Hurry up, a tap with a stick, and that was all. There were a few nurses because the people were very excited. Every time when a woman or a child would raise their voice crying, the whole Vélodrome, as many as there were, would cry with them. The destruction of the temple!

I personally could not cry anymore. I had a sheet of iron on my heart. It wasn't that I had courage. I was simply prostrated. The children would bring a bit of water, a bit of tea. Every day some people were selected and went away, those with children to Pithiviers, single persons to Drancy.

Meanwhile my husband hurried to a good friend of his who worked for the Germans, a furrier, who had the right to get [people] out of the Vélodrome. There was a large loudspeaker in the middle of the place on the Vélodrome, and they called out the names. Those families who were arrested whose men worked for the Germans and had certificates would be set free immediately. I saw a lot of families being set free. [But the announcer] gave our name wrong. Instead of Marcus F., they called out, "Marcus Marcus." My husband gave them his name, but they thought his last name was Marcus. Well, he [the French announcer] was stupid.

During the five days at the Vélodrome the place was terribly dirty. One didn't see any water for washing purposes. The toilets, if you excuse me, had overrun. At the gates, a lot of acquaintances who were not arrested stood around, with bundles, to send in food for the children. But the Frenchmen fired at them and did not permit a single bundle to pass.

And so, the fifth day came. Our turn came, and they took us to Pithiviers. They led us out from the Vélodrome at five o'clock in the morning. Twenty large busses stood on the square, and at the gate stood about fifty gendarmes and policemen and inspectors, and they led us just like they lead criminals. Of course, that [the early hour] was so that nobody should see how they proceeded with their "fine" business. The police, Frenchmen, stood there and looked at us very indifferently, as if they were thinking, "That is very good. Now the time has come when we will get rid of the Jews because the Jews are our misfortune here in France. They are taking away our business. They eat up everything, and we just stand there and look on. Now we are the masters. We shall get rid of them." Cold, with tight lips, they stood there like murderers. Indifferent. And they laughed, they were amused at us. We were taken to a train. On the side stood passengers, French men and women, who saw us disembark from the busses and led into the train. They laughed. The cars were locked, without windows, without air, just like beasts are transported. Cattle! Alors! We all got in. It was very high to climb. We finally picked ourselves up, one shoving the other.

The youngest child felt nauseated. She wanted, excuse me, to throw up. And there was nowhere to do it. Above a little window. I stuck out her little head, and she threw up. And she caught some air, and she got better. I set her down next to me, and we arrived at Pithiviers. At the station they ordered us all to disembark. They would bring our things, [they said]. Because we had to walk quite a distance. On both sides [with sarcasm] the honors were beautiful. On the one side, gendarmes; on the other side, inspectors, police. We are led like criminals, like murderers. Children cried, mothers fainted. We were led to a large square, fenced all around with barbed wire higher than a man. A big black gate opened for us, and we saw in the distance a big black barracks knocked together from plain thin boards. Between one board and the other, one could stick through his head and look outside. It just looked like a *sukkah*.[3] A *sukkah* is even better, more stable. Inside of this big barracks were a few bundles of straw, and the guards told us that we had to stay there. "Each one of you may take a bit of straw and lie down on the floor." And there was no floor; it was plain dirt.

And your things?

We got our things in a couple of hours. We spread out a bit of straw. People were fighting for a bit of straw. Everyone wanted a little bit more and even—

Were there men, too?

Men, women, children, old ones and young ones. All were there. Somehow, a space was fixed for me. They spread out a bit of straw. Everyone had some rags, a blanket, a little towel. I even saw some foolish people who had dragged feather-beds with them. They busted their guts dragging them. They were all exhausted. What for? Just to salvage a few more things from home.

My child, the sixteen-year-old, was made to drag a quota of bundles. And the poor dear spread out on the straw, and I asked for something to soothe her. And she [the nurse] gave her some kind of a pill to put her to sleep. Well, she got pains

3. A makeshift shelter with a roof of foliage built by Jews in connection with the Feast of Tabernacles, *Sukkoth*.

dragging the bundles. I couldn't carry anything. I was very weak. I was taken from bed, sick. I had a gall bladder attack. But she dragged [bundles]. Everybody called her the beautiful Mara. She was so beautiful. A day passed, and Mara became a bit stronger, but she still was weak, and she lost all her courage. She said, "Mother, I feel that I will never get out of here."

[Mara was one of those transported to the East from Pithiviers. Two days later F. and her remaining two children were released.]

What happened? I have sent out a little message from the camp with some persons to my husband. [The message said], "You should know. Try. If you are not going to do something, we shall be deported with the children to Auschwitz." And the letter arrived. A French gendarme carried it out. If one would give him a hundred francs, he would take out a letter, throw it in the mail box, and it would get to the people. And the letter arrived, and my husband managed to get the paper from the prefecture that they should let me out with my children. As we were getting out we were inspected three times. Three times! They suspected that people were sending out diamonds, jewelry or such things, but we did not take anything like that because they had announced, "Those who are so fortunate to get out, if they carry anything out of the camp, will be shot on the spot."

Mrs. F., will you tell me now what happened to your oldest daughter, the one who was nineteen?
With the older one it was like this. One "fine" morning a man came and asked, "Does Charlotte F. live here?" I said, "Yes." My child was in bed sleeping. It was eight o'clock in the morning. What has happened? A French woman has reported on my child that she went to the *Étoile*[4] and didn't wear the yellow star and went to the movies. Don't you know it was regulated when to go to the store? Children couldn't go out to play! You could buy things only in the afternoon between 1:00 and 2:00 and from 3:00 to 4:00. Summertime we had to lock ourselves in at eight o'clock. We could not go out in the street. One couldn't go out to a railroad station. The Jew could not go out in the large parks. The Jew had no right to travel in the first-class car of the subway. On the railroad a Jew could not travel. So I asked who had reported her? So he said he doesn't know. It was reported directly to the German commandant's office.

Was the man who came to call for her a Frenchman?
A policeman. He spoke French. I can't be sure whether he was an Alsatian or a Frenchman. I was upset. That was still before the rest of the family were taken to

4. A famous section in the city of Paris.

Pithiviers. He says, "You have time, don't hurry. Drink your coffee. Don't hurry. It isn't so bad. A Frenchwoman has reported that you don't wear your star, that you go to the movies. Well, you will explain, and they will let you go."

Well, I made coffee for my child. It was her last coffee with me. And the man was joking and laughing. To him it was a kind of an everyday event, like lighting a cigarette. She got dressed and left. When she arrived, she found some other people there who had been arrested, Jewish people who had also been reported by the French. From there they were soon sent away to a prison. I ran around to the prefecture; by trying hard I found out where she was.

I arrived there with a package of food, to pass it to her because for the three days that the child was away she had nothing to eat, no money, nothing. And they didn't even let me near her, just like she was the greatest criminal, the worst murderer. I [also] brought her a change of clothes, and four days more passed. Then I received a letter to come and look for her in such and such a place. The prison had been a big armory. I did not find my daughter alone. I found about 500 or 600 people!

Men and women together?

Men and women in the same prison but separated from each other. Among them fourteen-year-old girls. All of them Jews, but later Gentiles were added. I asked my child, "What is going to happen?"

Did they allow you to see each other alone?

No, not all alone. There was a visiting hour, and those who had relatives in prison were able to see them, say, twice a week during the visiting hours. They would be led out into a large hall with benches and tables, and members of families could come in and talk to them.

Did they watch you so you should not pass something on to them?

No, we could give them everything. There were gendarmes and police who watched, of course, trying to catch a word of the conversation. There were spies among them, also Gestapo agents. There was among them a German woman from the Gestapo—which they found out later—but they did not know then that she was from the Gestapo. They thought she was also a prisoner. When I came, I found that my child was also so foolish [taken in by the woman].

So I said to her, "My child, you are so naive. Don't you recognize that she is from the Gestapo, she being a German? She is here to spy on you. In case you say a word that is not just so, they will put you in the lockup." And I made it clear to her that one should not talk about improper things. "And you should not talk with that woman at all."

In all the child was there two weeks. In these two weeks we saw each other twice. She, alas, knew that they would be sent to Germany. There were some French gendarmes who had a bit of heart, so they told them. But there were exceptions, people who remained there six months, and there were a few others who remained there for a year. But my child was just out of luck, and she was deported.

A day passed, and I received a letter from my child. She managed to obtain a scrap of paper and a pencil, and when they put them on the train for deportation, she managed to write down a few words to her mother. She knew that we all were still home. "My dear parents, we are being deported in an unknown direction. We have no food, nor drink. We have no things. However, our morale is good, and we are strong. I am in the best of health. Don't cry, mother, and tell the children not to cry. I will come through. I am young, and I hope we will see each other again. I kiss you. And see that you do not fall into the hands of the German. Hide yourselves. Get away from Paris. Hide in a village. Hide so they should not trap you as they have trapped me." To this day I have not seen my child. Four dark years have passed, and I don't know where her bones rest.

Who brought you the letter?
The letter carrier brought it to me. She threw the letter out from the moving train, and the people who work on the tracks found the letter and dropped it in the mail box. And the letter was delivered. I had the letter, but there were constant raids by the Germans. They used to search around the house for various papers.

My husband said, "I am afraid to keep such a letter. We can all be killed for such a letter. Because if they are in the train, they were not permitted to write anymore." So my husband took the letter and burned it. It was the first and the last message I had from my child, written in German. She wrote German beautifully.

Didn't you tell me before we started this interview that you were in a concentration camp twice? Tell me about it.
A year passed [after her release from Pithiviers]. My husband worked at his trade for the Germans, and we had the proper papers.

What kind of fur coats was he making?
Vests, short vests. For the soldiers. He had to do it. That was forced labor.

Did he get paid?
Yes. While my husband was slaving there, he got a certificate that we could safely live in our home and that nothing should happen to us. One night we heard the police coming. They smashed our door and told us that we were under arrest. We had to go to a camp.

Who?

The French. My man worked on the night shift. He was not in the house. I was alone with the children. What was there to do? I dressed with the two children. I prepared two bundles. My husband returned from work early in the morning, and the concierge woman told him that they had taken me to Drancy with the two children.

Meanwhile I arrived at Drancy. Sixty or seventy families were there, all the same kind as we. There were armories at Drancy, six or seven stories high all around! As soon as we arrived they pressed a little piece of bread into our hands, and men dressed in prisoners' clothing came to help us drag our bundles into the blocks, and they assigned us to some cots. Each one got a cot for two people. The cots were small. You couldn't turn around. Black, dirty.

Did they separate the men from the women?

Yes. My son was taken with the men. I remained with the little girl. They gave us straw mattresses. Excuse me, thousands of prisoners had been lying on these mattresses. These mattresses were soaked in tears. Dirty. The place looked just like a stable. There was a trough like for horses. Everybody goes to it, lets a little bit of water run, washes off a bit of his grief. They brought us a kettle with some black water. It was supposed to be coffee, and maybe once it was. The next morning they brought a kettle with a bit of soup. They gave each one a ladle of soup, each one gets one potato, and 200 grams of bread for twenty-four hours.

Were the potatoes peeled?

They were with the peelings. The next time they would give not a potato but a kind of turnip and a little sardine, a small salted one. With that we were to last from dinnertime until seven o'clock at night—with 200 grams of bread. I wasn't there very long, about eight days. There were people [who had been] in Drancy six, seven months. They were established there as if they expected to stay for years. The beds stood one over the other, three-level bunks, a bit of straw. There were some very small cots given to a single person. Otherwise we had two persons on a bed because the beds were somewhat wide. [Later] we saw transports arriving from the free zone.

You mean from unoccupied France?

Yes. Young people, like sheer skeletons. They cannot stand on their feet. They had kept them for six, seven weeks in those camps and did not give them something to eat more than five or six times. Young people who were caught on the street in Free France and they were not permitted to take anything from home, but were dragged straight from the streets into the trucks and taken to prison.

From Drancy they were [to be] deported to Germany. When they were brought into Drancy, they told us that they were now in a paradise. When they got a little bit of soup and something was spilled on the floor, they would get down on all fours and lick up that soup from the mud. They were crazy from starvation, plain crazy. Their things were so messed up that one could not tell whether they were clothes or rags. They had slept in them six or seven weeks.

They kissed our hands, pleading for a little piece of bread. Because we were still fresh—we had been there only eight days, and we had taken something from home—and we shared with them, but one couldn't give away everything. We did not know yet that we would go free. And although we knew that they would be deported, we had to save something for our children.

And so we saw two transports go away. Why did they have to deport them to Germany? To bury them? They could bury them there. Dead, young exhausted skeletons. They gave each one a little ration of beans, a little piece of bread, a little piece of cheese for their journey. I saw with my own eyes how they dragged ninety-year-old women out of Drancy for deportation. The police supported them under their arms because they couldn't drag their legs. And they put them up in line for the count. Women with children! I saw little girls, little boys, who went into the cars with their mothers, and they were sent away to Germany.

At the time of the third transport an order came that all families of those men who worked for the Germans should be freed. Now the French wanted to appear "nice" since the people who would leave would start telling. So they told us [in a mocking tone], "You are going free. What a pity for these people who remain. Give them your food. You are going home. They are being sent away. One cannot tell how long they will be en route." So we should give them the food that we had. They tried to appear decent so that when we should go out we would say, "The French are nice people." They told us to give away our food. Do you understand?

Did you do it?

Whatever one had, everything was given away. Young people [and] a number of women of my acquaintance, many with infants, were sent away with this last transport.

Have they returned?

No. Almost nobody has returned. There were two hundred families in our neighborhood. A single man and a single woman from our house have returned. Nobody else.

We were taken to be released through a small gate, and from the other side people were led into the railroad cars for deportation. That is how things came to pass, Monsieur Professor. Here were people standing for deportation, and we were led out, all those who had been arrested and had certificates that they were working for the Germans, which were about sixty or seventy families. They let us all go.

This was not to the liking of the French. They were wondering, "What do we need Jews for? If they have already been arrested, why let them out again?" We told them that the Germans have done that for us. "Our men are working for the Germans, and that is why we were released." They were such anti-Semites, and they could not savor it.

And so I got out with my two children, Monsieur Professor. I spent a few months at home, and again they came pounding at the door. The Germans were having bad luck. They didn't need any more fur jackets. They no longer needed anybody to work for them, but what they did need was that all people who had worked for them to go to Auschwitz. And so the third time—the good angel wanted it that way—we didn't sleep at home. We slept in another house. We were forewarned. Somebody came and told us that they would raid again. They heard about it in advance.

Who came?

Policemen, who were taking lumps of money, and when they knew something, they would come and tell the people. "Tonight there will be a raid. Do not sleep at home, hide."

So where did you go to sleep?

With another family. Jews. In another flat, in another district. Do you understand? Indeed, there was a raid. Those who did not hide, who did not heed the warning, were "nicely" taken. Afterward, in a few weeks we ran away from Paris to a village, and we hid there until liberation.

How did liberation come? How did you find out in a village that liberation had come?

We were hiding. The highway isn't far from the village. Do you understand? Here already the bombs were falling.

It happened that the bombs did not fall where we were, but thousands of Gentiles were killed, and thousands of homes were demolished. Our house just remained standing.

And who came in there?

The Americans. We had seen how the Germans ran away. We were not far from their quarters. And yonder was the highway. We heard how the Germans were running away in their trucks. We heard it all, and the next day the Americans arrived.

Did the French begin to behave better after that?

Monsieur Professor, you will return to America. Tell them what a foolish woman has told you, that the French envy if the Jew accomplishes something. The anti-Semitism that we have seen from them, their militia, their beatings, their exploitation—they were worse than the Germans. If the French had not helped the Germans, maybe they would have taken 50,000, [but] not 150,000. "Take the Jews," the French said. They betrayed us.

Slovakia

31 Baruch F.

Zionist fundamentalism inspired suspicions of non-Jews that complicated Jewish-Gentile relations in normal times but served Jews well during the Holocaust. Baruch F.'s Zionist convictions caused him to disbelieve official stories about relocating the Slovakian Jews in 1942 and instead to flee to the forest with his younger brother. Their parents, merchants and farmers in Kurima, either believed Slovakian and German lies or acquiesced in their fate, as did most Slovakian Jews. The brothers hid with the aid of a Gentile acquaintance and, after the deportations stopped, reported voluntarily to one of several work camps for Jews set up by the Slovaks. It turned out to be agreeable as such camps went in those years, but the brothers' suspicions were hardly allayed. They made contact with anti-German partisans in the forests and armed themselves against a renewal of anti-Jewish measures.

These preparations paid off during the Slovak National Uprising against the Tiso regime, August 28 to October 27, 1944. Baruch F. and his brother were freed along with the other Jewish inmates of work camps. Although they helped fight German and Slovakian forces in the liberated zone, and F.'s brother died in combat, F. himself was deeply ambivalent about both the uprising's prospects of success and the attitudes toward Jews of even anti-Nazi Slovaks. Following the suppression of the uprising, F. again took to the forest, this time with a sizable band of partisans made up of Jews and Gentiles. In February 1945 they broke through to the Russian side. Baruch F. then returned to his village only to find his family gone, their home looted, and the fields taken over by neighbors. All this confirmed him in his determination to leave for Palestine. Boder found him living at Tradate, the home in northern Italy for young displaced Jews who had formed a kibbutz. (Boder noted the F. had a number of aliases, including "Abram P.," which he used at the time of, but not during, the interview.)

We begin with the transportation of Jews from Slovakia to Poland in the summer of 1942.

In 1942 Slovakian transports of Jews lasted the entire summer, until about September. About July, I hid in the forest with my brother. I was twenty-three years old then. [My] brother was younger by two years. Even before the transports began I had a premonition that Hitler's plan was so strong that something bad would come unto the Jews. I wanted at least a part of the family to save itself. My parents were not too much for it because they wanted . . . that what would happen to everybody would happen to me. But I said, "No. A part of the family must remain so that at least somebody should survive." There should remain, so to speak, a living seed of the family.

Didn't you think that if you remained with your parents you perhaps could save them?

I begged them to come. I did not ask them once, I asked them many times. But they could not conceive that all those people were led simply into the crematoria. And they did not want to know it. And I have foreseen that it can happen. So I said, "At first one should go [into hiding]." At first I went by myself. Then I dragged my brother along. I was so persistent that my brother came, too. Transports were going continuously. We had been hiding at home for a while. One night [we] decided we were going to the forest. I gathered the rucksack which I had ready, which every Jew had ready, and went to the forest at night.

At first we were hidden in a kind of cave. We had taken along a tent. We put [it] up in the forest, and there we lived under the open sky. We took along food for a week's time. Bread and canned milk and so forth.

How far was the forest from your home?

It was around five kilometers. And there we were alone for about a week. Entirely alone without communication, without anything.

Where did you find something to drink?

There are little springs there. And also for washing. Later we began making a closer connection there with a Gentile of our acquaintance. Quite close, since we began to realize that alone one cannot exist in the forest. The thing might drag on for very long. He took us in. At the beginning [there were] difficulties, but we promised that we would give him money and various articles which were still in the house. Then we sent a note to our parents that they should give him some things from the house, and in return he should hide us there. We asked that they should come there, too, because now we already had some sort of a place for them to hide. But they did not want to come. They said what would happen to all Jews should happen to them, too.

For a time it was quite comfortable. We spent the whole day studying [modern] Hebrew. We had taken along books. Even though our nerves were very tense; we knew that for the present we had to live like cattle. We made up our minds not to think about anything, even though the situation was difficult. Only to live.

Were you Zionists?

Yes, we were all Zionists. My father was an old Hassid. Not a whole Hassid, but half a Hassid. He was not for and he was not against [Zionism].

And so then we received information that our parents were gone, taken away with a transport. And then we had a still harder task. We remained helpless, because by then they were not sending anymore gifts from home for that Gentile.

Who went along with your parents?

The whole town. I still had two more sisters and two more brothers. I know that they arrived at Majdanek. Afterward the chairman of the Slovakian rabbinate informed me that they perished in Majdanek.

So I stayed there with that Gentile till around February 1943. For material and financial reasons, I had to get away from there. I could not pay him anymore, so I reported voluntarily to a Slovakian labor camp because Jews from Slovakia were not being transported anymore but remained in Slovakian labor camps. Seventy thousand Jews had left, and the rest had remained because of graft; it was possible to buy off the Slovakian government.

And so I arrived at the Vyhne camp on the 3rd of February 1943, along with my brother. We lived pretty well there in the beginning. We worked a little, and the Slovakian Jews who were on the outside [of the camp] supported us so that living was quite good. [It was] a purely Jewish camp but under Gentile management.

How many Jews were there?

About 300. We lived five boys in one room. It was a former hotel, a health resort, and we lived there rather well. There were beds and decent blankets. Not like a camp in Auschwitz, no. I only want to bring this out. The entire area is mountainous, so we began looking for a contact with the partisans. And we talked over the possibilities in case some day the transports would start moving again, so we should be sure of not going to Auschwitz or Treblinka.

Now tell me a little about the partisans. Did you later go over to them?

In the beginning we made our own plans. We went into the woods, made underground bunkers, procured weapons.

How could you go into the woods? Were you allowed to leave the camp?

We would go—it was not far from the forest. And sometimes on a Sunday, when we did not work, we would tear ourselves away.

What did you work at there?

People worked mostly at trades there. I am by trade a letter and sign painter, so I worked at painting. There was toy production, so I worked at it there. It was not bad. I cannot say that it was bad all the time. The Germans had absolutely no access there. The Slovaks were influenced by the Germans, but they were not that bad.

We lived that way till the 25th of August 1944. Then we were already in contact with the partisans and already had our own weapons, pistols. So that if it should come to a transport, we were organized to offer resistance.

And those partisans were Jews or Christians?

The partisans were mostly Russians who had crossed over to Slovakia. We came into contact with the main [partisan] contact in Bratislava. On the 25th of August the Slovakian uprising came.[1] A host of partisans came and liberated us, the whole camp, and took us right away. Everyone was released. And many of our youngsters voluntarily joined the fight against the Germans. The Germans put up many divisions against that. That brought about the occupation of Slovakia by the Germans. Large contingents of Jews came together, not only from our camp, [but] also from the Novaky camp. Four or five hundred Jews went against the Germans and also the Slovaks who sided with Tiso.

Would you describe to me everything that happened in all the details?

Well, I will begin with a day earlier. On the 23rd of August I was in Bratislava. I was to bring various pistols and munitions from Bratislava.

Were you there legally?

Yes. I had received a permit from the leader of the camp, but for a different reason, to shop for caps and so forth. For commercial reasons. During my journey back I heard [a rumor] that the Germans were occupying Slovakia. I did not know whether I should return to the camp or not. What if I returned [and] the Germans arrived there too? I came to the conclusion—I had a brother there, and I had to go to him. What would happen then I did not know. On the train I had heard that the Slovaks were rendering resistance. At night when [I] arrived—it was around twelve o'clock—the whole camp was awake. No one slept [for] excitement. What was going to happen? Some said, "Done for! It's all done for! We're as good as dead." Some still had a little hope because we thought that we would offer resistance, or that we would decide to join the partisans.

But something different was happening. The uprising, which had been organized so that the whole of Slovakia should be liberated, had [only] partly succeeded in the area around Banska-Bystrica.[2] The partisans, along with the Rus-

1. The date is probably a bit off. The uprising did not begin until August 28, 1944.

2. The town in east-central Slovakia that served as capital of the liberated zone during the Slovak National Uprising.

sians, disarmed the troops of the surrounding region, and one town garrison after another surrendered. In Banska-Bystrica they captured the radio station and announced a free Czechoslovakia. This was on about the 24th. On the 25th partisans from all those groups came to our camp, Vyhne, and liberated us, too, and they immediately took a part of the entire youth on a forced march for the forward push against the other part of Slovakia, which sided with the Germans. My brother and I did not join at first. We thought there was still time. We did not know yet. Maybe a more difficult moment would come.

We left then to live in Zvolen. Hundreds of youths fell because they threw themselves straight into the fire in the fight against the Germans and the Hlinkavites.[3] They were not trained. They just received a weapon; they were hardly shown how to shoot. So they all fell like flies. A very great number. While they were in the camp there were no possibilities for proper training. And a part of the Slovaks themselves did a lot of betraying in the uprising. In Bratislava, for instance, the bridge was supposed to have been blown up, and because of that [failure to do so], the uprising did not succeed. In Preskow in eastern Slovakia the uprising did not succeed either, also because of the treachery of the Slovaks. So the center remained in the area of Banska-Bystrica, a small area and difficult to keep.

Then the Germans drew away troops from the east in order to crush the uprising, because [it had] lasted about two months. And so I and my brother decided to join the army in Zvolen, the Twentieth Regiment. Then we fought simply the way we could fight. My younger brother fell there. And I did not know what to do. I saw [that] the Slovaks did not fight for themselves. They just wanted Jewish blood [to be] spilled. A lot of anti-Semitism was present. So I was of the opinion [that] I should not fight. What should I fight for? I saw the anti-Semitism. I saw that more and more the uprising was failing.

Within two months the entire uprising went completely to naught. Jews who had concentrated there from all corners of Slovakia, who had wanted to save themselves there, remained helpless and did not know what to do. What everybody did I did too. I still had arms, so we went into the forest and began partisan life. Around fifty Jews and thirty Gentiles went in, organized, with weapons.

And who was the commander?

A Gentile, a certain Lieutenant Mayer. As long as he was going to hide with us we figured that we could trust him. Were he a traitor, I think he would not have gone to hide.

---

3. The Hlinka Guard, the militia of the ruling Slovak People's party, named after Andrej Hlinka, a right-wing Catholic priest and fanatical Slovak nationalist.

And how did it show up later?

That he really was straight. After that, large transports began again. The Germans had come and occupied the whole of Slovakia. Of the 15,000 Jews who had remained, they dragged out another 10,000 to Auschwitz. Of them a part did remain alive, because by that time the crematoria were already a little weaker.[4]

We had come to that forest around November, and it began to snow. We began making preparations. We made holes for ourselves underground, bunkers guarded on all sides with weapons, and we settled in. [We] picked out a suitable point so that when the Germans came, we should be able to attack them and save our lives. Many times it happened [that] a German patrol noticed us. And so immediately alarm was sounded. [We] surrounded them and immediately shot them all. The Germans eventually knew that there were still partisans there. For many months after, they constantly, constantly searched all the woods, but they did not trust themselves to go directly in. They knew that a lot of partisans could fall upon them suddenly and do a lot of damage to them.

Did they not try to beg you not to shoot them? Did they not want to surrender?

We knew the German type. The Germans knew well that if they fell into the hands of a partisan, they were dead. So they fought for their life. There were many cases [in which] Germans were captured, let us say, a group of ten—not by our group; by other groups. So nine were killed with a brutal death, and one was released so that he should be able to tell his remaining comrades what ugly deaths they had died.

What do you call a "brutal death"?

For instance, a man was taken, and a nail was driven between the two eyes while still alive. They were all tormented. Because of that, they were very much afraid to fall into partisan hands.

Every night, or every second night, we went around into the neighboring villages, which the Germans did not trust themselves to enter because they knew that there they might be attacked by the local partisans. And the population received us very well. They gave us something to eat and to drink and let us wash, and sometimes we would even risk staying overnight, too. The population was not too bad because they knew that it was also in their interest, because there were many Gentiles, too, not just Jews.

4. The last gassings at Auschwitz occurred on October 30, 1944. The Slovak Jews F. refers to arrived after that date.

What sort of weapons did you have?

Mostly automatic pistols, Russian ones. The Russians had supported the uprising. And hand grenades. And there were also about six light machine guns and one heavy machine gun which could not be used readily because it was heavy to carry. Mostly we used just the light machine guns. We still had ammunition from the uprising.

We lived that way a pretty long time, until something happened. The front was very close. This was already in the year '45, around January, and we were waiting for the Russians to come and liberate us. But then the Russians stopped in Brezno, twenty kilometers from us, and did not move forward. We did not know what to do. The front there was a very difficult one. The German patrols were constantly passing and walking about. They sensed that there were partisans. They knew it. Occasionally they used mortars on us. We were in a very difficult position.

It happened that a strong German patrol which was close to the front passed by and noticed us. We shot at them, [but] we had not been able to surround all of them, and many escaped. They did not know how large a force there was, so they began to shoot at us with mortars in order to chase us away. Immediately our commander had a conference with headquarters—it was at 11:00, forenoon—and at 4:00 in the afternoon we made a decision to cross the border. He worked out a plan, and we circled the entire front. There were Rumanians, too, who were fighting against the Germans. And we found them. And at about 4:00 in the morning we crossed the front line and went over to the Russians along with the cables.[5] They received us at once and we became free.

To this I still want to [add that] we had been prepared for a battle. Had it come, naturally, we would have offered resistance. That crossing was accompanied with great difficulties. The snow was deep, about two meters. [Additionally there were] the high mountains to go up and down. But in spite of that, we were not deterred. There were also many women among us who suffered greatly. But still we did cross over successfully. It was on the 12th of February 1945.

At headquarters we were questioned about where we came from. [Our] officer described how the Germans were situated. And everyone received confirmation from the Russians that he was at liberty to go home. And everyone went home— free. Volunteers who wanted [to do so] remained with the Russians or reported to the Czechoslovakian army. At that time it had come from Russia, and one had to report in Kosice.

How many in your partisan group were officers? How was all that carried out?
There were three officers. Gentiles.

---

5. F.'s unit had been listening in to German telephone conversations. See below.

Gentiles. Why?

Because they had the technique, the real training. We, among ourselves, also had a Jewish leader, Greenbaum. We had a radio apparatus for receiving. That is how we knew all the news. And we also had an intercepting apparatus for listening in on telephone conversations. We listened in on all the front communications between the Germans. And then the chief commander turned it over to a larger partisan group. We were just a small section, but there were hundreds and hundreds of partisans in the whole area. Sometimes there would be a task to blow up a bridge or a train. But all this was one's duty. This one and this one have to go. And we went.

How many partisans were killed?

In the whole time about four people were killed. Not more. There were no Jews among them. One was wounded. One died a normal death.

So then you came home?

Yes. This is what happened. When I arrived home, I found nothing. From the whole family only myself. What does one do here?

And who was in the house?

Nobody. Everything was deserted, the windows broken, the house broken. Everything, everything in ruins, because the house had been standing empty, [and] people had gone there and tossed everything around, broken up everything. So that the whole house had remained completely, totally empty. We had fields there, too. All the time the Gentiles cultivated the fields. When I arrived home, .I thought that we would enjoy a little more consideration. I saw nothing [of the sort]. I considered some [of the people] whom I knew had committed misdeeds against the Jews. I wanted to avenge myself on them. I thought I had some right because of having been a partisan, [but] I was laughed at. Why? Because among the leaders of the Slovakian government were these same anti-Semites who were [there] before that. So that I did not trust myself, and I decided [to] leave everything, the house, the fields, and go to my goal. I am going *home*.

Did you not sell the house?

No. One cannot. To this day Slovaks have not returned their properties to the Jews. And everything is still as it used to be. So I decided—what was I waiting for? More evil might come. And many times we heard about the pogroms against the Jews. Here someone is beaten, and there someone is beaten. If one wanted to get some justice, many times people would pay with their lives, too. So I crossed into Germany and from there on to the goal, toward *Eretz*.[6]

6. Israel.

Tell me, how did you go to Germany, and how did you arrive in Italy?

With a transport of Jews. When I arrived in Prague, I received certain directions. At such and such a time a transport was going over to Germany. As far as the border by train, and across the border [illegally] on foot. The UNRRA aided, and we received help from the Joint. Some pants, a jacket, and a shirt. The less one has the better. It is easier to walk. And there in Germany I sat around four months. And then it came to personal distribution, who should go to *Eretz*. I was one among those. And I went across with the others, also with a transport, here to Italy.

32   Helena T.

Much of what we know about the operation of Auschwitz comes from prisoners who worked in its offices and lived to tell their story. Helena T.'s skills as a commercial artist came in handy when the Germans were developing ways of identifying and numbering prisoners in the early days of Auschwitz II (Birkenau). This led to her appointment as a kind of unofficial draftsperson in the camp headquarters, which shielded her from selections and murderous work details to the very end of the camp.

Helena T. was a native of Bratislava, which in 1939 became the capital of Slovakia. Three years later, at the age of twenty-three, she was among the first Slovakian Jews deported to Auschwitz. (Jewish women from Slovakia, among the first women sent to Auschwitz and often fluent in German, were well represented among the Auschwitz office workers. Of the twenty-seven women included in Lore Shelley's *Secretaries of Death*, fifteen arrived from Slovakia in 1942.) At first she lived in the original camp, Auschwitz I, while helping to construct the new facilities at nearby Birkenau. Then, in August 1942 she was transferred to the women's camp there. Almost immediately she made herself indispensable to the SS by painting stripes and printing numbers on the prisoners' clothing. Later, installed in the camp offices, she kept records of deaths and workforce allocations for the administration. This position gave her an overall view of the camp available to few of its prisoners. Who else, for example, could have arranged a personal visit to the "little white cottage," a former farmhouse where the first gassings took place at Birkenau before the construction of four modern crematoria during the first half of 1943? Nor could she miss the boundless cynicism in the Nazi deception of Gypsies and Czech Jews in 1944, holding out false hopes of salvation to the very end. Although "Zippi" (as she became known in the camp and subsequently) was always conscious of being in hell, she took a certain pride in her efficiency and the recognition it won from her German bosses. Immersing oneself in work was one way of forgetting for a moment the flames just outside the door.

Evacuated to Ravensbrück and then to one of its many satellite camps in Mecklenberg, Helena T. slipped away from her guards during the last days of fighting and lay low, waiting for the Russians to liberate her. Upon her return to Bratislava, she found just one brother there. Everyone else in her family had perished. She might have stayed there—conditions for survivors in Bratislava were evidently quite different from those in rural areas—but for her decision to marry another survivor who planned to join relatives in South America. She and her new spouse lived at the DP camp at Feldafing, near Munich, where she was interviewed in September 1946. We begin with the story of her deportation to Auschwitz in March 1942.

Slovakia was given its independence by Hitler. As a price Vojtech Tuka[1] put 60,000 Jews at the disposal of the Germans. First of all women up to forty-five years [of age] were called upon to present themselves voluntarily to an assembly point in Bratislava. That was the Patronka.[2] Not much was told to them, but [they were informed] that most of them were assigned to agricultural labor in northern Slovakia. Immediately the same day we had to surrender our identification papers. We were permitted to take 50 kilos [110 pounds] with us, and we had to commit ourselves to put the things that we had left behind at the disposition of the state. Of course we didn't find out what became of them since a week later we were transported away, cut off from the whole world.

My parents were still at home. In general all parents remained at home. The first transport consisted of unmarried girls who were called upon to cooperate in coming. And in case they were not to come, measures would be taken, and the parents taken instead. For this simple reason no girl dared not come, because for everyone the parents were to be considered. Since one had the worst premonitions about these matters, one was ready to sacrifice herself.

Who guarded you?
The Hlinka Guard. These were the counterpart of the SS at that time in Slovakia. The Germans themselves took over this assembly camp the last day, got the people up, and conveyed them with the transport. The trip lasted a night and a day. When we saw that we arrived in Poland, we were of the opinion that we possibly might go to work [there] because already there were rumors that field laborers were needed in Poland [and] even the Ukraine. We did not think much of it because we were promised our return home within two months. And we were gladly ready to work these two months just to protect our parents.

1. Tuka was prime minister of Slovakia during World War II and a proponent of full cooperation with the Germans on Jewish affairs.

2. The Patronka was an abandoned factory that was rented by the Bratislava Jewish Community to furnish temporary housing to Jews made homeless by the actions of Slovakian authorities. Its railroad siding became the assembly point for deportations of Slovakian Jews to death camps and forced labor centers.

Did you in general already know what was happening in the camps? Were these things known in Slovakia?

Actually hardly anything was known. We knew about the German concentration camps for the simple reason that a large part of the German immigrants were tolerated in Czechoslovakia at that time, and most German Jews knew what a German concentration camp was. But never in our lives had we dreamed that we, completely harmless [people], would be put in a concentration camp only because we were Jews. We were unable to orient ourselves because Auschwitz was completely unknown to us as a concentration camp.

The train stopped. We only heard a howl, because the railroad cars were locked. "Out! Faster!," and so on and on. When the turn of our car came, we were chased down. Before us stood people in uniform, the kind we did not know before because in Slovakia we had no opportunity to see actual "skulls." The uniform was a normal SS uniform, dark green,[3] ankle boots. The tunics were marked with "SS," and on the cap one saw a skull. We were hurriedly lined up in rows of five and [led] in the direction of the door.

And your things?

We never saw our things again. On the way we saw something that I hardly could describe anymore today. It was a most peculiar sight. Half-finished stone blocks surrounded with barbed wire. On the roofs, at the windows, stood striped, living corpses. I can't express myself differently. People without facial expressions, like . . . like made of stone. Next to them stood sentries who guarded these prisoners. When they [the prisoners] saw us, when they in some way directed their attention at us, they were yelled at, so that they would not dare turn their head, and continued with their work. As I now understand, at that time Auschwitz was being constructed for us, for the women, because most of them were up on the roofs.[4] Ten blocks were assigned for the women, stone blocks one story high with basements and attics.

We entered the camp. [We] saw a crowd in front of the last block. We did not know at first whether these were girls or women or even human beings. They stood there in old Russian uniforms, their hair shorn, wooden slippers on their feet. They just stood and stared at us. Then suddenly shouts were heard. Certain

3. SS men on normal duty wore gray uniforms, and it seems likely that T. misspoke. On the other hand, officers in construction units of the Reich Ministry for the Occupied Eastern Territories wore green uniforms, and it is possible that she saw some of them on the day of her arrival at Auschwitz.

4. The men's barracks already existed at Auschwitz I in 1942. T. refers to the construction of women's barracks.

girls had recognized girl friends, sisters, or the kind. They [were the ones who] had arrived a day earlier. We could not talk much because we were surrounded by SS, but we understood that these women were our neighbors from Slovakia. That was enough for us.

What we still had left, an overcoat, clothes, shoes, stockings and such, was taken away, and in groups of a hundred we came to a block which was called the bathhouse where our hair was shorn. We were given the Russian men's uniforms, old ones. And in a few hours we were made equals to the arrivals who preceded us.

[She backtracked.] One moment. Before the first Jewish transports arrived from Slovakia, a thousand German prisoners arrived from Ravensbrück.

Men or women?

Women, because there were only women in the women's camps. We had no contact with men. This was not permitted at all. These were women prisoners who had been imprisoned already for three or four or five years and as punishment were transported from concentration camp Ravensbrück. These women then clothed us, bathed us, shore our hair, [and] handed us over to the SS.

Did any SS men come in?

The camp manager of Auschwitz, Captain [Hans] Aumeier, and many others whose names are today not known to me, came in to inspect us like cattle. It was going on like a cattle show. They turned us this way and that.

While you were nude?

Nude. Besides there was the SS camp physician, Dr. [Franz von] Bodman, who looked us over and, I don't know, inspected us and put us through the normal process of bathing and hair shearing. The hair was cut from all places, wherever there was hair on the body, our eyebrows and . . .

With scissors or with . . . ?

Partly with electric shearing machines, and when these failed, scissors were used which most often were half dull. A few weeks later, after thousands of prisoners were brought from Slovakia [and] Poland, they started with the tattooing in order to organize things a bit. The early methods in fact failed. The early methods corresponded to a stamp. They arranged needles in the form of numbers [and] simply pressed it on the arm and spread India ink over [it]. But in a few days the tattoo was gone. Then followed the normal tattooing with the double needle which was applied to the left forearm of every prisoner in consecutive numbers beginning with "one."

How was that done? Did they scratch it?

No, just by touching. That is a double needle, one needle longer, the other shorter, dipped in India ink and then stamped.

Does that hurt much?

Hurt? We did not feel pain anymore because the removal of hair from the head of a woman, all that, the whole transformation hurt much more. It was as if we were transformed into stone. Nothing whatever affected us anymore because we knew that we were completely cut off from civilization, from mankind, and that we were on the "other side" of life. The first night we were lodged in this stone block, crowded together because the camp was not in fact exactly ready. There were old straw sacks from the men's camp, thoroughly rotten; there were not even enough straw sacks available then. These were spread out on the floor and one lay down wherever there was room. Fixed up with a piece of bread, we spent the night.

Who tattooed you, men or women?

The thorough tattooing was really performed two months later. The first was also performed by prisoners. Men. Always men.

The next day—it was still dark—we were aroused by whistles and yelling. We heard the words "roll call," for us something completely unknown. At the time we thought roll call was something for soldiers, so maybe they also wanted to make soldiers out of us. We got up [and] were chased out into the yard by SS women. We did not know exactly what to do. We were lined up in a way they could count us, after much fuss. Naturally, it did not come to a count because there was terrible chaos. The "report leader," Margot Drexler,[5] did not know what to do at all at the beginning. She did not yet have any experience. She had the people lined up, and as soon as they attempted to recount us, the number never was the same because people ran from one group to the other. One's sister stood in one group, possibly one's cousin in another. In one group the number [became] larger, in the other smaller. Hence in the first days it was totally impossible to arrange a correct roll call. [It could take] as long as four hours.

A prisoner was selected to assist the count leader, that is, worked with that SS woman. During the first year this prisoner was, I should not say an illiterate, but she could hardly figure. There was no consideration for efficient work, and she was not at all interested that the prisoners be counted promptly. In the year 1943 for the first time a Jewish woman was appointed report clerk. She attracted attention [by the fact] that right from the beginning she was appointed block senior and proved to be good. She was a clerk by profession. She could figure, could write

5. An SS supervisor at the women's camp at Auschwitz.

and read, and was interested in helping her fellow human beings. And thanks to her many, many prisoners are alive today from our country as well as from other countries. She often managed to complete roll calls in ten minutes, and in rain or severe cold the prisoners could disperse in a few minutes.

In August our number had reached about 7,000, and spotted typhus and malaria [claimed] their first victims. The SS camp leaders decided to have the women's camp moved four kilometers away to Birkenau. More than 2,000 women prisoners who in some way were not well remained in Auschwitz [I]. The rest were relocated to Birkenau.

Where were the crematoria? In Birkenau?

Crematorium I was a modern crematorium in Auschwitz [I] which served only to burn corpses. The little white building which stood in Birkenau in the forest was nothing but an "innocent little cottage." In the winter of 1943–44 I myself had a chance to step into that little cottage. Because this cottage has all our Slovakian brothers and sisters on its conscience. This little white cottage had a couple of windows, a large iron door, and a sign, "To the Bath." People were chased into that "bath," according to stories of prisoners whom I encountered, men of the Sonderkommando [who] were compelled to drive people into the gas chambers, to transport the dead to the crematorium, and to burn them. I had a chance to ask someone from the Sonderkommando how the people were gassed. And he showed me the iron door and the barred window. The people were driven in. It was one room. The iron door was slammed shut. Gas was passed in, and the window shut, until the people were dead. They were put on lorries, and nearby there were pits where the people were burned.

The first weeks I was in the wrecking commando in Birkenau. There were still a few shot-up houses in Birkenau which had to be demolished. We lived in Auschwitz [I] and walked barefooted some four kilometers to Birkenau for demolition [work].

In time they directed special attention to me. After the Russian uniforms which we were given did not suffice anymore, it was decided to give us civilian clothes. Civilian clothes were, of course, sufficiently available, because the baggage was taken away from all the women and the worst clothes selected and put at the disposal of the prisoners. But in order to distinguish us from the civilians [in the event of] escape, Aumeier ordered that a vertical red stripe be drawn on the back from top to bottom. Since they did not want to send painters from the men's camp to the women's camp, they were on the lookout for a woman who in some way was acquainted with paints. There were tints and the proper oil, and they wanted that the women help themselves to it. I was then the only one who reported for it. I did not know at all for what purpose. They looked for a woman painter. And since I am by profession also a sign painter, I reported.

I got red powder paint and a pot of varnish and brush shoved into my hand. I was ordered to mix the paint. And later prisoners were led before me and I got the order that a vertical stripe be af[fixed]. From dawn to dusk I was fully occupied. I had to make the red stripe, and every prisoner could then report and be tattooed.

Oh, that was before the tattooing?

Yes. Now, however, it was a number affixed to the left forearm. But in order to recognize us better, and to recognize us adequately in case of a checkup, they had the numbers which the prisoners had tattooed on the arm printed on cloth in the men's camp, which by that time already had a printing apparatus. In order not to be dependent on the men's camp, I was given a printing apparatus, and I printed numbers from one to eight thousand on linen tape. We were that many at that time [in the women's camp].

I was then shoved into the receiving office where every newly arrived prisoner was asked for his personal data, and as soon as the prisoner was through with the complete registration she automatically received a number pressed in her hand, and it was her duty to sew this number on her dress. The printing of numbers soon came to an end because other painting tasks were given to me. For example, I had to paint signs, numbers on a cabinet for the camp leader.

[In September 1942 T. fell ill with spotted typhus and went to the sick ward where she was scheduled to be gassed. Her work for the camp administration saved her.]

Camp leader Müller[6] was alerted by his woman secretary—a prisoner who then worked for him for reasons of race pollution[7]—that I, too, was among the prisoners who were in block 27. And I, before my illness, painted a few numbers for the camp leader on a box and was unable [then] to finish them. So he came up to me and asked what I was doing there. I replied that I was free from fever and would like to work again. So he said to me [using the formal, courteous form of address], "Good. Then you go over there. That is the Aryan infirmary. Let them take your temperature, and if you have none, you remain, and if you have any, you go with them."

A German nurse worked there, a German political prisoner with whom I previously had a little contact. She knew exactly what it was all about, and she assured me when she said, "Zippi, even if you had 43 degrees of fever, I shall say nothing."

6. Paul Müller, the first director of the Birkenau women's camp.

7. It is unclear whether T. means that the woman had been arrested and sent to Auschwitz for "race pollution" or that the SS officer had made her his mistress. "Race pollution" was the Nazi notion of the results of sexual intercourse between Aryans and "subhumans."

And indeed, in five minutes Müller came, and she reported that I was free from fever. I was not free from fever. I was given valerian in order to calm myself and still had to sit there in the room for three hours and wait. Then I saw through the window how all my girls with whom I lay sick were chased up into the truck and driven out through the gate. I was immediately instructed to begin with my work in the office. Feverish, half blind, half deaf after typhus, I began with my work. I weighed barely 70 pounds then. Now I weigh 52 kilos [115 pounds].

The idea that on that day I was the only remaining survivor out of 4,000 girls gave me the strength and faith for further endurance. I was a hundred percent sure that the girls were gassed; we in the office established a number book in addition to the card index of names. Every prisoner who had died was marked up with a red cross—every number. And prisoners who were gassed [were marked] with a black cross. This way I had what happened in black and white. Weeks later I recuperated. Meanwhile transports of the girls from the camp still departed daily. In February 1943, of 33,000, of whom more than 20,000 [were] Jews, 1,500 remained. Those not gassed perished from typhus, without treatment, without medicines; perished in part from starvation.

I want to give a little example. There were about 2,000 typhus cases in the hospital. The camp inquired in Berlin whether it would be permitted to gas the 2,000 typhus cases, that is the 2,000 Jewish girls. In about three months the reply came: "Yes." Meanwhile, however, 40 percent of these girls had gotten well. But the number 2,000 had to be gathered up. So they took all Jewesses from the hospital, without exception, whether they had scabs or any other little thing. The SS went through the blocks [in order to bring the total up to 2,000]. They took a fancy to the barracks service detail who looked well, so they took [it]. They took girls who at the moment were on their way to the toilet. They took whomever got in their way. The number 2,000 was reached, but that was not enough for them. They took advantage of the "special action" and raised the number to 3,000, and these girls all went into the gas. I know because I marked their numbers in the number book with black according to a list which we received.

Well, but it never said in the number book what black means.
It did, indeed. We knew: "SB"—"*Sonderbehandlung*" [special treatment].[8]

It did not say "gassed"?
No. Always "special treatment." The detail who worked at it was also called the Sonderkommando. And according to orders from Berlin, Jews who came with RSHA transports could not be gassed.[9] Jews who came from prison were treated

8. The official Nazi euphemism for extermination.
9. T. points to one of the more bizarre anomalies in Nazi procedures. Jews previously

as registered in the card index and were protected against "special treatment." But if by some mistake such a Jew would go to the gas, then a death certificate was simply made out, a normal death certificate [stating as cause of death] acute intestinal inflammation, etc. That, to a large extent, is the reason why we possibly see weak, older people who are alive today. Thanks to the fact that they were card-indexed; that means prisoners from jail. These were privileged. Indeed, it was paradoxical. The people who came from prison had definitely, consciously committed something. The others came into the camp harmless and innocent, only because they were Jews.

So then the criminals, so to speak, remained alive.
Correct. A large part of them. Or they were at times whipped to death [or] killed at work. That happened not only to Jews. So were many others, thousands of others, non-Jewish prisoners.

[Later in the interview Boder asked an open-ended question about T.'s deepest impressions of Auschwitz.]

What I am unable to forget is the fire by day and night. Four chimneys were active day and night. And the pits which were installed in the year 1944 when Hungarian transports were arriving rendered a sight which does not yield to description, because one imagined oneself in a living hell. One was encircled all around by fire. At our camp there was just a wire fence, and thirty meters beyond was crematorium II, so it was not far. One could see if one *wanted* to see. There were cases when one could see people stride in on foot or on trucks and a few minutes later naked corpses being carried out of the bunkers on litters. And what could one think about it? One saw fire and smoke. One saw little figures among the silhouettes—they must have been children. One saw only . . . one could . . . one can imagine how the devils in hell treat their sacrifices.

Now tell me this. You worked in the office as a clerk. Did you hear anything about the Gypsies?
Of course. The Gypsy camp was established in the year 1943. The Gypsies witnessed the procession of all the Jewish transports into the crematorium. They witnessed the burning. They were located within about two hundred meters. When they were ordered to mount the trucks, they hesitated and replied, "We don't

---

arrested for any infraction, even a comparatively minor one such as failure to wear the Jewish star, were on the records of the RSHA (Reich Central Security Office) and had to be accounted for. Hence they could not simply be gassed along with the other arrivals without elaborate efforts to falsify the cause of death for the files.

want to be burned with the Jews." They were let alone for about two or three weeks, and then they were deceived.[10] Young Gypsies were assembled. They were embarked in railroad cars in front of the Gypsy camp. The rails were laid up to the crematorium, and the Gypsies saw that their relatives were journeying in the opposite direction. (And indeed I happened to meet these women Gypsies again in 1945 in Ravensbrück.) On the same day the old Gypsies then regained a bit of hope and said that they too would be shipped away. But the transport went to the crematorium. And what happened that night . . . [she wept]. The prisoners who worked in [section] IIB told about that. Frightful scenes took place. A day later the Gypsy camp was empty, and the Hungarian Jewish transports that followed were lodged [there].

Not far from the Gypsy camp was the Czech camp consisting of Czech Jews who were sent with their families from Theresienstadt. They were kept together, could write letters [and] send packages. And what happened after six months? The whole Czech camp, young and old, well and sick, were gassed. One day before they were compelled to write to Theresienstadt with a date one month ahead, and when London [the BBC] reported the gassing of the Czech camp, the Germans denied it: "How come? The mail from Birkenau has arrived from those whom you consider dead." And because of that the Jews of Theresienstadt were deceived.

I personally sent news of the crematorium to Theresienstadt so that people would know where the road leads to. Unfortunately the leadership in Theresienstadt incriminated itself very deeply. They were afraid for themselves. Because afterward I met a gentleman who came from Theresienstadt, a Dr. Vollmeier, who only heard whispering [about Auschwitz] but could not learn much more.

I still want to mention a little event. One evening 2,000 women were transferred to us from the isolation camp. All of the 2,000 were bathed, dressed, and prepared for transport. We in the office knew that only 1,000 women were to be transported to a work camp. The other[s] were marked as "SB" [special treatment]. And how did the transport and the deception actually proceed? Before the camp stood railroad cars, and trucks stood behind the railroad cars. First 100 girls stepped out. It was evening. They were driven into the railroad cars. The next hundred on the trucks, the third hundred into the cars, the next hundred on the trucks. The prisoners in the cars did not know where the trucks were going, and those in the trucks did not know where the railroad cars were going. And then it started. The railroad cars actually went to another camp, and the other thousand were gassed. First, the same clothes came back, and second, we had to check-mark: *Sonderbehandlung*. So one never knew how one stood. Never.

[Boder brought T. back to her work in the camp office.]

10. The events T. describes in this section happened between May 15 and May 25, 1944.

I completed the few numbers on his wardrobe for the camp leader, and as the only one [still alive] out of 4,000, they [the Germans] took notice of me. "This prisoner was favored by Herr Müller." They did not know why. And when it subsequently came to any kind of selection, they used to "forget" about me. Besides, I performed, in the course of time, tasks which no other woman was [capable of] doing, because I was a professional. They were pleased by a proper looking card index, with little things that I did for them time and again according to instructions, exactly like any other prisoner who had to do the work that was assigned.

Later on I worked as a prisoner in the office, always doing what was indispensable. Then came First Lieutenant Hössler,[11] who [had just been sentenced to be] hanged in the Bergen-Belsen trial. I want to say a few words in connection with Hössler. At the selections which were performed at the arrival of a transport, of which 90 percent went in to the crematorium, Mr. Hössler was also present. At times Mr. Hössler, at times Dr. Mengele, at times Supervisor [Therese] Brandl, at times Supervisor [Margot] Drexler. It depended, alternating. That went on automatically, left, right, left, right. Whoever was lucky got into the camp. And only those who got into the camp were tattooed, got their number, and were entered in the card index. Mr. Hössler, too, took part in these selections exactly like all the others belonging to the SS. But thousands of male and female prisoners could possibly be thankful for their lives to Mr. Hössler because he was the one who undertook a most radical campaign of delousing. In all the men's and women's camps the typhus louse disappeared. And in this manner prisoners were spared.

How did he accomplish that?

He ordered the clothes to be put into steam boilers where the typhus louse was killed, [including] the eggs [and] the larvae. Often the prisoner was shorn [and] taken through a bath. He [Hössler] went so far as to provide enough water and soap, and such delousings took place every month. Thus there was not a single prisoner in Auschwitz or Birkenau who was not submitted once a month to a delousing.

Hössler, like the others, took notice of me as the draftswoman of the camp, put paints at my disposal, and arranged a small room for me next to the office where I worked. Then I got the first, larger task of drawing up a diagram of the labor force, that is, of everything that took place in the camp—the daily changes in the [labor] force, the daily additions, the labor force in the armament industry, in agriculture, and wherever else prisoners worked—to present that monthly in the form of a diagram which would then go to Berlin. I made that diagram once

11. Franz Hössler succeeded Paul Müller as commander of the women's camp at Birkenau.

for him, [and also a copy] for myself. And on the last day, the 18th of January 1945, I threw a roll of duplicates of the diagrams behind the bookcase in Birkenau, section IIB. I think it has fallen into the hands of the Russians.

Why could you not take it yourself afterward?
We had to evacuate, and right before [that] all papers, all the principal books, everything was burned. And nobody knew anything about these diagrams.

In order to kill time in some way, I undertook in this little room to reconstruct [a model of] the Birkenau camp in plastic. I obtained the proper tools and all that was needed for it.

You slept in a general block?
I slept along with all the other prisoners. I was not [officially] privileged. I was not a band carrier.[12] I was simply recognized as draftswoman of the camp.

What did you get to eat?
Exactly the same as any other prisoner. In the morning there was coffee. Then a quarter of a loaf of bread, about 500 grams [18 ounces]. It constantly changed. One time the [loaf of] bread was for four people, another time it was for five. It was Wehrmacht [army] bread. It was baked [fresh] every day. The men's camp at Auschwitz had a bakery. Auschwitz was self-sufficient. The most diverse shops. . . .

Now where was I? Yes. I decided to mount [a model of] Birkenau in plastic. And indeed, after three months of this work with another woman prisoner who assisted me, we presented the camp on a surface two meters by eighty [centimeters]. Afterward it was placed under glass and carried over to the commandant's office. I still have this plan in my head. Because the construction authority was always so busy, and the gentlemen of the camp constantly wanted schematic plans. And so they came to me, and in this manner they regularly kept me occupied.

How did you draw, with India ink or . . . ?
I always provided myself with most necessities. Everything was available because draftsmen also came with the transports. Artists also came who were not so lucky to get into the camp, but their things remained. There was one [section of the] camp in the midst of all the crematoria, camouflaged with trees, in which the clothes and everything that the people brought with them was piled up. And I fetched the things precisely from there.

12. Presumably a reference to an armband designating some prisoner official.

Now then, where did you go to from Auschwitz?

The 18th of January 1945 came. From afar we already heard explosions. We knew exactly—those were the Russians. The last crematorium was blown up on orders of the SS, and the prisoners were evacuated, I among them. We went in the direction of Breslau, accompanied by SS men. Right and left we saw dead prisoners. The men who marched ahead of us were, in large part, shot down. The SS at that time was especially selected for this transport, in large part ethnic Germans.

Ethnic Germans—who were they?

All Germans who *feel* German by nationality, claim to be such, but are not Reich Germans [citizens of Germany proper]. Yugoslav Germans, Sudeten Germans, Ukrainians who call themselves Germans, and so forth. Ethnic Germans were in the large majority worse than all the others. We were chased by them north, then south, then east, then west, away from the Russians. When we were in one place, it was said that the Russians were five kilometers away, so we had to turn south. When we got there, we had to turn north. And so after a day and night we arrived in the city of Breslau where we were confined in open cattle cars, 100 in each [car]. The trip proceeded just like the march on foot, without provisions, in a storm, without toilets, with nothing.

Still, you were not in fact without any food during that time.

Among about 100 women who were in one railroad car, two loaves of bread and a can of canned food [were supposed to] be distributed, but only about 50 percent of it was because the SS themselves were hungry. The first day each one received a thin slice of bread and maybe 100 grams [3 ½ ounces] of meat. The rest consisted of snow which we licked. Later on, near Berlin, the population did not exactly know who we were so they brought us hot coffee or hot water.

[The trip ended at concentration camp Ravensbrück.] On me personally Ravensbrück made the impression of Auschwitz [as it was] in 1942: cold, disorder, dirt, famine. They did not have any idea what to do with us. We were again transported away to smaller camps which were planned for a thousand people. Three thousand came! One can imagine how the conditions for living and nutrition looked up to the day of liberation.

The last camp was a small work camp, Mirow [?]. But it did not last long anymore because two weeks before the end of the war the Swedish Red Cross sent busses and officially removed [some of] the prisoners. I don't know what motivated them [the Germans] that they set some prisoners free, and that aroused a bit of hope in us. I remained there. The 1st of May came, [and it] was celebrated in our heart as the day of freedom. And on the 1st of May we were, indeed, evacuated from the camp by the SS. And we had an inkling, we knew, that this road might, indeed, lead to freedom.

People were on the highway—soldiers, prisoners—whoever still had hands and feet was heading for Lübeck. I and two other girls made ourselves disappear into the crowd. Before [escaping], we got rid of the red stripe from our clothes.

How did you do that?

I prepared for it by always painting my stripe, not with oil paint but with simple red watercolor which, however, was adequate; with a brush the stripe could easily be removed. We mingled with the crowd. That was not difficult because there was too much confusion, too great a state of nervousness among everyone, even the SS. And in the afternoon I found a little farm house where I saw that the German Wehrmacht was moving out. And so I went to that farm and went to sleep in a barn.

Whom were you with?

The two girls. But we found other people there who had arrived at exactly the same [idea]. These were mostly French war prisoners, some Russians, even members of the SS who had thrown away their insignia and did not want to continue [fighting]. There was a conglomeration of people. The night was passed in a barn.

What were you talking about?

There were debates. Should we move on? Why move on? We were driven toward the Americans. Why should we not be liberated by the Russians? For us prisoners that should be all the same, whether by the Americans or Russians or English. We [just] wanted to be liberated. And it was a pity to give away our last strength; we were almost too exhausted to continue at a running pace. We knew that the day of liberation [would] be *our* day no matter what nation did it.

And what did the SS men say?

They were ready to stay there and let themselves be taken prisoners. There were also two Danes, or [maybe] Dutchmen, two tall [SS] men who were quite undecided. They wanted to get away. And with quite strong persuasion I told them that it was not worthwhile because eventually they could be shot by the Germans as well. They remained. And indeed, at night we heard the thunder of cannon in the forest.

In the morning we were hungry. There were potatoes in the yard. We boiled some for ourselves, and all at once we saw a soldier. I asked him, "Who are you?" He did not answer me. I noticed the Soviet star on his cap, and I asked him in broken Russian, "Are you a Russian soldier?" "Yes." "Are the Russians here already? Are we free?" "Yes." And there was an advanced Russian detail who looked around and inspected the whole site and wanted to ascertain what was going on. In about ten minutes several tanks, horses, soldiers, trucks appeared on the highway. Since they knew that we were prisoners, they supplied us with provisions, candy, and the kind. They had no qualms when occupying a city or village to requisition things and give them to us. Because the prisoners were half naked, half starved, and were in need of the things.

The same night I decided to go home to Slovakia. It was the 3rd of May. I stopped an automobile which was going back from the front in order to fetch [something]. There was a Russian captain. I asked him to take us with them.

All three [of you]?
All three.

Were these Jewish girls?
No, two Polish girls. He took us as far as the city of Waren where he let us off and brought us food and provided us with lodging [in] a private dwelling. And he told us we should rest up for a few hours. [He said that] any automobile had orders to accept prisoners and transport them wherever they wanted.

In Waren we met various prisoners of all nations. For the first time I saw strangely uniformed [men with] carts, horses, and bundles like all the others. I asked them who they were, and they replied they were American war prisoners who now were liberated and that their destination was the American Zone. And so they asked me about my nationality, and I told them that I was from Slovakia. They had one among them whose parents years ago had emigrated to America who was of Slovakian origin and even from near my hometown Bratislava. He was introduced to me, and he still knew a bit of broken Czech. We chatted for a while. Then we took leave and endeavored to go ahead with our journey. On the road we met a great variety of people, and all were nice and helped us with whatever they could. On the 28th of May we arrived home through Poland.

Not by train?
By train only from Poland. Sometimes on horses, sometimes on foot, sometimes by automobile. To us it was all the same. We wanted [to get] home. I arrived, and right the first day I found my brother, the only one remaining from the three. He himself was sentenced to two years in the Bratislava prison beginning with January 1942. Then he was sent to a Jewish distribution camp from which he fled and put himself at the service of the partisans. He spent a year and a half in the hills.

Did you return to your apartment? What did you find there?
The apartment had been rented [to others] for a long time. We did not possess much before the war. A Czech who saved my things for three and a half years brought them back to me and returned them without my having to ask.

Now, tell me what kind of camp do you have here?

Feldafing is a camp founded right after liberation by Lieutenant Irving Smith, an American Jew. This camp was seized because he was a witness that thousands of prisoners stood half-starved without knowing what to do. Lieutenant Smith quickly created a block for the undernourished. Smith proceeded with the nourishment of the people gradually, starting with gruel and ending with solid things. The nourishment was controlled. The people were starved, and it was difficult to get [them] back on their feet. Day and night he worked for the good of the people here in cooperation with my present husband and others as well. After weeks they recuperated, and Feldafing had the smallest death [rate] of all the camps. Afterward the UNRRA took the camp over. And the people, in spite of everything, are already very impatient because everyone has only one single aim in view, to leave the country which once was hell for him.

Tell me, do you have any contacts with the Germans around here?

Contact with the Germans? Actually no, because the Germans of Upper Bavaria have no desire to establish contact with us. They have no intention whatsoever to feel in some way guilty. We understand. There are innocent German children, as innocent as our children were, who also perished in multitudes. But we feel that we are actually still hated. In Germany we shall never feel well. There is nothing for us in this country.

Hungary

33   George K.

Before Hitler took over Hungary in 1944, young Jews like George K. were excluded from the draft but required to work in factories or special Jewish labor gangs instead. He was working in Budapest when the Germans marched in, and although he had false papers supplied to him by the Zionist underground, he limited their use to visiting his family in the provinces. Using them at all was risky, and instead of posing as a Gentile and chancing discovery, K. gambled that joining one of the Jewish labor batallions would prevent his deportation. He lost.

Sent to Auschwitz, K. spent most of his time there at the camp associated with the Buna works at Monowitz, at first digging fortifications for the German Army and then stringing cable in the Buna factory itself. He describes mingling of Gypsies and Jews at the time of his arrival at Birkenau that was not typical and invites further research. He also makes some useful distinctions between his treatment by Wehrmacht and SS men and between Jewish capos, Polish overseers, and professional criminals in the camp hierarchy. It is clear from his unusually lucid narrative that cleaning up for his block senior provided him with extra nourishment that enhanced his chances of living. K. notes that the barracks were infested with fleas and bedbugs, but he credits the Germans with stringent and successful measures to eliminate lice. It was not typhus but an infected foot that landed him in the sick ward at the end of 1944. He must have sensed that the hospital was the safest place for him to be since he feigned slow recovery from an operation to assure a prolonged stay. That is where he was when the SS panicked during the evacuation of the camp and left the sick behind. He was one of only a handful of survivors of Auschwitz III who managed to be liberated by the Red Army in January 1945.

Returning with difficulty to his hometown after the war, the twenty-two-year-old survivor went to work for the American Jewish Joint Distribution Committee, aiding refugees who were in worse shape than he. His interview, held at the kibbutz DP camp at Tradate, Italy, reveals a man refreshingly free from self-pity and eager simply to get on with his life in Palestine. We join the interview with his labor batallion's removal from Budapest to a nearby small town, Hatvan, probably in April 1944.

Within two minutes from there, in a sugar factory, there was a small ghetto where the Jews of the city lived. We arrived there. It was pitch dark. We were ordered to put our baggage down on the floor and sit down. Nobody should say a word; nobody should tear anything up—money or documents; and one should be very quiet.

How many of you were there?

We were 150 Labor Service [men] there. We noticed that in another place there were bundles which we recognized as the baggage of people from other Labor Service [units]. We were sitting there for half an hour, and they trumpeted the end of the air raid. Then a German officer came with Hungarian officers and policemen, and then a Jewish policeman, and told us that all valuables and all documents we had on us should be put down on the floor. We did so. We didn't know yet what would happen to us. The gendarmerie came and searched our pockets for things we still might have had in them. We were afraid. We knew that if we did not give them up, we would get a bad beating. We surrendered everything, and they took it for themselves. We ourselves saw them putting it in their own pockets.

After we had surrendered our things, a German officer came who wasn't really a German but a Hungarian officer [in German uniform], the famous Captain Zoeldi who ordered the pogroms in Ujvidek of which the whole world has been talking.[1] He told us, "Jews, you are here in the ghetto. We shall transfer you to a work camp. You will work there, and you should behave well. Now go into these barracks. You will remain there until morning, and [then] you will learn what will happen next." At 6:00 in the morning the Jews in the ghetto got up, and we were given a warm vegetable soup and saw that the Jews were crowding together. A policeman came and asked what was going on, and they said that today the whole ghetto would be shipped away. Yesterday a transport had gone, and today the rest were going. Again the SS officer [Zoeldi] appeared: "Those who are not Jews and those who are citizens of other countries, who are not Hungarian citizens, should step forward."

Jews or non-Jews?

Jews too, if they were not Hungarian citizens. Three people stepped forward. One had a Swedish passport; he took him and led him away. Two Jews stepped forward and said that they were Christians. So he said, "Do you have documents?" So they said, "But yesterday you took our documents away." So he said,

---

1. Hungarian army captain Marton Zoeldi was responsible for the 1942 massacre of hundreds of Jews at Ujvidek in the Sajkas area of northern Yugoslavia annexed by Hungary in 1941. During the German occupation of Hungary he worked closely with the SS in anti-Jewish actions. In 1946 he was sentenced to death by a Yugoslavian court.

"I haven't *taken* away any documents; you gave them to me. Step forward, I shall examine you whether you are Christians or not." And so in the presence of everybody he started to examine "their race." He examined their eyes, hair, face. He did not examine anything else. Only the face. He said, "You are not of the Mongolian race; you are of the Jewish race. My friend, it may be that you are a Christian, a convert, but your father was a Jew, and you are also a Jew." And he beat them with a stick that he had in his hand.

Why "Mongolian"?
The Hungarian race belongs to the Mongolian race. We did not remain in the ghetto for long, only twelve hours. At twelve o'clock [noon] we were ordered to take the sacks that we still had and take them to be inspected. [There they] took everything of value from the baggage. We really didn't have anything. When we entered the Hungarian Labor Service, we took some clothes and some underwear and such things with us which we needed just for work. We thought that later they could send us some things [from home], that we would remain in Hungary. Then without food and with nothing to drink we were pushed into the railroad cars, eighty-five to the car; the train was not a Hungarian train but the German State Railroad train.

Where did they get so many people?
In the ghetto there were two or three thousand [Jews] from Hatvan and the surroundings. At twelve o'clock we got into the cars, the cars were sealed, and first of all someone was named commander of the car. And they didn't give us any water or anything. The Hungarian gendarmerie with the police stood next to the cars and walked with their guns and nobody could get out. We just had to sit inside. And we sat there and were thinking where they would take us. One said they would take us to Austria; another said they would take us somewhere in Hungary, or they would take us to the German Labor Service. But we didn't know anything about Auschwitz. The Hungarian Jews had not heard about Auschwitz over the radio, and when Polish or German Jews would come [and tell us about it, we] would say, "No, that is impossible. It is not possible that they are burning German and Polish Jews in Auschwitz." We did not believe *that*.

What did you say about the radio?
We had not heard about Auschwitz over the [Hungarian] radio. We heard about it secretly, from the London radio. It was said that Jews were being burned. We still believed that it was just propaganda. We did not believe that they burned Jews.

At four o'clock in the afternoon the train departed. We arrived at Miskolc at night, [and] they took on [Jews from] the Miskolc ghetto. We left Miskolc at

12:00 at night, and at one station still on the Hungarian side the train slowed down. In the train people said, "Comrades, we could save ourselves. We could jump out of the car."

They were sealed?

They were sealed, but high up there were iron bars. We had a little saw, and we sawed them through, and five men from our car jumped out, and these five men saved themselves—afterward, when we returned from the camp, we talked to these men. The cars were watched by the Hungarian gendarmerie up till the Hungarian-Slovakian border, up to Kosice. The Hungarian gendarmerie were sitting on top of the cars, and from there they could see what was going on in the cars. Up to Kosice the cars were not opened even once. It was a trip of twenty-four hours. We were in the cars, one standing, the other lying down. The people had already grown beards, looking like wild animals. We already had two dead people in our car. There were three or four who went completely insane. They couldn't speak anymore from thirst. The eighty-five people had to satisfy their needs inside the cars. It was a cattle car. We took our bowls, our dishes that we brought with us for food, and we went into them, and threw *it* out the windows.

We arrived [at Auschwitz and] walked over to the gate. An SS chief physician stood there—later we found out the name, Dr. Mengele—and said, "You are going to work, and whoever feels that he is strong enough to work should march. Those who do not feel strong enough to work, and are not strong enough to walk, should go over to the other side. They will be taken by truck to another place where they will get easier work." And there went the mothers with small children, and there went women and old people and people who said, "My leg hurts, I can't walk." And of the whole 4,000 people of the transport, 1,000 remained.

I did not go with the feeble ones. I had a feeling that if I was taken to work, possibly I would pull through. And I went with the transport, and we were led into the washroom. And before we entered the washroom, out on the street we heard music. There were prisoners who played trumpets. A whole musical orchestra. They played jazz music.[2] So we asked what was going on. "Yes," they told us, "a new transport comes, and they play so that one shouldn't suspect anything." And the men told us we shouldn't ask so many questions. And we saw people running and asking, "Jews, where are you from?" And the only thing we ask was, "Jews, can one drink the water here?" "Yes, but don't drink too much."

[After being shaved and disinfected, K.'s group was placed in Block 13 in the Gypsy camp.] Gypsies who lived in Hungary. The Gypsy musicians, the Gypsies from Germany, those who were not of the so-called race of Germans. These were

---

2. Unlikely, given the Nazi opinion that jazz was degenerate. K. probably means German popular music of the day.

wearing very funny clothes; the big hats that were taken away from the rabbis. Chassidic hats. And [they were] dressed in suits, and their suits had a large red cross on the back so that they should not escape. That was a mark that they, too, were prisoners.

Tell me, were there women with the Gypsies?
Their women, their children, were there with the Gypsies. We also saw Gypsy women there who were pregnant. [The Gypsies were] all in the same block, living together. Our block trustee was also a Gypsy. And we were ordered to lie down. We were 1,500 [*sic*] people who remained from the 4,500 from the transport. All in one block.

And how many Gypsies were there?
There were no more Gypsies in the block, only the block senior with his large family.[3] About the block I also have to tell you that Birkenau was a riding stadium before the war; there were horses there before the war.[4] We were told, "Jews, lie down on the ground, and things will proceed." And we wept. "Bring us something to drink!"

And so a Hungarian-German interpreter came—he had it written [on a band] on his left arm—along with a Gypsy and our block senior. He stood up on a box and made a speech: "Jews, you have come to Auschwitz, to Birkenau. This is an extermination camp. He who cannot work will be burned, and whoever can work will work as long as he can. Here you cannot hide anything. I have brought a lamp with me." An SS man had come with a lamp. "This is an X-ray lamp. Look again and see whether you still have on you some guldens or valuables or things that you are [not] permitted to possess." He also brought pliers and hammers and he ordered us to tear the soles from our shoes. "Maybe *you* have hidden something away there, and we may not have noticed it when you came into the block." And he came around, and the Jews took off their soles, and gold appeared, money appeared. And one Jew pulled out a work book—a German work book. He said, "This is my work book. I am a working man, and I shall work." And he [the interpreter] said, "Just drop it here." Pictures of our mothers, fathers, that we had managed to save, I don't know how, in the shoes or wherever—*I can't describe it.* I really cannot imagine how they hid them after such a thorough search.

3. K. left the subject of the Gypsies unclear. It seems likely that the Gypsies were being cleared from the block at about the time of his arrival. If so, it seems strange that a Gypsy remained as block senior.

4. A myth. Birkenau had been a tiny agricultural hamlet, and if there had been horses, they were farm animals. K. does not indicate why he made such a point of this. Perhaps he wanted to underline the unsanitary conditions in the camp.

And then he said, "Has everything been surrendered?" And the Jews said, "Yes." Then he said, "Yes, I see you are Hungarian Jews. You haven't anything on you. You are the kind that are afraid. Hungarian Jews are all afraid. I shall not search you with the X-ray lamp." Later we learned that it was no X-ray lamp. It was a plain ordinary large lamp that he brought in. And he took the guldens, and two days later we learned that he had bought bread and fat from the Polish workers who did not live in the camp but just came there to work, and from the SS soldiers.

Didn't he get enough to eat otherwise?

No, he was getting just his ration. He only had food that he could steal from the Jews. And he said, "Soon they will bring black coffee. Everybody will get coffee." And sure enough, they brought the coffee, and he said, "Jews, you are not permitted to leave this place. You may step out two paces. There is a box inside the block for your small needs, and outside the block two paces away is another box where you can satisfy your big needs. But do not go any farther because beyond that are the wires and the SS people in the big towers which have those large reflectors [searchlights] and the dogs. If one takes three paces, they grab him and shoot him immediately." And we again lay down on the ground, without blankets, without anything, and we slept. That was the first night after the railroad cars that we could sleep a bit.

At 6:00 in the morning there was a bell to get up for roll call. We stepped out. We were counted up [to ascertain] how many people we were. Then we were told that now we had to scrub the block. We were given mops and brooms to clean it up well. At 10:00 they brought the first soup. That was a German soup in which they threw everything possible together. It was served for ten people together in a large pot. The pot was dirty. It was a pot that was taken out from the railroad cars where the Jews were, without washing them out. We knew what these pots had been used for. The Jews had "gone" into them while in the cars. And we had no water to wash them out. A few people did not eat. I said, "I shall eat what they give me," because I knew that if I didn't eat, I wouldn't have the strength to go on with the work. And there were two people, diabetics, who became so ill that they said, "We need injections." And they were led away, and we haven't seen them anymore.

By eleven—we already dared to make a few steps outside—we saw something burning. It burns, it burns, it burns. We saw flames, and [there was] an awful stench. We asked the Gypsies, "What are they burning?" So they said, "They are burning the clothes that you brought with you since it cannot be used. It is none of your concern what is burning." And afterward they told us, "Now go and lie down again." We did nothing. Another day passed, [and] an SS man came. We were told to get up. The SS man looked us over and ordered those who were soldiers before the war to step forward, those who were strong people, for hard work. And they stepped forward. They divided us into two groups, the strong people and the not very strong people.

And where were you?

I was among the strong men. And with us were two stout men, very stout—100 kilos [220 pounds]. And the SS men said, "Are you strong?" So they said, "Yes." "Well, then I shall arrange a bout. You shall fight each other, box each other. The one who is stronger will go on the side with the strong people, and the other one will go to the other side." And the Jews even laughed about it. What did they know about what was going to happen? And there were 500 of us strong men who were lined up.

What happened to those two stout people?

That I don't know. They remained there. Some months later I met one of them in a work camp where he was assigned, and he told me they were taken to Auschwitz [I] to work in a factory.

By that time we were approached by the Polish Jews who wanted to barter with us for our shoes. One wanted to give a piece of bread with *other* shoes. And they told us that shoes there amounted to life. Whoever had shoes lived. And we didn't want to barter. We were taken to quarantine, because there was scarlet fever in the Gypsy camp. And we were in the quarantine camp four days.

Afterward an order came after the roll call that all of us had to move on. So these 500 men marched in formation, four abreast, holding each other's shoulder. Ten SS men marched with us with guns in hand and led us through [the town of] Auschwitz, through the streets. We saw stores, people walking the streets, the Poles. There were some who looked at us with sadness. There were some who laughed at us. And we marched ten kilometers. We entered a camp which was called Buna. That belonged to the I. G. Farben Industry, a big plant [making] synthetic rubber. The block senior soon lined us up at the roll call square and said, "Get ready to go into the washroom." And again we were led into disinfection chambers. Again they took away the clothes which we had gotten before.

We came out to the "clean" side again. There stood a doctor who examined us, and we were given very bad things, again these blue-white striped things, but in very bad condition, torn ones of small sizes. We were led into the quarantine block, and they told us, "Men, you shall remain here, and you are not permitted to leave until you are assigned to details in the camp." [That was] because we had come from a camp where there was scarlet fever. And for whatever reason, we didn't know, we were assigned to the *punishment* detail, a detail that worked outside the camp, six kilometers away. We were building fortifications for the Germans.

Why did they call it the punishment detail?

Because we marched barefooted. We had to take off our shoes before we left and walk barefooted the whole way on stony roads, and at times we had to run, at times we had to walk slowly, and every time we started out we had to fetch our food for the midday meal in 50 liter barrels. Two people had to carry the hot food on the road barefooted [for every] two or three hundred men. Those who carried the barrel had to run at the same pace as the others. They were not permitted to fall behind the group. And we went out there and worked. There was only one SS man. The rest were the Wehrmacht. Old people. And we talked to them, and they talked to us. They were quite good to us, and now and then they would hand over a little piece of bread. They themselves didn't have much to eat. But when the SS [man] would approach, the Wehrmacht men would immediately tell us, "Now work, here come the SS," and we worked hard, very hard.

[At] 4:00 in the morning when we were getting up, everybody had to wash in the washroom, and then there was breakfast. At breakfast we were given 300 grams of bread with 20 grams of margarine, not the synthetic margarine that did not contain fat. *German* margarine. And that was all the breakfast.

What was the synthetic margarine made of?

We don't know. It had no fat content. It smelled pretty good and tasted pretty good, but it had no calories. And we got bitter black coffee. At the Buna plant one couldn't drink the water because one would get typhus, and also [it tasted] very bad. And [so] we would go out to work. First we would go out to roll call at five o'clock. It lasted the whole hour until 6:00. At 6:00 they counted the men, and each one reported the number he had in his detail; and if the number was not correct, we had to stand until the number was correct.

We marched out. At the exit, at the gate stood a physician; and the ones who felt sick stepped before the physician, and anyone who was really sick could remain in the camp. If the illness lasted only two or three days or a week, he went to work again. But if he had an illness that could not be treated, he was taken by truck to Auschwitz [II] and burned.

How do you know that?

We know it because people would come who had met others who came from there. And later we talked to some Hungarians who had worked in the corpse disposal detail. The burning detail. People worked at this only three months, [and then] they were relieved and transported away to other camps.[5]

5. Here, of course, K. speaks of the Auschwitz Sonderkommando. Its members were not, however, "transported away" but rather gassed. Only a few of the last group survived.

We went out the gate to work. We were counted again, taken to work, and worked until 12:00. At 12:00 we went to eat. The food consisted of a half a liter of soup, [really] half a liter of water. And from 12:00 to 1:00 we were free and would lie down on the grass and sleep a bit. At 1:00 we would return to work until 5:00. Later on when [it grew dark earlier], we didn't work so late anymore. We always worked as long as it was light. At dusk we would get back into the camp with the [other] details, assemble at the roll call square, and were counted again. We had already been counted at the entrance, but we were counted again. And after the count everybody had to wash, and after washing we would get the evening meal, three-fourths of a liter of soup, a little heavier, not so thin, and it had some potatoes or turnips cooked in it. Turnips that in Hungary used to be served to cattle, red turnips and white turnips.

And after eating, once a week we had to shave. The hair was clipped down completely with a zero clipper, and every week we were shaved. They used two knives to shave two or three hundred men without sharpening the knife. Each shave was [a surgical] operation. And the people would get the so-called beard eruptions, infections, and because of the infection one would look terribly ugly. And people with such infections were not shaved anymore, so that these people would walk around with months-old beards and they looked very, very ugly. After that we would lie down and sleep. It was a very bitter life. We had two-deck beds. There were two blankets on each bed and nothing else. Two people slept on each cot, one with his head at the other fellow's feet, and the other one on the other side. The cots were approximately fifty centimeters wide. These beds were full of vermin, fleas, and bedbugs.

Lice?

There were none in the camp. Four times every week there was louse control. Everyone had to carry his shirt to the doctor. In every block there was a doctor who inspected the shirts, the underpants. One marched completely naked to the inspections, and if one had lice he would get a very, very bad beating, and all his things were taken away immediately for disinfection together with the beds. Everything was disinfected. I was in the camp a whole year, but I never had lice.

Every week we washed our shirts once. We did not have any [decent] shirts because we were selling our shirts outside, when at work, to the Polish workers. We would get 2 or 3 kilos of bread for a shirt. So we didn't have any shirts. We had only the clothes on us.

Wouldn't they ask you what became of your shirts?

At first we were ordered to surrender the old clothing every two weeks; afterward only every month. And we would take in a rag and say that the shirt had gotten torn, and we surrendered the rag and were given other shirts. These *other* shirts were also torn. We washed our clothing every week, once, twice, depending on how dirty [it] was. We had a little piece of soap every week.

You speak about the Poles. What kind of Poles were they?
These were Polacks, not Jews. Polacks that just worked there, work foremen.

People saw to it that they would get some kind of special assignment in the camp. Everyone who had some function in the camp got a bit more food. I personally worked for the block senior. I washed his underwear and darned his socks. I was a textile worker. I had learned to knit socks, to make new socks and knitted underwear, and other such things. But I was already accustomed to having to work, and I washed the block senior's shirts and darned the socks, and in return I was getting supplementary food every day, a double portion of three-fourths of a liter of soup.

How about bread?
Bread I wouldn't get. That was impossible; 300 grams of bread was all, and we ate it right away in the morning. All of it.

And so our life went on for about two months, that is, until August [when] they started to select. They asked who had a trade, and such a man was placed in the trade details that consisted of locksmiths, engineers, or bookkeepers or carpenters, glazers, painters; and these worked outside the plant. Approximately 100,000 worked in the factory. It was one gigantic camp. There were not just Jews there. There were Polish correctional camps. There was a camp for Germans who were there for punishment. Communists who took part in the Spanish revolution—that kind of Germans. There were [men of] the French Labor Service. There were English [and] American soldiers, prisoners of war who lived in the vicinity of our camp. There were also free Polish and German people, and we Jews, and Ukrainians, Belgians, and all kinds of people from all over the world in the Buna works.

I was then assigned to a locksmith detail, a detail of technicians. I went to work at the power plant, not as a locksmith but as an electrical worker. I worked there with the [German] General Electric Company, which supplied the whole plant with electric power, and we handled the connections there; we worked on the high-tension equipment, on the cables. I had it pretty good there. We worked from blueprints, and it was very pleasant work. I worked alongside Christian Poles who would give me stale bread or some food. They did not have much themselves, but they gave [some to] us, and every day I went to clean up the office, and I would pick discarded tomatoes out of the garbage can; because I always used to say, "I must eat what I see, because when I eat, I have the strength to go on working."

But the capo was not pleased to see that I got something to eat there, and he assigned me to his detail, to heavy work. I later worked laying cables five stories underground; the whole plant [Buna] was built five stories underground. It was very, very cold. It was already September. Our nerves had become completely apathetic. We were not thinking anymore. We knew nothing. Now and then we would find a German newspaper to read, but they were full of German [business]. We saw terrible things in the camp. During roll call we saw people hanged, three Jews at once, because [they] had stolen bread from the storehouse during an air raid. A little bit of bread, not much, and they were hanged.

Right at the roll call square?

We arrived at the roll call square, and there stood the gallows, three next to each other. In the evening, about 6:00—it was already September, it was already dark. And never before in my life had I seen a human being going "kaputt." And I asked, "What is going to happen?" "Oh, Jews will be hanged," is what I heard. We stood there for an hour. They led up the three Jews, their hands tied; the SS man brought them to the gallows and told us in German that by order of Himmler three Jews were to be hanged because they stole bread during the air-raid alarm. "Jews, you should know that during an alarm you should not steal. You are getting enough to eat, and you should eat what you are getting." And the [condemned] Jews were standing there and shouting, "Comrades, we are the last ones. Keep your heads up. All the fascists will die. The Russians are coming. The Russians will liberate us." The SS man approached and beat them right at the gallows. And they called out three Jews [for each condemned man], if a Hungarian [Jew], they called three Hungarian [Jews], and they had to stand and watch.

The gallows were so constructed that there was a lever, and he [the SS man] stepped with his feet on the lever, the scaffold would fall down, and the Jews were hanging. And we looked on. After ten minutes one [of the three] still wanted to pull his neck out of the noose. The others went "kaputt" immediately and their faces became gray. Afterward all the work details had to pass by the gallows, and everyone had to look at them. If anybody wouldn't look, he immediately got badly slapped in the face by the SS. And afterward—we all saw it—a capo came from the hospital and cut the rope. The dead men fell down, and right away he took a pencil, spit on the stomach, and wrote down his number with an indelible pencil and also wrote down his number on his legs; and the body was taken to Auschwitz [II] to burn. We had to look on [at executions]. And it happened not once, it happened very often. They often hanged people.

For what?

For nothing, for attempts to escape from the camp and from the plant. They would try, the Polish Jews who could speak the Polish language. There was a

Polish physician with me who previously had lived three kilometers from the camp. And he could see his home from the roof. They had possibly a way to get away, but they were always caught, and for that the penalty was death.

Was the physician also hanged?
Yes, we saw him hanged. After the hanging, we went to eat, and everybody ate. There was such apathy [that] everybody ate and did not talk about what they had seen anymore.

We continued doing hard labor until December [1944]. It was frightfully cold. It was raining, and we were wet through and through, [dressed] just in the only suit we had, made of cotton, that blue- and white-striped suit, in December, standing at 5:00 in the morning on the roll call square, and going out to work.

What exactly were you doing there?
I hung up overhead cables. They were very big cables of large width, and I had to hang them up on the walls. I already felt that I had a fever, but I did not want to go to the sick ward because I feared that whoever was going in there was not being cured. And I was already so sick that I couldn't work anymore. I had blood poisoning on my leg, and I couldn't put my shoes on anymore. I went into the dispensary, and the physician took my temperature. I had [a high] fever, and the physician told me that I should go to the hospital the next day. It was a rule that if one was assigned to the hospital, the list was given to the block senior [who] brought the people in the morning. I was not on the list. I wept, and I went to the hospital and told the physician that he should accept me. I was going around barefooted with [a high] fever in December. I could not put my shoes on anymore because my feet were so swollen.

I was accepted in the hospital. That was not so easy. We were examined; then came the SS chief physician who admitted us. All the clothing we had on was taken away, and we entered the disinfection hall naked. We were disinfected and then led to the division where the [particular] illness belonged.

How were you disinfected?
There were showers, and we were all rubbed with kerosene, and again we were completely shaven. And so we got in. There was a stench. In a small hall there were 300 people, all with surgical sicknesses. One was already operated on, the other one was still sick or dead, or people who were little short of dying. I went in there, two people to a bed; completely naked. I lay down. Steam was coming in from the plant, so there was a bit of heat. There again we had only two blankets. The comrade who was lying with me in the same bed—pus was flowing from his hand, and I was lying in the same bed with him. At first they gave me compresses on my feet for two days, and the third day I was operated on. That was on Christmas day.

It happened this way. I was listed for the operation. Every morning they made a list of twenty or thirty people to be operated on. These were selected by a physician who would say, "These are the people to be operated on today. They should go and 'do' their necessary things, toilet affairs." And so, naked as we were, we went in to be operated on, each one waiting for his turn. The operation took place in the same room; only a curtain was provided that separated [the operating table] from the rest of the room. There was a Hungarian physician from Kosice, and I begged him to operate on me after putting me to sleep. I was given an anesthetic, and he operated. He cut open the bottom of my foot and bandaged it up. After the operation I had to go back, naked, on one foot. They did not carry me out. My feet are cured now. They are now very well.

Did he operate on both feet? Were both swollen?

No, only one foot. It was Christmas day, [but] the food in the hospital was not better [that day]. We got 300 grams of bread in the morning and a half a liter of soup at midday and three-fourths of a liter in the evening. We drank the soup from the bowl. We had no spoons, and no knife to cut the bread. [The patients] believed that on Christmas, the great holiday of the Christians, we would get some additional rations; but we got nothing. I was lying there until the 3rd of January. The 1st of January was my birthday. I went to the block senior and told him, "Mr. block senior, today is my birthday. I want to ask you, give me an additional portion of food today." And he gave me another portion. The other people saw that, and they said, "I too have a birthday." But he had our card indexes, and he would say, "Good, you get food, but if it is not your birthday you will be killed." And I saw him beating a sick person with a whip . . .

There in the hospital?

In the hospital, because he had said it was [his] birthday, and he should be given another liter to eat.

After that I got a bit better, but I still could not stand on the other foot. I was taken to another room where the patients already had been operated on and felt a little better, and I remained there until the 10th of January. They wanted to move me out from there because my wound was healed, but I myself would scratch the wound before the [doctors made their] rounds so that they wouldn't see that it was healed. And they took my temperature, and I also heated up the thermometer. I rubbed it on the blanket so that it should go up.

Where did you have the thermometer, in your mouth or . . .

Under my arm. I knew that if I left the hospital, I would die from the frost, and afterward we heard people talking about the Russians coming.

Who would talk?

The block seniors. They were already packing their things. The physicians and people were already sewing knapsacks from blankets. Things were being distributed for the hospital, medicines and boxes to pack up the whole hospital. One day, the 15th of January, the camp did not march out [to work] anymore because it was ten or fifteen degrees of frost, but we already knew that the Russians were coming and that the camp would be evacuated. And one night at 8:00 all people were lined up for roll call. They handed out 600 grams of bread, 40 grams of margarine, 20 grams of some kind of liver sausage, and they said: "You are going to march out." Those who could not walk were left there. The camp marched away that evening at 12:00; only a few hundred remained. The prisoners at the Buna works numbered 10,000 people. We remained there without clothes, without anything, entirely naked.

And the physicians?

The physicians also departed. Only the sick were left. And among the sick [were] some physicians. [But the Germans had taken] everything away, medicines, surgical supplies, everything. We also got a ration, [the same as] given to those who went. They told us to distribute it, because it was the last food they were giving us.

Did they tell you then that they were leaving you to the Russians?

No, they said that we should remain, and the SS detail would be sure to come and "take care" of us. They knew that "taking care" of us meant they would destroy us. Early the next morning I covered myself with a blanket and stepped out barefoot from the block to look for clothing. I found some old pants and wooden shoes that had been thrown away [by] the people who left. They couldn't take these things with them. Only one change of clothes. And I dressed, and I had the nerve to go farther outside. I knew my life wasn't worth anything. We would be destroyed, or destroyed trying to get away; and it so happened that I dressed and stepped into the clothing storehouse.

There were no SS?

Yes, ten SS remained in the whole camp. They didn't even come in to us. And then I went in to explore what was going on in the kitchen. We always looked [for] a turnip or something there; and everything that the Jews from the hospital could find, those who could walk a little bit, [was] collected in one place. They dressed, those who could, and hid the things under the beds. I found quite a few things. I dressed up like a civilian; under the civilian clothes I still had the striped clothing. I went into the shop where they repaired the automobiles of the SS and found several pairs of pliers there. Nobody was working there at that time. We took the pliers and hid them away, too. There was a Hungarian engineer in bed with me. And we said, "We will cut the wires," because the wires were still loaded at high tension, "and we will get out into the bunkers."

The same night there was a great American-English [air] attack. We were in the hospital in wooden barracks, and bombs fell within a few hundred meters, and the whole barracks was shaking. Large bombs, small bombs, and afterward incendiary bombs. The last bombs fell on the camp, and the camp was hit by an incendiary bomb, and the wooden barracks were burning, and there was no electricity in the wires anymore. And the Jews all went outside. And the SS came and said nobody should go out. If one went out, he would soon be dead. The fire engines from the plant came and extinguished the fire. And a miracle happened. The fire reached as far as the hospital, but the hospital did not burn down. The whole camp burned down, only the hospital did not.

Did the hospital have a red cross on the roof?
No, no, no, no, no, no. The hospital did not have a red cross. And we, my comrade and I, had already taken our things into the bunker. The SS used this bunker before, during the air-raid alarms, and we took our things there. During that night the SS came and asked us whether we had any water that was left in the canteen. There was some mineral water, and we gave it to the SS—two bottles. And they departed, and after that we saw no more of the SS. And we remained in the bunker.

Why did you need water?
The water system was all bombed out. There was no more water, no more current, nothing to eat, nothing. And we saw a stream of vehicles coming along the road; crowds of SS men, soldiers marching, trucks, tanks at high speed, and Polish people and ethnic Germans with wagons. We saw that something was in the offing, that liberty was coming for us, and we walked away from the bunker. We entered the first village, went to [the house of] a Polish peasant, and told [him] to let us in. He could see that the Germans were running away and that the Russians were coming. He took us into his house and gave us a bit to eat. He himself did not have much.

For two days we were hiding with this peasant, and at night the Russians arrived, [and] we ourselves went back to the camp, and the people [there] were rejoicing. But of the 400 people only about 200 remained. The others had died from starvation, from typhus which started to ravage there, and we had nothing on our bodies. We already had long beards, three or four weeks old, and there were these "Moslems" who had only bones and flesh. Flesh did I say? They had nothing, only bones and bones. The Russians photographed it all and gave us food. Bread. They slaughtered a whole cow and brought us the meat, and we cooked it.

[K. made his way back to Budapest with help from the Russians.] In Budapest I still saw the dead on the streets. At the time Budapest had just been liberated from the Germans. The Russians were there. Conditions were very hard. There was no food. And I didn't find any of my relatives. And I went to the American Joint which had already started to work there and found work with them. And from there I was sent to Szombathely, to my hometown. Again I worked for the Joint at the [train] station for the deported people. We gave assistance there, and I, who had been through all these experiences, did it with all my heart and without pay, and I did it readily.

What do you mean "without pay"? Didn't the Joint pay?

We did not get pay from the Joint. We only got our food and quarters and clothing, and we did it without money. I did not find anybody of my relatives. Nobody remained from the large family that we had. One cousin lives in New Zealand. I have nobody. I got married there in my hometown Szombathely, and I told the Joint I wanted to go on to Palestine. And from Hungary I came illegally through Yugoslavia to Italy.

Why to Italy?

Because from Italy we knew the *Aliyah* goes to Palestine.

"Aliyah"?

Aliyah means to depart, to travel forward, in Hebrew.

How did you make connections with the kibbutz?

Long before the war I belonged to a youth organization of the Zionists in Hungary. Finally I arrived here; one is not sent out of Italy. The UNRRA registers one, and in this way the people become legalized.

How many people are there in the kibbutz?

Now there are seventy people.

Have you a room for your wife and yourself?

No, we are thirty-six people in one room, men and women together. All of us are married. The next bed is ten centimeters away. It is very hard, but we readily live that way because we know that possibly the time is not so far away when we will have a free life; we shall be in our country, where we are striving to go. In Palestine we will be human beings again, we will be able to work and won't eat the bread of UNRRA and the Joint anymore.

Does the UNRRA know that you live that way?

UNRRA knows. Medical inspectors came. They measured out the room and said it is possible for so many people to live in one room.

But men and women? Are there children in the same room?

Yes.

Well, did nobody request that you get better living conditions?

There are no better living conditions. We know it, and *now* we don't want any better living conditions. We want better conditions in *Eretz*, in our country. We don't want to be here for long. We want to go ahead. Many of my comrades have gone. They went illegally.

And now since the English are taking them to Cyprus, to concentration camps?

Still, we will go. Legally or illegally. And if we are taken to Cyprus, we will go anyway because we know that [eventually] we will be taken to *Eretz*. It won't be long in Cyprus.

How does one get the ships to go?

I don't want to talk about that.

34 Adolph H.

Adolph H. was born in Czynadowo, Czechoslovakia, to parents who owned a large farm and ran a lumber business. In 1939, when the boy was twelve, Hitler arranged the transfer of that part of Transcarpathian Ukraine to Hungary. That transfer meant that instead of being deported with the majority of Slovakian Jews in 1942, H., his mother, and two brothers were ghettoized and sent to Poland only after the Germans occupied Hungary two years later. H. recalls Germans taking these actions, but Hungarian officials were most likely the major participants in the whole procedure. They certainly made the decision to keep his father behind in one of Hungary's notorious labor batallions for adult Jewish males. Adolph's father was not among the few survivors of those units.

At Auschwitz Adolph and one of his brothers were separated from the rest of their family and sent to the Jawiszowice coal mine, which supplied the factories in Auschwitz. He spent eight months there. This and other coal mines in the region were infamous for their hellish conditions, but Adolph H. recalls Jawiszowice as being less unbearable than the camps he experienced later in Germany. He mentions that his block senior protected him, without providing many details. H. was evacuated with the rest of the Auschwitz contingent in early January 1945. Taken on foot and by train to Buchenwald and then on to a satellite camp near Nordhausen, he fell ill and could not join the death march to escape the approaching American army. Miraculously, at the last minute the Germans supplied trucks to evacuate at least some of the sick to Buchenwald. His inclusion probably saved his life, since a very large proportion of those marched out of Ohrdruf did not have the strength to finish the journey, and those left behind at Ohrdruf were massacred by the SS. At Buchenwald H. unhesitatingly attached himself to the young people's barracks which was liberated by the Americans a short time later. In his description of the events, H. provides another variation on the story about the commandant's tardy telephone call so dear to the memory of the survivors.

For reasons that can no longer be determined, Adolph H. volunteered little about his personal life either before or after the Holocaust, and Boder made no effort to draw him out on the subject during the interview in Geneva. We begin with H.'s description of the German occupation of his home village in March 1944.

We saw the German occupation with the army, and all of a sudden it became black before the Jews' eyes. And two weeks later one morning they [the Germans] came, and we did not know why the houses were occupied, and they said in two hours everybody had to be packed up to be taken away. We did not know where to. People were driven together into a large building and [then] taken in trucks to the Mukachevo ghetto. There were large barracks of a brick factory, large wooden barracks where the bricks were stored, and we were quartered there. It was very crowded. We could not stand it, because there were terribly many people. Three thousand persons lived in one barracks.

Men, women, and children together?
The families were still together. We were in the brick factory four weeks. The *Kehillah* [Jewish Community] still supported itself. All the food supplies which we still had had to be taken along. We did not have much anymore because everything had been taken away. And what was short was brought from the town. Not everything was taken away yet due to [the payment of] protection money and so forth, so they permitted us to bring in some food supplies.

[That lasted] four weeks. One morning they said that whoever had citizen's rights in such and such city could be released. And so everybody brought his papers. We, too, showed [ours], all valid papers. They were taken away. And suddenly we saw him [an unspecified official] making a big fire with those papers. They were just making fun of us. And the next day, in the morning, we were not permitted to leave the barracks. We saw a great number of railroad cars arriving. And they packed a hundred people in a car, without food, without anything, and we were transported—where to, nobody knew.

We were riding and riding, two weeks in the train. And then we arrived in Auschwitz. We did not know about any Auschwitz, about extermina. . . . We saw people dressed in prisoner clothes, but we did not know what it meant. Only afterward we found out the entire story.

All right. And so let us go back a little. What kind of railroad cars were they?
Freight cars for cattle. Not passenger cars. And they were very crowded, without any water. They had taken away our bundles. They had taken everything away. We lay on the bare boards. We had a few pots, so we made a toilet in the pots and poured it out through the window. There was a small opening covered with wire. We could barely put our hand through. We had received 2 kilos of bread per person, and we lived on this the whole time. It was very far from enough, but what

could one do? One said we are being taken *there*, and one said *this* will happen. We did not know ourselves. We were completely mixed up. We were already not normal from everything that had happened.

Now tell me, when the train arrived, what happened then?

An SS officer was standing there, and he separated the older people and the children to one side, and those who looked very capable of working to the other side. My brother and I stood on [that] side. Mother and the smaller brother were taken away to the other side with those not capable of working. Where they were led, no one knew. Only the next day we saw the huge flames and the smoke from the crematorium where they were being burned.

My brother and I went to bathe. And after we were bathed everything was shorn off, and we were led into a barracks. We were dressed in the prisoner uniforms just like the others. We did not know what was going on there. When we came out, we already saw clubs flying over backs and heads.

Who was beating you?

The SS and the German professional criminals. They were worse even than the SS men themselves. They were appointed as capos there. That means they would be over the prisoners in the camp.

We were driven into a barracks. And the second day we still did not get anything to eat, and we couldn't sleep, either, because it was cold. It was on stones [i.e., built on a stone floor]. It was still in Birkenau, not yet in Auschwitz. It was the quarantine camp for Auschwitz.[1] We were then asked what occupation one had, and they said we would be sent to work. I reported that I was a locksmith, because I knew that it is always better to have a trade than to work some place on a field, but . . .

Did you know anything about locksmithing?

Yes. I went to a school at home. I always liked to play around with these things. And I knew very well that they needed locksmiths. Anyway, I had no luck; I was not accepted for it. And on the next day we were called out and taken to Auschwitz [I]. It was already the third day, so everyone received a liter of soup, and we were taken to be tattooed.

In what was the liter of soup given?

There were various broken bowls which had been collected from the transports; they [the Jews] had taken along pots, and the soup was given in them.

1. H. was confused. The "quarantine camp" was part of Birkenau (Auschwitz II), which by 1944 was quite self-sufficient.

We stayed there two more days, and on the third day we were taken away. I was separated from my brother and taken to work in a coal mine eight kilometers from Auschwitz, Jawiszowice.

And so, were you given hammers?
Yes. The same as every worker. We had to carry lamps in our hands. The lamp weighed 6 kilos. The lamp itself was taking one's strength. Not carbide lamps, but large [battery-powered] electric lamps so as to last the twelve hours. We only worked eight hours, but they had to burn for ten hours [for us] to come out.

Had you ever worked with coal before?
No.

And how deep did you go down?
Four hundred and sixty meters. We went down in a lift.

Who showed you how to work?
Everywhere there was a Polish civilian, a foreman. They were still worse than the Germans themselves. They treated us much worse than the Germans. They informed on us. They beat [us]. It was terrible the way the Poles treated us there in the coal mines. They beat us to death.

Did you not try sometimes to hit back?
Who had the strength? We were completely worn out. Completely starved from that liter of soup and 200 grams of bread.

All right, go on. How long did you work there in the coal mines? And where did your brother go?
I knew nothing more about my brother.[2] It lasted until the Russians arrived. That was in '45.

When you came out from the mines, what would happen then?
We were counted [to see] if everybody was present, and we were led into the camp. There we bathed every evening. That was a good thing, that bath. And after the bath we got supper, which was a piece of bread and black coffee, and we went to bed. They were wooden plank beds, four levels high. Four or five people slept on one [square] meter.

2. Earlier, in a section of the interview deleted from this anthology, H. indicated that he had received news that his brother was alive in the USSR but that he had not been able to make direct contact with him.

Did you take off your clothes?

No, it was too cold for undressing. We had one blanket, and sometimes not even one.

Did you have lice?

There is no question about it. We had a lot of lice. We bathed, and still there were lice. Because we did not have enough soap, and lice always remained in our underwear and in the beds. When we would come home, we always lay down in the same things. Not much was done about it, because there was a very great crowd of people. In one barracks there were two or three hundred people. Care was taken to make [the lice] go away, but not enough care could be taken.

What happened when someone became sick?

He was taken away, or he was given an injection to make him die faster. And if not, he [might] even request it [a fatal injection] himself because life was not that good that he should desire to recover. And if one was not so critically ill, there was a sick ward, and the wounds would be bandaged when one would hurt himself, or something like that.

And so you worked all the time?

We had no free Saturday or Sunday. Always working.

Was there any holiday that you did not work? Christmas?

Christmas, no. On New Year's we had a free day.

There were three shifts. I always worked on the noon shift. We got up at eight o'clock in the morning and washed up and got black coffee. And until dinner we idled around. I was young, and I was able to get along, so I went to a block to sweep up. I had a little protection from the block senior, so I would always get a little extra soup. And that kept me going.

Aha! But you worked for it.

Yes, I did extra work in the camp for it.

We walked three kilometers [to work]. At eleven o'clock we ate dinner. Everyone got the liter of soup, and we went down to work. We marched out by details, guarded by the SS, and we went down.

Did you sing while going to work?

We were not in a singing mood.

Yes, but it is said that the SS demanded it.

They did not demand it from us. There were camps where they did demand it just to make fun, but not from us. They just yelled all the time. The people were falling on their feet, so they would call, "Left, two, left, two," to keep in step. And then we would ride down. There [in the mine] everyone knew his workplace. The civilian [foreman] arrived, too, and we worked in the props. That means in the coal—it was sixty centimeters high. And there we had to work lying down the whole eight hours and shovel beneath yourself. Every eight hours the shift was changed. The others came, and we left. We arrived in the camp, and we bathed and went to bed again.

You told me you had a free day on New Year's. What did you do on that day?

We caught up on our sleep. We were happy that we could get some rest. Everyone slept the whole day.

In December of '44 the Russians made an attack on the region. So we started to be taken away from there. We left the coal mines on foot. We were eight kilometers from Auschwitz, so we saw Auschwitz burning. They demolished everything.[3] In the last moments everybody was able to loot bread and everything, because everything was open. So everyone grabbed a loaf. We killed each other for a piece of bread. And we walked on the road. There was a half meter of snow, and we were not dressed well. But of course we had to walk very fast because they were afraid that the Russians would catch up with us. They were afraid that we would tell all those stories so that the whole world would know. And then we were of use to them for work.

We walked a hundred and forty kilometers on foot in two days. And one night we slept, because the SS themselves could not walk anymore. They were healthy, it is true, but they, too, had no more strength, because we made eighty kilometers. We were chased into a field of snow, and there they began to shoot, and they said for everybody to lie down, because they did not want us to stand. And there was no room in that field. And they said to lie down. And they began to yell. One simply fell on top of another, because they were shooting over our heads. Many also fell [died] there. And all lay down. And there was snow and a severe frost. The night was terribly cold. I had fallen into the snow, and I slept there. In the morning I arose completely wet, because the snow had melted. I am surprised today how I pulled through that night. And in the morning we got up, and 50 percent remained lying there in the snow. We had to dig ditches and bury them there. Whoever was not able to walk was shot and thrown into the grave.

3. In their haste to depart the Germans left Auschwitz largely intact. H. probably saw the bombed Monowitz factories burning in the distance.

There were also many people on the road who were not able to walk anymore, so they would place a blanket over their head and sit down. The SS man would pass by and finish him off with a shot.

The next day, after we buried them, we walked on. They said we still had fifty kilometers to a train. Many people could not make it. And we, who were still able to make it, arrived there—it was Breslau, I believe.[4] And after several hours—we sat there in the snow—railroad cars arrived, and we boarded. But the cars were also terrible because [they] were completely open, without roofs. The journey to Buchenwald took eight days.

And where was the SS [guard] standing? Also in the snow?

There was an SS man in each car, but he, of course, was well dressed. And they were constantly changing [the guard]. At every station others would take over. And at the end [of the train] there were two passenger cars which were heated, and the SS were living there.

Well, if you were together for so many days, didn't people talk to the SS man? Didn't he himself talk?

Yes. There would be a good one [who] wanted to talk, and there would be a mean one who would take the rifle and beat one if one said a word to him. In the camp they would also play the same trick. One would be walking along, and he [the prisoner] greeted him. So he [the SS man] would come over and ask whether he was his comrade, since he had greeted him. If he [the prisoner] did not greet, then he would ask why he did not. [Either way] he would beat him. So we ourselves would not know what to do.

After eight days on the train we saw that we were arriving at Buchenwald. We were already very weak from the journey. We were bathed there, because with the Germans those arriving in another camp were bathed. Disinfection. After the bath my head was spinning. I became weak. The hot bath sort of melted my bones, because I was completely frozen. I was hardly able to walk over to the bath. So I sat down for a little while and more or less came to myself. Then after the bath again our hair was shorn off all over, and we were led into barracks. And we were there for two days. Suddenly we heard we were going to another place again. And we were chased out early one morning in the snow. The whole block was called out, and we were not told where we were going, and we were packed into railroad cars. We rode one day; it was good that it did not take any longer.

We arrived in a camp [that] was much worse yet than in the coal mines. There

4. If H.'s estimate of the distance traveled is correct, the station was probably located at Oppeln.

were munition depots. We lived in a cellar, in underground bunkers. In a forest. And the treatment there was much worse than anywhere else.

Why?
Because there we did not bathe. We had no water. Three months passed that we did not have any water whatsoever with which to wash ourselves. And the lice ate us up completely.

What did you do there?
Worked. Dug various ditches. Loaded munitions. They were building a large factory there underneath the forest. I talked to some people from Poland who had been there already for six years. They said they had gone through the worst camps—Majdanek, Treblinka—but they were never in such a place. Then I, too, became sick from the many lice, in the last two weeks before the liberation. When I became sick, I went to a doctor for eight days, always in the evenings, pleading that I could not work. He did not want to believe me.

Was he a Jewish doctor?
Yes. A Jew from Poland. He was a very mean one. There were also very bad people among the Jews themselves. Very brutal persons. And then he spared me, because, after all, I was young. I was then seventeen years old. He put me in the sick ward. I was there eight days. Then I was sent on a transport that was being sent to the crematorium. Eight kilometers from there was another camp, Ohrdruf. They had set up a crematorium there.

Did they gas people there?
No. They were already half dead anyway. So they were killed there with rifles and burned. And when we arrived, it was already the last transport. They did not have any more time for it. They were busy with themselves, because the Americans were already approaching. We lay there another eight days, and we were supposed to remain there until all the people were shot, or the camp blown up, or something like that. And then at the last moment trucks came and the sick were loaded on and taken away. And that was our luck.

In Buchenwald we were put near the crematorium, so we believed that we were being taken *to* the crematorium, but luckily we were [taken] to the old camp [and placed] among the people who were in quarantine and lodged there a few days. But we knew that the Americans were already near, because they were advancing rapidly. Every night we could hear the shooting. And Buchenwald, too, began to be evacuated, I don't know where to. Because I still remained there. And it was said that those who could walk [would] go, and who could not walk . . . , then the camp would be destroyed at the last hour. And the healthy people went, but our block said we were *not* going. They should kill us there, we were going to stay.

The next day—it was on Sunday—the SS came and began to throw [us] out through the windows and drive [us] to the roll call square, and from there we should be taken for evacuation.

Why through the windows and not through the doors?

Because nobody wanted to go. Everyone was reluctant to be evacuated. And they poured water over these people [the SS men]. They told them to their faces to shoot them. But they did not shoot. I do not know why. The next day, the same story. Finally they succeeded. They assembled the people on the roll call square. And I went up there, too. I saw a transport of young men standing there. They had been selected to remain in the camp. They were not suitable for transport. I, of course, am young, too, and I went over and mingled in, and returned to the camp. And these [other] people left on a transport. This was on Tuesday.

[After the liberation], we heard that the commander had telephoned from Weimar to demolish the camp, one hour after the liberation. He did not know that the camp had already been liberated. It was at half past four. So the camp senior—he as a prisoner—answered him that he should telephone the Lord God and not us. If we had not been liberated an hour before, they would have demolished the camp.

And so we were liberated. But many people also died after the liberation because they received very rich food. They completely ruined their stomachs. They got stomachaches, and they died from that, too. And then I was taken away to a youth block, and there I fell sick with spotted typhus. I lay there four weeks, and then I heard about the transport going to Switzerland. So I reported for it, to go to Switzerland.

Glossary of Terms

action: German raid to round up prisoners for deportation to slave labor and killing centers

Agudah: Orthodox Judaism

Aryan: Nazi term for a mixture of supposedly superior Germanic races. In practice it meant non-Jews.

block: The barracks that served as sleeping quarters for prisoners in forced labor camps

block senior: The prisoner trustee in charge of each block

BVer: Abbreviation for "Berufsverbrecher," the professional criminals among the prisoners

Canada: Auschwitz slang for the sector of the camp where the prisoners' belongings were sorted and collected for shipment to Germany or use by the prisoners

capo: The prisoner trustee in charge of a work detail in a slave labor camp

DP: Abbreviation for "Displaced Person," here referring to homeless refugees stranded in Western and Central Europe after World War II

Eretz Israel: Literally, "The Land of Israel," the preferred Zionist designation for Palestine before the creation of the state of Israel in 1948

General Government: Nazi term for the sectors of occupied Poland that were not annexed directly to Germany in 1939

Gestapo: Nazi Germany's "Secret State Police," under the control of SS boss Heinrich Himmler. Holocaust victims commonly spoke of any German unit as "the Gestapo."

HASAG: Abbreviation for Hugo Schneider Aktiengesellschaft Metalwarenfabrik, a privately owned German armaments manufacturing concern that employed concentration camp labor

Joint: Short for "American Jewish Joint Distribution Committee," a charitable organization that extended considerable aid to refugees in DP camps after the war

KZ: Abbreviation for "Konzentrationslager," German for "concentration camp"

Moslem: Concentration camp slang for a prisoner who had lost the will to live

organize: Prisoner slang for stealing food or other necessary items in the camps

ORT: Abbreviation for the "Society for Manual Work," founded in Russia in 1880 to train Jews for jobs in modern industrial societies

OSE: Abbreviation for "Working to Save the Children," a worldwide Jewish public health and child care organization that did relief and recovery work in Western Europe after World War II

SA: Abbreviation for "Sturmabteilung," the Nazi storm troopers

selection: The act of choosing prisoners to be deported or to be gassed

Sonderkommando: A "Special Commando" of prisoners forced to work in the gas chambers and crematoria of the extermination camps

SS: Abbreviation for "Schutzstaffel," the chief instrument of terror in Nazi Germany and throughout German-dominated Europe

UNRRA: Abbreviation for "United Nations Relief and Rehabilitation Administration," which aided displaced persons after the end of World War II

Wehrmacht: The regular German army in World War II

Glossary of Ghettos and Camps

Aschersleben: Labor camp south of Magdeburg, Germany

Auschwitz: The largest killing center and forced labor camp, located in southwest Poland, consisting of the original camp and administrative center (Auschwitz I), Birkenau (Auschwitz II), and Monowitz (Auschwitz III)

Barth: Labor camp near Wismar in northern Germany

Bedzin: Ghetto in Upper Silesia, northwest of Auschwitz

Bergen-Belsen: Detention camp, later a concentration camp, between Hannover and Hamburg, Germany

Birkenau: An extension of Auschwitz, housing four large crematoria, vast barracks, and various workshops

Birkenheim: Labor camp run by Organisation Schmelt in Lower Silesia

Buchenwald: Concentration camp near Weimar, Germany

Buczacz: Ghetto in southeastern Poland

Budy: Agricultural subcamp of Auschwitz

Buna: *See* Monowitz

Burgau: Subcamp of Dachau

Busk: Ghetto in southeastern Poland

Czestochowa: Ghetto and labor camp southwest of Warsaw in the General Government

Dabrowa-Gornica: Ghetto in Upper Silesia, near Bedzin, Poland

Dachau: Concentration camp near Munich, Germany

Dora-Mittelbau: Subcamp of Buchenwald, near Nordhausen in the Harz Mountains of Saxony

Drancy: Transit camp for Jews from France, located in a suburb of Paris

Flossenbürg: Concentration camp east of Nuremberg, near the Czech border

Fünfteichen: Subcamp of Gross-Rosen in eastern Germany, attached to the Krupp Ordnace Factory

Fürstengrube: Subcamp of Auschwitz, near Katowice in Upper Silesia

Girsdorf: Labor camp in Upper Silesia

Gogolin: Labor camp in Upper Silesia

Görlitz: Subcamp of Gross-Rosen, in eastern Germany

Gräben: Subcamp of Gross-Rosen, for women

Gräditz: Labor camp near Gleiwitz in eastern Germany

Grodno: Ghetto in eastern Poland

Gross-Rosen: Concentration camp in Lower Silesia

Grünberg: Subcamp of Gross-Rosen, for women

Hatvan: Ghetto in Hungary

Hirschberg: Subcamp of Gross-Rosen in Upper Silesia

Jawiszowice: Coal-producing subcamp of Auschwitz

Kamenz: Labor camp near Dresden, Germany

Kirkheim: Subcamp of Dachau

Kovno: Ghetto in central Lithuania

Krakow: Ghetto in the capital of the German-occupied General Government of Poland

Krasnik: Subcamp of Majdanek

Landsberg: Subcamp of Dachau in southern Bavaria

Lippstadt: Labor camp near Paderborn in western Germany

Lodz: Large ghetto in western Poland, annexed to Germany during World War II

Majdanek: Large camp combining killing and slave labor facilities, near Lublin in eastern Poland

Markstadt: Labor camp of the Organisation Schmelt in eastern Germany

Messenthin: Labor camp near Stettin in northeastern Germany

Miedzyrzec Podlaski: Ghetto in eastern Poland

Mielec: Subcamp of Auschwitz in southeastern Poland

Mirow: Subcamp of Ravensbrück in northern Germany

Monowitz: Heavy industrial sector of the enlarged Auschwitz camp, often called "Buna" after one of its chief products, synthetic rubber

Mühldorf: Subcamp of Dachau in southeastern Germany

Mukachevo: Ghetto in northern Hungary

Neustadt: Subcamp of Ravensbrück in northern Germany

Nordhausen: *See* Dora-Mittelbau

Novaky: Labor camp in western Slovakia

Ohrdruf: Subcamp of Buchenwald

Oranienburg: *See* Sachsenhausen

Pithiviers: French concentration camp

Plaszow: Concentration camp near Krakow in southern Poland

Ravensbrück: Concentration camp for women, north of Sachsenhausen

Sachsenhausen: Concentration camp just north of Berlin, originally called Oranienburg

Skarzysko-Kamienna: Labor camp in central Poland

Sosnowiec: Ghetto and transit camp in Upper Silesia

Starachowice: Ghetto and, later, a labor camp in central Poland

Stutthof: Concentration camp near Danzig in East Prussia

Tachau: Labor camp near Leipzig, Germany

Theresienstadt: Ghetto and concentration camp in northwestern Czechoslovakia

Treblinka: Killing center northeast of Warsaw

Trawniki: Subcamp of Majdanek, southeast of Lublin
Vyhne: Labor camp in southern Slovakia
Warsaw: The largest ghetto, in the former Polish capital
Weidenburg: Labor camp of the Organisation Schmelt in Lower Silesia
Wolfsberg: Subcamp of Gross-Rosen

Selected Bibliography

Abzug, Robert H. *Inside the Vicious Heart: Americans and the Liberation of the Nazi Concentration Camps.* New York: Oxford University Press, 1985.

Adler, H. G. *Die verheimlichte Wahrheit. Theresienstädter Dokumente.* Tübingen: J. C. B. Mohr, 1958.

————. *Theresienstadt, 1941–1945.* Tübingen: J. C. B. Mohr, 1960.

Ainsztein, Reuben. *Jewish Resistance in Nazi-Occupied Eastern Europe.* New York: Barnes and Noble, 1974.

Bartel, Walter, ed. *Buchenwald: Mahnung und Verpflichtung.* Berlin: Kongress Verlag, 1960.

Bauer, Yehuda. *The Jewish Emergence from Powerlessness.* Toronto: University of Toronto Press, 1979.

————. *Out of the Ashes: The Impact of American Jews on Post-Holocaust European Jewry.* Oxford: Pergamon Press, 1989.

Bergmann, Martin S., and Milton E. Jacovy. *Generations of the Holocaust.* New York: Columbia University Press, 1990.

Boder, David P. "The Adjective-Verb Quotient: A Contribution to the Psychology of Language." *Psychological Record* 3 (March 1940): 310–43.

————. *I Did Not Interview the Dead.* Urbana, Ill.: University of Illinois Press, 1949.

————. "The Impact of Catastrophe: Assessment and Evaluation." *Journal of Psychology* 38 (1954): 3–50.

Boehm, Erich, ed. *We Survived.* Santa Barbara, Calif.: Clio, 1966.

Bondy, Ruth. *"Elder of the Jews": Jakob Edelstein of Theresienstadt.* New York: Grove Press, 1989.

Braham, Randolf L. *The Politics of Genocide: The Holocaust in Hungary.* New York: Columbia University Press, 1981.

Bridgman, Jon. *The End of the Holocaust: The Liberation of the Camps.* Portland, Oreg.: Areopagitica Press, 1990.

Browning, Christopher R. *Ordinary Men: Reserve Police Battalion 101 and the Final Solution in Poland.* New York: HarperCollins, 1992.

Burney, Christopher. *The Dungeon Democracy.* New York: Duell, Sloan and Pearce, 1946.

Butnari, I. C. *The Silent Holocaust: Romania and Its Jews.* New York: Greenwood Press, 1992.

Charny, Israel W., ed. *Holding on to Humanity—the Message of Holocaust*

Survivors: The Shumai Davidson Papers. New York: New York University Press, 1992.

Cohen, Elie A. *Human Behavior in the Concentration Camp*. London: Free Association Books, 1988.

Czech, Danuta. *Auschwitz Chronicle, 1939–1945*. New York: Henry Holt, 1990.

Des Pres, Terrence. *The Survivor: An Anatomy of Life in the Death Camps*. New York: Oxford University Press, 1976.

Dobroszycki, Jucjan, ed. *The Chronicle of the Lodz Gehtto, 1941–1944*. New Haven: Yale University Press, 1984.

Feig, Konnilyn G. *Hitler's Death Camps: The Sanity of Madness*. New York: Holmes and Meier, 1981.

Fein, Helen. *Accounting for Genocide*. New York: Free Press, 1979.

Friedlander, Saul. *Memory, History, and the Extermination of the Jews of Europe*. Bloomington and Indianapolis: Indiana University Press, 1993.

Gilbert, Martin. *The Holocaust: A History of the Jews of Europe during the Second World War*. New York: Holt, Rinehart, and Winston, 1985.

Goldhagen, Daniel Jonah. *Hitler's Willing Executioners: Ordinary Germans and the Holocaust*. New York: Alfred A. Knopf, 1996.

Gutman, Israel. *Encyclopedia of the Holocaust*. New York: Macmillan, 1990.

Gutman, Yisrael, and Avital Saf, eds. *The Nazi Concentration Camps*. Jerusalem: Yad Vashem, 1984.

Gutman, Yisrael, and Michael Berenbaum, eds. *Anatomy of the Auschwitz Death Camp*. Bloomington: Indiana University Press, 1994.

Gutman, Yisrael, and Shmuel Krakowski. *Unequal Victims: Poles and Jews during World War Two*. New York: Holocaust Library, 1986.

Hackett, David A. *The Buchenwald Report*. Boulder, Colo.: Westview Press, 1995.

Heller, Celia. *On the Edge of Destruction: Jews of Poland between the Two World Wars*. New York: Schocken Books, 1977.

Henige, David. *Oral Historiography*. London: Longman, 1982.

Hilberg, Raul. *The Destruction of the European Jews*. New York: Holmes and Meier, 1985.

———. *Perpetrators, Victims, Bystanders: The Jewish Catastrophe, 1933–1945*. New York: HarperCollins, 1992.

Hirschfeld, Gerhard, ed. *The Policies of Genocide: Jews and Soviet Prisoners of War in Nazi Germany*. London: Allen and Unwin, 1986.

Hyman, Abraham S. *The Undefeated*. Jerusalem: Gefen Books, 1993.

Kautsky, Benedikt. *Teufel und Verdammte*. Zurich: Gutenberg, 1946.

Kogon, Eugen. *The Theory and Practice of Hell*. New York: Berkley Books, 1980.

Krakowski, Shmuel. *The War of the Doomed: Jewish Armed Resistance in Poland, 1942–1944*. New York: Holmes and Meier, 1984.

Kraus, Ota, and Erich Kulka. *The Death Factory*. Oxford: Pergamon Press, 1966.

Krausnick, Helmut, et al. *Anatomy of the SS State*. New York: Walker and Company, 1968.

Kuchler-Silberman, Lena. *One Hundred Children*. Garden City, New York: Doubleday, 1961.

Laqueur, Walter. *The Terrible Secret: Suppression of the Truth about Hitler's Final Solution*. Boston: Little, Brown and Company, 1980.

Langer, Lawrence L. *Holocaust Testimonies: The Ruins of Memory*. New Haven, Conn.: Yale University Press, 1991.

———. *Versions of Survival: The Holocaust and the Human Spirit*. Albany: State University of New York Press, 1982.

Lederer, Zdenek. *Ghetto Theresienstadt*. London: E. Goldston, 1953.

Levi, Primo. *The Drowned and the Saved*. New York: Summit Books, 1988.

———. *Moments of Reprieve*. New York: Summit Books, 1986.

———. *Survival in Auschwitz*. New York: Collier Books, 1961.

Levin, Dov. *Fighting Back: Lithuanian Jewry's Armed Resistance to the Nazis, 1941–1945*. New York: Holmes and Meier, 1985.

Loftus, Elizabeth. *Memory*. Reading, Mass.: Addison-Wesley, 1980.

Marrus, Michael R. *The Unwanted: European Refugees in the Twentieth Century*. New York: Oxford University Press, 1985.

Marrus, Michael R., and Robert O. Paxton. *Vichy France and the Jews*. New York: Schocken Books, 1983.

Marszalek, Jozef. *Majdanek: The Concentration Camp in Lublin*. Warsaw: Interpress, 1986.

Matussek, Paul. *Internment in Concentration Camps and Its Consequences*. New York: Springer-Verlag, 1975.

Matzner, David. *The Muselmann: The Diary of a Jewish Slave Laborer*. Hoboken, N.J.: KTAV Publishing, 1994.

Mendelsohn, Ezra. *The Jews of East Central Europe between the World Wars*. Bloomington: Indiana University Press, 1983.

Mueller, Filip. *Eyewitness Auschwitz*. New York: Stein and Day, 1979.

Parkin, Alan J. *Memory and Amnesia: An Introduction*. Oxford: B. Blackwell, 1987.

Proudfoot, Malcolm J. *European Refugees, 1939–52: A Study in Forced Population Movement*. Evanston, Ill.: Northwestern University Press, 1956.

Rabinowitz, Dorothy. *New Lives*. New York: Knopf, 1977.

Ringelblum, Emmanuel. *Notes from the Warsaw Ghetto*. New York: Schocken Books, 1975.

———. *Polish-Jewish Relations during the Second World War*. Jerusalem: Yad Vashem, 1976.

Rittner, Carol, and John K. Roth, eds. *Different Voices: Women and the Holocaust*. New York: Paragon House, 1993.

Roland, Charles G. *Courage under Siege: Starvation, Disease, and Death in the Warsaw Ghetto*. New York: Oxford University Press, 1992.

Ross, Bruce M. *Remembering the Personal Past*. New York: Oxford University Press, 1991.

Sack, John. *An Eye for an Eye*. New York: Basic Books, 1993.

Segev, Tom. *Soldiers of Evil: The Commandants of the Nazi Concentration Camps*. New York: Berkley Books, 1991.

Shelley, Lore. *Secretaries of Death*. New York: Shengold Publishers, 1986.

Spence, Donald P. *Narrative Truth and Historical Truth*. New York: W. W. Norton, 1982.

Tec, Nechama. *When Light Pierced the Darkness: Christian Rescue of Jews in Nazi-Occupied Poland*. New York: Oxford University Press, 1986.

Tory, Avraham. *Surviving the Holocaust: The Kovno Ghetto Diary*. Cambridge: Harvard University Press, 1990.

Troller, Norbert. *Theresienstadt: Hilter's Gift to the Jews*. Chapel Hill: University of North Carolina Press, 1991.

Trunk, Isaiah. *Jewish Responses to Nazi Persecution*. New York: Stein and Day, 1979.

———. *Judenrat*. New York: Macmillan, 1972.

Yahil, Leni. *The Holocaust: The Fate of European Jewry, 1932–1945*. New York: Oxford University Press, 1990.

Yerushalmi, Yosef Hayim. *Zakhor: Jewish History and Jewish Memory*. Seattle: University of Washington Press, 1982.

Young, James E. *Writing and Rewriting the Holocaust: Narrative and the Consequences of Interpretation*. Bloomington: Indiana University Press, 1988.

Index

Buczacz, Poland, 224, 225–27
Budapest, Hungary, 236, 373, 388
Budlen Institution, 158
Budy (camp), 180
Buna. *See* Monowitz
Bund, 319
Burgau (camp), 222
Busk, Poland, 162

Camp seniors, 15; duties of, 37–39, 302;
    Jews as, 293, 294; Gentiles as, 299, 310
"Canada," 15, 52
Capos, 15, 383; Jews as, 32–36, 39–41, 47,
    53; Gentiles as, 42–45, 73–74, 257, 264,
    295
Catholic Church, 151, 157–59, 208, 327
Central Committee of the Jews in
    Poland, 21, 118–19, 125, 134
Chelmno (camp), 11
Chemnitz, Germany, 201
Children, 20, 108, 112; in camps, 20,
    103–5, 118, 122, 159–62, 167, 171, 220,
    306, 314; as orphans, 20–21, 151–52,
    154–60; deportation of, 28, 95, 96, 252,
    335; in ghettos, 50–51, 109–11, 141, 157,
    158, 206, 216, 247, 252; assist partisans,
    157; saved by Gentiles, 204, 206–7,
    213, 231, 314, 324; as DPs, 231
Christian Dierig (firm), 296
Coburg, Germany, 259
Cologne, Germany, 259
Cremona (DP camp), 137, 238
Crystal Night, 8, 289, 291, 300, 389
Czechoslovakia, 7, 11, 283, 286; prisoners
    from, 43, 108, 115–16; DPs in, 134;
    Gentiles help Jews in, 368
Czerniakow, Adam, 141
Czernowitz, Poland, 230
Czestochowa (camp), 170, 187–89, 221
Czestochowa, Poland, 187, 189
Czynadowo, Czechoslovakia, 390, 391

Dabrowa-Gornica, Poland, 27–32, 41
Dachau (camp), 19, 81, 83, 264, 266
Dalin, William Z., 291
Death marches, 9, 16–17, 46, 54, 62–63,

122–23, 132, 180, 264, 297, 319, 366,
    395–96; escapes from, 18–19, 78, 323,
    326–31, 366–67; at war's end, 201–2,
    309–10
Displaced persons camps, 3, 6, 21–22,
    369; conditions in, 135–37, 234,
    236–40, 369, 388–89
Doctors, 15; German, 52–53, 95, 101,
    103, 316, 357, 376, 380; Jewish, 101–2,
    111–12, 188, 397
Dora-Mittelbau (camp), 76, 126, 132
Drancy (camp), 314, 323, 324, 332, 339–41
Dresden, Germany, 56
Drexler, Margot, 358
Dror Habonim (kibbutz), 136, 237
Dunant, Paul, 287

Eastern Upper Silesia, 9, 10, 27–56
Ehrlich (Gestapo officer), 206
Eichmann, Adolf, 1, 5
Einsatzgruppen, 10
Elkes, Elchanan, 244, 246, 248–49
Estonia, 249–50
Ethnic Germans, 9, 102; and Jews, 107,
    142–43, 163–64, 183, 197
Extermination centers. *See* Auschwitz:
    as extermination center; Belzec;
    Chelmno; Majdanek; Sobibor;
    Treblinka

Feldafing (DP camp), 21, 369
Final Solution, 9, 22
Flossenbürg (camp), 47, 55–56
France, 11, 18; deportations from, 11, 338,
    340–41; Jews in, 289, 292, 313, 314,
    323–24, 332–42; anti-Semitism in, 289,
    332–42 passim; forced labor in, 332,
    338–39
Frick Industries, 294–95
Friedmann, Desider, 280
Fünfteichen (camp), 13, 27, 41–47, 54
Fürstengrube (camp), 294–95

Galinsky, Edek, 313
German Armament Works, 191
Germans, 9, 88, 124, 221, 369; aid Jews,

267, 394, 397; administration of, 15, 106, 221; nonprisoner workers at, 33, 38, 42, 45, 54, 59, 91, 92, 106, 188–89, 309, 392; conditions in, 34–35, 36, 38–40, 43, 44–45, 67, 296, 394; shootings and body disposal, 44, 82–83, 294, 295
Landsberg (camp), 222–23
Latvia, 3
Leipzig, Germany, 3
Lemberg. *See* Lvov, Poland
Lewis Institute, 3
Lichtenbaum, Marek, 141
Liepaja, Russia, 3
Lippstadt, Germany, 211–12
Lithuania, 7, 217, 243–53
Lodz, Poland, 174, 183, 196, 197; postwar return to, 118, 124–25, 138, 149, 213
— Ghetto, 9, 10, 303; deportations and liquidation, 9, 175–79, 182, 185–86, 198–200; conditions in, 11, 174–76, 178, 182, 184–85, 187, 198, 303–4; formation of, 182–84, 197
Lowicz, Poland, 154
Lublin, Poland, 12, 129, 217. *See also* Majdanek
Lvov, Poland, 161, 165, 167–68, 215, 234–36

Madagascar plan, 8
Majdanek (camp), 12, 22, 103; conditions in, 94, 99, 108, 112–13, 131, 215, 218, 219–20; executions and body disposal, 102, 103, 120–21, 217–20
Mandel, Maria, 316, 318
Markstadt (camp), 13, 27, 28, 32–41
Mengele, Josef, 376
Merin, Monek, 10, 27, 28–29, 47, 49
Messenthin (camp), 298
Miedzyrzec Podlaski, Poland, 94–95, 97–99
Mielec (camp), 81, 82
Mirow (camp), 366
Miskolc, Hungary, 375
Mixed marriages, 11, 268–72
Moll, Otto, 317n

Monowitz (camp), 126, 131–32, 134; conditions in, 262–63, 373, 379–86; evacuation and destruction of, 373, 386–87, 395. *See also* Auschwitz
Mühldorf (camp), 266–67
Mukachevo, Hungary, 390
Müller, Paul, 360–61, 364
Murmelstein, Benjamin, 273–80

National Armed Forces, 156
Neustadt (camp), 123
Nordhausen (camp), 132, 390, 396–97
Novaky (camp), 248
Nuremberg, Germany, 268–69, 272

Ohrdruf (camp), 390, 397
Olchowek, Poland, 151, 152–54
Oranienburg. *See* Sachsenhausen
Organization Schmelt, 13, 31n, 289, 294n
Organization Todt, 266
ORT, 28, 82, 86, 87, 138–39, 143–45
Oschatz, Germany, 326–29
OSE, 117

Paris, France, 313, 314, 322, 324, 332–41 passim
Partisans, 228–29, 348; Jews join, 18, 161, 165–66, 235, 345, 349–52
Patronka, 355
Pister, Hermann, 19
Pithiviers (camp), 332, 334–36
Plaszow (camp), 103–4, 162, 169
Poelitz (camp), 298
Pohl (General), 245
Poland, 8; prewar anti-Semitism in, 6, 196, 332; Jews of, 6–7, 9, 18, 71–73, 162–65, 204, 215, 290; postwar anti-Semitism in, 6–7, 48, 79, 118, 124–25, 150, 152–60, 170–71, 230; Jews return to, 79, 107, 118, 124–25, 134–35, 138, 149, 151, 154–55, 166, 213, 224, 230
Poles, 18, 94; betray Jews, 88, 154, 189, 215, 216; aid Jews, 94, 96, 108–11, 138, 145–48, 162–66, 204, 207–8, 387; Jews pass as, 149, 151–54, 168, 205, 209, 215
Police, 163, 238, 239, 249, 281, 287; Ger-

Ujvidek, Yugoslavia, 374
Ukraine, 161–63, 236
Ukrainian Insurgent Army, 236n
Ukrainians, 55, 65; as camp guards, 8, 87,
90–93, 221, 236–37; in DP camps, 21,
135, 234, 236–37, 239; SS volunteers
from, 97, 109–11, 112, 116, 128–30, 217,
310
United States, 21, 369
United States National Health
Service, 5
UNRRA, 116, 181; aids DPs, 21, 78, 95,
136, 215, 234, 237, 238, 240, 356; and
DP camps, 239, 240, 369, 388–89

Vienna, Austria, 11, 273, 274–76
Villach (DP camp), 237
Vilna, Russia, 3
Vlasov, Andrei, 250
Vogel (capo), 74
Vyhne (camp), 347–49

Waedenswil (DP camp), 85–86
Wannsee Conference, 9
Waren, Germany, 368
Warsaw, Poland, 145–48, 149; postwar
return to, 124, 134–35, 138, 224, 230
—ghetto, 16; labor in, 9, 10, 119, 139,
144–45; conditions in, 17, 138–43, 158,

216; uprising in, 18, 22, 110, 126–29;
deportations from, 94, 95, 108–11,
119–20, 140, 143–44
Weidenburg (camp), 59
Weimar, Germany, 19, 77, 190
Wielikowski, Gustav, 141–42
Wiener, Fischel, 298, 299
Wiesbaden, Germany, 290, 291
Wolfsberg (camp), 297
Women, 12, 15–16, 19–20, 151–54, 155–59;
resistance by, 22, 92, 126, 128, 152, 313,
317–18; in labor camps, 40, 59, 92, 215,
218; with children, 51, 161, 163–64,
300, 306; pregnancies and births, 91,
103–4, 320–21

Yad Vashem, 3
Yugoslavia, 374n

Zakopane, Poland, 155–59, 161, 167,
170–71
Zimetbaum, Mala, 22, 313, 317–18
Zionism, 1, 21–22, 196, 197, 234, 345–47,
373; inspires DPs, 20, 21, 48, 86, 107,
118, 124–25, 151, 159, 196, 202–3, 234,
239, 388–89; and Orthodox Judaism,
21, 118, 225, 231–33
Zoeldi, Marton, 374–75
Zvolen, Slovakia, 349

DATE DUE

APR 1 9			
FB 2 8			
APR 3 0			
MAY 1 3			